Britannia's Zealots, Volume I

Also available from Bloomsbury

Colin Jordan and Britain's Neo-Nazi Movement: Hitler's Echo, by Paul Jackson
Conservative Moments: Reading Conservative Texts, edited by Mark Garnett
*Neo-Tories: The Revolt of British Conservatives against Democracy
and Political Modernity (1929–1939)*, by Bernhard Dietz

Britannia's Zealots, Volume I

Tradition, Empire and the Forging of the Conservative Right

N.C. Fleming

BLOOMSBURY ACADEMIC
LONDON • NEW YORK • OXFORD • NEW DELHI • SYDNEY

BLOOMSBURY ACADEMIC
Bloomsbury Publishing Plc
50 Bedford Square, London, WC1B 3DP, UK
1385 Broadway, New York, NY 10018, USA

BLOOMSBURY, BLOOMSBURY ACADEMIC and the Diana logo are trademarks of
Bloomsbury Publishing Plc

First published in Great Britain 2019

Cover image: A vintage postcard published to commemorate the Coronation
of King George V and Queen Mary in London, 22nd June 1911.
(© Paul Popper/Popperfoto/Getty Images)

A catalogue record for this book is available from the British Library.

Library of Congress Cataloging-in-Publication Data
Names: Fleming, N. C. (Neil C.), author.
Title: Britannia's zealots : tradition, empire and the forging of the
conservative right / N.C. Fleming.
Description: London : Bloomsbury Academic, 2019– | Includes bibliographical
references and index.
Identifiers: LCCN 2018011573 (print) | LCCN 2018025483 (ebook) |
ISBN 9781474237864 (ePDF) | ISBN 9781474237857 (ePUB) |
ISBN 9781474237833 (v. 1 : hardback)
Subjects: LCSH: Conservatism—Great Britain—History—20th century. | Conservative Party
(Great Britain)—History—20th century. | Great Britain—Politics and government—20th
century.
Classification: LCC JC573.2.G7 (ebook) | LCC JC573.2.G7 F64 2019 (print) |
DDC 320.520941—dc23 LC record available at https://lccn.loc.gov/2018011573

ISBN: HB: 978-1-4742-3783-3
        ePDF: 978-1-4742-3786-4
        eBook: 978-1-4742-3785-7

Typeset by RefineCatch Limited, Bungay, Suffolk
Printed and bound in Great Britain

To find out more about our authors and books visit www.bloomsbury.com
and sign up for our newsletters.

I Euriana

Contents

Illustrations

Acknowledgements

The long gestation of this book has inevitably incurred a large number of debts. Two semesters of research leave awarded by the University of Worcester, in 2013 and 2017, provided the necessary time and space for archival research and writing. This was further assisted by a Visiting Fellowship, St Catherine's College, University of Oxford; Senior Associate Membership, St Antony's College, University of Oxford; and the Caird Research Fellowship, National Maritime Museum, Greenwich. Additional financial support towards archival research was provided by the Scouloudi Research Award, Institute of Historical Research, University of London; and research grants from the Historic Society for Lancashire and Cheshire and the Leicestershire Archaeological and Historical Society. The Institute of Humanities, University of Worcester, generously covered the copyright and reproduction costs of two illustrations. Practical and institutional support was provided by an Associate Fellowship, Institute of Commonwealth Studies, School of Advanced Study, University of London; and an Honorary Research Fellowship, School of History, Archaeology and Religion, Cardiff University.

The book has benefited from the assistance of staff at the Arts and Social Sciences Library, Cardiff University; the Bodleian Library, University of Oxford; the British Library, St Pancras; the Caird Library, National Maritime Museum, Greenwich; Cambridge University Library; the Churchill Archive Centre, University of Cambridge; Durham County Record Office; the Hive, University of Worcester; the House of Commons Library, Westminster; Lancashire Archives, Preston; Liverpool Record Office; the Parliamentary Archive, Westminster; the Public Record Office of Northern Ireland; and Worcestershire Archives.

For access to manuscript sources, and permission to quote from them, I am grateful to the British Library; the Bodleian Library, University of Oxford; the Viscount Boyd; the Conservative Party; Dr Jeremy Hogg; Mrs Elizabeth Meynell; the Warden and Scholars of New College, Oxford; the Chairman of the 1922 Committee; the Parliamentary Archive, Westminster; and the Earl of Selborne. In some instances it has not been possible to trace the owners of copyright material, for which I apologize. Permission to use material from articles previously published in *Parliamentary History* and *History* was kindly granted by Professor David Hayton and Professor Emma Griffin respectively.

I have been very fortunate that Professor Stuart Ball CBE, Professor D. George Boyce, and the anonymous reviewer commissioned by the publisher, all agreed to read the entire text and offer their valuable insights and corrections. Likewise, Professor Dilwyn Porter and Dr Roland Quinault kindly agreed to read individual chapters. Any errors or shortcomings remain my own. The late Dr Alan O'Day was supportive throughout, not only as a friend, but also by providing accommodation during successive terms at St Antony's College and St Catherine's College, and the other occasions when I consulted archival material at the Bodleian Library. In the book's early stages of development, valuable help in securing a publisher, research grants and fellowships was given by Professor Ball, Professor Boyce, Professor Philip Murphy and Professor Simon Potter.

I have benefited also from the encouragement and assistance of many colleagues and experts including Professor Roger Ainsworth, Professor Maggie Andrews, Catherine Armitstead, Frances Arnold, Professor William Beinart, Dr Robert Blyth, Dr Jeff Bowersox, Professor Michael Bradshaw, Rosemary Cameron, Dr Ian Cawood, Angela Coss, Professor Peter Coss, Professor Nicholas Crowson, Dr Jody Crutchley, Professor John Darwin, Lizelle de Jager, Emily Drewe, Professor John D. Fair, Professor Sam Goodfellow, Dr Rob Havers, Merv Honeywood, Professor Stephen Howe, Dr Brian Jackson, Dr David Jarvis, Dr Martin Johnes, Professor Bill Jones, Peter Keelan, Professor Liam Kennedy, Dr Harshan Kumarasingham, Sue Littleford, Beatriz Lopez, Dr Donal Lowry, Professor Elaine McFarland, Jeremy McIlwaine, Professor Hugh McLeod, Professor Margaret Macmillan, Dr Paddy McNally, Dr Mehreen Mirza, Duncan Montgomery, Professor R.J. Morris, Professor Marc Mulholland, Dr Siân Nicholas, Professor Darren Oldridge, Dr John Parham, Megan Parry, Professor Antonia Payne, Professor Robert Pyper, Dr Nigel Rigby, Dr Nini Rodgers, Professor Suzanne Schwarz, Professor John Stewart, Dr Paul Stocker, Dr Toby Thacker, Rowan Thompson, Dr Anne-Marie Tindley, Dr Gerry Webber, Dr John-Paul Wilson and Dr Conor Wyer. Above all, I received the support of my wife, daughter and parents, without whom none of this would be possible.

Abbreviations

BUF	British Union of Fascists
EIA	Empire Industries Association
ICS	Indian Civil Service
IDL	India Defence League
IER	*Indian Empire Review*
IES	Indian Empire Society
IML	Imperial Maritime League
IRA	Irish Republican Army
JSC	Joint Select Committee
NCA	National Constitutional Association
NCU	National Citizens Union
NL	Navy League
NSL	National Service League
RAF	Royal Air Force
TRL	Tariff Reform League
UBC	Unionist Business Committee
UVF	Ulster Volunteer Force
UWC	Unionist War Committee

Introduction

The Conservative party has from its inception contained a section fundamentally opposed to change and reform. Unable or unwilling to agree with those Conservatives who argue that reform and preservation are not antithetical, they have defied a succession of party leaders, from the first Duke of Wellington to Theresa May. Referred to variously, as 'ultras', 'diehards', and 'Tory rebels', *Britannia's Zealots* argues that the behaviour and attitudes of this 'Conservative Right' are observable from the origins of the party through to the present. Their ranks have included authoritarians, traditionalists, populists and advocates of 'constructive' social policies, as well as opportunists and transient supporters. This variety in background means that the Conservative Right has never been able or willing to articulate or develop a comprehensive ideology. It is characterized instead by what Rodney Barker describes as themes, that is, a 'cohering or unifying concern, form of argument, or intellectual predilection whose character is historical rather than logical, and which has a coherence which can be rhetorical or ascetic, as much as logical.'[1] These include a shared hostility to the trimming and pragmatism required of Conservative statecraft. The Conservative Right regards bipartisanship and moving in the direction of political opponents as fundamentally misguided and counterproductive. It holds that straying from Conservative principles aids and abets the enemies of Great Britain, at home and abroad, so that the reformist tendencies of other Conservatives are viewed as symptomatic of national decline and a contributor to it. Yet for all its preoccupation with Conservative principles, the nature of the Conservative Right has changed over time and in fundamental ways. For much of the nineteenth century, orthodox Toryism was defined by its steadfast adherence to the rights and privileges of the established churches and unreformed constitution. By the twentieth century, the Conservative Right was defined instead by its belief in the need to maintain Britain as a great power.

These contrasting ideas of Conservative first principles existed in parallel during the Edwardian period, fomenting its 'crisis of conservatism', and producing a complex set of reactions on the right of the party, ranging from mutual cooperation and convergence through to reciprocal hostility.

To identify the Conservative Right, the focus here is primarily on Conservatives who actively and visibly defied their party leaders, as distinct from those who might have sympathized or agreed with their outlook, especially on single issues, but who took no action to express doubts or objections. This method is open to challenge, of course. G.C. Webber's *Ideology of the British Right* is a compelling case for examining ideas over activities.[2] Illuminating insights on political attitudes are also emerging in the fields of social psychology and genetics.[3] Nonetheless, the historical method adopted here is justified on the basis of focus, evidence and practicality. Unable to exercise power on its own, the Conservative Right has had to operate within the political coalition that is the Conservative party. Its perennial misgivings about democracy have been to some extent ameliorated by a sympathetic hearing in sections of the popular press, and a level of support amongst grass-roots Conservatives which is disproportionate to the strength of dissidents in Parliament. Marshalling these forces, the Conservative Right has on occasion created political crises. These have rarely succeeded in their aim of defeating reform or vetoing policy, but they have contributed to a climate which, to varying degrees, and by shaping public attitudes to controversial questions, circumscribes the room for manoeuvre afforded to Conservative leaders. However, the historiography on British Conservatism in the twentieth century has generally underplayed or overlooked this dynamic process, not least because treatments of the Conservative Right have been relatively brief and in most cases related to a specific short period or theme.[4]

Britannia's Zealots is primarily a history of the right wing of the Conservative party. The constellation of journalists, writers and thinkers which orbited the party also feature, though their influence is placed in its appropriate context. As a result, the evidence presented in the forthcoming pages does not reveal an ideologically driven subset of Conservatives. For one thing, the party has survived and thrived because it is adaptable and flexible. As a 'doctrine of power', Conservatism has necessarily reacted to great transformations, from revolution and reform in the late eighteenth and early nineteenth centuries, to liberalism and democracy from the mid-nineteenth to the early twentieth centuries, and since then to communism and social democracy.[5] These shifts produced regular internal divisions about the purpose and identity of the Conservative party. The position adopted by its 'right' has therefore always been relational, in so far as it is bound up with and defined by the position of the 'centre' – that is to say the front bench, for the most of the nineteenth and early twentieth centuries, and the bulk of MPs since then – on any given issue at any given time.[6] As such, a longitudinal history of Conservative Right ideas would be hard to distinguish from a history of Conservative political thought. Put simply, the rhetoric and ideas of the Conservative Right, *qua* Conservatives, shifted in response to specific and changing temporal contexts.[7] This helps to explain why the Conservative Right rarely acknowledges its own antecedents.[8] In 1910, for example, the *enfant terrible*, Henry Page Croft (1881–1947), called for a party leader in the mould of Wellington, seemingly unaware that the victor of Waterloo had faced some of the party's largest back-bench rebellions. The crisis of conservatism provoked by Croft and others appears to have escaped the memory of Ian Colvin, a journalist at the diehard *Morning Post*, whose 1934 account of Edwardian politics claimed that the party 'had not yet begun its latter-day practice of selling its friends to placate its enemies'.[9] In like manner, Conservative Right MPs in the 1930s and 1990s were wont to invoke the memory of Benjamin Disraeli as a standard bearer of Conservative principles.[10] Such nostalgia seemed unaware that in his own time Dizzy was no stranger to back-bench accusations of betraying the party's beliefs. Ahistorical readings of history such as these allow successive generations of the Conservative Right to believe that there remains ground to be defended in the name of tradition, despite generation after generation lamenting the passing of all they hold dear. If it is bemusing to historians, it nevertheless helps to explain why the Conservative Right remains a potent force to the present day.

II

The Conservative Right plays a conspicuous if background role in most histories of the Conservative party. These have until relatively recently tended to be dominated by biographies and studies of high politics which focus on a narrow party elite. As Bruce Coleman observes, this has the habit of conflating erroneously government with party, and to downplay their subjects' essential conservatism by highlighting instead the party leadership's contributions to progressive causes.[11] Opponents within the Conservative party are of course acknowledged, but there has long been a tendency to treat them as aberrations and reach for reductive epithets rather than detailed explanation. After all, if we follow Cicero's sage advice, 'only a fool would risk shipwreck by holding to the original course rather than change and still reach his destination'.[12] Yet such dismissiveness downplays the conservatism which united all wings of the party, and risks also overlooking the sometimes considerable efforts of party leaders to manage dissentients on the backbenches. Few historians today, of course, would subscribe to Maurice Cowling's dismissal of 'backbenchers and party opinion . . . as malignant or beneficial forces with unknown natures and unpredictable wills'.[13] Stuart Ball has done more than most to repudiate this assertion. For him, the importance of the Conservative Right is clear, it typified 'something fundamental which the party could not afford to dispense with . . . the impulses of its heart, even if the head decided to face another way', and he cites the revealing admission of one local party chairman in 1922 that 'every true Conservative man or woman had something of the diehard in his or her constitution'. The right, Ball continues, was 'important for keeping the party in contact with its core support, and for denying any competing political force further to the right the space in which to grow'.[14] This points to something often lost in the greater scholarly preoccupation with the extreme right over the Conservative Right: the political significance of the Conservative Right remaining within the Conservative party.

This is clearer when comparing the British experience with what occurred in other European states. As E.H.H. Green observes, many continental conservative parties fractured during the transition to mass democracy, most notably in France and Germany, with far-reaching consequences for the stability and viability of their democracies.[15] Indeed, it was their wariness of faction which helped to keep Britain's Conservative Right within the Conservative party. The Edwardian 'crisis of conservatism', on its own, offered an abject lesson to the interwar 'diehards', but so too, as Andrew Bonar Law warned in 1922, did the history of the party throughout the nineteenth century. When the Ultra Tories tried to form their own party in the early 1830s, they faced what Robert Stewart calls the 'peculiar difficulty which afflicts the right wing of conservative parties' in two-party systems. Whereas a radical can break up his party 'without sacrificing the world which he hopes to create', the 'extreme Conservative has less scope'. Breaking with the party 'not only loses his immediate object . . . but he also weakens the force of Conservatism, hands power to his opponents, and thereby assists radical triumphs which are almost certain to be permanent'.[16] However much the Conservative Right might bristle with unease about their party leadership, it recognized, as Ball explains, that political parties were 'at the very least a necessary evil' and that there were 'powerful pragmatic reasons for remaining within the fold'. Behind the Conservative Right's high-flown language about maintaining Conservative principles, disputes between it and the party leadership very often boiled down to differences of opinion over methods and strategies.[17] The importance of remaining attached to the Conservative party was underlined by its electoral success after 1918, a feature which was accompanied and supported by the dominance of a very particular idea of mass democracy – 'English constitutionalism' – which thereafter came to define the domain of acceptable political behaviour.[18] Conservatives had always identified themselves with the constitution, but the increasingly extreme positions adopted by the party in the Edwardian period called into question their fidelity to constitutionalism. The claims of Conservatives at the time that the constitution had been suspended seemed naive and self-serving, for these ignored the nature of electoral politics and the long-established supremacy of Parliament in general and the House of Commons in particular. After this period of aberration, the party, especially under the leadership of Stanley Baldwin, renewed its strong identification with the constitution. His emphasis on the sovereignty of Parliament was not so much a return to the past, however, as a means of reaching out to Liberal voters and casting socialists, communists and fascists as enemies of the constitution. The resulting shift away from Conservative shibboleths naturally frustrated the Conservative Right, but the Baldwinite project to transcend class, gender and denomination was undeniably successful with the electorate and popular amongst Conservative MPs.

The real significance of the Conservative Right is its accommodation within the Conservative party, whose survival and unity Ross McKibbin describes as the 'crucial datum' of British political history since 1918.[19] The wider relevance of this is underlined by Brian Girvin's observation that 'the Conservative Party was closer to a liberal constitutional model of politics than to the authoritarian style predominant in many other European states'.[20] The pronounced tendency of historians to look in the opposite direction, at possible links between the Conservative Right and the extreme right, has found little that might compare in political significance. As Martin Blinkhorn observes of European right-wing politics between the wars, there is a subjective difference between the 'radical right' and the 'conservative right'.[21] Girvin concurs: 'Whatever sympathy there may have been between the conservative and radical right in terms of their relationship to capitalism, monarchy and religion, the determining difference between them is the acceptance or rejection of liberal democracy'. Girvin's analysis of the adherence of Conservatives to democracy is useful for understanding the dynamic forces also at work on the Conservative Right. He argues that whilst conservatism draws 'its intellectual strength and political power from pre-modern forces, it cannot be separated from the process of modernity itself'. Moreover, although 'conservatism works against modernity, it also operates within it, and by doing so modifies, influences and changes that structure.' Crucially, its dynamic role in politics leads 'to a blending and influence ... which has had a decisive impact on the evolution of democratic politics'. The willingness of Conservatives, and therefore the Conservative Right, to use modernity as a means of opposing it, and even to utilize 'progressive issues' to 'generate bulwarks against modernity', does not mean that they were progressive or even a force for modernity.[22] It is always necessary in judging such behaviour to draw a distinction between 'progress', a positivistic concept, and 'modern', which grants space to a wide range of moral judgements.[23] It demonstrates, rather, that political tactics could, on occasion, give the appearance of contradicting the core beliefs advanced by the Conservative Right.

In spite of Cowling's dismissal of back-bench opinion, he admitted, albeit in passing, that the Conservative Right of the 1920s and 1930s had some political influence, chiefly as 'a party of propaganda', and that the success of their sporadic campaigns depended on the efforts of individuals.[24] He conceded also that their campaign of further opposition to extending Indian responsible government eroded Baldwin's authority in the party and forced the government subsequently 'to appease critics in other directions'.[25] A number of other historians similarly conclude that the influence of the Conservative Right has been largely confined to the press, though some accept that it might also have affected the calculations of ministers, and that it could even express the dissatisfaction of many more backbenchers than those openly defying the front bench.[26] It is possible to develop this still further by following Bill Schwarz's call to 'think through the transactions between mass politics and mass culture ... for these two forms are intricately connected'. He advances this to examine 'authentic crises of Conservatism', which occur when 'national sentiment points one way, and the requirements of state management point another'.[27] This has utility in understanding the capacity of the Conservative Right periodically to undermine front-bench authority. As Ball observes of the interwar diehards, they were unable on their own to determine party policy or remove the party leader. They had to persuade other right-of-centre Conservative MPs, as well as the moderate centre, or as he describes them, the 'ballast of the party'. It was only 'if events should confirm their constant complaints, or if their outlook on any major issue should come to be widely shared within the parliamentary Party' that the Conservative Right could provoke a party crisis.[28] Yet outward expressions of loyalty to the party leader were an intrinsic element of remaining within the

Conservative fold. In spite of privately held frustrations and objections, the Conservative Right was obliged to couch its concerns and criticism in the language of fidelity to the leader and party. They knew well that such loyalty counted for much among the rank and file, and that as a result, party leaders were adept at maintaining their hold over the voluntary party at times of crisis by appearing to give them a fair hearing.[29] In trying to uncover the influence of the Conservative Right, therefore, it is not the aim of *Britannia's Zealots* to suggest that it dictated or otherwise determined party policy let alone government policy. Rather, it tries to observe something more subtle and easily overlooked, namely, the Conservative Right's relationship with the grass roots and press and how it brought these to bear on the party leadership; and as a result of this, the Conservative Right's occasional capacity to influence the delivery of policy; and on rarer occasions, even prevent party leaders adopting a certain course of action for fear of the backlash it might provoke.

The term Conservative Right is employed to lend a measure of clarity to a subject which has attracted a proliferation of labels. This is inevitable given that scholars have examined specific episodes or offered summarizing syntheses. Moreover, the adoption of terms such as 'Radical Right', 'Radical Conservative' and 'Radical Tories', is not always consistent, especially on whether or not these labels can be applied exclusively to members of the Conservative party. E.H.H. Green helped to popularize 'Radical Conservative', which he distinguished from 'radical right … in order to differentiate developments in the "British Right" from those on the continent', where the tendency has been to apply it to 'proto-fascist groups and ideas'.[30] Alan Sykes, in contrast, has employed the term 'radical right' for this very purpose.[31] If confusion over labelling poses a problem for the historian of right-wing conservatism, it is also a complicating factor in longitudinal histories of conservatism generally. The parliamentary party, in recognition of its relationship with the Liberal Unionists, referred to itself as the Unionist party from the late–1880s, and reverted back to Conservative in the 1920s, though not all local constituency organizations went along with either change, and some even preferred alternative labels such as 'constitutional'. Unionists in Scotland retained the name until the 1960s. The task is considerably more fraught for those examining the party in the late eighteenth and early nineteenth centuries. Then it lacked an official or agreed name: Pittite, Tory, Blues, loyalist, country party, and Brunswickers were all in circulation. Historians have preferred 'Conservative' or 'Tory', for convenience, to describe the parliamentary party, sections within it, or to account for the modern Conservative party's antecedents. It follows that those on the right of the party in this period are also described in numerous ways, with Robert Blake alone offering 'Ultra', 'doctrinaire Tory', 'antediluvian', 'country party' and 'stern and unbending Toryism'.[32]

Whilst historians struggle to agree a consistent nomenclature, there is greater consistency on the existence of a binary divide within the party and its attendant and competing political outlooks. Sykes, for example, proposes that British conservatism 'evolved with two different, even conflicting, traditions, which exist in varying degrees of tension within a single political party, and even within individuals'. On the one hand, there is 'a rationalist approach, seeking the greatest happiness of the greatest number in a society in which anarchy is just below the surface and authority is needed to preserve any happiness at all', and what he describes as 'a "divine" view, in which the actual social and political order is seen as part of a larger supernatural order'.[33] Harvey Glickman identifies the two strains as positional and doctrinal.[34] For Coleman, the contrasting outlooks are presented as the 'cerebral and the more atavistic'.[35] 'King Henry' and 'Prince Hal' fulfil these roles for Rodney Barker, the former representing the 'normal, central, mainstream tradition of political thought', the latter taking 'the guise of a bold and rebellious voice crying in a wilderness laid bare by orthodoxies either socialist or liberal'.[36] T.F. Lindsay and Michael Harrington discern the two viewpoints as 'Conservative' and 'Tory'. The former surpassed the latter they argue, but with Toryism still casting a long shadow which to some extent blended with Conservatism. They regard Toryism as rooted in feudal tradition, making it hierarchical, authoritarian, paternalistic and collectivistic. Tories 'were the party of Church and King, and this special concern for the position of the Church [of England, Ireland and of Scotland] and the Monarchy has continued to be an important feature of Conservative politics'. Conservatism, in contrast, 'has no real objectives'; its 'way of looking at politics can best be approached through [Edmund] Burke's reaction against the French Revolution ... reason is a fragile and unreliable guide, prejudice represents the accumulated wisdom of generations'.[37] The waning influence of Toryism on conservatism exercised the diehard Conservative MP, Viscount Lymington (1898–1984):

> the difference between modern Conservatism and Toryism is that the modern Conservative too often ceases to regard history after it has disappeared from living memory. The Tory takes a deeper view, in that instinctively he tries to discern between the growth and the decay of functions in the application of history to modern issues. Thus to the Conservative what has become an established fact in the last twenty-five years, becomes if it has any pretence at all to conform with Conservatism, an object for indiscriminate conservation.[38]

Three decades later, and from a contrasting position in the party, the veteran Conservative minister, Rab Butler, provided a bittersweet take on the binary division which no doubt drew on his personal experience:

> The range of defensive response has always varied widely in degree of sophistication – all the way from the dunderhead stand-patters thundering '*on ne passe pas*' while dying in penultimate ditches, to the supple and subtle intellectuals who, each in his or her own very different way, have said: 'alas, feudalism and monasticism and lordship and kingship and vicinage and other features of the organic society cannot conceivably survive the impact of the almighty machine, but the *values* of that older society can and must somehow be made to survive'.[39]

Philip Norton and Arthur Aughey present the most detailed breakdown of the dualism at work within British conservatism. They take exception to the first Baron Coleraine's claim that conservatism is a golden mean of the 'Tory concept of original sin and the Whig concept of human improvement', on the basis that it ignores pragmatic decisions to lean one way or the other. But Norton and Aughey still take the Whig and Tory elements posited by Coleraine to embody the coalition of interests within British conservatism. The former, they aver, 'gets down to materialistic basics and appears to brush off all the old moralistic *faux frais* of Toryism'. The Whig element 'desires to anticipate change, to be in the van of economic and political reform and thus to mould events in a way that most efficiently preserves the equilibrium of the productive dynamism of capitalism'. This element 'tends to elevate intelligence and intellectual rigour above mere deference to tradition', it believes that 'a balanced constitution will come about naturally so long as the economy is producing the material goods', and that 'morals should be left to archbishops'. Toryism, in contrast, 'is the desire to maintain the social and political system that exists at any one time or even to restore privileges that have been lost'. It believes in 'a harmonious and well-disciplined society'. It is compassionate and concerned 'for the moral as well as the economic wellbeing of the people'. In contrast to Whig reason, Toryism 'appeals to the heart and soul', and is 'sceptical with a touch of fatalism'. Within Toryism, they argue, it is possible to delineate four general tendencies: a pessimistic or fatalistic strain, which appears aloof and cynical, and holds to nostalgic myths of a golden age, but lacks any 'defined or operative alternative to what exists'; a paternalistic strain, characterized by *noblesse oblige*; 'progressive Toryism', an updated paternalism which articulates explicitly 'the emotional thrust of that strain in terms which appear relevant to modern political debate';

and combative Toryism, which criticizes 'any attempt to undermine values and standards in society' and that 'tends also to be inherently suspicious of fashionable new ideas and of establishment "pinkishness"'. In Whiggery, Norton and Aughey divine two strains: corporate Whiggery, whose 'keynotes are efficiency, bigness and rationalisation'; and 'neo-liberalism', which 'asserts that the State should play only a very limited role in the economic affairs of the nation.'[40]

The proliferation and inconsistency of labels on this subject highlights the difficulty of defining the Conservative Right primarily through ideas or ideology, especially in a longitudinal survey. Defined rigidly, the people and groups examined could potentially be too few to be meaningful, and the analysis couched in exceptions and caveats to explain why the examples given on occasion defied the confines of those labels and disagreed with one another on particular issues. The fourth Marquess of Salisbury (1861–1947), for example, lamented in 1904 about reactionary Conservatives adopting a 'catastrophical theory of politics' in their attitudes to Labour and international relations.[41] Yet Salisbury was one of the most reactionary of his generation when it came to traditionalist causes such as the established churches. Conversely, the sixth Earl Winterton (1883–1962), MP for Horsham, was amongst the biggest troublemakers on the pre-war right; yet after 1918 the Irish peer shifted to become a critic of 'reactionary' elements of the party.[42] Defined too broadly, then the importance of these ideas in helping to explain and contextualize the attitudes and behaviour of right-wing Conservatives is lost, and the category becomes too wide-ranging to be meaningful. As Blinkhorn observes, 'the definitions, typologies and taxonomies beloved of social scientists tend to fit uncomfortably the intractable realities which are the raw material of the historian ... what is needed is rather a valid and useful *working approach* which will assist our understanding.'[43] This accounts for the working approach outlined above. Through this it is possible to acknowledge principles, preferences and attitudes, as well as how these could be moderated, negotiated and even shifted as a result of the political calculations required of parliamentary politics and changing societal attitudes.

III

The Conservative Right's abiding anxieties about the influence of socialism at home and imperial decline overseas embodied considerably older concerns about social order, political economy and Britain's global status. This is not a completely novel observation. Coleman highlights strong continuities in

Conservative politics throughout the nineteenth century, either side of the ruptures of the Great Reform Act and the downfall of Sir Robert Peel, in personnel, interests and sentiment.[44] More pertinent to this study, Gregory Phillips notes that the 'diehard' or 'ditcher' peers – those who opposed the 1911 Parliament bill to the last ditch – 'continued an established Tory tradition', stretching back to the repeal in 1846 of the corn laws, 'of periodically criticizing the party leadership for lacking vigour or for abandoning conservative principles'.[45] And John Charmley argues that Conservative divisions in the 1930s over India were the latest stage in an 'age-old struggle between those who argued that accommodation with change was necessary to preserve what could be preserved, and those who knew that tactical concessions always led to strategic ones'.[46] *Britannia's Zealots* sets out to examine properly these continuities and by doing so demonstrate the deep roots of the Conservative Right.

The 'Ultra Tories' of the early to mid-nineteenth century can be regarded either as the ancestors or precursors of the Conservative Right. A crucial difference between the two is that for Ultras the Protestant constitution, not the possession of an empire, symbolized and embodied all that they held dear. Other than this, Ultras held many of the same underlying concerns and exhibited similar fractious behaviour in their attitude to the party and its leaders. Ultras too were regarded by contemporaries as defensive and destructive, engaged in a hopeless struggle to oppose change. Anthony Trollope offered a wry take on their politics in *The Eustace Diamonds*:

> His father was a fine old Tory of the ancient school, who thought that things were going from bad to worse, but was able to live happily in spite of his anticipations . . . They feel among themselves that everything that is being done is bad – even though that everything is done by their own party. It was bad to interfere with Charles, bad to endure Cromwell, bad to banish James, bad to put up with William. The House of Hanover was bad. All interference with prerogative has been bad. The Reform bill was very bad. Encroachment on the estates of the bishops was bad. Emancipation of Roman Catholics was the worst of all. Abolition of corn laws, church rates, and oaths and tests were all bad. The meddling with the universities has been grievous. The treatment of the Irish Church has been Satanic. The overhauling of schools is most injurious to English education. Education bills and Irish land bills were all bad. Every step taken has been bad. And yet to them old England is of all countries in the world the best to live in . . . To have been always in the right and yet always on the losing side; always being ruined, always under persecution from a wild spirit of republican-demagogism – and yet never to lose anything, not even position or public esteem,

is pleasant enough. A huge, living, daily increasing grievance that does one no palpable harm, is the happiest possession that a man can have. There is a large body of such men in England, and, personally, they are the very salt of the nation. He who said that all Conservatives are stupid did not know them.[47]

Invoking seventeenth-century politics to explain conservatism was not out of place in nineteenth-century accounts, as demonstrated in Benjamin Disraeli's *Sybil*.[48] That historians have been more cautious is understandable given that the Tory party of the seventeenth to mid-eighteenth centuries is not the same as the Tory party of the late eighteenth and early nineteenth centuries. Not only had the old Whig–Tory cleavage gone into abeyance in the second half of the eighteenth century, but the emergence of a Left–Right dichotomy in response to the American and French revolutions was between radical Whigs and conservative Whigs. Accusing the latter of being Tories was intended as a slur, linking the followers of William Pitt the Younger with an anachronistic and controversial political legacy. Yet if Pitt's adherents in Parliament did not regard themselves as Tories, their ministries had a distinct political identity and purpose which echoed Tory precursors. James Sack argues that there may even have been a basis to the slur, at least amongst Pitt's supporters out-of-doors, through their common preoccupation with 'churchly matters'. Moreover, far from being absent, late eighteenth-century Toryism continued to exist, he argues, albeit 'in a largely religious context, in the revival or nurture, often by conservative Whigs, sometimes by avowed Tories who clung to the old name, of right-wing political and especially spiritual attitudes in the press, in pamphlets, and in sermons.' This, Sack avers, gave ' "the Right" its identity and its abiding character'.[49] It certainly helps to explain why a significant section of Pitt's adherents, after his death, refashioned his political outlook to make it fit their enduring anti-Catholic and anti-latitudinarian outlook. As a result, Pitt's successor as 'Tory' leader, the second Earl of Liverpool, was judged against a myth and not unexpectedly found wanting. His chief accusers in this regard were the thirty or so parliamentarians identified as Ultra Tories.

Ultras have received relatively little scholarly attention. Part of the difficulty is that the appellation is just as problematic as Tory. Its application by contemporaries, at least in the 1820s, was confused and inconsistent; after all, the Ultras' preoccupation with the Protestant constitution suggests that they were the successors of conservative Whigs and not old Tories. Their intellectual lineage aside, Ultras were in practice closely bound up with the faction of parliamentarians commonly labelled Tory. Their difficult relationship with Tory ministries is explained by the fact that front- and backbenchers did not belong to a single coherent party. Tory ministers nevertheless depended on the support of Ultras, amongst others, in parliamentary divisions; mirroring the reliance of Whig ministries on radical MPs. The Ultras' preoccupation with preserving the status quo invariably led them to venerate the Glorious Revolution in the manner of old Whigs, but they represented a political tradition, located also in the press and established churches, which was primarily confessional and agrarian. As ideal-based conviction politicians, Ultras were committed to upholding values and institutions which protected the traditional social order. Content to settle for a minor role in the House of Commons, leaving leadership to the natural men of government – typically the more wealthy, powerful and talented – Ultras nonetheless remained vigilant. Fitful efforts to break with this pattern, by launching what amounted to a coup, were doomed to failure, such as the attempt in 1830 by the Ultra MP, Sir Richard Vyvyan, then twenty-eight years old, to form a ministry.[50] Ultras differed from front-bench Tories in style, strategy, organization and tactics. The resulting tensions occasionally flared up in parliamentary debates and in the journalism of Ultra sympathizers across the country. On three famous occasions it led to clashes which brought down Tory ministries: over Catholic emancipation; the subsequent reform crisis; and the repeal of the corn laws. *The Times* in 1830 expressed the governing caste's contempt for such men:

> This party, characterized throughout the United Kingdom as 'Ultra Tories,' consist of the ancient, inveterate placeholders – the most narrow minded, servile, and thorough-going courtiers – the most insolent and exclusive advocates of every shade and form of monopoly, whether game-laws, alehouse license laws, anti-Catholic penal laws, anti-Christian corn laws. No matter what modification of monopoly the grievance complained of may assume, if only it be complaisant enough to the wealthier classes, and sufficiently oppressive to the poor, these men are sure to be its supporters, with a zeal and pertinacity worthy of the noblest ends, but by them perverted to the most iniquitous.[51]

In acknowledging that the Ultras offer a point of comparison with the twentieth-century Conservative Right, is it possible to point to deeper connections and not merely comparisons? Robert Stewart's contention that the Ultras ceased to exist in any meaningful sense by the late 1830s suggests that the answer is no.[52] Richard Gaunt, in contrast, answers in the affirmative, citing the fifth Duke of Richmond as 'the most conspicuous link' between the 'country parties' of 1830 and 1846.[53] As Richmond's political career demonstrates, the accommodation of

Ultras within the more coherent 'Conservative party' which developed from the mid–1830s was hardly likely to eliminate their instinctive hostility to certain measures. To address this question properly, it is necessary to acknowledge what Jeremy Black calls the 'long-term, seemingly inherent assumptions, the emotions of policy, that help create the context for the politics of the shorter term'.[54] Applying this deep history approach, it is not only possible to examine the longer-term influence of Ultra politics on the Conservative Right, but also to trace its origins back to the late seventeenth century. In doing so it is important not to suggest that the Ultras were a coherent or organized faction. Ultra Tories existed in an age before political parties had fully developed. They were identified by their behaviour and attitudes; individual Ultras shifted position on certain issues and their passions varied. In attempting to develop a deep history of reactionary conservatism, therefore, it is instructive to utilize Douglas Simes' categorization of the elements of Ultra politics: Protestant constitutionalism, patriotism, pastoralism, protectionism and philanthropy.[55]

IV

Devotion to the Protestant constitution defined the Ultras. Rooted in a particular interpretation of the historic development of the established churches, Ultras held that state institutions which embodied or upheld the values of the national religion must also be protected. It shaped their responses to almost all major political questions, domestic, foreign and colonial. The strength of popular Protestantism meant that Ultra ideas transcended class as well as the three kingdoms. Reverence for the Protestant constitution, of course, was also a characteristic of conservative Whigs, and at first glance it seems at odds with the old Tories' stance on the exclusion crisis of 1679–81. The latter's fidelity to James, Duke of York, after all, reluctantly tolerated his Catholicism and that of his potential heirs, on the basis that parliamentary interference with the royal succession risked undermining the entire social, political and religious order. But the ultimate loyalty of the old Tories was to the divinely ordained authority of the Crown and established churches. It was this outlook which saw the Tories through the difficult years of the 1688–89 Glorious Revolution to enjoy a revival during the reign of Queen Anne. A minority, however, following Anne's death, could not be completely reconciled to the crown passing to the House of Hanover. The first Viscount Bolingbroke was among those who attempted to persuade King James II's son and namesake to embrace Anglicanism, in order to render him more acceptable to Parliament. The Old Pretender's refusal substantiated Whig allegations that Tories were lenient on Catholicism and allowed Whig ministers to persuade George I of the necessity of excluding all Tories from any advancement under the Crown.

Decades later, when George III lifted his grandfather's proscription on Tory officeholders, the label had ceased to be a meaningful party attachment. But Tory ideas survived in the journalism and pamphleteering of High Churchmen and populist Protestants. The Rev. Henry Bate Dudley's output, for example, was anti-dissenter, xenophobic, anti-Semitic and 'quirkily humanitarian', expressions of an old Toryism which led him in due course to support the anti-radical policies of Pittite ministries, and the latter to return the favour through government patronage.[56] This embrace was one of convenience, for disagreements persisted between Pitt and his followers, both on the backbenches and out-of-doors, about two of the most important questions of the day, Catholic emancipation and electoral reform. Pitt's death in 1806 helped to strengthen the Protestant element in the broad coalition he had marshalled in Parliament, so that the 1807 general election became the first in which the Anglican clergy figured prominently as a distinct interest.[57] As great landowners it is hardly surprising that the established churches tied their colours to Pitt and his heirs, but this common cause was deepened by their mutual suspicion of radicalism and the growing numbers and influence of dissenters and Catholics. Given the hostility of these Tories to other denominations, it is noteworthy that the anti-Semitic strain of old Toryism became less pronounced in this period. A majority of the Tory press supported an end to Jewish disabilities by 1829, with only a small number of organs, such as *John Bull* and *Fraser's Magazine*, continuing to peddle racial slurs.[58]

In contrast to their English counterparts, Irish Tories remained loyal to the Hanoverian succession; their controversial proprietorship of the land depended on the settlement of 1688–89.[59] The fidelity of Irish Tories to the Glorious Revolution was over time fortified by strong connections to the Orange Society. Originating amongst small farmers in south Ulster, Orangeism spread from Ireland to Britain during the wars with France. The Society's hybrid political ancestry and popular base both attracted and repelled Ultras in Parliament. The Duke of Cumberland, fifth son of George III, presided over its English grand lodge. Other Ultras, however, including the fourth Duke of Newcastle and the first Earl of Eldon, distrusted the democratic and freemasonic character of Orangeism. The Society's prominent defence of the sanctity of marriage during the Queen Caroline affair of 1820, in defiance of George IV, his ministers and bishops, further concerned a section of Ultras wary of imbuing ordinary people with political agency.[60] Such suspicions prevented Ultras from co-opting the Orange Society, and its offshoot Brunswick Clubs, as a popular base for their parliamentary activity. Orangeism nevertheless left an indelible mark on popular Tory politics which continued through to the twentieth century, especially in Ireland and parts of Britain with significant Catholic Irish settlement.[61] This missed opportunity for a 'democratic' Ultra Toryism is all the more noteworthy given their shared attitude to the perceived change in style of Lord Liverpool's administration. Improving economic conditions, decreasing political unrest and the adhesion of several prominent Whigs to his ministry in the 1820s heralded a decline in political repression. Ultras feared a revolution, especially after a Catholic Relief bill successfully passed through the House of Commons in 1825, only to be blocked in the House of Lords following the intervention of the king's brother, the Duke of York and Albany. The 1826 general election demonstrated that public opinion in Britain remained hostile to Catholic enfranchisement, but Ultras were still not ready to consider harnessing democratic forces; even after Catholic emancipation was passed in 1829 few Ultras were prepared to take that step.[62] This aside, tensions between Ultras and front-bench Tories over the Catholic question and other policy areas contributed to Liverpool's stroke in 1827, the break-up of his ministry and the brief lifespan of the coalition ministry which followed.

The administration formed in 1828 by Wellington and Peel was meant to restore unity. But Wellington's indifference to Ultra concerns led them to accuse him of being authoritarian, militaristic and in the mould of Oliver Cromwell.[63] They cast him also as an 'apostate' for introducing the 1829 Catholic Relief bill, an action which led some to consider replacing him with Cumberland. Ultras were not alone in opposing the measure. In addition to the 2,000 or so petitions submitted to Parliament, George IV, and around 200 Tory MPs and 100 peers, all attempted to block the bill, requiring Wellington to rely on Whig support. As if this was not enough, Wellington accepted the tenth Earl of Winchelsea's challenge to a duel. Submitting himself for re-election at Oxford University, Peel too faced an unwelcome contest. Wellington lived and received an apology; Peel was defeated by Sir Robert Inglis, the leading spokesman of the fifty MPs who made up the High Church party. This political crisis effectively undermined the political alliance between Wellington and the Ultras and fatally weakened his ministry. It limped on until the end of 1830, coming asunder following a last-ditch effort by Wellington to rally Ultra feeling by declaring against parliamentary reform. Not that Ultras were kingmakers. As noted already, Vyvyan's attempt to fashion a ministry, containing the unlikely combination of Cumberland and several Whigs, came to nothing, for although Ultras were capable of undermining Tory ministries, they were singularly incapable of forming alternatives. Indeed, their fundamental weakness lay exposed just as the passage of Catholic emancipation undermined their rationale and coherence as a parliamentary grouping. Yet anti-Catholicism remained a pronounced feature of Conservative politics throughout the nineteenth century. It was periodically inflamed when governments at Westminster, Liberal and Conservative, sought to conciliate Irish Catholicism, so that it remained a factor in ministerial calculations about the likelihood of disaffection amongst the party rank and file.[64]

Sitting on the opposition benches in the 1830s restored a measure of coherence to Tory parliamentarians. Indeed, the recovery of the Tories' political fortunes in that decade paralleled and was bound up with the emergence of a more assertive Anglicanism.[65] Yet Tories remained prone to divide in response to certain measures laid down by the Whig ministry. Its 1833 Irish Church Temporalities bill provoked Cumberland and Wellington to take opposing positions, though Tories united to defeat the Whigs' 1834 measure to admit dissenters to the universities. Unity was further assisted by the inclusion of six Ultras in the 1834 ministry assembled by Peel and its improved performance – under the newly adopted name of 'Conservative' – soon after at the polls.[66] The Conservative party's religious identity was reinforced at the 1837 general election when the Church of England again lent its support. These developments, which favoured the party's greater cohesion based on state Protestantism, posed an obstacle to Peel's efforts in reaching out to conservative Whigs, especially as Conservatives in the House of Lords reacted angrily to his government's suppression of the Orange Society. Wellington warned the Ultra peers – the most prominent of which included the Dukes of Cumberland, Buckingham and Newcastle, and Lords Londonderry, Falmouth, Winchelsea and Lyndhurst – that sabotaging these and other government measures might precipitate its collapse and replacement by radicals. This logic had never been especially successful amongst Ultras but it convinced the majority of Conservative peers to fall into line, even on religiously sensitive questions such as a permanent Ecclesiastical Commission to organize church revenues, tithe commutation and the right of dissenters to marry according to their own rites. Wellington's burden was lightened considerably in the late 1830s following Cumberland's departure for the throne of Hanover.

Peel's belief in the inevitability of social and economic change coupled with an elitist and high-handed attitude to ordinary MPs ensured continued tensions between the front and back benches into the early 1840s. The latest attempt to conciliate Irish Catholicism again produced one of the most spectacular clashes. Peel's increase to the state grant awarded to St Patrick's College, the seminary at Maynooth, provoked anti-Catholic objections as well as complaints that the established churches required additional support. Peel pressed ahead regardless, despite arousing popular Protestant feeling across the country and especially in Ireland where Orangeism enjoyed a revival. Conservative MPs divided 149–148 against the measure when it was brought before Parliament, necessitating Whig support to secure its passage. Aggrieved by Peel's betrayal, the old Ultra, Winchelsea, led a secession from the Carlton Club along with eighteen MPs; their new National Club claimed by 1851 to have a membership of 45 MPs.[67] Likewise, Lord Ashley's Protestant Association dedicated itself to repealing the Act.

The ground was thus prepared for the devastating party battle over the repeal of the corn laws. Even after that clash, when the majority of Conservatives defined themselves against the free-trade Peelites, Protestantism proved to be more dependable and meaningful than protectionism in rallying popular support. Shorn of the Peelites, the narrow religious outlook in what remained of the party became apparent in its treatment of Lord George Bentinck. He had assumed a leading position following Peel's departure, but his support for the 1847 Jewish Disabilities bill provoked an angry response on the back benches and led to his resignation. Adherence to sectarian politics therefore helped Conservatives at the polls but limited their capacity to recruit a talented front bench. As such, the party's electoral fortunes revived during the 1850–51 papal aggression crisis and indirectly brought about its brief return to office in 1851, following the collapse of Lord Russell's Whig government. As noted in section VI of this chapter, the fourteenth Earl of Derby's new ministry disappointed backbenchers on protection, but its decision to ban Catholic processions on the eve of the 1852 general election, triggering disturbances across the United Kingdom, at least satisfied the party's compromised stance on state Protestantism. Indeed, Derby's decision to abandon protection left Protestantism as the party's primary badge of identity. It was not enough, however, to dislodge the third Viscount Palmerston from his long spell in office as prime minister, not least because Conservatives in the constituencies struggled to fault his patriotic credentials.[68] This weakened the Conservative party in Scotland though it continued to prosper in Ireland where sectarian politics remained bound up with the preservation of the 'Ascendancy'.[69] Here then, Ultra politics enjoyed something of an Indian summer, for electoral success encouraged Irish Conservatives to believe that fidelity to Conservative orthodoxy paid dividends. If this promoted solidarity in their ranks, it also bred paranoia about the party's front bench at Westminster.[70] And in the aftermath of the Second Reform Act, it left Irish Conservatives on the back foot and clinging onto Protestant strongholds in Ulster and County Dublin.

The distrust felt by Irish Conservatives towards the front bench was not entirely unfounded. The latter remained committed to identifying with the established churches, but its desire to wrest conservative Whigs from the Liberals meant that over time it became less disposed to translating this into positive assistance or exclusiveness. Protestantism still mattered out-of-doors, especially in areas of significant Catholic Irish migration. Indeed, as Walter Arnstein argues, the trend towards 'religious liberalization', from the 1820s through to the 1870s, 'did as much to rouse ultra-Protestant fears as to allay Roman Catholic dissatisfaction'.[71] As such, the strength of the Fenian movement in Manchester encouraged Orangemen and clerical controversialists to fan sectarian feeling in Lancashire in advance of the 1868 general election, contributing to the populist character of the Conservative party in the county and the revival of its electoral fortunes.[72] The remaining rump of High Church Tories at Westminster were ill-disposed to these 'Extreme Protestants', but in their contrasting ways both groups sought to perpetuate the Conservative party's connection with religion.[73] The declining influence of both was dramatically if temporarily altered when William Gladstone went to the polls in 1868 calling for the disestablishment of the Church of Ireland. Not only did this reanimate the rhetoric of 'church in danger', it led Derby to adopt a posture of defiant opposition which placed him at odds with Conservatives seeking to reach a negotiated compromise.[74] After Derby's death in 1869, his place in this specific capacity, in response to the Liberals' University Test Act and Education bill, was taken by the third Marquess of Salisbury. Disraeli, in contrast, abandoned attempts to craft a new ecclesiastical politics in deference to the increased electoral strength of nonconformity.[75] However, in contrast to Trollope's fictionalized version of Disraeli, Mr Daubeny, who shocks his party by adopting the disestablishment of the Church of England, the real leader of the Conservative party did not forsake religion as a badge of party identity.[76] This much is clear from his famous 1872 addresses at Manchester Free Trade Hall and the Crystal Palace. The following year, widespread objections to Liberal legislation that sought to establish a Catholic University in Dublin proved to be a handy peg on which to eventually bring down and replace Gladstone's ministry, and the accompanying revival in Protestant politics helped to return Disraeli to office at the 1874 general election.[77]

The oft-noted success of Disraeli's ministry in keeping party conflict to a minimum did not extend to religious questions, which even exposed divisions within his own party. The Public Worship Regulation bill, proposed by the Archbishop of Canterbury, obliged Disraeli to declare a stance which offended High Church Conservatives.[78] The 1876 Education Act was meant to appease them but it never went far enough, and they were further irritated by the 1880 Burials Act. Even so, Disraeli prevailed because most of the parliamentary party by this stage 'wore their religion rather lightly'.[79] This shift in attitude led bishops to 'rebel' when Conservative parliamentarians advanced the interests of the brewers.[80] These tensions aside, doctrinal divisions within Anglicanism meant that it now struggled to speak with one voice in public, let alone on the Conservative benches. Pan-Protestantism increasingly took its place in Conservative rhetoric, and became a necessity following the alliance forged in 1886 with the Liberal Unionists. Irish Unionists readily adapted to this transition though not without friction. There was friction too at Westminster given the contrasting positions taken by Salisbury and Joseph Chamberlain on Welsh disestablishment, tithes and denominational education.[81] The pan-Protestantism of Unionist politics, and its more subtle influence on imperial sentiment, helped to take the edge off these lingering intra-Protestant tensions. As a corollary, of course, it helped also to sustain an enduring anti-Catholicism amongst sections of the party into the twentieth century, for a Unionist whip could note in 1910 that it was 'very lucky' that it fell to a Liberal government to alter the king's accession declaration, making it less offensive to Catholics, as the 'No Popery drum is being beaten very hard'.[82] It exerted its influence also in Unionist opposition to the third home rule bill, as well as the parallel campaign in 1913–14 opposing the disestablishment of the Church of England in Wales, causes which demonstrated that rallying to the 'Protestant constitution' could still mobilize party supporters.[83]

V

Simes identifies patriotism as the second of element of Ultra politics. It took the form of a specifically English belief in the perfection of its national church and unreformed constitution, as well as a broader British outlook which stressed Protestantism. In both cases, Britain's prosperity, liberties and greatness were laid at the door of its faith, so that Protestant Britons were identified as a chosen people. Domestically, Irish Catholics were held to be incapable of forming part of the British nation. In international relations, it meant that Britain had to avoid multilateral arrangements – such as the Holy Alliance or the Concert of Europe – with Catholic states. The depth of the Ultras' anti-Catholicism could even lead them to express cautious support for liberal movements across Europe which challenged Catholic monarchies.[84] The assumed uniqueness of the established churches, however, prevented this from developing further; Ultras were unable to develop a 'sense of identity of interest' with Conservatives elsewhere in Europe.[85]

The Ultras' xenophobic patriotism drew on an older tradition, albeit one that was markedly less hostile to Catholicism given the old Tories' fidelity to 'James III'. As the Old Pretender lacked a common religious affiliation with the majority of his British subjects, his 1743 appeal, in advance of his son, Charles Edward, landing in Scotland, pandered instead to a sense of national identity which linked royal nativism with political morality. George II's connection to Germany, the appeal claimed, exerted a corrupting influence on Britain and its national interests, including 'the preference and partiality shewn on all occasions to foreigners'. The restoration of the Stuart line would bring this state of affairs to an end and rescue the people from 'their present deplorable situation ... convinced they can find no relief but by restoring their natural born Prince'. The House of Stuart's Catholicism and alliance with the French court compromised its patriotic credentials, so the former was not addressed, and the latter excused as a necessity to protect Britain from 'shoals of foreign mercenaries, with which the Elector fills the kingdom whenever he thinks himself in danger'.[86] Such calculated ambiguities were easily denigrated by Whig opponents committed to Protestant solidarity against Catholic France.[87] Clearly, Ultras in the early nineteenth century were more assertively Protestant, but the Old Pretender's invocation of nativism, national exceptionalism, xenophobia and Whig corruption remained important elements in the Tory critique of Whig government. Crucially, it helped Toryism to move beyond a fixation with kingly rights by placing a greater stress on the national community. Excluded from office, Tory propagandists emphasized the detrimental effects on the nation exacted by the Whig state's heavy taxes and bloated civil service.[88] This echoed the claim made by the Old Pretender, in his 1743 appeal, that Whig misrule encouraged financial venality, political bribery and the decay of manufacturing and trade, resulting in a 'universal corruption and dissolution of manners, encouraged and countenanced by those, whose example and authority should have been employed to repress it, and a more than tacit connivance given to all irreligion and immorality'.[89]

Bolingbroke developed this line of reasoning into a broader critique of the Whigs' supposed denigration of the British Crown and churches. Under his tutelage, Tories sought not only to restore the House of Stuart, but also a 'nostalgic

vision of an ideal society which had never really existed'.[90] As Jacobitism declined
in importance amongst Tories, it was this wider application of restoration which
remained a potent force especially among the Ultras. Bolingbroke's defence of
constitutional tradition and social hierarchy, government based on prescriptive
not contractual rights, and belief in the superiority of country politics over
urban politics, were important influences too, though these were hardly confined
to the Ultras given that they were taken up and developed by the conservative
Whig, Edmund Burke.[91] The consensual patriotism that reigned in Britain
following the defeat of the 'Bonnie Prince' in 1745, framed by a common
Protestantism and propelled by colonial expansion and successive wars with
France, meant that it was not until the American and French revolutions that the
longer-term influence of Bolingbroke's writings on patriotic duty came into
sharp relief.[92] His Tory vision became manifest in the repression undertaken by
Pitt's ministry and its cultivation of loyalism through the press, political
associations and armed volunteer corps. This bred a 'habit of authoritarianism'
that Ultras clung to longer and harder than the Tory front bench.[93] It obliged
Liverpool to pass the repressive Six Acts in the wake of the 1819 Peterloo
Massacre, but the receding experience of war, along with stabilizing agricultural
conditions, meant that the 1820s saw sections of parliamentary opinion that had
previously turned a blind eye to counter-revolutionary excesses now question its
appropriateness.

The gradual recovery of Conservative unity in the 1830s was helped in part
by renewed anxiety about radicalism. Country party MPs looked on favourably
as James Graham at the Home Office responded to Chartism with repression. In
Ireland, the government suppressed the Repeal Association and banned Daniel
O'Connell's mass meeting at Clontarf. However, Peel employed repression as a
tactic, whereas for Ultras it remained a disposition. This could even produce
unexpected alignments. The quiescence of Conservatives during the long period
of Whig and Liberal government has already been noted; it was aided in part
by Lord Russell's measures against Chartism and the Young Irelanders, and
Palmerston's patriotic foreign policy. The situation returned to more traditional
lines of antagonism following Gladstone's accession to the Liberal leadership.
The new government's stance on Irish disaffection and a series of setbacks in
foreign and imperial policy enabled the Conservatives to wrest back the patriotic
banner which had long been carried by Palmerston.[94] Disraeli's 1872 Crystal
Palace speech even expanded the application of patriotism by criticizing the
Liberals' failure to halt the settlement colonies' drift towards self-determination,
through countervailing measures such as imperial tariffs and defence

coordination. As prime minister from 1874, Disraeli did not live up to his rhetoric about imperial organization, but he certainly succeeded in placing imperialism at the heart of the Conservatives' evolving definition of patriotism.[95]

Grandiloquence alone would not have satisfied all Conservative backbenchers. The deepening party antagonism over patriotic questions therefore served Disraeli well. In contrast to Gladstone, Disraeli offered Irish nationalists and land campaigners only coercion. Bestowing the title 'empress of India' on Victoria was largely symbolic but it served also in driving a helpful wedge between Conservatives and Liberals. More consequentially, if the authoritarian patriotism of a previous age was no longer acceptable in Britain, it could still be vented in policies towards Ireland and India that critics charged with being antithetical to liberty.[96] Even still, Disraeli's more bullish and showy patriotism managed to upset older fealties in the party. The Bulgarian question was closely associated with Gladstone's Midlothian campaign, but High Church Conservatives too were concerned about their government's continued support for the Ottoman Empire. If there were doubts here, then Gladstone's responses to the Irish land war of 1879–80, and controversial relationship with the Irish nationalist MP Charles Stewart Parnell, allowed Conservatives to unite and claim the patriotic high ground by depicting the prime minister as being in thrall to rebels, agitators and dynamitards. This naturally overlooked the fourth Earl of Carnarvon's secret soundings of Parnell in 1885; a reminder that Irish Conservative paranoia was not altogether groundless, and that reactionary elements in the party – Carnarvon was a prominent opponent of the Second Reform Act – were not united or coherent in practice across all issues. The Tory democrats of the Fourth Party – which sought to harness the voluntary party in order to challenge the party leadership – also gave Irish colleagues cause for concern when Lord Randolph Churchill and John Gorst offered a favourable hearing to certain of Parnell's demands.

Having approved Carnarvon's earlier overtures to Parnell, Salisbury nevertheless felt that his room for manoeuvre was very limited, ruling out a devolved central council for Ireland as he would not 'play the part Sir Robert Peel had in 1829 and 1845'.[97] The Unionist ministry formed in 1886 gave no ground on the exclusivity of the Westminster Parliament. And in matters of law and order, Arthur Balfour's tenure at Dublin Castle earned him the sobriquet 'Bloody Balfour'. The party's strong stand on the union helped to boost its standing in Scotland after decades of weak performances at the polls.[98] If Irish Conservatives could take some satisfaction from these events, they were still expected to swallow a series of unpalatable measures – most significantly in land reform and local government – intended to kill home rule with kindness. The number of Conservatives actively opposed to such legislation was kept low through the generous terms always offered to landowners, and the remaining minority handled deftly by party managers in the House of Lords. The alliance with the Liberal Unionists in 1886 was followed in 1895 by the two parties forming a coalition government, and their merger in 1912.[99] The long-term impact on the Conservative and Unionist party's orientation and identity was manifested in its reactions to significant crises in Irish affairs, in 1912–14, 1921–22 and at certain points between 1968 and 1998.

In imperial affairs too there was some concern at the edges of the party. Certainly, Chamberlain at the Colonial Office earned praise from Conservatives.[100] But the existence of the Imperial Federation League and the Navy League, both formed in the 1890s, revealed an undercurrent of dissatisfaction, at least in certain quarters, with the Unionist government's capacity to address rivalry with other great powers. Defence was a particularly sensitive question. It had provoked ire amongst Unionists in 1886, when Lord Randolph Churchill at the Treasury faced significant opposition to proposed cuts to army estimates.[101] The arrival of the Navy League, and later the Army League, signalled that anxiety about defence was no longer confined to Parliament but deliberately cultivated in the press and public. John Darwin observes that declining empires contain elites who 'dig themselves in' and 'enlist the support of other factions and groupings to form a grand coalition, to defend a status quo from which they are chief gainers'.[102] Notably, it was not the leader of the Unionist party who fulfilled this role in Britain, nor for that matter any of his successors in that post. Salisbury and his senior colleagues might claim that theirs was the party of empire, but it was outside of Parliament that the politics of imperialism were 'most openly and vigorously debated'.[103] Rising patriotic fervour, or jingoism, could be an asset, as demonstrated by the Unionists' success at the 'khaki election' of 1900. But Salisbury's willingness to mobilize the 'villa vote' did not prevent him from despising their ultra-patriotism, and he had greater cause to do so as the South African War dragged on and the government stood accused of incompetence.[104] It became increasingly clear that the passions whipped up by imperial patriotism, cultivated by journalists, party activists and the patriotic leagues, slid easily into criticisms of the Unionist party, and reinforced parallel concerns about the capacity of Unionist leaders to defend the union with Ireland and the empire more generally.[105] As the Liberal Unionist A. V. Dicey declared, 'imperialism is to all who share it a form of passionate feeling; it is a political religion, for it is public spirit touched by emotion'.[106]

As the French case demonstrates, it does not necessarily hold that imperial patriotism is synonymous with right-wing politics.[107] Yet the increasing emphasis given to imperial patriotism by the right of the Unionist party recalled the heyday of the Ultras in several ways. The pressure exerted on the front bench has already been noted. It also further implicated the Unionist party with increasingly controversial positions on civil and constitutional liberties, albeit relocated to Britain's overseas territories. The vitality of the British as a nation and global power might now be more explicitly expressed through the prism of empire, but its references to mission, providence and sacrifice indicate that it was not that far removed from a *Protestant* patriotism.[108] The importance of journalists in this endeavour also evoked the role of the patriotic press during the wars with France; it was from that period, after all, that empire first made a marked feature in the emergence of British national identity.[109] The rise of jingoism was not, however, an exclusively Tory affair. It was bolstered by the adhesion of Liberal Unionists, bringing with them a distinctly Liberal tradition of imperialism foregrounded in free trade, representative government and religious tolerance. Right-wing imperialist discourses employed some of these themes in their attempts to foster kith and kin solidarity, and misappropriated them also for the purpose of giving greater emphasis to imperial defence and racial hierarchy.[110] Nonconformist militarism, with its roots 'outside the theatre of the Empire and the professional armed forces', also fed into what Anne Summers calls the 'remarkable shift from evangelism and nonconformity to military and patriotic allegiance'. Imitated subsequently by 'Anglican militarism', these movements, especially popular among the young, helped to lend Edwardian militarism moral and religious qualities.[111] There was still an important difference, however, for whereas Ultra politics prized its exclusivism by keeping even plebeian supporters at arm's length, the Unionist politics of imperialism deliberately and successfully sought to harness working- and middle-class electors.

VI

Pastoralism is the third element of Ultra politics identified by Simes, and inevitably it is bound up with the fourth and fifth, protectionism and philanthropy. There was little to distinguish Ultras from the 'country party', and it was in the guise of the latter that the agrarian elite sought to defend its political and economic privileges against the growing influence of the industrial and commercial bourgeoisie. The traditional system of landholding, they believed, embodied hierarchy and order, promoting both national stability and traditional values, and it was invariably juxtaposed with the supposedly deleterious effects of urbanization and industrialization. Bolingbroke had framed this dichotomy in the early eighteenth century, but agricultural unrest and reform agitation a century later gave such ideas obvious immediacy to country party MPs. Agricultural protection was the economic expression of pastoralism. It also bore closely on their patriotism as it favoured autarky, proved its merits during the Napoleonic Wars and lessened Britain's dependence on foreign suppliers. Pastoralism likewise shaped the Ultras' attitude to franchise reform as it threatened to diminish the agrarian interest and promote that of the industrial and commercial classes. As noted already, Ultra MPs in the 1820s were concerned about the moderating style of Liverpool's government. A ginger group, known as Boodle's Cabinet, kept a keen eye on ministerial interference with the corn laws. Front-bench ministers, after all, were generally wealthier than the average backbencher and less reliant on agricultural rents.[112] Worse still, they were increasingly disposed to listen to industrialists. Back-bench opposition to the 1827 corn bill, Catholic emancipation, and the Great Reform Act therefore featured a familiar cast of country party MPs and their allies in the House of Lords.

The significant number of abstentions in the House of Lords which allowed the Great Reform bill to pass was in no small measure due to William IV's agreement to pack the upper house. The reluctant acquiescence of Tory peers helped to preserve their chamber, and unexpectedly, it soon became clear that the reformed system served to boost landed representation of the counties and even the small boroughs. The latter was checked to some extent by the 1835 Municipal Corporations Act, but overall the trend was towards a gradual recovery which culminated in the Conservatives' victory at the 1841 general election. Peel's gradualist steps towards freer importation were watched with concern by country MPs; the two sides having already clashed in 1834 over the former's Irish tenant bill. The Duke of Richmond's agreement in 1844 to head the new Agricultural Protection Society demonstrated that old Ultras could learn new tricks, for it sought to win over public opinion throughout the country. As such, Peel's decision the following year to repeal the corn laws met with organized opposition. The benefit of harnessing local opinion became clear as protection associations brought pressure to bear on Conservative MPs to prevent their sanctioning a new ministry under Peel.[113] It was not enough, however, to prevent the legislation passing with Whig assistance in 1846, and abandoning many of their most talented ministers on this question left Conservative MPs rudderless.

It is a signal irony that Lord Stanley, afterwards fourteenth Earl of Derby, soon emerged as their champion, for his political career up until that point had been characterized by its fluidity between Whig and Tory administrations. Country MPs benefited too from another unlikely advocate, Disraeli, whose bitter attacks on Peel provided the eloquent voice most of them lacked.

The subsequent improvement in agricultural prices undermined the protectionist cause. Nevertheless, 1849 witnessed a renewed push for protection with the formation of the National Association for the Protection of British Industry and Capital. The emphasis again was on harnessing democracy, not ignoring it. There were two further innovations: working with like-minded allies representing colonial and shipping interests, and emphasizing the socially positive applications of protective tariffs.[114] Even this was not sufficient to check the growing realization of senior Conservatives that their party's commitment to protection had become an electoral liability. Barely three years after the formation of the National Association, Derby took the bold step of abandoning protectionism. It was part of a more general strategy – during Derby's brief minority ministry of 1852 – to demonstrate that Conservatives were not simply a rump of reactionaries incapable of government.[115] Most Conservatives understood Derby's rationale, though zealots like the veteran Ultra, J.W. Croker, remained steadfast. Similar calculations were at work over a decade later when Derby and Disraeli stewarded through the Second Reform Act. Steeled by the long sojourn in opposition and the prospect of a Liberal measure should Conservatives break on the issue, Conservative opposition was confined to forty MPs and three cabinet resignations: Carnarvon, General Jonathan Peel and Viscount Cranborne, afterwards third Marquess of Salisbury. Attempts by Carnarvon and the sixth Duke of Rutland to undermine the bill in the House of Lords were outflanked by Derby and reversed in the Commons.

The Second Reform Act did not signal the abandonment of the Conservative party's landed interests in the way that protection had been jettisoned in 1852. Certainly, it was meant to minimize extensions to the counties by making concessions to the Liberals regarding the borough franchise. But Disraeli remained committed, where possible, to maintaining the political authority of the landed elite, opposing household suffrage in the counties and Gladstone's Ballot Act. Yet the new political dispensation inevitably influenced how the front bench balanced town and country, especially in response to Conservative electoral success in the former. Disraeli's opposition to the Ballot Act, for example, was necessarily muted, as urban Conservatives regarded it as a means of diminishing the influence of Liberal employers.[116] He was quiet too about the

Gladstone ministry's other legislative sorties on landed privilege, on Irish landlords, education in the counties and army commissions, though the disarray of Conservatives in the House of Lords following Derby's death was also a factor.[117] Disraeli's reference to imperial tariffs in his 1872 speech at the Crystal Palace was not a backward glance to his former protectionism; it looked forward instead to harnessing popular sentiment for his party under the banner of imperial patriotism. In office, the 1875 Agricultural Holdings bill attempted to balance the interests of tenant farmers and landowners by granting the former compensation for improvements, but only if both parties agreed to the statutory framework. The 1876 Education Act to some extent addressed landed concerns about their eroding influence in the counties. Following Gladstone's return to office in 1880, Disraeli again displayed cautious ambivalence about defending the landed interest, allowing the 1880 Ground Game bill to pass the House of Lords but rejecting a measure to compensate for disturbances in Ireland.

After Disraeli's death in 1881, Salisbury in the House of Lords and Sir Stafford Northcote in the House of Commons faced the same dilemmas about how to conduct opposition. Salisbury proved to be more bullish than his colleague but did not always get his way. Initially an opponent of Gladstone's 1881 Irish Land bill, despite the support given to it by a section of Irish landlords keen to avoid another land war, Salisbury was subsequently obliged to find a compromise. He was again undermined by a section of Irish peers the following year, when they readily acceded to the Arrears bill that Salisbury had hoped to oppose in order to force a general election. In 1884 Salisbury at first opposed the latest measure of franchise reform – equalizing the counties and boroughs – against the wishes of other senior Unionists, and again compromise was reached, on the question of redistribution. By the time he headed his own ministry in 1885, Salisbury exhibited a conversion, as he joined the ranks of those seeking to deal with Irish land by facilitating tenant purchase, albeit on generous terms to landowners. In doing so he faced a number of rebellions from a different section of Irish landowners: those committed to opposing tenant rights.[118] He was fortunate that these Irish peers rarely succeeded in depicting the measures as an attack on all property and not *sui generis* to pacifying Ireland; the first Earl of Halsbury's 1889 Land Transfer bill was a notable exception resulting in its withdrawal by the government.[119]

Salisbury also inherited the dilemma of how to balance party supporters in the counties with the growing strength of Unionism in the boroughs and cities. The 1880s had witnessed a revival of Conservative agitation for protection under the banner of the Fair Trade League. Around sixty MPs supported the league's campaign for tariffs on agricultural and manufactured imports and motions to this effect were presented at National Union meetings into the 1890s. If nothing else, these fruitless gestures demonstrated that the National Union was not simply a creature of urban Conservatives.[120] More significantly, the polls in 1885 and 1886 heralded a remarkable reorientation as Unionists increased their strength in the boroughs and Liberals increased theirs in the counties. This inevitably made the task of balancing agricultural and industrial interests even harder. There was also the City of London to consider, Unionism having largely recovered the support of the financial class lost in the 1830s over the Tories' response to reform.[121] Under such competing pressures, Salisbury failed to live up to his earlier principled defence of the landed interest. He might have achieved the upper hand with Chamberlain over social reform in the second half of the 1890s, but free trade remained an article of faith for the Unionist government, and the urban bases of both the Conservative and Liberal Unionist parties could not be dismissed lightly.[122] The twelfth Earl of Winchelsea's National Agricultural Union tried in vain to challenge this development.[123] Still, the friction between the aspirations of the old agricultural interest in Unionism and newer sources of support created considerable instability in the party in the longer run. This should not, however, suggest a simple binary conflict between town and country. There were tensions within urban Unionism, between Conservatives and Liberal Unionists, brewers and social reformers, Protestant populists and those making an inclusive appeal, so that it lacked a single powerful register to challenge the landed elite. Moreover, Unionists in towns and cities across Great Britain demonstrated a peculiar veneration for the old order through the archaic medieval pageantry of the Primrose League.[124] And measures such as the Unionists' 1888 Local Government Act could satisfy both town and country, the latter after some persuasion from Salisbury that landowners should use its machinery, and his agreement to maintain separate poor-law boards. Salisbury's management of his party's majority in the House of Lords might also be read as preserving an important institution of the old order by 'appropriating a set of quasi-democratic arguments to bolster its veto'.[125] The agricultural interest in Unionism was certainly a shadow of its former self, but it remained a significant element of the party's identity and electoral strategy. Its accommodation within the Edwardian Tariff Reform League – which sought to harness import duties to the cause of imperial unification – even held out the hope that it might find new relevance in the battle against radical Liberalism.

Philanthropy is the final element of Ultra Tory politics identified by Simes. A subsidiary of the Ultras' Protestantism, pastoralism and protectionism, it was manifested in the practice of *noblesse oblige* and expressions of concern about the negative consequences of industrialization on agricultural workers and child labourers. Habitually paternalistic, it led sometimes to innovation, such as the schemes of social improvement implemented on the Buckingham and Winchelsea estates.[126] In the political sphere, it supplied an increasingly defensive justification of the organic society that Ultras tried to maintain and justify. Its advocates included a milieu of Tory journalists and writers, ranging from the romantic neo-feudalism of the young Disraeli to the concerns for industrial labour found in the Orange press. Sack identifies the latter with 'Tory humanitarianism' and places it within the Jacobite-Tory tradition. These 'Tory radicals' waned as a force in the years leading up the abolition of slavery in 1833, their anti-slavery stance being overwhelmed by Tory proponents of slavery.[127] Liberal hegemony in the mid-nineteenth century, agricultural decline and depression, the resulting indebtedness of estates, and local government reform, all took their toll on the defence of the old order and its ability to properly fulfil its philanthropic functions. Its place in Conservative politics nevertheless survived in a number of contrasting ways. In its purest form, as a defence of hierarchy and landownership, it survived into the Edwardian period when it was employed by the ditcher peers.[128] It endured too in the local practices and customs of county life. It also supplied a tradition and precedent which helped Conservatives to justify their party's démarche into social questions in the wake of the Second Reform Act. These forays onto Liberal territory, of course, were hardly in keeping with the Ultras' rejection of measures which undermined their authority. Even if some were involved in the Agricultural Protection Society, demonstrating that a section of Ultra opinion in the 1840s was moving in this direction, the negative reaction of Conservative backbenchers to the New Social Alliance of 1871, and the Fourth Party a decade later, suggest that old Ultra reflexes also survived.

However distasteful to sections of the Conservative backbenches, these initiatives pointed to a political necessity. It seems likely that the New Social Alliance, despite its brief life, was one of several factors that encouraged Disraeli to adopt social reform in the 1870s.[129] And he of all people could situate this project in the Tory humanitarian tradition. Its importance intensified in response to pressure from urban Conservatives, especially those representing marginal seats, as well as Liberal Unionists after 1886. As noted already, the rising importance of urban Conservatism did not set out to eliminate or denigrate the values of the old agricultural order. It even generated a convergence of sorts that gathered momentum in the final decade of the nineteenth century. There were, of course, advocates of urban social reform within the Unionist party, but there was a far more prevalent wariness amongst ratepayers of expensive schemes that imposed upon local rates, and an instinctive hostility amongst Conservatives to 'state interference'.[130] Some of this was grounded in the lingering survival of anti-government radicalism, but the shifting political sands meant that by the middle of the Edwardian decade the ratepayers movement was an adjunct to Unionist politics.[131] The alliance was cemented by the notion that all property owners had a common interest which had to be mobilized and defended, reinforced by the growing strength of Labour and radical Liberalism in both rural and urban constituencies.[132] Salisbury put it into practice in the second half of the 1890s by frustrating Chamberlain's demands on social policy. The resistance in Parliament to Chamberlain's 1897 Workmen's Compensation bill not only included manufacturers, but also landed magnates with interests in coalmining, such as the sixth Marquess of Londonderry.[133] Yet the greater public profile given to urban slums in the 1880s and 1890s could not be ignored altogether. In fact, Unionists embraced these problems with renewed vigour in response to the South African War. The ditcher peers, in many respects the Ultras' latter-day successors, were drawn in significant numbers to the panaceas offered by tariff reform and the patriotic leagues. The leagues' emphasis on social policies might have been focused on winning over urban support, but the accompanying discourses on the obligations of property ownership, character, self-sacrifice and leadership recalled the philanthropic ideals once championed by the Ultras.[134] As with the other elements of Ultra politics identified by Simes, their attitude to philanthropy continued to have bearing on subsequent generations, if only in an attenuated and considerably modified form. And like them, it fed into the Edwardian 'crisis of conservatism' which had been brewing since the last days of Salisbury's premiership.[135]

VII

The crisis of conservatism was not so much the beginning of modern reactionary politics as a significant marker in its long development. Nor was it a resurgence of reactionary forces. Rather, it was a product of the Conservatives' late-Victorian success in accommodating new interests and expectations, which found expression in an assortment of right-wing campaigns. Nevertheless, the themes outlined above are observable in the responses of the varying types of right-wing dissidence which arose in this period. As Chapter 1 examines, these became manifest in three distinct vectors of dissent within the party: the empire-first Unionists; the legion of leagues; and the ditcher peers. Overlapping in theme, personnel and ideas, they nevertheless remained distinct expressions of Unionist discontent through to the First World War. United only by a shared desire to see the party's front bench adopt a more assertive and principled approach to parliamentary opposition, each vector – and even within each vector – experienced disagreements about the definition and application of those principles. Still, their influence was felt in a number of ways. In the short term, right-wing discontents helped to remove the party leader and bring about a change in the style of leadership, and their activism was a significant factor in the decision to reorganize the party machine. In the longer term, the assortment of groups and causes on the Right supplied many of the attitudes, ideas, behaviour and personnel which went on to define the interwar Conservative Right.

Chapter 2 analyses the response of right-wing Unionists to the political upheaval wrought by the First World War. The crisis acted as a restraint on the party's right wing, but it failed to diminish the tensions and divisions which had plagued Unionism since the turn of the century. If anything, these were further inflamed by the demands of political cooperation between the Liberal and Unionist front benches. The resulting back-bench unrest encouraged paradoxically the Unionist front bench to formalize this cooperation in a wartime coalition, and to reorganize that coalition in its favour later in the war when right-wing back-bench dissidents threatened to undermine wartime government. Their influence was strengthened by the organization of back-bench committees, but the heightened anxieties of wartime meant that the most zealous right-wingers were never fully satisfied with the Unionist leadership and even the party. The contrasting fates of the different elements of right-wing politics are charted, from the struggles of traditionalist Conservatism and the legion of patriotic leagues, through to the decision of the most fanatical tariff reformers to breakaway and form the National Party.

The continuance of the Unionist–Liberal coalition after the First World War and its role in the creation of a more coherent 'Conservative Right' is the subject of Chapter 3. These 'diehards' were shunned by many Unionist parliamentarians, but the seemingly principled position they articulated found support beyond Westminster, to the growing consternation of influential figures in the party. The Conservative Right's emergence as a distinctive, cohesive and purposive body of politicians was in part a product of their common rejection of the post-war evolution of imperial policy, as well as their pronounced hostility to government spending, and stimulated by the ill-fated attempt by leading Unionists to fuse the two governing parties. It was sustained and developed thereafter through the series of domestic, imperial and diplomatic political crises which beset the post-war coalition and called into question its purpose and longevity. Indeed, it was the fear amongst junior and middle-ranking ministers and party officials that the diehards might achieve some sort of ascendancy in the wider party that convinced them in the end to break with David Lloyd George and return to the old party system.

Having achieved this measure of unity and sense of purpose, Chapter 4 charts how the diehards understood and interacted with post-war democracy. Whilst some were attracted to the indigenous forms of fascism which emerged after the First World War, the overwhelming majority were convinced of the need to work within the Conservative party. There was considerable unease with Stanley Baldwin's attempts to shift the party to the centre, but on domestic reform at least, most diehards acquiesced, even if reluctantly. Subjects which had once defined reactionary Conservatives no longer appeared to arouse the concern of most, from the sanctity of monarchy, to preserving the Protestant constitution, opposing the extension of the franchise and defending the agricultural interest. The further development of back-bench organization proved effective in reining in and integrating the diehard MPs. Nevertheless, there were serious rumblings about Irish policy in the early to mid–1920s, and it was imperial policy that eventually drew diehards out into the open as sworn opponents of the broad liberalizing agenda pursued by their party leader. This was first evident on tariff reform, so that breach opened in 1930 further widened in the years that followed in the bitter and prolonged intra-Conservative battle over the future government of India.

In the wake of the clash over India the diehards appeared to lack the unity of purpose and coherence which had been forged after the First World War. As Chapter 5 demonstrates, there was no single 'diehard' position on how to deal with Nazi Germany. Like most Conservatives, the diehards believed that Britain needed to rapidly rearm and that Germany posed a direct threat, but it produced two contrasting outlooks in their ranks. For a sizeable minority, Britain could only preserve its great-power status by checking German aggrandizement in Europe. The majority, however, assumed that conflict with Germany, even if Britain emerged victorious, would weaken British power to the advantage of other rivals. But both drew on peculiarly diehard readings of recent history. Opponents of Neville Chamberlain's policy of appeasement regarded it as further evidence of Britain's decline, and out of line with its stance in the 1910s; whereas supporters of the policy believed that it was rendered necessary due to years of weak Conservative leadership and two Labour governments which had left Britain unable and unwilling to fight. Even so, this division should not obscure the diehards' unity and role in the promotion of rearmament, or indeed, their concerted campaign to prevent the transfer of British administered mandates to Germany.

1

Edwardian Crisis, 1900–14

I

The Edwardian period stands out as an aberration in the history of the Conservative party. The circumstances of the Liberals' assumption of office in 1905, their landslide victory at the 1906 general election, the Unionists' defeat at two subsequent general elections and the government's radical programme combined to produce an especially overwrought period of introspection on the political right. The frustrations of opposition were further intensified by the Liberals' reliance, after the January 1910 general election, on Irish Nationalist and Labour MPs, and especially following the December poll, which returned 272 Unionists to 271 Liberals.[1] Thereafter, successive Liberal defeats at by-elections convinced Unionists of the need to force a general election by breaking Herbert Asquith's ministry. The Ulster question was employed to this end, bringing Unionists dangerously close to endorsing armed resistance to Parliament. As noted in the Introduction, this 'crisis of conservatism' was also the culmination of a decades-long convergence of different economic and social constituencies under the Unionist banner. Yet the acrimonious debate about whether or not to adopt tariff reform in place of free trade was not simply the latest incarnation of the century-long tension between the party's agrarian and industrial interests. Nor was it a dispute that divided Conservatives from Liberal Unionists. It was especially complex and intractable because leading protagonists on both sides hailed from land and business as well as both parties.[2] At one level, therefore, the crisis of conservatism was a debate about parliamentary tactics and electoral strategy, but this lay atop a deeper conflict over the party's identity and purpose.

If this suggests a Manichean struggle for the soul of Unionism, it is important to bear in mind that those challenging the status quo were far from united in purpose and objectives. This is easily obscured by the towering figures of Joseph Chamberlain, MP for West Birmingham, and the first Viscount Milner, and the seemingly ubiquitous presence of journalists Leopold Maxse (1864–1932) and Arnold White (1848–1925), and the politicians Henry Page Croft and the nineteenth Baron Willoughby de Broke (1869–1923), in a number of right-wing campaigns and patriotic leagues. Certainly, their output provides rich pickings for those seeking to identify the challenge posed by Britain's 'radical right', yet the scholarly application of such a category has been contested from the outset. When Arno Mayer argued that it was the Right, not the Left, which threatened liberal democracy before 1914, he claimed that in much of Europe it was spearheaded by traditional agrarian elites and other pre-industrial groups.[3] Overlooking Britain, and therefore G.R. Searle's study of the national efficiency movement, Mayer's intervention encouraged Searle in due course to clarify the nature and place of a 'radical right' in Britain and its relationship with national efficiency proponents and 'traditional' Conservatives.[4] Searle acknowledges that these groups were fissiparous and prone to splinter, that individuals could shift from one to the other, and that his typology carried the 'risk of some oversimplification', but he argued nonetheless that 'it makes sense to distinguish between three different responses to the crisis and between three corresponding groups within the Conservative party'.[5] In this schema, traditional Conservatives sought to preserve national institutions by working within parliamentary democracy to apply a brake on radical change. National efficiency proponents and radical rightists, in contrast, held that the social and imperial problems exposed by the South African War required a different approach on the part of Unionist leaders, especially in response to the electoral progress of 'socialism', the label Unionists applied to the collectivist policies of 'new liberalism'. However, the two responses differed in their attitude to partisanship. Radical rightists opposed all bipartisanship, whereas proponents of national efficiency sought to establish a national government that combined the talents of experts from all parties. Searle places the empire-first groups, the ditcher peers and individuals associated with the patriotic leagues within the radical right category. Noting that radical rightists hailed from both the Conservative and Liberal Unionist parties, Searle defines them as a 'collection of super-patriots unable for one reason or another to identify with their "natural" party, or as a movement of rootless nationalists who felt alienated to a lesser or greater extent from *all* the major political organisations of the day'.[6]

Searle's taxonomy of the Edwardian Right has been influential.[7] However, its depiction of amorphous groups has drawn criticism for increasing the size of the radical right and exaggerating its influence; more specifically, for interpreting the willingness of Unionists to consider adopting 'social imperialism' as evidence of the radical right's influence when for many Unionists it was a tactical ploy to provide the party with a means of countering what they regarded as radical legislation.[8] A similar criticism has been levelled at E.H.H. Green's study of 'radical Conservatives', despite his applying this label to the broad tariff reform movement and not the more extreme empire-first elements within it.[9] These issues with Searle and Green aside, there is another reason to be cautious about approaching the Edwardian Conservative Right as a study of the radical right. The latter is often used by scholars of British fascism and of necessity tends towards the conceptual and theoretical, helping to bring coherence to the motley assortment of small and marginal extreme-right parties and groups that have operated from the 1920s to the present.[10] The same approach, however, tends to be unhelpful when applied dogmatically to Edwardian Unionists. Yet it would be wrongheaded to overlook the relevance of identifying a set of right-wing 'responses'; such neglect, after all, is typically the behaviour of high politics approaches to history which demonstrate the same indifference to the subjects of this study. It is clear that the ideas and worldview identified by a number of scholars as radical right had a purchase on elements of Unionist discontent in the Edwardian period, in particular the empire-first campaigns and prominent figures associated with the patriotic leagues. The important thing is not to infer the wider purchase in the party of the ideas they expressed.

Searle's original sketch is cautious enough. His radical right is identified by certain attitudes: bitter discontent with the party leader, Arthur Balfour, suspicion of front-bench collusion, obsession with Liberal hypocrisy and corruption, preoccupations with external threats to Britain's global power and its internal enemies – financiers, bureaucrats, aliens, intellectuals and high society – and a cult of violence manifested in militarism and invasion scares.[11] Difficulties with the application of the label are more obvious in Alan Sykes' survey of British fascism, which by his own admission prefers the term 'radical right' to 'fascist' as it focuses on 'ideas'.[12] This radical right is elitist in that it believes that an elite within the nation should lead and that Britain is an elite among nations; purposive in striving to regenerate existing society through the transformation of its political and social structures, and the regeneration of individuals, physically, mentally and morally; restorative, by seeking to restore values from the past though not necessarily the conditions of the past; and organicist, in that it conceived of society not as an aggregate of individuals but an organism in which individuals were part of a greater whole. Its outlook was therefore anti-materialist, anti-individualist, anti-liberal, anti-democratic and anti-internationalist. Sykes identifies the radical right's attitude to racial politics in terms similar to Searle: preoccupations with the physical and moral fitness of the British people, alien immigration, and Jewish influence in high society and the City of London.[13]

As noted already, the application of these generalizations to the actual behaviour of Edwardian Unionists is not so straightforward. The label of 'traditionalists' could just as easily be applied to agricultural protectionists as free-traders. The collectivism and social thought of radical right and national efficiency proponents might have challenged contemporary Conservatives, but it drew on the organicism and paternalism which underpinned old Toryism. Frustrations about the appearance of front-bench fraternization were common, but those identified with the radical right were not necessarily more extreme in their attitude. The prominent empire-first Unionist, Lord Winterton, for example, hosted in 1911 a fancy dress ball at Claridge's attended by both the prime minister and the leader of the opposition.[14] Likewise the attention given to race by those identified as radical rightists was uneven and their attitudes did not exist in isolation. Eugenics undoubtedly had an appeal to empire-first Unionists; Willoughby de Broke argued that:

> the whole vast problem of Heredity and Environment, have got to be faced if we would keep our place among the Nations ... Let us rely on National Character, and aim at preserving it by breeding from the best stocks and bringing to maturity the greatest possible number of mentally and physically sound men and women, reared among healthy surroundings in the ideals of Religion and Patriotism, equipped with a trade education, protected by Tariff Reform ... [and] trained to bear arms.[15]

Yet the ideas and assumptions of eugenics informed Liberals too; the government's 1913 Mental Deficiency Act placed the 'feeble-minded' in institutions to prevent them having children. Across Europe and beyond, eugenics influenced ostensibly progressive causes such as the advocacy of birth control, family allowances and improved housing.[16]

Anti-alien rhetoric was more unambiguously associated with Unionists. Since the 1890s, it had featured prominently in the party's populist appeal to working-men in London's East End.[17] The especial concern of empire-first Unionists with gaining working-class support drew on this tradition, combining it with several basic ideas first sketched out by Chamberlain. His attitudes to race drew on mid-nineteenth century liberal philosophy and served the function of legitimating his policies at the Colonial Office and later advocacy of tariff reform.

Chamberlain's imperialism, which preferred the settler colonies to India, reflected and reinforced what James Belich labels the ideology of 'settlerism', and what Bill Schwarz highlights as the privileged role of whiteness in Britain's overseas territories.[18] But racial thought was not a prominent part of Chamberlain's political ideas, nor did he work out a systematic or coherent racial theory. In part, as Hugh Cunningham highlights, identifying the supposed uniqueness of kith and kin across the oceans was difficult to accommodate neatly in simple language in the manner of Englishness or Britishness.[19] As such, Chamberlain applied the language of race to imperial crises and international relations, using it to promote social integration, the maintenance of security through order and prosperity, and greater economic cooperation between the 'Anglo-Saxon' dominions. His invocation of the British as a 'governing race' was common currency amongst imperial proconsuls, and like them Chamberlain's interpretation of 'race' was expressed in the 'language of character'.[20] According to Wolfgang Mock, Chamberlain's racial politics as a consequence remained 'undifferentiated', enabling a range of interests and ideological projects to identify with his views.[21] The Navy League, for example, cited a public letter from Chamberlain to Glasgow shipowners, in which he criticized pilotage arrangements, to lend weight to its own campaign to prevent 'aliens' from working as harbour pilots.[22] Croft more readily than Chamberlain attempted to sell the tariff reform gospel to working-class audiences, and this often employed racial slurs, such as his denunciation of Liberal amendments to the Unionists' 1905 Aliens Act, for allowing in 'hordes of people, disease stricken, immoral, and without a penny in their pockets, and who by sweating undersold the British working man'.[23]

A comparison between out-of-doors campaigning and speeches at Westminster suggests that the invocation of race politics was more likely in the former. Perhaps an explanation might be found in the observation of Lord Winterton that the Aliens bill, 'before it was passed, was a platform asset ... but after its passage, I do not think that the Act gained us a single vote'.[24] Parliament certainly heard passing references to racial fitness and immigration, but with the notable exception of the Liberals' 1911 Aliens bill, a legislative attempt to curb anarchist violence, these interventions tended not to be the subject of specific debates. Even on that bill, only two 'radical right' MPs, Edward Goulding (1862–1936) and Rowland Hunt (1858–1943) were sufficiently exercised to address the House of Commons.[25] In his study of the Unionists and anti-Semitism, Harry Defries observes that views in the party were complex; anti-Semitism was by no means confined to its right wing, and even ostensibly pro-Jewish

Unionists could be anti-Semitic.[26] Then there is the case of the Jewish radical rightist, Harry Marks (1855–1916). Fifth son of the Reverend Professor David Woolf Marks, head of the Reformed Congregation of British Jews, he stood unsuccessfully at the 1892 general election for Bethnal Green, taking a hard line on immigration. Marks secured a narrow victory three years later, standing in St George's-in-the-East, no doubt helped by a moderated position on immigration calculated to accommodate the constituency's significant Jewish population.[27] In truth, far from being the sole preserve of empire-first Unionists, racial politics was employed across the political spectrum, including the Liberal anti-imperialism propounded by J.A. Hobson.[28] And when radical rightist interventions were forthcoming, they could draw on the plethora of official, quasi-official and amateur commissions, committees, reports and studies on the physical condition of the British people triggered by the South African War.[29] As David Glover argues, the 1905 Aliens Act attracted support from a complex range of supporters, and by intertwining liberal and illiberal reflexes, ensured that the politics of anti-Semitism developed alongside the growth in democratic politics.[30]

Race politics was pursued with greater persistence by journalists identified with the radical right. Leopold Maxse and Howell Gwynne (1865–1950), editors of the *National Review* and *Morning Post* respectively, achieved notoriety in this regard, as did Arnold White at the *Referee*. An active member of the eugenicist movement, White was particularly preoccupied with racial fitness and undesirable aliens.[31] Also a prominent navalist, his ostensibly progressive campaign for the improvement of conditions below decks can be better understood in the context of the Navy League's campaign to reduce the presence of 'lascars' in the merchant marine.[32] In addition to targeting vulnerable minorities, White excoriated the elite for its failings as a governing caste during the South African War.[33] He attracted criticism for being anti-Semitic, from other journalists as well as the first Baron Rothschild, so it is notable that White was at pains to deny such accusations.[34] He could certainly contort his derision for Jews into backhanded complements about their resilience and purity as a race.[35] Yet his denials exposed a visceral racism: 'Never was I a Jingo or an anti-Semitic', he informed one critic. 'The quality, not the quantity, of alien immigration, whether Gentile or Jew, has always been the objective of my attacks on the policy of free entry of undesirables to the United Kingdom.'[36] White's influence outside of eugenicist and navalist circles should not be exaggerated. His patron, the eleventh Duke of Bedford (1858–1940), was a peer of little political consequence; White himself was a failed Unionist parliamentary candidate, for North

Londonderry in 1906; and he remained isolated from the empire-first Unionists marshalled by Croft. Anti-Semitic and eugenicist politics did not develop into significant issues before the First World War. Attacks on Jews were sporadic and negligible, and biological ideas of race remained marginal.[37] In contrast to Germany, the very small size of the Jewish population in Britain enabled the host community to accommodate 'Jewish influence without suffering from an identity crisis'.[38] As such, the Marconi scandal was the only politically significant incident to feature anti-Semitic slurs in the right-wing press; though, again, these were largely confined to unconventional writers on the margins of the right, such as the Chesterton brothers, G.K. and Cecil, and their Anglo-French, ex-Liberal and Catholic collaborator, Hilaire Belloc.[39] Maxse too joined in this clamour, a marked departure from the support he gave as a young journalist to Alfred Dreyfus.[40] For the majority of Edwardian Unionists, however, concern about the British 'race' found an outlet instead in defending the 1905 Aliens Act from Liberal amendments, as well as the youth training schemes promoted by the Navy League, National Service League and the twelfth Earl of Meath's Empire Day movement.[41] Race had no significant place in the rhetoric of Unionists during the Ulster crisis, often held to be the violent culmination of the crisis of conservatism; a noteworthy departure from the late-Victorian habit of citing the inferiority of the 'Celtic race in Ireland'.[42]

As the above example of race suggests, the agency of individual Unionists and the patriotic leagues gets lost in prescriptive understandings of an Edwardian radical right. A shared frustration with Balfour's detached and intellectual style of leadership did not amount to a common ideological outlook. That this tapped into wider unease in the Unionist party about its stewardship, organization and policies does not demonstrate the influence of so-called radical rightists or a victory for their world view. The majority of Unionists, including empire-first MPs and ditcher peers, remained outwardly loyal to the party leader. Even when support for Balfour fell away in the autumn of 1911, the party quickly demonstrated the same outward loyalty to his successor, Andrew Bonar Law. The journalism of right-wing zealots should not be automatically conflated with the groups and causes they supported. Membership of the legion of leagues, from ordinary people through to parliamentarians, was motivated by a range of factors and cannot be taken to imply support for a political revolt led by radical rightists. After all, Maxse and Croft's efforts to associate themselves with the defiance of the ditcher peers in 1911 was never fully reciprocated, and the Halsbury Club which attempted to harness this association quickly dissipated as differences of emphasis became clear. Undoubtedly, these various expressions of

Unionist discontent influenced the shape and outlook of the Conservative Right which emerged after the First World War, but history must not be read backwards. To untangle and explore the complexity of these relationships, therefore, it is instructive to distinguish between three vectors of active and visible right-wing discontent associated with the Edwardian Unionist party: the empire-first groups, the legion of patriotic leagues and the ditcher peers.

<h1 style="text-align:center">II</h1>

The principal empire-first vehicles within the Edwardian Unionist party were the Confederacy, Reveille and Imperial Mission. This succession of campaign groups presented themselves as a vanguard of younger, active and constructive parliamentarians striving to reform and rededicate their party in pursuit of tariff reform and imperial unity.[43] They quickly earned the enmity of Unionist free-traders, but their methods and political style meant that even old protectionists like Walter Long – for much of this period the spokesman of Irish Unionists – regarded them with suspicion, and that they were on occasion disavowed even by the Tariff Reform League.[44] These groups undoubtedly had a long-term influence on the forging of the Conservative Right, in personnel, outlook and methods, but they should not be written off as 'radical right' nurseries. A committed core of the membership certainly followed Croft into his breakaway National Party, established in 1917. And some even achieved notoriety in the 1930s for their reactionary politics, including the Blackpool MP, Wilfrid Ashley (1867–1939), afterwards the first Baron Mount Temple, and the Liberal Unionist MP for West Staffordshire, George Lloyd (1879–1941), afterwards the first Baron Lloyd of Dolobran. But facing these men, all staunch opponents of the post-war Liberal–Conservative coalition, were empire-first Unionists willing to serve in that administration, including Leopold Amery (1873–1955), James Fitzalan Hope (1870–1949), William Hewins (1865–1931), Arthur Lee (1868–1947), afterwards the first Baron Lee of Fareham, Oliver Locker-Lampson (1880–1954), Leslie Orme Wilson (1876–1955), William Mitchell-Thomson (1877–1938), Arthur Steel-Maitland (1876–1935), George Tyron (1871–1940) and Laming Worthington-Evans (1868–1931).[45] Steel-Maitland even considered in 1921 becoming a Liberal.[46] The reason for this contrasting outcome in many instances can be found in their membership of the Compatriots Club, which sought the same ends as the Confederacy, but was avowedly intellectual in tone and approach.[47] A similar observation might be made about the journalism of the empire-first Unionists. If scholars have plumbed the output of Croft, Maxse and Willoughby de Broke for a distinctive 'radical right' ideology, the empire-first campaigns included better regarded and considerably more well-known journalists, scholars and writers. In addition to Amery, these included Ralph Blumenfeld (1864–1948), the American-born editor of the *Daily Express*; William Hewins, noted already, a professor at King's College, London; Arthur Lee, MP for Hampshire and formerly a military college professor in Canada; H.J. Mackinder (1861–1947), professor of geography at the University of London; Harry Marks, mentioned above, proprietor and editor of the *Financial News*; the author Sir Horatio Parker (1862–1932); and Henry Spenser Wilkinson (1853–1937), journalist and professor of military history at All Souls, Oxford. That this variegation in the makeup and output of empire-first Unionists is overshadowed by Croft, Maxse and Willoughby de Broke is not altogether surprising. These three depended on the empire-first campaigns to make their influence felt in the Unionist party, whereas most of those mentioned above regarded the vehicles as merely adjuncts to their primary political activity.

Henry Page Croft was the central figure in the establishment and management of the Confederacy, Reveille and the Imperial Mission. His family bridged land and commerce. The Pages' maltsters business brought wealth and employment to the gentry Crofts, providing them with a family seat at Fanhams Hall, in Ware, east Hertfordshire, and supporting Henry with a job after several years at Trinity Hall, Cambridge. This foot in the commercial world helps to explain why Croft came under the spell of Chamberlain rather than the local magnate and prime minister, the third Marquess of Salisbury. Croft's family is likely to have also influenced his strong views on military and naval questions, for although he had only modest military experience in the local regiment, at least until the First World War, his father was a long-serving officer in the Royal Navy, and his brother an invalided veteran of the South African War. Shortly after the formation of the Tariff Reform League (TRL), on 21 July 1903, Croft founded a branch at Ware, followed by others across the county. His belief in the need to win over working-class support quickly brought him into contact with the veteran protectionist Henry Chaplin. Croft energetically launched himself into two controversial contests to secure nomination as a potential parliamentary candidate.[48] Locally, Croft mobilized Unionist and TRL branches to apply pressure on the sitting free-trade Unionist MP, Abel Henry Smith.[49] With an eye also on the city of Lincoln, Croft did the same there, against the incumbent Liberal Unionist and free-trader, Charles Seely. The disruptive effects of these interventions outlived Croft's adoption in 1907 as the candidate for Christchurch in Hampshire.[50] Ensconced there, it was not long before he played a leading role in establishing the Confederacy.

Croft was joined in this endeavour by Leopold Maxse, editor of the *National Review*. His father, Admiral Frederick Maxse, proved to be a great influence, not only as an idiosyncratic Liberal turned Liberal Unionist, but also in purchasing the *Review* after his son failed to enter Parliament. As a youth, Leopold came into contact with the future Confederates Goulding and Bernhard Wise (1858–1916), as well as Austen Chamberlain. After Cambridge University, where he was president of the Union, Maxse's position at the *National Review* provided him with a platform to critique party politics and intrigue with Unionist backbenchers. The marriage of his sister, Violet, who succeeded him as editor of the *Review* in the early 1930s, into the Cecil dynasty, and later to Milner, did not blunt Leopold's criticisms of both, especially in the wake of the South African War and 1906 general election.[51] Salisbury's party, he informed Violet in 1900, 'don't care a tinker's cuss for the British Empire as long as they win the . . . general election.'[52]

Figure 1 Lord Willoughby de Broke

The extreme language of Maxse's journalism, especially when applied to opponents, lent it notoriety which helped to overcome the *Review*'s limited circulation of around 11,000, and its inability, as a monthly, to respond quickly to political developments.[53] The sheer relentlessness of Maxse's attacks on Balfour made other critics, such as Gwynne and Croft, appear reticent by comparison, but Maxse's genuine belief in the importance of cultivating grass-roots opinion ensured that he was a popular figure at party conferences.[54]

Lord Willoughby de Broke was not involved with the original Confederacy, but his decision to join the Reveille and Imperial Mission represented an important link between empire-first Unionists and the ditcher peers. An unenthusiastic MP for Rugby in his twenties, it was only in later life that his passions for fox hunting, horse breeding and the theatre were joined by a renewed interest in political affairs. Penning a number of articles which combined throne-and-altar Toryism with the rhetoric of social imperialism, he eagerly joined Croft to campaign in the industrial north of England. Willoughby de Broke's political objectives nevertheless remained rooted in defending aristocratic privilege. Even if he denied that it was 'a device for dishing the Radicals', his strong commitment to the tariff reform cause, like the lukewarm support lent to it by most Unionists, was regarded primarily as a means of attacking the 1909 People's Budget.[55] Revealingly, he later expressed regret about taking a stand on this rather than waiting for the third home rule bill, as the latter 'could have been comfortably rejected without a catastrophe'.[56] As a latter-day Ultra Tory, Willoughby de Broke staunchly defended the traditions of county life, and was far more at home helping to organize the ditcher rebellion against the 1911 Parliament bill, and drumming up recruits to resist home rule by force of arms, than in the campaign for tariff reform. Still, Willoughby de Broke's participation in the Reveille and Imperial Mission, and presidency of the Imperial Maritime League, sat comfortably with his reputation as a notorious and insubstantial reactionary, for these were widely regarded as noisy groups on the fringes of Unionism.[57]

It is striking that the empire-first campaigns contained a significantly active cohort with connections to Ireland, a reflection, perhaps, of the long-term disenchantment of Irish Conservatives and their wariness of the party's front bench at Westminster. The fifth Earl of Malmesbury (1872–1950) was instrumental in Croft's adoption at Christchurch. Born at his mother's family home in County Down, Malmesbury later took a BA in History at Christchurch, Oxford, before serving in the Hampshire Regiment. He was at the Colonial Office for a brief period during Chamberlain's tenure, when he served as an unpaid assistant private secretary to the fourth Earl of Onslow.[58] Edward 'Paddy'

Goulding was also born in Ireland and educated in England. His poor skills as an orator belied his experience as president of the Cambridge Union and subsequent call to the bar. Deriving his wealth from the family's Irish chemical fertilizer company, Goulding's talent lay in organization and intrigue, making him the 'prince of backbenchers' according to his *Observer* obituary.[59] Sitting as the Unionist MP for Devizes until 1906, and for Worcester from 1908, Goulding was chairman of the TRL's organizing committee between 1904 and 1911. Others with strong connections to Ireland included Viscount Duncannon (1880–1956), from 1910 the MP for Cheltenham, and from 1913 for Dover; Patrick Hannon (1871–1963), a prominent figure in the militarist leagues; Ronald McNeill (1861–1936), MP for Kent from 1911; the third Baron Oranmore and Browne (1861–1927); Hugh O'Neill (1883–1982), later a Northern Ireland MP; Geoffrey Skeffington Smyth (1873–1939), a South African War veteran; and Lord Winterton, MP for Horsham. As a source of right-wing politicians and politics, Ireland featured prominently across the vectors examined in this chapter.

The Confederacy was the first and most controversial of the empire-first campaigns.[60] For all its notoriety, however, the Confederacy's outlook and methods adapted or developed ideas and strategies already utilized by Joseph Chamberlain and the TRL.[61] Indeed, its short life reflected its emergence and submergence within the ranks of that league. And the intolerance and vigour which characterized the Confederacy's campaign to 'purge' the Unionist parliamentary party of free-traders – later described by Winterton as 'severe and even brutal' – was hardly distinguishable from the position adopted by the TRL.[62] Like it, Confederates sought to mobilize grass-roots Unionists to exert pressure on their MPs and prospective parliamentary candidates. Cajoling reluctant converts to recant their faith in free trade was a shared tactic, as was misrepresenting Balfour's carefully worded support for fiscal reform as support for tariff reform. The latter was mischievously employed to depict free-fooders as disloyal and to justify purging them from the party. The Confederacy's only significant innovation from the TRL, therefore, was the aura of secrecy surrounding its emergence and membership.[63] This had utility in increasing anxiety amongst Unionists about the cabal's potential reach and influence. It also provided a useful foil to Unionist free-traders reluctant to attack the highly popular figure of Chamberlain, though this potential benefit to party cohesion was outweighed by the animosity and suspicion the Confederacy sowed in Unionist ranks.

The Confederacy's real and only positive achievement lay in reviving the TRL. The league's purges had begun in early 1904, ostensibly in response to a statement from the president of the Unionist Free Food League, the eighth Duke of Devonshire, that Unionist voters at two by-elections should not support candidates advocating the policy of Chamberlain and the TRL.[64] The duke further aided the cause of his opponents by laying the groundwork for cooperation between Unionist free-fooders and the Liberals.[65] After the 1906 general election, 109 out of the 157 Unionist MPs returned supported tariff reform, 32 favoured Balfour's compromise formula of retaliatory tariffs, and only 11 were committed free-fooders, with 5 unattached to any camp. Yet, even with Balfour's failure to win his seat, Chamberlain was reluctant to take over the party owing to back-bench suspicions about his radical past and statist inclinations.[66] Weeks of intrigue only ended when the two men reached the so-called Valentine compact on 14 February 1906. Balfour agreed to acknowledge fiscal reform as the first plank in the party's platform and Chamberlain recognized that tariff reform could only be implemented gradually. Thereafter the fortunes of the TRL seemed to be riding high until Chamberlain's sudden stroke on 11 July. The refusal of several high-profile Unionists to take up his mantle, and concern about the commitment of tariff reform MPs, led some of Chamberlain's younger supporters to seize the initiative. In the autumn of 1906, Croft, Bernhard Wise and Thomas Comyn-Platt (1875–1961), a former diplomat and Unionist parliamentary candidate, held a meeting at Fanhams Hall in Ware, followed by a second attended also by Maxse and another dozen like-minded tariff reformers. Out of this emerged the Confederacy. Its gatherings were confined to small groups so that few had knowledge of the entire membership; Amery's memoirs, somewhat disingenuously, merely recollect it as an occasional dining club which dealt with 'constituency problems'.[67] Several historians have attempted to draw up a membership list with Larry Witherell producing the most substantive to date.[68] Out of a total of 51, over half were forty years of age or younger; only 12 sat in Parliament in 1906 or before; 28 attended Cambridge and Oxford universities; 19 had some form of military service before 1914; 14 were landed, and an equal number came from commercial or industrial backgrounds; 12 were called to the bar; 8 were pressmen, and 5 academics. Twenty-six of their number stood for Parliament in the general elections of 1910 with only four failing to take seats.[69]

The existence of the Confederacy was cited soon after by the second Viscount Ridley, president of the TRL, to warn Balfour of back-bench malaise about his lack of leadership on the fiscal question.[70] Now returned to the House of Commons, Balfour responded by holding a series of meetings with prominent tariff reformers including Bonar Law and Austen Chamberlain, as well as the

Confederates Goulding, Hewins and Lee. Within weeks the press reported Balfour's first public statement on the fiscal question for almost a year, but he disappointed zealous tariff reformers by cautioning against becoming 'a party of one idea'.[71] Further disappointment followed in response to Balfour's handling in Parliament of the question of colonial trade, leading his private secretary, J.S. Sandars, to reassure backbenchers that the party leader would harass the government.[72] The *Daily Telegraph* identified the Confederacy with the unrest and accused it of being 'so historically naïve and politically immature as not to see the parallels to the "round-robins" of the 1850s and 1860s who tried to unseat Disraeli as leader of the party ... These Confederates ... are simply reproducing the petty malevolence of small sections of partisans which have earned a passing notoriety on the morrow of all great political reverses'.[73] Unable to push Balfour decisively towards its own unequivocal position, the Confederacy's reputation for disruptiveness increased in the months that followed. It sought to increase tariff reform representation on local and national party committees and commit these in turn to that cause. The Confederacy reached new heights of indiscipline in June when Winterton plotted with others to place a 'shibboleth' before all Unionist candidates to test them on tariff reform. These developments inevitably encouraged the TRL leadership to be more strident as well as issue timely and self-serving denials of having any knowledge of or authority over the Confederacy.[74]

If it was not clear to the Confederates, Unionist free-fooders realized that the tide was turning against them. Balfour in effect gave a free hand to the Confederacy's local agitation by declining to intervene in the affairs of constituency associations, citing their prized independence in the matter of candidate selection. The worsening economic situation also encouraged the party leader to edge closer to the position occupied by tariff reformers.[75] On 15 July 1907 the Unionist front bench bowed to back-bench pressure by supporting a vote of censure on the government, for its failure to 'consider favourably' ideas for colonial preference raised by dominion premiers at the recent colonial conference convened in London. The vote also obliged free-fooders to fall into line to avoid accusations of disloyalty.[76] They were required to do so again at the annual party conference held at Birmingham in November 1907. On that occasion Balfour finally endorsed a resolution declaring that tariff reform should be the party's first constructive policy, though he took care to warn against the 'ostracism' of those 'who cannot yet accept tariff reform in its entirety'.[77] The party's remaining free-fooders – since 1906 five had crossed the floor to join the Liberals and twenty-three had retired, gone to the Lords or died – reluctantly adhered to the new policy or attempted to reach personal positions on fiscal policy that might call off the Confederacy's attack dogs.[78]

These events were clearly a victory for the TRL and its leaders, Austen Chamberlain and Lord Ridley, but the role of the Confederacy appears to have encouraged a section of its membership to take the bold step of publishing their views in *The New Order: Studies in Unionist Policy*.[79] Nominally edited by Malmesbury, the book contained essays on a range of subjects of varying quality and length.[80] Far from being a 'radical right' manifesto, there is little in the way of bitter partisanship or racial politics. In his introduction, Malmesbury confessed that while the Unionist party required a systematic theory:

> the present volume makes no pretension to satisfy this want ... The writers do not imagine themselves to be philosophers ... They propound no logical theory; even in regard to practical policy their views are not always identical in matters of detail, and no one of them is in any degree responsible for opinions here expressed by others, though they approach the consideration of public affairs from a standpoint of substantial agreement.[81]

The volume succeeds in most instances in presenting a constructive face to Unionism, as Malmesbury put it, 'consistent with Unionist traditions, and at the same time without hostility to reasonable innovation'. Viscount Morpeth's defence of the constitution aired ideas such as referenda and life peerages that were then in circulation. Winterton in contrast favoured extending the representative peer system beyond the Scottish and Irish electoral colleges, and making dominion prime ministers and the heads of major religious denominations de facto members of the House of Lords. O'Neill's chapter on Ireland relayed standard Irish Unionist objections to home rule and familiar recommendations, the latter including abolition of the viceroyalty, continued land purchase and the consistent enforcement of law and order. Wise counselled that schemes for empire unity required Britain to learn from the mistakes of the Imperial Federation League by acknowledging the dominions as equals. Comyn-Platt's examination of 'foreign policy' advocated a strong hand in India, though he swam against the tide of recent Unionist opinion by advocating isolationism.[82]

If the aforementioned contributions were far from radical, others went beyond what traditional Conservatives would have regarded as 'reasonable innovation'. Writing on religious education, Michael Temple called on Unionists to abandon the Conservative High Church tradition by acknowledging the principle of an agnostic state. Alan Burgoyne's (1880–1929) chapter on the navy might have reflected advanced opinion in the Navy League, of which he was a prominent member, but its demand that the authority of the First Sea Lord be increased at the expense of the government and Parliament challenged the Unionists' vaunted fidelity to the latter. The National Service League's call for a citizen army was represented in a chapter penned by Croft, and flatly rejected in Wilfrid Ashley's chapter on the army. John Rolleston and E.G. Spencer-Churchill put forward the TRL position, the latter arguing that: 'The function of the Government should be to regulate circumstances so that the interests of the individual and of the nation lie in the same direction.'[83] He was echoed in G.L. Courthope's chapter on land. If Mayer's 'agrarian elites' hitched onto protection as a means of preserving vested interests and restoring the place of landownership in society, Courthope's contribution was far from a defence of their cause.[84] Instead, he called for greater regulation to encourage the 'right people' to go 'back to the land', the state to take a greater role in research and education, and expressed admiration for agricultural cooperation. In like manner, Steel-Maitland surveyed the labour question, damning laissez-faire practices for abuses, and recalling the mid-nineteenth-century Conservative Factory Acts to argue for some modest regulation. McNeill, on 'Socialism', also invoked the Factory Acts to call for 'government interference in industrial organisation'. He attacked American 'tricks of the trade' and the corruption of its municipal government, and championed 'peasant ownership of the land' as a means of 'strengthening the foundations of private property and free industry'. In a striking admission, McNeill acknowledged the usefulness of the Marxian critique of the ill effects of laissez-faire, though he concluded that a social state would be a 'tyranny tempered by corruption'. Prefiguring Friedrich Hayek, he claimed that 'the temptation to bribe and the temptation to blackmail would be infinitely increased under a system in which the Government official would be omnipresent as well as omnipotent'.[85] Publication of *The New Order* in the spring of 1908 did not materially help the Confederacy as a group. It may even have added fuel to back-bench disquiet, especially amongst traditionalists, about Austen Chamberlain's growing influence in the party and its implications for the emphasis traditionally accorded by the party to the union and established churches.[86] However, the *New Order* at least contributed to the more variegated approach to Unionism evident in this period and probably assisted sections of the party in developing targeted and pluralistic campaigns across the country.[87]

Working through the TRL, the Confederacy's local campaigns of intimidation continued, though overall activity seemed to slacken in the wake of Balfour's conversion. This was reversed abruptly on 18 January 1909 when the *Morning*

Post published a blacklist of Unionist MPs suspected of being hostile to the party policy of tariff reform.[88] It naturally alarmed those identified and brought forth condemnation even from tariff reformers; the *Daily Mail* denouncing it as 'jesuitry'.[89] Ridley of the TRL issued a public repudiation of any link with the Confederacy.[90] The impact of the blacklist was ostensibly negative, as the wall of criticism emanating from the Unionist press provided space for those blacklisted to declare their loyalty to Balfour and in some cases even express support for the full programme endorsed at the Birmingham conference. For his part, Balfour was conspicuously silent, a reflection of his prior approval for the *Post* article, and belief that it was not worth coming to the rescue of free-fooders when they contemplated breaking with the party. Moreover, the grip of tariff reform over the Unionist party was tightened after the appointment in April 1908 of David Lloyd George as Chancellor of the Exchequer, as fear of his 'socialistic' intentions further increased the appeal of tariff reform and kept lingering free-fooders in the party fold. Several even joined forces with tariff reformers in the recently established Anti-Socialist Union.[91] Tariff reform was therefore a central plank in Balfour's platform during the January–February 1910 general election campaign.[92] The policy helped to revive the party's electoral fortunes in the south and midlands of England, and its proponents claimed credit for the Unionists' significant gains at the polls. But their cause was dealt a blow by the failure of the party to take sufficient seats in the industrial north. Many Unionists blamed this on the 'food tax' scare raised by Liberals. The 275–273 result in favour of the Liberals – with Irish nationalists and Labour effectively holding the balance of power – was sufficiently ambiguous to sustain the steadfast faith of advanced tariff reformers against the travails which followed soon after, especially given that the Unionist party had beaten the Liberals in the popular vote.

Returned to the House of Commons with only 731 votes over his Liberal rival, Croft preferred to depict his polling as the 'biggest majority ever known in Christchurch'.[93] Along with other Confederates, he looked on anxiously during the party truce that followed the death in May 1910 of Edward VII. The presence of Austen Chamberlain in the secretive inter-party conferences that followed seemed not to abate Confederate anxieties about the abandonment of their political principals. Even efforts to explore areas of agreement that might prevent the Irish nationalists from holding either party to ransom proved too frustrating. At the time, Willoughby de Broke suspected that the conferences might be a 'trap' to saddle Unionists with 'responsibility for an unfavourable issue'.[94] He later recalled:

A real quintessential Die-hard, although he may not say so, never entirely trusts his leaders not to sell the pass behind his back. On this occasion neither the extreme left of the Radicals, nor the extreme right of the Tories, liked the idea of their own champions sitting in secret round the same table with the champions of those to whom they were temperamentally and diametrically opposed ... a great principle was at stake; and there is nothing so wicked as a compromise about a principle.[95]

Croft's call to arms was published in the *Morning Post* on 30 August 1910, with the aim of harnessing wider Unionist unease during the summer recess.[96] Presented as a 'Reveille', it labelled the party truce a 'sleeping sickness', called for a strong leader like the first Duke of Wellington, and demanded that the party place tariff reform and imperial unity at the forefront of its policies. A week before the inter-party conferences resumed, around forty of the Confederates, along with some new adherents, met on 6 October to launch a fresh empire-first campaign which adopted 'the Reveille' as its name. In contrast to the secrecy of the Confederacy, the meeting was attended by the party's chief whip and chief agent.[97] Its openness probably accounts for the Reveille's smaller membership, at forty-two, as it is likely that some former Confederates were reluctant to identify publicly with Croft and Maxse.[98] Conversely, Maxse was initially hostile to the presence of senior party officials but was reassured by Croft that the Reveille remained independent.[99] Criticism followed from other quarters. Lord Londonderry – later a prominent figure in the Ulster Unionists' controversial preparations to defy Parliament – compared the behaviour of the Reveille to that of the impetuous young royalist commander, Prince Rupert.[100] The Liberal Colonial Secretary, Lewis Harcourt, used the Reveille's appearance to characterize the Unionists' fiscal policy as 'badger my leader' and 'in confusion after the reveille on the tin trumpet'.[101] The unfinished business of the inter-party conference, especially as it discussed the Irish question, even prompted expressions of concern from other 'whole-hoggers' – those committed to tariffs on food imports – on the wisdom of launching such an organization.[102]

On 8 November Unionist leaders broke off the inter-party conferences. It was not the Reveille, however, which impelled this outcome, but Balfour's concern that any significant movement on the Irish question would fail to carry his backbenches.[103] If the Reveille's dramatic appearance was fuelled by back-bench frustration with the party truce, the conclusion of the conferences saw it struggle to make itself heard. Reveille members tried to counter this by campaigning in the north of England and throwing themselves into two by-election contests. But its imperial preoccupations appeared increasingly out of step with wider party opinion and the urgent questions which now faced Unionist parliamentarians. On the same day that the Reveille announced its first manifesto, Balfour flaunted his patriotic credentials at Glasgow in a speech on naval defence, declaring that 'What matters it if we proclaim our devotion to an Imperial ideal if the very foundations on which any Imperial ideals rest are shaking under our feet?'[104] He remained firmly in harness in the weeks that followed as the party prepared for the second general election of 1910. To the delight of the Reveille, he initially appeared to defend the policy of tariff reform, but in advance of his next speech on the question, scheduled for 29 November, the confidence of the Reveille was shaken by calls on Balfour, most notably from nominal tariff reformers, to pledge that a future Unionist government would hold a referendum on the issue.[105] Reveille spokesmen were obliged to declare that they had nothing to fear from a referendum. The December poll had the two parties almost evenly tied. With the Unionists again ahead in the popular vote, and the party's share of the poll almost constant, the ambiguity of the result allowed the Reveille to blame the failure of Unionists to secure a parliamentary majority on the referendum pledge. It published a revised empire-first manifesto soon after which restated its diagnosis of the party's ills, but even this had to acknowledge the shifting attention of Unionists by giving greater attention to the House of Lords and Ireland.[106]

An expanded treatment of the question followed in January 1911 with a series of articles by Croft in the *Morning Post*. His medicine was a mixture of party democracy and centralization, populism and traditionalism. On party reorganization, Croft advocated the creation of local women's and youth associations, as well as defence clubs to steward rowdy public meetings. Parliamentary candidates must no longer pay their own election expenses, he argued, and their suitability for constituencies should reflect their professional background. Central Office would undertake periodic inspections of constituency associations, appoint full-time agents and distribute party literature. On policy, Croft took care to defend the constitution, established church and the union. Not unexpectedly, he criticized Balfour for not giving a clear lead and for failing properly to consult the party on the referendum pledge. More provocatively, Croft attacked the party's focus on the People's Budget as it tainted them as a landlord party, and he criticized the belated attention of the peers on the need to reform their House. In addition to the customary demand that tariff reform be implemented in full, Croft called for British emigration – which he attributed to the increasing number of aliens in Britain – to be channelled into the British dominions rather than allowing Britons to move to the United States.[107] The frustration expressed by Croft about party organization was widely felt, but he was too marginal, and his record too controversial, for his intervention to make a decisive impact. He was in any case unlikely to win many allies given his inference about the suitability of backbenchers to their constituencies, especially after several years of unwanted scrutiny by the Confederacy. It was not so much the Reveille, therefore, as the third general election defeat in a row that prompted the announcement on 1 February that the party's former chief whip, Aretas Akers Douglas, would chair a new Unionist Organisation Committee. But the inclusion of several Reveille members on that committee – Ralph Glyn, Willoughby de Broke and Goulding, along with the former Confederate, Steel-Maitland – suggests that the party leadership recognized the need to bind the restless empire-first Unionists to this process.[108] In due course the committee recommended the rationalization and reorganization of Central Office and its integration with the National Union. The changes were implemented in November 1911 under the supervision of the party's first chairman, Steel-Maitland.[109]

Throughout the period of the committee's deliberations two issues dominated politics, the House of Lords and Ireland. This made Croft even more determined to draw the attention of Unionists to empire unity, and in particular, the threat posed to it by the announcement in January 1911 that Canada and the United States had agreed a trade deal. But with Reveille members on the party's organization committee, tariff reformers divided on food taxes, and Balfour gaining approval for his strong stand on the upper chamber, Croft declined Maxse's suggestion in February that they inaugurate a campaign calling on Balfour to stand down.[110] Reveille MPs were still active, however, condemning the government – and by implication the Unionist front bench – as 'treasonable' for failing to woo Canada out of the arms of the United States.[111] Striving to grab attention, Croft now put his other empire-first organization, the Imperial Mission, at the forefront of campaigning. It had begun life in the spring of 1910 as the Imperial Pioneers. In contrast to the Confederacy and Reveille, it sought to harness the collective influence of like-minded parliamentarians from across the empire, as well as former governors and officials.[112] The *National Review* publicized its activities and by early 1911 it claimed to have addressed around 400 meetings.[113] Those in the East End of London attracted counter-campaigns. The rowdiness of these encounters led Croft to hire boxers from the famous Wonderland hall, and when this proved impractical, he was offered the services of the paramilitary Legion of Frontiersmen.[114]

Croft aspired to develop the Imperial Mission into a political party, albeit through establishing a new binary in British and dominion politics on the question of imperial unity. However, in contrast to his other empire-first ventures, the Imperial Mission could only muster a dozen Westminster MPs by September 1911.[115] It was dealt a blow soon after when the Canadian parliament rejected the trade deal with the United States, as this outcome deprived the Imperial Mission of the urgency which had propelled its modest advances.[116] Its identity too became blurred in the latter half of 1911 as the involvement of several ditcher peers – the first Baron Leith of Fyvie, the ninth Duke of Marlborough, Lord Milner, the first Baron Northcote and the second Earl of Selborne – raised the profile of that issue at its meetings and thereby undermined its avowed aim to focus on empire unity.[117] This was evident at the Imperial Mission's mass demonstration at Chelsea Town Hall on 17 October, when Maxse used the platform to condemn Balfour's handling of the Parliament bill and call on Unionists to take back their party.[118] Balfour's resignation the following month brought further satisfaction but not success. Struggling for funds, the Imperial Mission limped on, holding meetings and boasting that it had a thousand members.[119] However, the latter, if accurate, underlined its limited impact, for it was easily dwarfed by the major patriotic leagues.

III

The Imperial Mission entered a crowded field in 1910. That same year, the TRL had around 600 local branches and the Navy League (NL) around seventy.[120] The National Service League (NSL) boasted that it had 62,000 members.[121] Even the fringe Imperial Maritime League (IML) had over a thousand members.[122] The phenomenon of the 'legion of leagues' has been presented by historians in various ways; as a 'nationalist agitation', 'popular imperialism', or as specialized pressure groups favoured by the 'radical right'.[123] What should not be lost, however, is that there were important differences in the size, influence and outlook of the leagues, and as a result there existed a measure of inter-league rivalry. The NL and the breakaway IML were by definition bitter rivals, divided in their attitude to political partisanship. Their common 'blue water' position on defence was challenged by the NSL's call for a citizen army. The navalists could retort that theirs was a traditional British defence policy which transcended the political divide. In contrast, campaigners for conscription, or 'national service', struggled with the stigma of it being perceived as foreign and illiberal. Placed on the defensive, Lord George Hamilton, a former First Lord of the Admiralty no less, countered that if Nelson were alive he would join the NSL.[124] As a member of the Unionist Free Food League, Hamilton's experience of inter-league rivalry was not confined to defence questions.[125] The NL appealed to both free-traders and tariff reformers as its campaign focused on maintaining the two-power standard in order to prevent 'national starvation'; in contrast to the other leagues it had significant support from Liberal MPs.[126] The IML, in contrast, faced accusations that it was connected to 'violent' tariff reformers, a charge it was keen to deny.[127] Navalists and the TRL alike encouraged anxiety about rivalry with Germany, but the naval race was considerably more clear-cut in comparison to the opacity and controversy surrounding fiscal reform, and Britain's victory in the former does not appear to have noticeably bolstered the tariff reform cause.

The leagues nevertheless had a common disposition to play up concerns about global rivalry and the threat of national decline.[128] This meant that they were overwhelmingly Unionist in membership.[129] There were some overlaps in personnel, especially in propagandists, ornamental vice presidents, and national and local committees. These included the likes of Maxse and Arnold White, though their peculiar motivations cannot be taken as representative of all supporters. Most ordinary members did not regard the leagues as 'primarily ideological'; a range of factors motivated their decision to join and maintain membership, including support for specific goals, material inducements and social attractions such as entertainment and personal prestige.[130] The relatively cordial if limited relations between the Unionist front bench and the leadership of the leagues recognized the potential for friction. This was especially so with the NSL, given the strong ill-feeling of its president, the first Earl Roberts, towards Balfour. The very existence of the leagues, after all, tested the patriotic credentials of the Unionist front bench, not least, as Willoughby de Broke admitted frankly, because the causes they advocated had no 'real chance' unless adopted by the 'party machine'.[131] And there were a number of Unionist parliamentarians willing to use the leagues to advance their own political careers by publicly scrutinizing the party leadership. Not unexpectedly, Salisbury had been reluctant to embrace the leagues, for they seemed to resemble the Liberal faddists which had long subjected that party to disorder and indiscipline.[132] Balfour too remained distinctly cool, particularly towards the militaristic leagues, and was aided to some extent by the widely held feeling in his party that its defence policy fell under his almost exclusive jurisdiction.[133] It did not help relations between the leagues and the party's front bench that a number of writers associated with the leagues attributed the impediments faced by their pet causes to the vicissitudes and calculations of parliamentary politics. Likewise, the scaremongering and Germanophobia evident in some of the leagues' rhetoric distressed Balfour and others with experience of the requirements of statecraft and diplomacy.[134] These tensions aside, the patriotic leagues remained committed to parliamentary politics. Their claims to be non-party, of course, allowed for a measure of tension to be occasionally vented at the Unionist front bench, but the need for Unionist policymakers to take on board their concerns also ensured that the leagues' frustrations with Balfour and parliamentary politics were generally kept beneath the surface.

The NSL can be regarded as a voluntary counterpart to the series of state commissions which investigated the army and recruitment following the South African War. Founded in February 1902 by journalists and Unionist politicians, the NSL's choice of name acknowledged the public's wariness of continental-style conscription as well as opposition from elements within the army. The driving force was George Shee, author of a famous tract advocating conscription. The first meeting was attended, among others, by Maxse, Amery, Colonel J.E.B. Seely, MP for the Isle of Wight, Field Marshal Sir Frederick Roberts and its first president, the fourth Duke of Wellington.[135] Other prominent recruits included Rudyard Kipling, Admiral Lord Charles Beresford and Field Marshal Lord Wolseley. Arnold White and Maxse were attracted to the league as it held out a means of subverting liberal individualism, but for this very reason it struggled to gain the support of Unionists let alone the wider public.[136] The NSL's fortunes changed only after the appointment in 1905 of the popular military figure, Field Marshal Roberts, as its president. This followed his decision to retire from the Committee of Imperial Defence, in response to Balfour's making public its view that an invasion of the British Isles had no hope of success. Under Roberts, the NSL attempted to rebut claims that it sought to emulate German militarism by promoting instead a 'Swiss' model of mandatory training: annual drill practice for adult males for purely defensive duties. There was a domestic tradition on which this more modest ambition could build, namely the enthusiasm for drilling in church youth organizations.[137] And the NSL's aims were promoted by sections of the Unionist press as a patriotic necessity. In 1907 the league claimed to have over 10,000 members, rising to 62,000 by 1910.

For all its growth, however, the NSL's strength lay in rural areas and reflected pre-existing support for volunteering in local yeomanry regiments. The challenge to this traditional form of military service posed by Richard Haldane's 1907 army reforms provided the NSL with a significant platform for its own ideas.[138] Inspired by the TRL, the NSL employed the language of social reform to lend its cause wider legitimacy.[139] It was aided also by the heightening anxiety which accompanied the naval race with Germany, although this proved to be a mixed blessing. If 177 Unionist MPs could indicate in December 1910 that they had 'sympathy' with the idea of military service, then the resolution afterwards of the naval race in favour of Britain diminished the urgency of the NSL's claim of a likely invasion.[140] In any case, the notion of compulsion remained the league's most pressing problem. It might be expected that the NSL would have a strong base of support in the House of Lords given that the chamber boasted many former and serving officers in the army and yeomanry, and the league had the patronage of high-profile figures such as Milner and the first Baron Curzon of Kedleston (1859–1925). But it faced considerable opposition there from the front bench as well as right-wing stalwarts such as the seventh Duke of Northumberland (1846–1918) and the Duke of Bedford. As a result, several private members bills introduced by Roberts came to nothing. The one bill that came closest to success, introduced in July 1909 and narrowly defeated 123–103, foreshadowed the bitter clash between the front and back benches over the 1911 Parliament bill, but it is noteworthy that the ditchers of 1911 were in 1909 divided, thirty-nine in favour of national service and seventeen against.[141] Even in March 1914, when the NSL claimed 270,000 members, an attempt by Willoughby de Broke to legislate for the compulsion of young men belonging 'to the higher professions', or enjoying 'means exceeding £400 a year', attracted only modest support.[142] After the start of hostilities in August that year, which Roberts privately greeted with exhilaration as the realization of his predictions, the NSL decided to suspend its propaganda and place its organization at the disposal of the government's voluntary recruitment campaign.[143]

The NL was considerably more successful than the NSL in gaining parliamentary support for its aims, but its studious avoidance of controversy led in 1907 to schism. The NL had emerged in 1894–95 in the wake of a naval scare propagated by Henry Spenser Wilkinson, then the military correspondent of the *Pall Mall Gazette*.[144] Its initial disposition to comment on government and Admiralty policy was so poorly received that it devoted itself thereafter to public education. A minority were never fully reconciled to this change of course. In the wake of the Liberals' 1906 election victory, these restless navalists became especially exercised about Admiral Sir John Fisher's revolution in naval organization and deployment.[145] Two in particular, Harold Frazer Wyatt (1859–1925) and Lionel Graham Horton Horton-Smith (1871–1953), attacked the league's political neutrality at meetings throughout 1907, attracting considerable support from other navalists though not enough to overturn the policy. In January 1908 Wyatt and Horton-Smith announced the establishment of the IML. Wyatt had devoted his life to campaigning on patriotic, imperial and defence questions. A graduate of Oxford, he published several essays on the necessity of war between nations.[146] Active also in Unionist politics around Portsmouth, he expressed bitter disillusionment with the Salisbury government's handling of the South African War.[147] Like the empire-first Unionists, Wyatt still recognized that the Unionist party was essential to his aims, and at the 1906 general election he stood unsuccessfully in Rushcliffe against its incumbent Liberal MP, John Ellis. In contrast to Wyatt, Horton-Smith's politics were originally Liberal Unionist. After Cambridge University, he practised at the bar, gained some military experience in the London regiment, and like Wyatt took to publishing his views in journals, though these for the most part dwelt on Scottish culture and antiquarianism.

Wyatt and Horton-Smith's criticisms of the NL were supported by a number of right-wing journalists, including Gwynne, Blumenfeld, Maxse, H.W. Wilson of the *Daily Mail*, and Fred Jane, also a parliamentary candidate for Portsmouth. At its foundation, the IML was supported by twenty-two Unionist MPs and thirty peers.[148] A strong start, certainly, but it is noteworthy that the new league failed to recruit the likes of Croft, let alone Fisher's arch opponent, Admiral Beresford. A number of empire-first Unionists did join the IML, including Courthope, Malmesbury and Winterton. Rowland Hunt, the Liberal Unionist MP for Ludlow, became the IML's chairman in 1910, and Willoughby de Broke was appointed its president in 1912.[149] But the IML singularly failed to harness all navalists identified with the 'radical right'. White remained in the NL, as did Alan Burgoyne, from January 1910 MP for North Kensington, and Patrick Hannon, who went on to reorganize the NL and further improve its standing amongst parliamentarians. The persistence of these divided loyalties before 1914 is all the more notable given that Croft, Wyatt and Burgoyne came together in 1917 to establish the National Party.[150]

The IML addressed the frustrations of its founders by launching a series of overtly political campaigns. The MP for Dover and IML member, George Wyndham, is said to have coined the famous slogan, 'We want eight and we won't wait', which Unionists intoned regularly to pile pressure on the government's dreadnought programme. The IML launched its own petition against the People's Budget and attracted 140,203 signatures, second only to the petition raised by Walter Long's Budget Protest League. The IML's campaign against the Declaration of London – an international agreement on maritime war – grew in strength throughout 1910 and 1911 culminating in Balfour's decision to address a major demonstration organized by the league on 27 June 1911.[151] This momentum dissipated, however, when the IML subsequently decided to petition the king to defer his assent to the declaration's ratification.[152] It was a bold step which went too far for most Unionist parliamentarians and underlined the IML's weak support at Westminster in comparison to the NL. Yet if Long could publicly express concern about the existence of rival navalist leagues, the IML's troublesome presence provided the necessary stimulus for the older league to overhaul its structure – including giving parliamentarians a greater role in its governance – and display more willingness to take on the government and Admiralty.[153] The IML's standing committee of MPs, under the chairmanship of H.S. Staveley-Hill (1865–1946), MP for Kingswinford, looked pale in comparison, and having concentrated on national campaigns the IML neglected to build up a network of local branches.

Reviewing the decline of his league in 1912, Wyatt blamed Unionist leaders for allowing the naval scare to dissipate, a result, he argued, of their being 'bound by the shackles of Parliamentary convention'.[154] He was no doubt frustrated that the attention of Unionists had moved on to the Irish question, yet Wyatt seems not to have recognized that Balfour had been willing to address the naval question far more readily than tariff reform, and that this had helped to create the necessary political pressure to secure British success in the naval race with Germany.[155] Wyatt's dissatisfaction with parliamentary politics was hardly new. It had been evident in his criticism of the Salisbury ministry. In May 1908 he warned in characteristically grandiloquent fashion that an opposition party which 'made no effort to expose the infamy which was being perpetrated would become the accomplices by that abstention of the authors of the crime. They would become accessories to the murder of the national safety'.[156] Wyatt's attitude to the party, like that of other maverick figures on the Right, was purely practical: 'The Unionist party alone', he argued that same year, 'has the means, the organisation, the number of speakers, and the prestige needed to arrest the attention of Britain and to penetrate the cloud of apathy and indifference'.[157] Wyatt and Horton-Smith resigned in 1913 as joint secretaries of the IML, and with its executive committee left to Hunt and Willoughby de Broke, the league entered a period of internal recrimination and decline. The NL, in contrast, claimed in 1913 to have 125,000 members. It nevertheless remained concerned, like the NSL, about its overwhelmingly middle-class membership and the continued indifference of the masses to its rallying cries. Britain's declaration of war on Germany certainly fulfilled the patriotic leagues' predictions of conflict, and their years of agitation probably contributed to the surge in patriotic feeling which accompanied mass voluntary recruitment. Yet the NL, IML and NSL all felt obliged to set aside their respective aims after the outbreak of war by offering their services instead to drumming up volunteers exclusively for the army.

IV

The ditcher or diehard peers are the third vector of active and visible right-wing discontent associated with the Edwardian Unionist party. In his reflections on the period, the first Earl of Midleton assessed the behaviour of Unionist peers: 'Our tactics for five years from 1905 were deplorable ... there was an excess of pugnacity.' He attributed this to poor leadership and 'the summary way in which reasonable amendments by the Lords on important bills had been rejected in the House of Commons'. This had the effect of enabling 'the vast body of back-benchers in the Upper House to override more reasonable counsels'.[158] The burden of managing Unionists in the House of Lords fell on the fifth Marquess of Lansdowne. It was rendered increasingly onerous and troublesome as the party's majority in the upper chamber offered a great temptation to Unionists looking for a last line of defence against unpalatable Liberal measures. Responding to the Liberals' dramatic gains at the 1906 general election, Balfour encouraged such an expectation by rousing the party faithful to make sure that 'the great Unionist party should still control, whether in power or opposition, the destinies of this great Empire'.[159] Salisbury had used the House of Lords for such purposes in the 1880s and 1890s. He justified his actions citing the doctrine of 'mandate' to declare that unpalatable legislation lacked popular support and required reference to the electorate.[160] Lansdowne too was prepared on occasion to use the Unionists' majority in the upper chamber for such purposes if it was tactically propitious. Most of the time, however, both he and Balfour sought to avoid directly challenging the democratic House for fear of endangering the Lords' constitutional privileges. This proved a difficult position to maintain in the wake of the Liberal landslide. Still, the House of Lords managed to reject only a small number of the 250 Liberal measures brought before it during the 1906 Parliament.[161] Amongst this number, however, was a highly symbolic education bill intended to satisfy the nonconformist vote. Frustrated by the obstruction of anachronistic vested interests, the Liberal prime minister, Henry Campbell-Bannerman, signalled the following year that his party was determined to tackle the Lords' veto, but even this did not initiate an all-out conflict between the two Houses.[162] Lansdowne, for one, worked to ensure that Unionist peers did not appear to stand in the way of legislation intended to address working-class grievances. For its part, the Liberal government avoided a showdown with the House of Lords in 1907 when it used letters patent to grant constitutions to the Transvaal and the Orange River Colony.[163] But a change in Liberal leadership in April 1908 – Asquith replacing Campbell-Bannerman and Lloyd George installed at the Treasury – heralded a more trying period for Lansdowne's stewardship of the upper chamber.

Before the House of Lords summarily rejected the People's Budget on 30 November 1909, Lansdowne had faced significant organized rebellions on only four occasions: in 1906 and 1907, over sensitive religious questions pertaining to education and marriage respectively; Roberts's national service bill in July 1909; and in October of that year in response to Irish land legislation.[164] There was also a potentially compromising clash with the Commons which arose in July 1908 over the Old Age Pensions bill, a signal in advance of the People's Budget that Unionist peers were now willing to challenge the convention of not opposing finance legislation from the lower chamber. A crisis was avoided on this occasion after critics of the measure in the Lords were persuaded to back down following pressure from party colleagues in the Commons; Lansdowne too tried to assuage their concerns, albeit by confining himself to accusing the government of adopting 'the most extreme interpretation of the doctrine of privilege'.[165] When another back-bench revolt loomed in November that year, marshalled by Lord Rothschild, in opposition to the Licensing bill, Lansdowne convened a meeting of Unionist peers at his London home at which a majority agreed to sanction the bill's rejection.[166] Meetings of all Unionist peers were a recent innovation, following the 1906 general election, to facilitate communication between the front and back benches. Yet, Willoughby de Broke later recalled that the summons to discuss the Licensing bill was the first time 'that the "backwoodsmen" ... were really taken into the private confidence of the leader of the House of Lords'.[167] Undoubtedly, the siege mentality felt by some peers increased in response to these run-ins with their own front bench, but the rebellions were disparate and transient. It was not until the 'betrayal' of 1911 that a phalanx of ditcher peers made preparations to organize as a permanent faction.

Opposition to the People's Budget united Unionists in both Houses, tariff reformers and free-traders alike. Even so, this atypical bout of Unionist harmony was policed by Long's Budget Protest League for any signs of equivocation on the part of Balfour and Lansdowne.[168] And the higher than normal participation of Unionist peers in the budget debate left no doubt that the decision to reject the measure lay not in the hands of the party's front bench.[169] The appearance of unity was maintained into the January 1910 general election. Curzon organized a 'Peers Campaign' to assist Unionist candidates on the hustings, inducing 'some of the obscurer members of the peerage from the south and west of England to explain their position to open meetings in the industrial north'.[170] Rejecting the Liberals' depiction of the contest as one of 'the peers versus the people', Unionist candidates and peers alike warned that a single chamber dominated by one party would result in tyranny. The general strategy, however, was to counter the Liberals' 'Holy War' on the Lords by downplaying the constitutional crisis and diverting the electorate's attention to the threat of 'socialism'.[171] Cracks in the Unionist façade over the future of the House of Lords became more evident against the backdrop of the 1910 inter-party conferences. In March, the future ditcher leader, Lord Halsbury, along with the fifteenth Duke of Somerset, issued a circular to Unionist peers urging them to maintain the hereditary principle, but mustered only sixteen colleagues against an amendment which questioned the automatic right of peers to sit and vote in Parliament.[172] The Duke of Bedford, in contrast, took the opposite view, favouring a wholly elected chamber. As the constitutional crisis rumbled on into 1911, divisions amongst Unionist peers persisted. An attempt by Lansdowne in May to propose indirect election to the upper chamber was savaged by members of his own party; Somerset professed to Halsbury that he was 'utterly disgusted' with the proposals which would end the upper chamber's role in checking the 'Socialist and revolutionary crew who now misgovern this country'.[173] One of Lansdowne's critics, Willoughby de Broke, nevertheless spoke in favour of the not too dissimilar election of hereditary peers, having conceded that the function of the House of Lords was more important than its composition. He even advocated that Unionists consider the tactic of proposing an elected senate as the 'obligation of opposing [it] would mercilessly reveal the true inwardness of the Radical attitude towards representative institutions'.[174] Sidestepping the issue of composition, many Unionist peers voiced approval of referenda as a means of settling disputes between the two Houses – as A. V. Dicey argued in 1892, these were believed to be 'in practice Conservative' – but this too exposed differences of opinion on the scope of such polls, and an attempt in March 1911 by the sixth Lord Balfour of Burleigh to introduce a referendum bill was dropped after only the first reading.[175]

On 6 July it became public knowledge that George V had given his assurance to the government that he would pack the House of Lords to allow the successful passage of the Liberals' Parliament bill. With Unionist peers unable to agree about proposed reforms, Balfour and Lansdowne had no time to prepare a viable alternative policy which might restore party unity. They inclined to abstaining, but faced dissension and 'violent' recrimination at meetings of the shadow cabinet, as the fourth Marquess of Salisbury and Lords Selborne and Halsbury refused to bow to the will of the majority.[176] Unionists split into two camps. The bulk of the parliamentary party became 'hedgers', reluctantly accepting the need to sacrifice the power to veto bills from the Commons if it prevented the peerage from being swamped and a further general election on the issue of the peers versus the people. Opposing them, a determined minority of 'ditchers' or 'diehards' vowed to fight such legislation to the bitter end. The dilemma facing Unionists was made worse by the likelihood that the bill's passage would be followed by a third home rule bill.[177] This was especially felt amongst Irish peers, though as in past controversies, a majority remained loyal to the front bench.[178] Much of the Unionist press also backed Balfour's reasoning, J.L. Garvin's *Observer* was a conspicuous exception, much to the annoyance of his fellow Irishman and proprietor, the first Baron Northcliffe.[179] As noted above, Maxse's *National Review* championed the ditchers' stand against what he depicted as front-bench collusion.[180] Croft expressed his support for the ditchers by summoning a meeting of nearly forty MPs. It called on Unionist leaders in both Houses 'to abandon the conciliation programme and start an agitation in the country'; it was necessary, the meeting resolved, to have a policy of 'fight, fight, fight'.[181] If Croft hoped that the ditcher peers might trigger his long-sought-after overhaul of the party, the Unionist whip, Robert Sanders, noted derisively that the meeting was 'rather laughed at'.[182] Even ditchers in the House of Lords were prepared to go along with attempts by Unionists to amend the bill before it returned to the Commons on 20 July.[183]

A shadow cabinet on 21 July revealed that eight out of twenty-two of its members intended to oppose the measure. Later that day around 170 Unionist peers gathered at Lansdowne House. Their host's plea for caution struck a chord with many present; ditcher support numbered only around fifty. It resolved to delay any further action until Asquith addressed the Lords' amendments to the Parliament bill in the Commons on 24 July.[184] The ditchers, however, were not prepared to wait, and instead issued their own manifesto on the danger of a 'sham House of Lords' partially concealing the 'uncontrolled autocracy of the House of Commons'.[185] Balfour noted in an unsent memorandum that the ditchers were 'essentially theatrical ... [the manifesto] does nothing: it can do nothing: it is not even intended to do anything except advertise the situation'. He conceded that 'Their policy may be a wise one, but there is nothing heroic about it; and military metaphors which liken the action of the "fighting" peers to Leonidas at Thermopylae seem to me purely for music hall consumption'.[186] Theatrics were foremost when the House of Commons met on 24 July to debate the Lords' amendments.[187] As Asquith began to speak, he was met with continual shouts of 'traitor' from ditcher-supporting MPs, and other 'unseemly and undignified' interruptions. Instigated by the Irish Unionist leader, Sir Edward Carson, and the prominent free-fooder, Lord Hugh Cecil, the fracas was joined quickly by the latter's arch opponents on the fiscal question. As Amery, a supporter of the ditchers, recorded at the time, 'the demonstration was undoubtedly meant quite as much to keep Balfour up to the mark as to defy Asquith, and to some extent did so'.[188] Sanders noted that 'General opinion on our side [is] that the row was a mistake', but two days later he acknowledged that a proposal by one Unionist MP to send a note to Asquith expressing regret 'was withdrawn as the idea had hardly a supporter'.[189] Also on 26 July, ditchers from both Houses held a dinner ostensibly in honour of their most eminent associate, the seventy-eight-year-old former Lord Chancellor, Halsbury. In practice, it served as a protest against Balfour and Lansdowne's acceptance of an unamended bill, though ditchers were reluctant to publish a list of supporters so that the front bench 'must discover for themselves the exact number of "black-legs" needed to consummate the ruin of the House of Lords and destroy the

Figure 2 The Earl of Halsbury

constitution for ever'.[190] What ditchers lacked in ministerial experience they made up for in energetic activity and aristocratic status; in comparison to other peers, their cohort was generally younger, from older families, and more likely to possess large estates.[191] Under Selborne's leadership, they quickly set about organizing a campaign to canvass Unionist peers; Willoughby de Broke and the fourteenth Baron Lovat served as whips.[192] In due course, a number of local Unionist associations and clubs passed resolutions in support.[193]

The ditcher campaign suffered setbacks from the outset as Curzon, Long and a number of others crossed over to the hedgers. That Curzon should switch sides was particularly ironic given that he had previously urged peers to 'die in the last ditch', the phrase which begot the epithet of 'ditchers'.[194] One such peer explained to Halsbury that 'Living in Ireland, with the dread of Home Rule always hanging over one, I cannot be a party to sacrificing even the short respite of two years which the new Parliament Bill affords us.'[195] It seems likely that Balfour also pulled some across through his gesture of laying down a censure motion on 7 August; defeated 365–246, it still made the point of criticizing the government's abuse of the royal prerogative.[196] But these peers may also have been pushed by the desperateness and hollowness of ditcher rhetoric, such as Halsbury's assertion that it would take months for the government to create sufficient peers, and Willoughby de Broke's humorous boast that he could convert the newly ennobled Liberals.[197] Maxse too appeared to be convinced that 'they will come over to our side as fast as they are made'.[198] The campaign was also troubled by attracting 'ne'er-do-wells and out-of-elbow individuals' asking for and receiving loans from Willoughby de Broke.[199] Yet the ditchers still presented the Unionist front bench with a serious problem. With a majority of the Unionist peers committed to abstaining, there was a risk that the ditcher peers would outnumber those voting with the government. Acting as Lansdowne's intermediary, Curzon secretly tasked the second Lord Newton, a back-bench peer and a co-founder of the NSL, to recruit a sufficient number of Unionists to vote with the government.[200] An open solicitation risked not only compromising the front bench but also provoking a number of reluctant abstainers, such as the sixteenth Duke of Norfolk, into joining the ditchers.[201] Edward Carson appears to have learned of the plan, for he warned Balfour of the harm it would inflict on the party as it 'would be looked upon as a tacit arrangement with the Gov[ernmen]t'.[202] The 'Judas Brigade', as one ditcher labelled them, proved to be decisive when the House of Lords divided on 10 August, 131–114, for the government.[203] Supporters of the bill included the two archbishops and eleven bishops, provoking the High Church Conservative, Hugh Cecil, to quip that his side had been 'beaten by a combination of the twelve apostles and Judas Iscariot'.[204] Willoughby de Broke later recorded that many ditchers wore sprigs of white heather sent by the Scottish-born Duchess of Somerset, a well-known symbol of good luck, but also, perhaps, a reference to the similarly doomed cause of the Jacobites.[205]

Feelings ran high in the weeks that followed. Willoughby de Broke considered the possibility that ditchers might constitute a new party, but Selborne applied the lessons of his Liberal Unionist party to highlight the problems with this course of action.[206] The imminent overhaul of the Unionist party machine also helped to check ditchers tempted to take steps that risked a permanent rupture.[207] This in turn intensified calls on Balfour to resign as party leader, the loudest of which was Maxse's 'Balfour Must Go' or BMG campaign.[208] Old party stalwarts like Halsbury had no intention of openly challenging Balfour let alone forming a breakaway movement. The 'diehard' organization which did emerge on 12 October, the Halsbury Club, sought to use the support of 'the great majority of the party' to 'influence the opinion and so the policy of the party'. A confidential memorandum drawn up by the club acknowledged that members were unlikely to agree on tariff reform and women's suffrage; Selborne and Willoughby de Broke were advocates of the latter, but on all other major questions they needed to 'support each other in our speeches'.[209] *The Times* reported that the Halsbury Club even managed to recruit some hedgers. The new group declared that it would 'insist on the revival and maintenance of principles which they hold to be vital to national and Imperial existence', mentioning in particular tariff reform and defence of the union.[210] This offered thin gruel to those like Croft who had hoped to harness the ditcher revolt to their own ends, for the immediate peril facing the union meant that it, not tariff reform, took priority. In any case, tariff reform was an unlikely rallying cry for the Halsbury Club given that it included free-fooders and older peers unable to shake off their suspicions about statist social reform.[211] As Austen Chamberlain, one of the club's more high-profile members, privately reassured a colleague, its object 'is to develop the fighting spirit and nothing else'. He added that 'Selborne was actuated by a desire to control the forward element, which but for this rallying point might have ended in an organised movement against the Chief'.[212] Selborne's efforts, of course, could not prevent the 'no surrender' example of the ditchers being harnessed by Maxse to call for Balfour's removal, and cited explicitly in his planned resolution for the party conference in November. Indeed, Selborne's efforts at containing the 'forward element' were quickly and fatally tested at the Halsbury Club's first annual meeting on 6 November. When senior members supported a resolution expressing confidence in Balfour, they subsequently threatened 'to leave the Club' if Winterton and other younger members insisted on making an amendment. Winterton agreed to drop the amendment only after F.E. Smith quietly assured him that Balfour was due to resign within days.[213]

Balfour did indeed step down shortly afterwards. A note in the second Viscount Esher's journal for 9 November records that the decision was reached owing to opposition from 'his "stalwarts" and his young wreckers'.[214] Balfour's private secretary, Jack Sandars, felt that it was largely down to the former, as the row over fiscal policy had kept Balfour in post, determined to avoid a split 'as fatal as the rupture in 1846'. He noted also that Balfour regarded the positions adopted by 'protectionists' and free-traders alike as grounded in 'tradition'. The breach over the 1911 bill, however, was 'not one of principle, but of mere party tactics'. As a result he felt 'badly treated' and resolved that under such circumstances it was 'useless for me to attempt the duties of leadership if my leadership is not accepted'.[215] These claims aside, Balfour had been in receipt of advice from a number of party officials that back-bench support for him was weakening. He was particularly devastated to receive a letter bearing this message from 'my oldest colleague, my professed friend and upholder', Walter Long; 'nothing of the Diehards could be compared with this for what is called disloyalty'. Balfour was said by a confidant to have attached particular importance to Long's advice, 'for it is most symptomatic of disquiet – which if it produces such epistles from "the most loyal of the loyal" cannot fail to be deep-rooted'.[216] Balfour had been considering retiring for several months, and had indicated privately in September that although the 'diehard agitation' was a factor, it 'was symptomatic of previous discontent'.[217] Without doubt, from Balfour's Olympian heights, the Reveille represented relatively junior and marginal figures in the party, whereas the split over the Upper House went right up to the shadow cabinet and included his kinsmen. Nevertheless, the recent years of party discord unleashed by the empire-first Unionists went some way to undermining backbenchers' faith in Balfour's capacity to recover from the Lords crisis. However it might be explained, it is hard to escape the irony that it was the Halsbury Club, which outwardly supported Balfour, that delivered the killer blow, and not the Reveille which had implicitly called for a change of leader.

V

In the contest between Long and Chamberlain to succeed Balfour, Sanders noted in his diary that Chamberlain's questionable loyalty to Balfour and connection to the Halsbury Club 'went against him'.[218] The compromise candidate, the Canadian-born Scottish businessman, Andrew Bonar Law, was famously accused by Asquith of introducing the 'new style' of politics. But Law's forthright and combative rhetoric was welcomed by those demanding a style of leadership that emphasized Unionist principles. Law also won over many Unionist parliamentarians through his preparedness to consult party colleagues, even to the extent of actively gauging the views of backbenchers.[219] The advent of Law's new style seemed to be exemplified by his support for the dramatic steps taken by the Ulster Unionists to resist the third home rule bill. Yet for all the outward show of party unity, Unionists remained divided. Not only did the fiscal question return to prominence in 1912–13, and almost lead to the resignation of both Law and Lansdowne, but the party was riven with internal tensions on its Irish policy. The last was manifested in the establishment of new leagues on the Irish question, which alongside the continued growth of the major patriotic leagues, underscored their respective organizers' wariness of placing too much trust in the new party leader.

Law's grandstanding on Ulster was largely tactical, focusing on the weakest point of the home rule bill as a means of forcing a dissolution of Parliament. It led him to endorse the raising of the Ulster Volunteer Force (UVF), the refusal of army officers to participate in the coercion of Ulster Unionists, and to consider amending the annual Army Act, actions that took his party close to treason and the country to the edge of civil war. Yet Law's focus on Ulster obliged him also to enter discussions with Asquith in 1913 and 1914 about a possible compromise on the province's exclusion from home rule, albeit confident that such talks could never satisfy all Liberals let alone their Irish allies. As he privately assured Willoughby de Broke, 'I do not think you need be afraid of compromise, for apparently the Nationalists will make that quite impossible.'[220] Law engaged with this risky and potentially reckless course of action for the sake of appearances; he did not want to seem completely recalcitrant in the eyes of the electorate, especially given his hope that the failure to reach any compromise would leave the Liberals' minority government with little choice other than to go to the polls. As such, speeches endorsing the defiance of Ulster Unionists called also for a general election or referral of the question to a referendum. The subtleties of Law's tactics were largely lost on those in his party who objected to any scheme of home rule. Various groups within it intrigued, often at odds with Law, throughout the two years that followed the House of Lords' rejection of the home rule bill. Ditcher peers were particularly incensed. Not only did Law's meetings with Asquith recall the distrust felt for Balfour during the

1910 inter-party conferences, but anger at the betrayal of loyalists left outside any proposed excluded area was especially felt by Irish peers in the ditcher ranks. Fears of such a settlement increased as Ulster Unionists shifted from opposing home rule outright to supporting the permanent exclusion of their province.[221]

Long and Willoughby de Broke's rival organizations, respectively, the Union Defence League and the British League for the Support of Ulster and the Union, propagandized and raised money in Britain for Irish Unionists, including the UVF. These served also as vehicles through which the two men could apply pressure on Law against a compromise that excluded Ulster. Weariness of the Irish question amongst the English made this a difficult task, but interest in the union was not insignificant, especially in strongholds of anti-Catholicism.[222] Willoughby de Broke dismissed the idea that the English were apathetic on the question, and even 'if opposition to Home Rule is "bad electioneering," then it ought not to be', as it was the duty of 'public men' to awaken 'the public conscience on this matter'.[223] Announced in March 1913, his league attracted 120 MPs and 100 peers, including many of his associates from the Reveille and Halsbury Club.[224] Bedford's appointment as chairman, despite his differences with Willoughby de Broke over Lords reform and national service, highlighted that preservation of the union commanded a greater degree of unity on the right of the party than other issues. The British League's 'call for service' placed in the *Morning Post* signalled its potential to become Great Britain's equivalent to the UVF. In both cases, the openness of recruitment was in marked contrast to the fleeting and secretive preparations for armed resistance which accompanied earlier home rule bills.[225] There were reports in the English press of league volunteers, though Willoughby de Broke's claim to have mustered 7,000 must be treated with caution.[226] Whether or not it was an empty boast, the figure is more revealing for demonstrating a notable disparity with the 831,000 men and 530,000 women who by July 1914 had signed Lord Milner's British covenant.[227] This counterpart to the Ulster Solemn League and Covenant of 1912 was shorn of that document's implicit commitment to unconstitutional and military resistance in an effort to gain high-level endorsement and popular support. Having initially declined to have any involvement with the British League, Milner accepted its presidency after Willoughby de Broke agreed to refocus its purpose to the promotion of Milner's British covenant.[228] A number of politically significant former allies, Salisbury, a veteran of South Africa, as well as Lord Robert Cecil and Austen Chamberlain, had similarly declined to go along with any warlike plans, and most Unionist MPs were opposed to Willoughby de

Broke's suggestion in March 1914 of amending the annual Army Act in an effort to prevent the military coercion of Ulster Unionists.[229]

Despite rhetoric to the contrary, therefore, Ulster was a place apart; supporting the militant stand of the Ulstermen did not necessarily extend to employing similar militancy on the other side of the Irish Sea, nor did it mean endorsing their shift towards exclusion.[230] Yet, for all his bluster, Willoughby de Broke confided to Halsbury that his opposition to 'the partitioning of Ireland' would relent if it 'avert[ed] a civil war'.[231] The lack of clarity and consensus on the party's right about the Irish question was not confined to the use of violence. The Scottish enthusiast for imperial federation, F.S. Oliver, was as reactionary and militant a figure as any in his disdain for democracy and relish for conflict with Germany: 'Nothing will save us', he informed his like-minded ally, Milner, 'except the sight of blood running pretty freely, but whether British and German blood, or only British, I don't know – nor do I think it much matters'.[232] But he dissented from the diehard line of opposing any change to the status of the union. Oliver was the most vocal proponent of 'home rule all round' in the United Kingdom as a step towards his wider goal, and he looked with hope on the inter-party talks that were convened to discuss the Irish question. He won over Austen Chamberlain, evinced the interest of Carson, and was to a limited extent echoed in Croft's musings on the same theme, though the idea inevitably became tangled up in acrimonious debates about exclusion.[233] As this suggests, the lack of any consensus on what federalism meant in practice ensured that it did not take hold of the wider party.

If Law's uncompromising rhetoric outwardly appeared to appease some of the most reactionary elements of his party, it caused alarm amongst others on the right, as well as sowing divisions and confusion in wider Unionist ranks about the lengths to which the party might go in playing the Ulster card.[234] Hugh Cecil informed Carson in 1914 that he was disturbed by Law's speeches on Ulster, fearing that they might 'incur the reproach of being irreconcilables'.[235] Law's underlying strategy, noted above, meant that he occupied a lonely position on Ireland; committed to an Ulster Unionist movement that became disposed to exclusion, but gambling on the failure of any proposed compromise on exclusion; and reining in right-wing opponents of exclusion who like him remained committed to supporting the defiance of the UVF. When this fine equipoise was threatened by the possibility of a compromise with Asquith at the end of 1913, Law intentionally undermined the likelihood of an agreement through an incendiary speech at Bristol on 15 January 1914, earning him the praise of Willoughby de Broke, the acknowledged standard bearer in Britain of the most hard-line position in opposition to home rule.[236] It took the outbreak of the First World War to extricate Law and his Unionist critics from the highly volatile situation facing the party and the country.

Tension between the right wing of the Unionist party and the Ulster Unionists was not confined to the question of exclusion. There was bad blood between the latter and George Wyndham, given that they had driven him from office in 1905. As Henry Lucy recorded at the time, 'I have not seen anything exceeding the virulent passion, the personal hatred, displayed ... by respectable-looking Ulster members denouncing a Unionist Chief Secretary, accused of having trafficked with the accursed thing, Home Rule.'[237] Wyndham's political career never recovered and found refuge only in right-wing campaigns such as the IML and ditcher peers.[238] Carson's prowess as a speaker was well known, but his all-consuming commitment to the union frustrated tariff reformers and empire-first Unionists as it prevented him from fully embracing their causes.[239] In January 1909 he irritated them further by sharing a platform with the prominent free-fooder, Robert Cecil, at his Marylebone East constituency; a gesture of solidarity against protests from militant tariff reformers. Carson's action moved two Irish Unionists with local connections, Lord Oranmore and Browne and Lord Bessborough, to boycott the event.[240] The Irish Unionist leader's sense of personal loyalty and code of honour also exposed him in 1913 to the ire of Maxse and other right-wing journalists when he defended in court, alongside F.E. Smith, afterwards the first Earl of Birkenhead, the two Liberal ministers implicated in the Marconi scandal.[241] Maxse's howls about Liberal corruption and anti-Semitic slurs tapped into considerable unease on the Unionist benches, and some even called for Law to take action against Carson and Smith.[242]

For their part, the Reveille and Imperial Mission were committed to the union, and individuals within these groups were prominent in its defence. Yet Croft sought to focus the aims of both on empire unity, not least to gain wider attention in the Unionist party when all else seemed to be focused on Ireland. Those associated with the Reveille and Imperial Mission achieved considerable if short-lived success in this regard through their contribution to the party crisis over tariff reform in 1912–13. Whole-hoggers had never reconciled themselves to Balfour's referendum pledge on food taxes. His replacement by Law, the shadow cabinet's decision to drop the pledge in 1912, and the party's need to offer an alternative to Lloyd George's agricultural campaign, appeared initially to restore the tariff reformers' fortunes. But their apparent victory – Lansdowne's declaration at the Albert Hall in November 1912 that the party was no longer bound by the pledge – provoked sustained pressure from Lancashire Unionists.

They had leverage over the wider party given that a significant number represented working-class seats. The vulnerability of these to 'New Liberalism', according to Peter Clarke, made Lancashire 'the cock pit of Edwardian elections', and disposed Unionists there to regard their cause as being hampered by the spectre of food taxes.[243] On 16 December, Law attempted to calm party feeling with a speech at Ashton-under-Lyne which declared that a Unionist government would wait for any initiative on food taxes to come from the dominions. It had the opposite effect, renewing internal party warfare between Chamberlain and the so-called king of Lancashire, the seventeenth Earl of Derby. The latter considered a breakaway movement if food taxes were not dropped, which had the effect of the forcing the TRL to yield ground.

In contrast to the NL and NSL, the TRL was in a weak state by 1913–14; still a popular movement with around 250,000 members, but beset by divisions between the central organization and northern branches wary of the full programme, as well as a decline in funds and activity.[244] Persistent pressure was maintained in its stead by whole-hog MPs and pressmen. Croft might have wound up the Reveille after Law succeeded Balfour, and reduced his ambitions for the Imperial Mission considerably, but in doing so he hinted about the possibility of a 'new movement ... divorced from party' should circumstances dictate, which was borne out in the subsequent party crisis over fiscal policy.[245] In response to the pressure exerted by Lancashire Unionists, Croft even revived the spectre of the Confederacy. Disappointed with Law's Ashton speech, Croft's dismay increased as the majority of back-bench opinion came out against food taxes, but he hardly helped his position by demanding that empire union not be sacrificed to save the union with Ireland. Law had little regard for the Confederacy. His support for tariff reform had always been practical and he came to regard its most earnest proponents as the greatest danger to party unity. Along with Lansdowne, he indicated his intention to resign the party leadership unless the advanced tariff reformers agreed to the policy outlined at Ashton. Carson rescued the situation – for the sake of Law's stance on Ulster – by working with Goulding to draw up a memorial to be signed by the Unionist parliamentary party.[246] Croft, Goulding and McNeill ensured that most of the whole-hoggers applied their names, even if reluctantly, and after some revisions to the text; only eight Unionist MPs refused outright.[247] The memorial effectively enshrined an agreement that, if returned to government, Unionists would pursue imperial preference immediately on manufactured goods, and that a further general election was required to extend preferences to agricultural imports. It was the first occasion that the party's grass roots, in this instance, the Lancashire Unionists, successfully exerted pressure on party policy, an irony given that Croft's Reveille had championed the mobilization of ordinary members. The TRL's grass roots, however, took exception to this at their 1913 annual conference by passing Maxse's resolution criticizing the memorial.[248] Chamberlain and Croft continued proselytizing through the TRL in a vain effort to apply pressure on Law.[249] The bulk of the party, however, remained focused on Ulster, though this was hardly a safe harbour for Law. He might have departed dramatically from Balfour by introducing the new style to front-bench politics, but his attempt to balance the various positions in the party was a continuation of and not a break from the troubled leadership of Balfour.

VI

The travails faced by Edwardian Conservatism make it one of the most examined periods in the party's history. The complexity of the 'crisis of conservatism' has produced contrasting approaches, from the high political to the history of ideas. Expressions of Unionist discontent tend to be relegated to the margins in the former and lumped together in the latter. In examining right-wing discontent with the Unionist leadership as three distinct vectors, this chapter seeks to restore their respective relevance to the high political drama that unfolded during these troubled years, and also to unravel the often tangled networks of disgruntlement and restlessness that stretched from Westminster to Fleet Street and beyond. This is not meant to underplay the overlaps in ideas, outlook and personnel between the vectors identified, but it is surely telling that not one of the groups or campaigns examined was able to embody and serve as a wider platform for the party's right wing. On the questions pursued with vigour by these elements, tariff reform, the future of the House of Lords, military preparedness and Ireland, it divided time and again on points of detail and on what to prioritize. The only organization to come close, the Halsbury Club, quickly revealed its lack of coherence. In the months following Balfour's resignation the club tried to regain focus and purpose by examining proposals for House of Lords reform, but with little hope of realizing such schemes it soon disappeared from view.[250] As Unionist discontents understood, the parliamentary party remained broadly Cecilian in outlook and temperament. This was demonstrated in the inability of empire-first Unionist parliamentarians to come out openly against Balfour, the patriotic leagues' low-level frustrations remaining just that, and the ditcher peers' insistence on declaring their loyalty to the party leader.

If there was a 'radical right', identified most readily with the empire-first Unionists, their allies in the press and a number of activists in the patriotic leagues, its size and influence was modest. The rhetoric employed by radical rightists, and in due course the Halsbury Club, was fundamentally Conservative in its exhortations that the front bench boldly state 'Unionist principles'. Moreover, the Unionist discontents examined here were not entirely out of keeping with Edwardian political culture. More than any period before or since, electoral politics before the First World War were disorderly and bitterly fought, with both Unionists and Liberals embracing vulgar populism to address the variegated mass electorate.[251] In any case, calling on the party to adopt Unionist fundamentals was not entirely helpful to or consistent with radical rightists advancing forward or 'radical' ideas, and it became clear that using coercion to make Unionist MPs and candidates adopt whole-hog tariff reform was insufficient to sustaining it as a policy. The urgent crises over the House of Lords and Ireland recalled the party's older fidelities and seized the attention of most Unionists, including the right of the party, to the detriment of those committed to the chimera of empire unity. Even when the tariff reform controversy revived in 1912–13, it was ultimately put in its place by Unionists in free-trade Lancashire, where the party's electoral appeal remained, as it had been throughout the nineteenth century, bound up with denominational identity.

If not in policymaking, then the influence of the empire-first Unionists can be detected in more subtle forms. Establishing a bridge to the ditcher peers prefigured the greater coherence of the interwar Conservative Right. The instability wrought by the Confederacy through the TRL was one of several factors that encouraged Balfour's shift towards tariff reform and his decision to overhaul the party organization, which in turn, along with the patriotic leagues, contributed to the revival and diversification of Unionist campaigning on the ground. The admiration of empire-first Unionists for the defiance of the ditcher peers, and the language of catastrophism evident in all three vectors of Unionist discontent, anticipated the new style of front-bench politics practised by Law. It also had a marked effect on the party's approach to opposition, culminating in its extreme brinkmanship over the Ulster question. This produced the most striking innovation, though not one sought by the empire-first Unionists. For the party of the constitution seemingly placed its own unity above the legitimacy of Parliament, not only risking civil war in Ireland, but potentially destabilizing Great Britain itself at a time of escalating international tension. The expediency of Unionist claims that Westminster had been captured by enemies of the constitution, that the constitution had been abrogated or suspended by the Parliament Act 1911, is evident in the ready abandonment of this line of reasoning after 1914. The three vectors examined here might not have secured obvious goals, but they were not without consequence. And if the Edwardian crisis of conservatism did not produce a coherent or unified faction on the right of the party, the experience of total war and coalition government stimulated its component parts to move slowly but decisively in that direction.

Patriotism Strained, 1914–18

I

The exigencies of total war did not dissipate the tensions and divisions which had plagued Unionism since the turn of the century. Although the crisis acted to some extent as a restraint on the party's right wing, cooperation between the Liberal and Unionist front benches inevitably inflamed those seeking an unadulterated form of conservatism. Paradoxically, the right's reflexive distaste for cross-party collaboration was partly responsible for significant advances along this course during the war. The decision of Andrew Bonar Law to enter into a coalition in May 1915 was motivated in large measure by the need to maintain party discipline, as was its reconstitution in December 1916. On both occasions he hoped to satisfy his party's determination to get back into office and take responsibility for making decisions in the crucible of war. Equally, Law addressed the right's demand for vigorous wartime leadership by helping to promote David Lloyd George to the premiership. Once in place, their partnership acquired new relevance and utility as Unionists contemplated the prospect of a vastly expanded electorate and post-war reconstruction. Both men were aware of the destructive potential of right-wing discontents, but for the most part they were able to contain it through a combination of their overwhelming parliamentary majority and timely concessions. This went some way towards incapacitating right-wing agitation. The war on the continent and the political situation at Westminster therefore did not fashion a more coherent grouping on the right of the Unionist party. Differences of opinion on a range of issues persisted, albeit with traditional conservatism increasingly marginalized. And some of the most zealous of tariff reformers removed themselves from the party altogether with the ill-fated experiment of the National Party. Little wonder that the earnest hope of many right-wingers for a leader of national standing remained unfulfilled.

II

The parliamentary truce agreed between Law and Herbert Asquith on 30 July 1914, followed on 28 August by a further agreement to suspend contests in the event of parliamentary vacancies, was calculated to take the heat out of British politics. Unease within Liberal ranks with declaring war is well known, but it also provided the party's front bench with renewed purpose. Unionists in contrast were thrown into confusion and disagreement about how to conduct 'patriotic opposition'. Added to this was the Unionists' frustration that Liberals now held only 260 seats compared with their 288. Resentful, suspicious and stranded on the opposition benches, Unionist MPs had little knowledge of the lengths to which Liberal ministers were prepared to go in order to achieve victory in the war. Removed from the difficulties and complexities of high-level decision making and restrained from criticizing policy, the frustrations of Unionists were channelled into making repeated calls for a more vigorous prosecution of the war. They also readily grasped the rare opportunities to criticize individual ministers provided by military setbacks and conflicts between ministers and service chiefs. The prominent right-wing backbencher, George Lloyd, was therefore unusual in deprecating the 'facile abuse of all politicians and all except soldiers ... My experience of both tells me that soldiers are, I fear, no more honest or wide-minded than the average politician – and their knowledge of foreign affairs is pitiable'.[1] Most right-wing Unionist MPs, in contrast, played a conspicuous and active part in stirring up disquiet amongst their back-bench colleagues. Unlike the pre-war period, though, persuasion had to take the place of cajoling and intimidation. This was aided by the emergence of new back-bench committees which increased the Right's influence in Parliament and lessened its reliance on patriotic leagues. Rather than end internal party strife, however, platforms such as the Unionist Business Committee (UBC) and Unionist War Committee (UWC) posed a direct challenge to the authority of the party's front bench.

Established in January 1915, the UBC gave institutional expression to the assumption that back-bench pressure was required to stiffen the party leadership. This was evident in the days leading up to the declaration of war. It was a matter of convention that questions of diplomacy, statecraft, defence and warfare were reserved to the party leader and his specialist advisors. However, on the weekend of Friday 31 July, as senior Unionists deliberated over the opposition's response to the international crisis, a parallel series of meetings took place between Leopold Amery, George Lloyd, Admiral Lord Charles Beresford, General Henry

Wilson and Leopold Maxse. All stalwart right-wing malcontents, they conspired with one another in the belief that the Unionist front bench lacked the necessary dynamism to demand an immediate and unequivocal declaration by the government in support of France.[2] Insisting on having their voices heard, Lloyd and Wilson were invited to a late-night meeting of senior Unionists at Lansdowne House. There it was agreed that the party would issue an ultimatum to Asquith the following day.[3] Regardless of whether or not this missive played a role in helping the prime minister persuade his cabinet to support war, and notwithstanding behind-the-scenes conversations between Arthur Balfour, Winston Churchill and F.E. Smith, the behaviour of Amery, Lloyd and the others, in their own eyes at least, appeared to be vindicated by the declaration delivered on 4 August to Germany.[4]

Further examples of such swagger might have been minimized had the Unionist leadership been able to establish a businesslike approach to patriotic opposition. However, Law's authority was undermined from the outset by Asquith's determination to pass bills for Irish home rule and Welsh disestablishment before proroguing Parliament. Facing calls from Walter Long and Lord Robert Cecil to use tactics which amounted to a return to party conflict, Law confronted an intemperate meeting of parliamentarians at the Carlton Club on 14 September.[5] He outlined the dilemma now faced by all Unionists: 'we cannot fight the Government now. They have tied our hands by our patriotism ... when the War is over the fight will be resumed, and it will, in my opinion not be less successfully resumed because we put our country now before our party'.[6] The following day, after Asquith addressed the Commons about the two bills, including his plan for a suspensory bill to delay their implementation until the conclusion of the war, Law and Sir Edward Carson vented the frustrations of their party in debate before the former led his MPs out of the chamber.[7] In doing so he followed the advice of Sir George Younger, chief whip of the Scottish Unionists, that backbenchers would prefer a strong protest to further party conflict.[8] Yet the gesture failed to quieten the shadow cabinet. Meeting on 16 September, Lords Halsbury and Selborne, Austen Chamberlain and Carson, all veterans of the Halsbury Club, won over a majority of those present to the proposal that unpalatable measures should be blocked in the House of Lords.[9]

Law was clearly vulnerable, but the position he outlined at the Carlton Club held in the months that followed. It helped that over a hundred of the party's younger MPs were serving in the armed forces and therefore absent from Westminster. The decision to wind down the party machine, and devote it instead to army recruitment, likewise assisted Law by depriving agitators of the opportunity to gain support in the voluntary party.[10] The Unionist press was another matter. It might be expected that censorship would prove more of a bind than patriotic opposition, yet as C.P. Scott noted in November 1914, 'The scurril press is still yapping at our heels ... The truce of the parties certainly doesn't apply to the party press. And it is all done by innuendo and epithets.'[11] Right-wing organs believed that they were rousing the country to the war effort, but this readily slipped into criticisms of government ministers.[12] Another by-product was the widespread adoption of an explicitly xenophobic style hitherto associated with the *National Review* and *Referee*.[13] Not only did this inflame public anger towards resident and naturalized Germans, high-profile figures were also targeted such as the First Sea Lord, Prince Louis of Battenberg, driven from his post in October 1914, and the first Viscount Haldane, removed from office in May 1915.[14] The resulting atmosphere obliged the one-time Confederate, R.D. Blumenfeld, editor of the *Daily Express*, to reassure readers that he was not and never had been a German.[15] Shrill and discordant coverage of the war by sections of the Unionist press inevitably drew attention to the relative silence of Unionist parliamentarians.

This finally cracked following the return of Parliament after the Christmas recess. When Lord Curzon rose to address the House of Lords on 6 January 1915, he signalled a departure from previous practice by adopting a distinctly critical tone in his scrutiny of war policy. Correspondence with Law and Long followed on the need for a more vigorous approach to opposition.[16] Law saw off this challenge with the help of Balfour.[17] But a more effective contest followed on its heels with the emergence of the UBC. Organized by the former Confederates, W.A.S. Hewins and Basil Peto, along with Ernest Pollock, MP for Warwick and Leamington, the UBC convened its first wartime meeting on 27 January. If only around forty MPs regularly attended its meetings, Law still recognized its significance by asking Long to serve as its chairman.[18] The preponderance of MPs with business backgrounds meant that it could not be easily overlooked by leading Unionists. Similarly, its expansive definition of economic questions revealed the committee's determination to become involved in many aspects of war policy through subcommittees on munitions, explosives, tariffs, shipping, food supply, contraband, blockade, aliens and the rationalization of industry. The UBC's latent influence became manifest in April in response to plans by Lloyd George to nationalize the liquor trade in a bid to accelerate munitions production. Against expectation, Law gave the idea favourable consideration.[19] The UBC's interest in munitions was already well established, but it was the brewing interest in its ranks which now came to the fore and threatened to revolt.[20] On 21 April, Hewins raised the matter in the Commons in what he described as 'observations which inferentially may be said to be critical of the Government'.[21] Law was remarkably candid when he addressed the House, acknowledging that he was 'constantly criticised by my own friends, in letters, because we do not criticise the Government enough'.[22] When Lloyd George subsequently turned his attention instead to a significant increase in liquor taxes, Law informed him frankly that his 'party was so much in the hands of the Trade that they must oppose these root and branch'.[23] In due course, on 6 May, UBC MPs and Irish nationalists, a remarkable combination in any other circumstance, combined to effectively defeat Lloyd George's proposal.[24] His authority already compromised, Law warned Lloyd George a week later that he could not restrain his party from attacking Churchill for the Dardanelles campaign if he remained First Lord of the Admiralty following the resignation of Admiral Fisher.[25]

III

The formation of a coalition government in May 1915 was meant to tackle the disruptive behaviour of Unionist backbenchers and restore the battered authority of Westminster over the civilian population and army alike.[26] It soon became clear, however, that its only tangible success was in postponing the general election, which was due to be held before the end of the year. Asquith's determination to retain overall control was demonstrated by the relatively modest level of Unionist input into the new administration. Churchill might have been thrown to the wolves, but his replacement, Balfour, was unlikely to reassure Unionist doubters. Haldane was removed for similar reasons, but replaced on the Woolsack with another Liberal. Most worrying of all, Law agreed to serve as Secretary of State for the Colonies, giving the impression that he had either been outwitted or was not willing to take on a greater role. If this was not bad enough, Unionist participation in the government did nothing to address the sense of exclusion felt on the back benches. As the party whip, William Bridgeman, remarked, 'he heard nothing whatever of what was going on; in fact he was more out of it than when he was a new member'.[27] However much Unionist MPs might grumble, there was no one of sufficient national standing around whom disaffection might coalesce. Leopold Maxse was especially frustrated: 'I only wish they [Germany] would invade us', he informed his sister. 'It would really wake up the country, and might even keep it awake for another generation. If we came through the war without being invaded, what hope is there for us?'[28] He later complained that the cabinet was saddled with 'the

International Jew in the shape of the Samuels and the Montagus'.[29] The situation changed following Carson's resignation on 19 October following a short spell as Attorney General. The Gallipoli debacle supplied him with the necessary pretext. His skill as an orator and reputation for uncompromising patriotism went before him as Carson demonstrated that he was just as prepared for the role of party rebel as that of leader in waiting. He was no stranger to defying the front bench, having resigned the whip in 1896 over Gerald Balfour's Irish Land bill. He had some modest yet not insignificant experience of party leadership too, not only of Irish Unionists, but also in managing the Unionist opposition in 1908 against Lloyd George's licensing bill.[30] Yet the casting of Carson as the standard bearer of true Conservatism is all the more notable given that his formative years were grounded in Irish Orangeism and Liberal Unionism. Something of Carson's unconventionality could still be discerned in his enthusiasm for Catholic higher education in Ireland, an issue which placed him at odds with many Unionists, and his surprising public denunciation of the decision to erect a statue of Oliver Cromwell at Westminster on the grounds that 'he was a murderer'.[31]

Figure 3 Sir Edward Carson

Carson's idiosyncrasies were initially of little importance to the disillusioned Unionists looking to him for leadership. Organized from January 1916 as the UWC, this new back-bench committee stood apart from the UBC in both its large membership and willingness to court publicity. It was founded by the Ulsterman and former Confederate, Ronald McNeill, and fellow right-winger, Sir Frederick Banbury (1850–1936), MP for the City of London. The UWC had the backing of the *Morning Post* and *National Review*, but far from being a purely partisan vehicle it tapped into the revived enthusiasm for Milnerite 'national' politics by working closely with the smaller Liberal War Committee.[32] Both war committees focused their efforts on demanding full conscription. Legislation passed around the same time of the UWC's formation had conscripted unmarried men between the ages of 18 and 41; a significant step for many Liberals, but one which failed to address near unanimous Unionist demands for 'equality of sacrifice'.[33] This reflected a popular view on the right that Unionists and Unionist sympathizers disproportionately filled the ranks of the army.[34] The UWC's conscription agitation eventually obliged the coalition to convene secret sessions of both Houses of Parliament on 25 April. The committee's MPs used the opportunity to savage government spokesmen, with the result that within a fortnight legislation was brought before the Commons to extend conscription to married men.[35] That day, over a hundred MPs honoured Carson at a special luncheon presided over by Lord Milner.[36] The former proconsul had already welcomed Carson into his inner circle of admirers, known as the 'Monday night cabal'.[37] To his supporters and opponents alike, Carson now appeared to be a figure of great significance. The *Morning Post*'s editor, Howell Gwynne, informed him that he was 'our fancy, and Lady Carson is, for the purposes of the simile, your trainer'.[38] Not everyone was taken in. At least one of Milner's acolytes, Amery, perceived a weakness in Carson which was confirmed soon after: 'He is a splendid leader if he has to sustain and advise unanimous followers. He can't quite control and make unanimous a body that is divided'.[39]

Unionists were united in condemning the Easter Rising mounted by Irish republicans but subsequent efforts by Lloyd George to reach a new settlement laid bare pre-war tensions about abandoning southern Ireland in order to safeguard Ulster. Carson and his nationalist counterpart, John Redmond, agreed with Lloyd George that home rule should be implemented immediately with exclusion for the six north-eastern counties, though the permanency of the latter provision remained ambiguous.[40] Two meetings of the Ulster Unionist Council, on 2 and 12 June, took the controversial step of abandoning the southern Unionists, including those resident in the three frontier counties of Ulster. Ulster Unionists in the abandoned counties felt 'sold and betrayed' and worked with Walter Long to put an end to the process.[41] Long canvassed opinion about forming a 'real Conservative Party', apparently without consulting Gwynne, for the editor was convinced that he stood with Lloyd George.[42] Carson now faced opposition from the very quarters which, weeks before, lauded him as a potential party leader. The UWC was divided, with Banbury opposing the settlement and McNeill siding with the Ulster Unionists.[43] A number of Unionist ministers rounded upon claims supposedly made by Lloyd George, that he had the agreement of the cabinet to bring the 1914 Act into operation, and that the settlement was necessary to appease American opinion. Selborne took the drastic step of resigning as president of the Board of Agriculture; Long and Lansdowne chose instead to remain in the government in order to frustrate the settlement.[44] There was unrest too at a meeting of back-bench Unionists on 22 June at the Carlton Club. Those in attendance summoned Law to a meeting there scheduled for 7 July. Hours before the latter convened, sixty Unionist parliamentarians met at Lord Salisbury's house, including the Duke of Norfolk, Lords Beresford, Cromer, Halsbury and Hugh Cecil, and the prominent right-wing MPs, Banbury and William Joynson-Hicks (1865–1932).[45] The Carlton Club meeting left Law in no doubt that a majority of Unionists were opposed to the deal.[46] In its wake, Lords Midleton and Salisbury, and Walter Guinness, MP for Bury St Edmonds, established the Imperial Unionist Association 'with a view to fighting the Government on their proposed surrender to Sinn Féin'.[47] On 12 July the *Morning Post* declared melodramatically that the 'Unionist Party is, in fact, dead; the cause for which it existed has been surrendered'.[48] There were, of course, Unionist MPs and journalists who decried the intransigence of the southern Irish Unionists and their allies in the cabinet, but the latter's opposition proved impossible to ignore. A cabinet committee established to examine safeguards for Unionists under a home rule settlement did not in itself pacify the revolt, but it succeeded in alienating Redmond and with that the only home rule settlement reached between the leaders of the Irish nationalist and Irish Unionist parties was dead.[49] Reviewing the episode, Salisbury wrote revealingly about his role in stiffening 'the back of our friends' and utility of delaying matters so that 'the real differences between the parties' became apparent: 'It is a beastly job this opposition of the independent Unionists. In the middle of the war our role seems to be putting spokes in the wheel of the Govt. But the machine does not seem to work without our opposition.'[50]

In the wake of the fallout over Ireland, the UWC was unable to maintain the promise of its early success. In part, the direction of the war moved significantly closer to its demands for the use of overwhelming manpower and munitions. As the deadly and drawn-out Somme offensive demonstrated, not even this could secure a decisive outcome. When the UWC next chose to stage a revolt, opposing a Colonial Office scheme to sell business interests captured from the Germans in West Africa, it lacked the unity and strength of purpose evident in its conscription crusade. Clearly, this went against expectation, for the 'Nigerian question' was meant to unite critics of the government. As Carson emphasized in his contribution to the debate, it was the Unionists' patriotic necessity to defend the recently acquired monopoly of Liverpool mercantile interests against the unpatriotic indifference of Law's department. Yet, at the crucial Commons division on 8 November, Unionist MPs divided 72–65 in Law's favour, revealing that a third of the UWC had failed to follow Carson's lead.[51] The Nigeria debate nevertheless demonstrated that the coalition had not succeeded in quelling unrest on the Unionist benches nor removed wider concerns about wartime governance. It stimulated Law, Carson and Lloyd George – an admirer of Carson since the Marconi affair – to enter discussions about the formation of a more compact ministry.[52] In their dealings with Asquith, Carson held out longer than the other two against the prime minister's attempts to retain power and circumscribe that of the proposed war council. Emboldened by the *Morning Post* and the Northcliffe press, Carson's defiance set in motion a series of resignations, and threats to resign, which culminated in Asquith's on 5 December.[53]

IV

The replacement of Asquith with Lloyd George betokened a shift in the style of leadership which went down well on the Unionist backbenches.[54] Most were reassured by the new prime minister's determination to win the war at all costs. Indeed, they were more likely to witness dynamic leadership from Lloyd George than their own party leader, whose adroitness, patience and stoicism as a parliamentary manager made him both a fitting counterpart and loyal lieutenant to the prime minister.[55] This did not amount to a continuation of the Balfourite restraint which had characterized Unionism in the Asquith coalition. Unionists had a majority in the new war cabinet. Its inclusion of Curzon and Milner sent a clear message to doubters in their party, as did Carson's agreement to return to government as First Lord of the Admiralty. As a result, the UWC ceased to pose any serious threat to the Unionist front bench, at least until Salisbury's takeover in 1918. The continued activity of the UBC was not a direct threat either, as it was merely one aspect of a resurgent campaign for tariff reform within and outwith Parliament. There remained, however, a hard core on the Right of the party that could not be appeased by the new arrangement. Initially, their energies were channelled into devising alternative schemes of 'national' government, before returning in the final year of the war to a more combative posture. These right-wing critics hoped that touchstone issues such as Ireland, franchise reform and tariff reform might upset the apple cart and lead to the formation of a 'national' government in their own image.

The Irish Convention which met at Dublin between 25 July 1917 and 5 April 1918 was intended, in part, to pacify American opinion by placing the responsibility for a new settlement in the hands of Irishmen on Irish soil. Unionist participation was secured by the government's agreement that conclusions would be non-binding.[56] But the Convention quickly laid bare divisions between Ulster Unionists and southern Irish Unionists, led by Lord Midleton, and thereby risked re-exposing tensions between Unionists at Westminster. Whereas southern Unionists now regarded Unionism as a lost cause in its traditional form, their northern counterparts were more determined than ever to secure the exclusion of the six north-eastern counties.[57] The Convention also strained the relationship between Ulster Unionists and British Unionists and within the former. When one of the Ulster delegates, the seventh Marquess of Londonderry, floated the possibility in November 1917 of a federal solution, then enjoying enhanced popularity amongst British Unionists, and Carson did the same again in February 1918, the leadership of Ulster Unionism stood firm in demanding nothing short of exclusion from home rule.[58] Lloyd George's attempt to offer Ulster special privileges under a home rule settlement was likewise rebuffed.[59] The split between the two branches of Irish Unionism was confirmed in March when delegates voted on a series of constitutional propositions, in the process also revealing a split amongst southern Unionists on the question of immediate home rule.[60] The latter was exacerbated by Salisbury's uncompromising motion in the House of Lords which ignored the Convention's deliberations by calling for the enforcement of law and order, economic development and conscription.[61] Salisbury's intransigence in turn exposed divisions in the UWC when it met to deliberate on Irish affairs, and his continued opposition to federalism was contested by Selborne.[62] As Unionism was riven several times over, it is not surprising that the tortuous, protracted and seemingly foredoomed proceedings of the Convention failed to provoke a party revolt similar to that witnessed the previous year. With even Lloyd George coming round to advocating the extension of conscription to Ireland, and the authorship of a fourth home rule measure placed in the hands of Walter Long, there was little possibility that Unionist discontents could successfully exploit the Irish question between 1918 and 1920.[63]

They struggled too during the drawn-out deliberations at Westminster over franchise reform. Having come out strongly in favour of extending the vote to wartime servicemen, Unionists broke with the ancient link between property and the franchise. It followed that the creation of a large electorate which might by exploited by socialists increased the appeal of a limited female franchise based on age and property. As with previous franchise reforms, the pill was sugared with an accompanying scheme of redistribution; Long used his influence as president of the Local Government Board to ensure that it benefited county seats.[64] Unionist discontent was further reined in by the convening in October 1916 of the Speaker's conference on franchise reform. Opposition, however, was not entirely absent, and three right-wing members of the conference, Banbury, Salisbury and James Craig, MP for East Down, all resigned. Following its report in January 1917, Banbury, John Gretton (1867–1947), MP for Burton, and other right-wing stalwarts challenged aspects of the resulting legislation when it was debated in the House of Commons.[65] The voluntary party too, from local associations through to its former chairman, Arthur Steel-Maitland, expressed grave doubts; though of necessity, given the need not to offend the likely new electorate, these were often couched in qualifications about out-of-date electoral registers. The right found an outlet for its frustrations and some satisfaction at the July 1917 meeting of the party's central council. Resolutions supporting the disenfranchisement of conscientious objectors and resident naturalized aliens from enemy countries – fuelled in part by reports of young Jewish men brought before conscription tribunals – proved to be very popular amongst delegates.[66] When the concerns embodied in these resolutions were subsequently presented to the House of Commons by McNeill, it led to embarrassing divisions in which large numbers of Unionist MPs chose to abstain rather than support the government.[67]

In contrast, efforts at the central council to link franchise reform with reconstitution of the House of Lords were headed off by the present and former party chairmen, Younger and Steel-Maitland.[68] Instigated by Halsbury, Selborne and the seventh Duke of Northumberland, this revival of ditcher politics enjoyed a measure of support amongst Unionist constituency associations.[69] It even possessed a progressive tinge when bound up with schemes for proportional representation. The latter ran into opposition from Long, however, who warned Halsbury that far from protecting Unionists, 'PR will only help Minorities who are highly organised and whose members are willing to obey the caucus and vote by the ticket, an objectionable method introduced from the USA and one which I earnestly hope Conservatives and Agriculturalists will never adopt.[70] In any case, House of Lords reform was ultimately undone by the imminence of the Representation of the People bill and the lack of a party consensus on what it meant in practice. When the issue was raised at the November 1917 Unionist conference, summoned in camera to demand answers from Law about the party's future, he promised to look at the issue if there 'was anything like agreement in the Conference'.[71] As Law's performance on that occasion was 'ineffective & very hard to hear', the party chairman obligingly moved a resolution which demanded that the party take up House of Lords reform following the report of a parliamentary committee established to examine the question.[72] When Selborne and Henry Chaplin, now first Viscount Chaplin, proposed an amendment which demanded reconstitution in advance of the franchise bill, Younger succeeded in dismissing it out of hand as an 'absurdity'.[73] Franchise reform might have stirred up anxiety amongst Unionists, but like Ireland, at least after 1917, it did not supply the means of launching a right-wing assault on the coalition. In view of his later decision to form a breakaway party, it is striking that Croft was both a member of the Speaker's conference and generally supportive of the government throughout the legislative process on franchise reform.[74] Lord Selborne too was disposed to some scheme of women's suffrage, to 'increase the general Conservatism of the classes of manual workers', and provide a 'steadying influence'.[75] In contrast, Curzon's National League for the Opposition to Female Suffrage was plagued by poor management, and it was utterly compromised by his decision to abstain when the House of Lords divided on its subject matter.[76]

Milner stood out amongst his ditcher colleagues by adopting a more constructive approach to the new electorate. The circumstances in which he was appointed to the war cabinet seem only to have reinforced his disenchantment with conventional party politics. Using contacts made in 1915 through the National Service League (NSL), Milner set about building an alliance with 'patriotic Labour' by helping to found the British Workers National League; from May 1918, the National Democratic and Labour Party. Injecting his personal wealth and liaising with Steel-Maitland in order to give the new party opportunities to stand unopposed at the 1918 general election, Milner's imprimatur was evident in its admixture of left- and right-wing policies and pronounced interest in moral and racial fitness. Not surprisingly, the party's ambiguous identity encountered hostility within the broader Labour movement. This problem was exacerbated by its receiving financial assistance from Patrick

Hannon's employers' organization, the British Commonwealth Union, and receipt of the 'coupon' – the letter of approval signed by Lloyd George and Law identifying candidates they wanted voters to support – at the 1918 general election. The party managed to secure 1.5 per cent of the popular vote and return ten MPs at that poll, but it was hardly the breakthrough desired by Milner and his attention moved elsewhere soon after. As for the National Democratic and Labour Party's remaining MPs, they stood in the 1922 general election as Lloyd George Liberals and all lost their seats to Labour.[77]

There was perhaps too much 'Labour' in Milner's party to attract significant support amongst right-wing Unionists. Nor were they attracted in March 1916 to the maverick and ultimately self-destructive right-wing politics of Noel Pemberton Billing, whose by-election victory over the Unionist candidate at Hertford caused a minor sensation. Those determined to oppose the successive coalitions headed by Asquith and Lloyd George tended to prefer instead Milnerite rhetoric about forming a 'national government'. Howell Gwynne was an early enthusiast and pioneer. In November 1915 he touted the idea of a 'League of Patriots' which might form a new government.[78] He circulated a memorandum by the *Morning Post* journalist, Ian Colvin, to Law and Carson, which called for a 'British, Protection, and National Service Party' to oppose the 'Free Trade, pro-German, and Voluntary Service party'.[79] Amery was another early enthusiast. He suggested that the British League for the Support of Ulster and the Union might provide a nucleus of supporters.[80] Collaborating with Gwynne, Milner, Carson and General Wilson, a meeting was organized for 12 January 1916 at the Constitutional Club to discuss Gwynne's 'suggestions for a National Policy'.[81] The simultaneous establishment of the UWC seems to have brought immediate satisfaction to many of the key figures in attendance, for Gwynne's efforts subsequently to enlist Lord Derby and Carson as front men for his 'national policy' met with little success; Derby rebuffed the idea as 'utopian' and Carson was reputedly incapacitated by ill health.[82]

Unable to make progress on his own, Gwynne supported the reconfiguration of the coalition in December 1916 which saw the elevation of his fellow Welshman to the premiership. This melted away in the months that followed. Like others of a similar disposition, Gwynne grew alarmed by a run of military setbacks. There were rumours too: Lloyd George intended to form his own 'national party', he wanted to invite Churchill and Asquith to return to government, and that an early peace with Germany was in the offing.[83] A core of right-wing MPs, including Lord Duncannon, Edward Goulding, Amery, Guinness and Croft, along with Maxse, now turned to Wilson as a potential leader, and plans were made to find the general a seat in Ulster where he had a family connection. Their scheme came to an abrupt halt in July 1917 when Law informed Wilson that it was impossible for him to join the war cabinet and that there was no point in him standing for Parliament.[84] Duncannon and Croft pressed on. They engaged the Liberal MP David Davies in a nod to the original ideal of a national party. But their determination to steer the new movement in a rightist direction was evident in plans to ask F.S. Oliver to draft its manifesto and for ditcher peers to head three of the seven planned district federations.[85] Croft hoped that the Tariff Reform League (TRL) would supply the new party's organization. He had some reason to be hopeful, having played an important role from 1916 – following his return from the Western Front as a brigadier general – in its revival. The crucial stimulus for the league's renewal, however, came from government. Its concession in autumn 1915 of limited duties on luxuries, and willingness to consider tariff reform in summer 1916, in the wake of the Allies' economic conference held at Paris, were calculated in part to appease the demands of the UBC and UWC for an effective form of economic warfare.[86] These developments understandably boosted the moral of the TRL. As Croft laid plans for the National Party, 5,000 members of the league attended its annual 'Chamberlain Day' in July 1917.[87]

Croft launched the National Party on 20 August. Only six out of the twenty-seven MPs who promised to join him actually followed through: the empire-first Unionists Alan Burgoyne, Duncannon and Rowland Hunt, as well as Douglas Carnegie, Sir Richard Cooper and Richard Rawson (1863–1918).[88] Eighteen peers also declared themselves as 'National'. Led in the Upper House by the second Baron Ampthill, a former Whig and one-time Governor of Madras, five were ditcher peers and two sat on the Imperial Maritime League's (IML) largely ornamental general council. With the qualified exception of Lord Beresford, almost all of them were political non-entities.[89] Despite this poor start, Croft pressed ahead with plans to merge the TRL with the National Party.[90] He encountered a further setback, however, when 400 members of the league gathered the following month for its annual conference. A resolution calling for amalgamation was rejected in favour of one welcoming the establishment of the National Party, and even this encountered 'strong opposition' although it managed to pass. The meeting thereafter descended into disorder, triggering the departure of those behind the attempted coup as well as prominent opponents. The TRL never recovered and was finally wound up in 1922.[91]

In comparison to other patriotic leagues, the TRL wilfully squandered the good hand it was dealt by the war. Against expectation, the NSL did not benefit from the conflict or growing calls for conscription. Scarred by pre-war accusations of militarism, the league remained committed to voluntary recruitment even as opinion began to change amongst Unionist parliamentarians. When it belatedly joined a conscription campaign whipped up by the *Morning Post* in August 1915, the NSL still met a largely negative reaction, from Labour MPs through to George V. The passage of two conscription acts in 1916 further dented its membership and finances. A crucial meeting on 16 January 1917 to decide its future overwhelmingly supported a motion to suspend its work; in doing so delegates rejected the efforts of Curzon and Hannon to find a new role for the league.[92] The IML too struggled to find a purpose and support. Its president, Willoughby de Broke, wrote desperate letters to raise money for its 'Villages and Rural Districts Enlightenment and Recruiting Campaign'.[93] Finding little satisfaction there, the league's co-founder, Lionel Graham Horton Horton-Smith, devoted himself instead to publishing a stream of pamphlets and letters vindicating the IML's pre-war campaigns.[94] Looking backwards did little to stem its decline. A meeting of the league on 2 April 1921 formally ended its existence 'owing to a lack of public interest'.[95] As for its larger rival, the Navy League, it also struggled with low membership and finances during the war, but it found a practical wartime role in countering 'socialist' agitation in the south Wales coalfields and guaranteed its long-term survival by concentrating on its celebrated sea-cadet training units.[96]

In the meantime, the National Party received ridicule early on for failing to live up to the Milnerite ideal suggested in its name, for it was less a government-in-waiting than a rump of zealous nationalists. Long compared it to the three tailors of Tooley Street.[97] But he conceded that the situation might be different if it attracted a leader of national standing; then, he argued, the 'great bulk of our Party would go over'.[98] The most likely candidate, Carson, was available, having resigned in July 1917 as First Lord, but he regarded the National Party as an embarrassment.[99] George Lloyd was less dismissive, seeing in it 'very great possibilities', but even he declined Croft's invitation to join. Lloyd informed a confidant that the National Party 'lack brains ... if one joined them one could only do so if one could bring with one a few people possessing brains as well as courage. Duncannon is *pour rire* – Page Croft a good fellow but a little too much of the platform hack to give dignity and weight to the movement'.[100] Gwynne acknowledged that the National Party was in want of a good leader, but as it was 'putting into practice what we have been preaching for the last two years', he made a virtue out of necessity by asserting that the 'big men' were 'all tarred with the same brush, and are perfectly incapable of being what the Salvation Army calls "born again"'. Invoking nostalgia, he further argued that 'To go back to the better days, when the leaders of the people told the truth to the people, is not possible with old hands. We must have new men to do it.'[101] F.S. Oliver too was not so convinced by the negative assessments of the new party, but he probably had the fate of the patriotic leagues in mind when he predicted that it 'stands more danger of being done to death by suffocation of enthusiastic adherents than by neglect, or derision, or abuse'.[102]

The National Party's failure, at its inception, to recruit more than half a dozen MPs was symptomatic of its most significant problem. The UBC and UWC had demonstrably proven that influence was best wielded from within the Unionist party. Moreover, the Lloyd George coalition went a long way to satisfying Unionist calls for a more dynamic and vigorous wartime leadership. Most ordinary Unionist party members appear to have been satisfied with this, though it is telling that the combined support at inner London by-elections for extreme right-wing candidates nearly rivalled that of coalition candidates; as Adrian Gregory notes, the victories of the latter owed something to adopting their challengers' anti-alien rhetoric.[103] A significant number of ordinary Unionists were closely involved in the government's National War Aims Committee established two months before the National Party. The committee's jingoistic campaigning targeted pacifist and other suspect meetings in an effort to head off the socialist revolutionary politics then playing out in Russia.[104] Participation was not for the faint-hearted as rival gatherings were known to turn violent, especially when the committee recruited the aid of the British Workers National League and the National Federation of Discharged Soldiers and Sailors.[105] Some Unionists expressed concern that these clashes hampered the war effort. And the reliability of the National Federation was called into question when its members heckled prominent figures associated with the government and Unionist party.[106] In this context, the National Party's hostility to conventional politics belied the fact that it offered nothing strikingly different from the government in style or substance. As such, its most potent criticisms focused on the prime minister's personal style, the 'sale' of honours, the appointment of the press barons to government and tensions with staff officers. Unionist backbenchers on the Right of the party were not immune to these concerns. As Selborne put it: 'We have a PM whom nobody respects, not one word of whom does anybody believe, whom most people cordially dislike, and yet hardly anyone wants to [remove] out of fear that Squiffy should come back.'[107]

Those remaining within the fold continued to make their voices heard. The UBC, in particular, sustained its demands for tariff reform. It secured a meeting with Lloyd George which if nothing else demonstrated that he was prepared to give them a hearing.[108] Law too received a delegation after the UBC took the uncharacteristic step of publicizing its 'anxiety' in July 1917 about the direction of war policy.[109] On 4 August a UBC motion in the Commons critical of the government narrowly lost by twenty-five votes, owing to a large number of abstentions. According to Hewins' account, Law afterwards admitted that he would have resigned had the government lost the division.[110] The UWC too remained a thorn in the side of the coalition. In the absence of Carson, and following its decision in June 1917 to admit peers, the UWC came increasingly under the influence of Salisbury and Selborne.[111] It gave vent to issues which also activated the National Party, contributing to the latter's redundancy, such as Churchill's return to government in July 1917, and the appointment in February 1918 of the press barons, Lords Beaverbrook and Northcliffe, as propaganda ministers. Austen Chamberlain shared the UWC's concerns, but the latent promise of enhanced influence for the committee that this suggested quickly evaporated. Salisbury's parliamentary motion on the matter went too far for

Figure 4 The Marquess of Salisbury

Chamberlain. If it won, it risked breaking the government, and if it failed, the result would be taken as an endorsement of Lloyd George's behaviour.[112] In the end, the prime minister managed to prevent the UWC revolt by stalling for time and assuaging its concerns directly rather than working through Law.[113] Political interference with the general staff continued to be a particularly sore point for the UWC, and personal regard for Henry Wilson was put to one side when Lloyd George substituted him as chief of the imperial general staff in place of Sir William Robertson.[114] Further meddling in May 1918 threatened to provoke a major back-bench revolt following the intervention of the former Director of Military Operations, General Maurice. Working through Salisbury, Maurice questioned the veracity of parliamentary statements on the war by Law and Lloyd George. But the general's grievance came to nothing when Asquith also decided to take up the matter. A large meeting of the UWC concluded that the former prime minister's involvement meant that it could take the issue no further.[115]

V

The limitations placed on right-wing agitation by the fear of Squiffy's return suggests that the initial promise of back-bench agitation faded under the second wartime coalition. So much for the old denunciation of political calculation in preference to principle. Even the National Party was not so much an exercise in idealist politics as a humiliating misjudgement about the durability of Lloyd George's government. Related to this, the right singularly failed to produce an effective leader. Carson came closest, but as Lord Crawford observed, too many of the government's critics 'are themselves open to rebuke – Carson for instance or Milner being "unsound" on the Home Rule question, Hugh Cecil being rotten on tariffs and so on'.[116] Indeed, the heterogeneity of the Right became even more complex towards the war's conclusion. Carson attended the crucial UWC meeting on Maurice having resigned from the cabinet earlier in the year. But his role on the government's Economic Offensive Committee further distanced him from the preoccupations of many right-wingers, as both he and its secretary, F.S. Oliver, arrived at the view that post-war Germany would not pose an immediate economic threat and that tariff reform was no longer urgent.[117] Beyond the party, the patriotic leagues withered, defying their leaders' expectations that war would increase patriotism and bring about national cohesion; it was the machinery of the state which had to be brought to bear in driving voluntary recruitment to the army and organizing anti-socialist campaigns.[118] Yet it is reductive to judge the effectiveness of the Right using only crude measurements such as its capacity to break governments and offer alternative prime ministers.

Put simply, Unionist party leaders could not ignore the UBC and UWC. For all their limitations, the two committees respectively brought about the demise of the last Liberal government and contributed significantly to the expiration of the first coalition. Lloyd George and Law might not have been able to give full and immediate satisfaction to UBC delegations, but the economic war waged against Germany brought the bulk of Unionists behind tariff reform to the extent that it was regarded as party policy and a condition of continuing to work with Lloyd George after the war's conclusion. As Robert Sanders informed the coalition Liberal whip, 'unless L.G. declares for preference and tariff against dumping it would be no good to ask Conservatives to back his candidates'.[119] Rumbling unease about the independence of the Unionist party was addressed by the formation of a policy committee in 1918 which included Younger and Long. In addition to tariff reform, it recommended that the party's platform include significant amendments to Welsh disestablishment and the Parliament Act of 1911.[120] Right-wingers were satisfied in other directions too. The enforcement of draconian anti-alien measures, and the harassment and censorship of pacifist and left-wing organizations has already been noted. Following protests from the UBC in August 1917, Law condemned the Labour party's leader, Arthur Henderson, his cabinet colleague since May 1915, for planning to attend a socialist peace conference in Stockholm.[121] Law again satisfied the militarist mood of his party a few months later by coming out 'very emphatically' against Lansdowne's proposal for an early peace.[122] In spite of its own shortcomings, back-bench organization clearly took its toll on Law's authority, as repeated threats to resign were a rough expedient for maintaining party discipline. Backbenchers could even circumscribe the leader's options. As Chancellor of the Exchequer, Law gave favourable consideration to a capital levy to tackle the country's depleted finances. This created a 'good deal of trouble' in a party that looked to reparations and tariff reform to fulfil this end.[123] After defending his right to look at such schemes, Law said no more on the subject.[124]

Influence was not all one way. Just as the war provided a political context conducive to the right wing's emphasis on sacrifice, urgency and impending cataclysm, it also expected Unionists of all hues to preside over increasing state interference in the economy and individual liberty. This was not so demanding for empire-first Unionists and those associated with F.E. Smith's Unionist Social Reform Committee. But even Cecilian Unionists came to recognize the need to address constructively the prospect of universal male franchise. Salisbury presided over a commission which recommended public subsidized housebuilding, and he was involved in plans, alongside the first Lord Sydenham of Combe (1848–1933), a former Liberal turned reactionary Unionist, with careers in both the army and colonial service, to settle returning soldiers on agricultural land. Carson's Economic Offensive Committee gave the state a role in shaping economic policy in both war and peace.[125] As with the Confederacy's *New Order*, these deviations did not amount to a revolution, and empire-first Unionists remained convinced that that the role of the state was simply to encourage 'men to better themselves'.[126] Moreover, departing from orthodoxy could be justified as a necessary response to the challenges of war and post-war reconstruction, and even legitimated with reference to the nineteenth-century Factory Acts and the venerable practice of *noblesse oblige*. These rationalizations, however, did not always prevent conflict with the party's traditionalist wing. A scheme devised by Milner and Selborne to fix grain prices was successfully opposed by Long and Chaplin.[127] Nor was Selborne recast as a progressive Unionist: his support for continuing the coalition into peacetime did not preclude challenging Lloyd George on Welsh disestablishment.[128] The experience of war challenged but did not eliminate traditionalist Conservatism as a distinct strand of right-wing Unionist politics, just as it perpetuated the fanatical element of empire-first Unionism with the creation of the National Party. At the war's conclusion the right of the Unionist party seemed more divided than ever. It was not the war, therefore, but a decision made during the war by the Unionist front bench to prolong the coalition into peacetime, which eventually brought a measure of unity to the Conservative Right.

Breaking the Coalition, 1918–22

I

An unintentional effect of the continuance of the Conservative–Lloyd George Liberal coalition after the First World War was the fashioning of a more coherent Conservative Right. Combining the personnel, behaviour and outlook of the ditcher peers with a section of empire-first Unionists, it gradually acquired a more uniform identity during these years which was captured in the contemporary epithet of 'diehards', a revival of the alternative label applied to the Edwardian ditcher peers. Shunned by many Unionist parliamentarians, the seemingly purist position articulated by the diehards found significant and growing levels of support amongst the party grass roots in this period and was echoed in sections of the Unionist press. At Westminster, whilst most Unionists deprecated the diehards' uncompromising rhetoric, there was concern that the underlying assumptions of the diehards' politics might increase in appeal in reaction to high-level support for the fusion of both governing parties, and when that prospect receded, by the series of political setbacks encountered by the coalition domestically and overseas. Like its component progenitors, the Conservative Right that emerged in this period made itself a thorn in the side of the government. Its sustained questioning of the purpose and longevity of the coalition, and concomitant concerns about the political identity and purpose of the Unionist party, struck a chord with many Unionists and contributed over time to the momentous decision by Unionist MPs in October 1922 to break with David Lloyd George. But the role of the diehards in this outcome was not a straightforward instance of the parliamentary party endorsing their case. On the contrary, it was the spectre of the diehards achieving some sort of ascendancy in the party which finally convinced influential figures of the need to go the polls as an independent party.

The 1918 general election returned 335 coalition Unionists, 133 coalition Liberals and 10 coalition Labour MPs. The negligibility of the scattered opposition, accentuated by the abstention of seventy-three Sinn Féin MPs, meant that the only viable and immediate threat to the survival of the coalition government came from the Unionist backbenches. This much was familiar given the dynamics of wartime politics. The context, however, had changed after the Armistice. The Unionists' reliance on Lloyd George was no longer due to parliamentary arithmetic. Rather, he was celebrated as 'the man who won the war', and widely considered as the only figure capable of overseeing the country's post-war reconstruction, not least in handling the trades unions. Front-bench Unionists regarded the government's overwhelming majority as a public endorsement of the coalition idea and an asset in facing an expanded and unfamiliar electorate in highly uncertain times. The voluntary party initially went along with it. There were a number of local disputes with 'coaly Libs' about designating the 'coupon' candidate to be supported by both, but not sufficient to call into question the principle of the coalition going to the polls. Right-wing critics of the coalition were outnumbered from the outset and as a consequence easily outmanoeuvred, yet these very same circumstances gradually helped to foster a greater sense of solidarity and coherence in their ranks. Over time the coalition supplied the 'other' against which they could define and promote 'Conservative principles', especially as leading coalitionists toyed with the idea of fusing the two anti-socialist parties. In these circumstances, the traits that united right-wingers came to matter more than what divided them.

II

It took several months before right-wing critics of the peacetime coalition government found their metier. Punishing Germany had featured prominently in Unionist appeals to the electorate in 1918.[1] But it was the right-wing press that maintained pressure on this question during Lloyd George's sojourns at the Paris peace conferences in the months that followed. In April 1919 Sir Edward Goulding and seven other backbenchers sent a telegram to the prime minister urging him to pursue 'the complete financial claim of the Empire'. Signed by 200 MPs, it purported to seek his assurance 'to meet innumerable inquiries from our constituents'. The gesture was presented as one which helped to 'strengthen the hand of the Prime Minister', but contrary to its authors' intentions, the sheer size of support given to the telegram proved to be its weakness, for it obliged them to avoid the appearance of 'disloyalty'.[2] Lloyd George exploited it to the full in his formal reply to one of the ringleaders, Kennedy Jones, MP for Hornsey, along with Jones's connection to Lord Northcliffe whose presses did so much to stir up discontent on this question. The prime minister returned to the theme following his return from Paris, denouncing Jones for his role in creating unease on the back benches and condemning *The Times* as a 'threepenny edition of the *Daily Mail*'.[3] His success in these skirmishes, however, could not completely settle the suspicions of ordinary Unionists about the government's leniency on Germany. This became evident at the National Union's annual conference in June 1920. The first to be held since the special conference of November 1917, it greeted with 'acclamation' Leopold Maxse's resolution attacking the government's 'singular and depressing absence of zeal ... to search the capacious pockets of Germans'. It was significant also for being the only critical resolution allowed by the organizers to proceed. *The Times*'s correspondent noted that others were 'dexterously put on one side, after they had been moved and seconded, by the simple process of proceeding to the next business without putting them to the vote'. He speculated that these resolutions would have received 'little support', but conceded that one delegate was responded to with 'cheers' after complaining that conferences served no purpose if the 'feelings and sentiments of ... a large proportion of their constituents' went unheard.[4] Days later, the newspaper reported 'that a very large section of the conference distrusted the Coalition'.[5]

This did not mean that ordinary Unionists were surly on all issues. Opposition to Welsh disestablishment, which before the war had provoked large rallies outside of Wales, was not raised at the 1920 conference.[6] Nor for that matter had it been brought up at the 1917 meeting between Andrew Bonar Law and the parliamentary party.[7] Even when it was raised by Lord Robert Cecil in November 1918, at the shadow cabinet which discussed prolonging the coalition, it failed to lead to a debate.[8] Undaunted, Cecil and other opponents were determined to use the opportunity to state their case provided by the Welsh Church (Temporalities) bill laid before Parliament in August 1919, which delayed the operation of the 1914 Act until 1920. Their revolt failed miserably. As Robert Sanders noted, 'The promised deal on the Welsh Church has also come off and seems to satisfy everyone except the Cecil clique. They are furious with the Bishops for accepting it'.[9] The uncompromising language adopted by the Cecils appears unwittingly to have accentuated the archaism of the controversy, from Lord Salisbury's criticism of the bishops as 'too simple minded for this wicked world', to Lord Hugh Cecil's attack on Law and other Unionists for conniving in 'robbery'. The latter went so far as to condemn his front bench of betrayal, 'who, willingly and knowingly, set their hands to an enterprise which their own lips have declared to be disgraceful, but which they lack courage and moral rectitude to turn away from'.[10] Lord

Robert Cecil made his protest by resigning from the government following the bill's safe passage in the House of Commons, 159–31.[11] The episode prompted Salisbury to revive the Association of Independent Unionist Peers, which in the short term became the principal diehard grouping in the House of Lords.[12] However, it had little effect in stemming the diminishing importance of the established churches to the Unionist party's identity and purpose, just as the pre-war cooperation between ditcher peers and empire-first Unionists did little to reverse the declining relevance of landownership. And as with land, the Church could not even unite right-wingers. For although many of Salisbury's future diehard collaborators in the House of Commons voted with Lord Hugh Cecil, a significant number did not, including the two National Party MPs, Henry Page Croft and Sir Richard Cooper. Conversely, if Unionist party managers and backbenchers hoped to restore the party's fortunes in Wales, they were to be disappointed. Outside of the anglicized south-east and some isolated redoubts, the party struggled throughout the interwar years to shake off its 'perceived identification with "Englishness" and "English interests"'.[13]

In contrast to Welsh disestablishment, concern amongst Unionists about the presence of aliens, particularly enemy aliens, increased considerably as a result of the war. From being a pet obsession of several patriotic leagues and certain right-wing organs, as had been the case before 1914, by the war's conclusion the issue had been taken up by Unionist-controlled local authorities and the National Union's executive committee.[14] The government responded in October 1919 with the Aliens Restriction bill, but when it was first put to the Commons, the measure was defeated by seventy-two votes for not going far enough; 66 coalition Unionists voted for the bill and 120 coalition Unionists voted against. A significant portion of the parliamentary debate focused on pilotage certificates, the subject of a pre-war campaign by the Navy League (NL), and taken up on this occasion by Sir Edward Carson. Citing his wartime tenure at the Admiralty, the former First Lord vindicated the navalists' long-held suspicions by claiming that 'eight or nine German pilots who had learned how to come into our ports by reason of the certificates we gave them' were 'afterwards found to be using that knowledge for naval purposes to blow up our ships'.[15] Nine of the bill's most prominent opponents were afterwards summoned to Downing Street with the result that legislative provisions for the deportation of aliens and a bar on their employment in the civil service were strengthened.[16] Contrasting the parliamentary revolts over German reparations, disestablishment and aliens, it was becoming clear that outraged jingoistic and xenophobic nationalism was considerably more effective in marshalling the Right of the party, and extending its influence beyond, than the churchly preoccupations of traditionalists.

This was confirmed by the post-war coalition's handling of Indian affairs. The 1919 India bill met with little effective opposition in Parliament. The alacrity of its passage, along with the government's willingness to accept amendments proposed by a joint select committee of both Houses, went some way to delivering this result. Unionists seem to have recognized its provisions for 'dyarchy' as a means of stemming the growth of Indian nationalism. Violence in the Punjab in early 1919, culminating in the massacre by troops of 379 protestors at Jallianwala Bagh, Amritsar, on 13 April, also provided an abject warning about relying only on the draconian Rowlatt Acts to deal with political dissent. Some on the Right demurred from this assessment, the *Morning Post*, predictably, but also the Northcliffe press.[17] However, most were reassured that the proposed constitution would leave overall control in the hands of the British whilst fulfilling the promise made in 1917 by the Secretary of State for India, Edwin Montagu, that Britain's goal was to increase Indian participation in every branch of the administration. As a result, and in contrast to the marked sympathy of Conservatives in the 1880s for British Indian opponents of Liberal reforms, most Unionists in 1918 appeared deaf to rumours of wholesale resignations from the Indian public service.[18] Opposition in the House of Lords was led by two former governors, Lord Sydenham and the first Baron MacDonnell, though its supporters there included proconsuls of far greater eminence, Curzon and Selborne.[19] Opposition amongst MPs was marshalled by Carson and Sir Frederick Banbury. They tried in vain to persuade Lloyd George and Law to give further time for consideration of the bill, and failed also to provoke a Commons division.[20] Rudyard Kipling wrote afterwards to one of the bill's opponents, Charles Oman (1860–1946), the Oxford academic and MP for the university, pinning the blame for what had happened on 'putting a Jew [Montagu] at the head of the India Office'.[21]

Details of the Amritsar massacre were kept out of the public eye during the deliberations of the joint select committee and the third reading of the bill in December 1919. In the meantime, the officer responsible for ordering troops to fire at Jallianwala Bagh, Brigadier Reginald Dyer, was sent off to fight on the Afghan frontier whilst an investigative commission determined his fate. Its report in March 1920 placed responsibility with Dyer. Montagu and the War Secretary, Winston Churchill, took the necessary steps to remove the brigadier from his post. Dyer's treatment by the two Liberal ministers provided the opening which critics of the government's Indian policy needed to turn attention away from Dyer's actions. Concerns about Montagu's knowledge and handling of the massacre, and his pronounced dislike of Dyer, lent a degree of plausibility to their case. It had a wider resonance too, for Dyer's treatment recalled tensions within the wartime coalition about civilian interference in the military, and critics and supporters alike drew parallels with contemporaneous political and military challenges to British authority in Ireland. Howell Gwynne arranged for Dyer to meet with MPs sympathetic to his cause on 8 June.[22] When the Commons debated the India Office budget a month later, Carson's amendment attacking Montagu's handling of Dyer attracted the support of 129 MPs. It was not enough to succeed, but it was an embarrassment to the coalition all the same given that many Unionists chose to abstain, making the government reliant on the support of Labour and Asquith-Liberal MPs.[23] When the House of Lords divided on a similar motion a fortnight later, 129–86 sided with Dyer.[24]

The Dyer affair was not a breakthrough for Unionist critics of the coalition, but it served as a demonstration of what was possible on certain issues and in particularly favourable circumstances. As Sanders recorded, 'a good many men voted against merely because Montagu had made them angry'.[25] Neville Chamberlain voted with the government 'but not very happily feeling strong disgust at having to endorse the censure on a man who made a bad mistake'. The ugly mood of the House, he wrote, was 'purely personal & does not signify any general hostility to the Govt'. Montagu, he observed, 'was hated for being a Jew and his speech was as tactless as possible getting everyone's back up and making the House feel that a Britisher was being thrown to the dogs by an alien'.[26] This anti-Semitic attitude was not unusual among Unionists. Bound up with the decades-old discourse about 'undesirable aliens', it was intensified during the war by alien scares and claims made about the role of Jews in the Bolshevik revolution.[27] On the issue of aliens, right-wing Unionists might have felt some sense of satisfaction that the parliamentary party appeared to move in its direction, for the xenophobia displayed on the Unionist benches during the passage of the 1919 Aliens Act was more intense in comparison to the bill's 1905 precursor.[28] Such attitudes were given renewed vigour by the 'race riots' witnessed in nine British cities between January and August 1919.[29] The heightened animus against ethnic minorities became entangled also with hostility to Lloyd George; in particular, his reputation for corruption and advancing his Jewish friends, and the rise of 'folklore' about war profiteers.[30] But anti-Semitism proved to be a blunt tool for the diehards in attempting to rally the party under their banner. Without doubt, they were at the centre of back-bench unrest over the Aliens Restriction bill. But Gwynne's publication in the *Morning Post* of 'The Cause of

World Unrest', a series of eighteen articles based heavily on his specially commissioned English translation of the so-called *Protocols of the Learned Elders of Zion*, unintentionally underscored the limited appeal among Unionists of politics foregrounded in anti-Semitism. Months in the planning, it was merely a coincidence that publication in July 1920 coincided with Carson's showdown with Montagu.[31] Yet in contrast to the *Morning Post*'s 'Appeal to Patriots', which raised a total of £26,317 1s. 10d. for Brigadier Dyer, the man it claimed had 'saved' India, its venture into the murky world of conspiracy theory met with little overt support.[32] And this despite *The Times* initially endorsing the veracity of the *Protocols*; it would be another year before the same paper demonstrated that it was a forgery. Even in advance of publication, Gwynne encountered opposition from otherwise friendly quarters. Charles Oman politely declined Gwynne's request to endorse the conspiratorial reading of history presented in the *Protocols*.[33] There was even opposition within the *Morning Post*.[34] Gwynne reported to the paper's owners, the seventh Earl and Countess Bathurst, that Lord Ampthill, a prominent Freemason and leader of the National Party in the House of Lords, took exception to conspiracy theories about the Jews and Freemasonry, but attempted to mitigate this by assuring them that Ampthill and other English Freemasons 'all agree that French Freemasonry is in the hands of the Jews. Any criticism of French and Italian Freemasonry would be cordially welcomed by the English Masons'.[35] This affirms Harry Defries's observation that 'it is not possible to discern ... a single Conservative attitude' to Jews, and the resulting ambivalence was replete with contradictions even at the level of personal relationships.[36] More pressing for Unionists seeking to restore their party's independence, it was evident that however widespread the prejudice against Jews, the middle classes were far more exercised about the 'working man'.[37] As subsequent events demonstrated, it would be anti-waste not anti-Semitism which advanced the diehards' cause.

Significantly for the post-war Conservative Right, the Dyer affair endowed it with greater clarity and coherence. Andrew Thompson argues that 'imperial weakness' was 'fundamental' to the 'mindset' of the post-war diehards.[38] However, they were not concerned with empire simply for its own sake. As Derek Sayers observes, the debate about Dyer in the press and Parliament invoked competing visions of 'British tradition', 'un-British behaviour' and 'national character'.[39] These were abiding concerns for traditionalist Conservatives, as indeed was their intuitive opposition to Liberal constitutional reforms.[40] At the same time, tensions within the 'constructive' element of pre-war empire-first politics were exposed by the adhesion of its most able advocates – typically those associated with the pre-war Compatriots Club, including Amery and Steel-Maitland – to the coalition government. Their preparedness to support a measure of Indian self-government was consistent with Lionel Curtis's Round Table movement. Tracing its roots to Lord Milner's 'kindergarten', the Round Table played an important role in replacing the mid-Victorian ideal of a single Anglo-Saxon global state with a federation of dominions, revised after the First World War to include India.[41] In this way they agreed with the quiet acceptance by Unionist leaders that a string of imperial controversies, from the Jameson Raid through to the South African War, underscored the need to resolve the perennial tension 'between *imperium* and *libertas*' in favour of the latter.[42] It extended even to the highly sensitive question of the party's attitude to Ireland.[43] As such, the Liberal view of imperial organization prevailed in the post-war years, one which, according to Ronald Hyam, 'pulled the administration of the Empire away from the more aggressive and centralizing methods' towards a 'loosely structured "Commonwealth of free nations"'.[44]

The diehards increasingly found relevance and cohesion in opposing this development. They remained an amalgam, of course, drawn for contrasting reasons to the oxymoronic tradition of 'new imperialism'. For traditionalists unable to realize the ideal of a premodern society at home, empire now stood in the place once occupied by the unreformed constitution. The Raj, above all, had an especial appeal after 1918, as David Cannadine observes, 'India's was a hierarchy that became the more alluring because it perpetuated overseas what was increasingly under threat in Britain.'[45] For those empire-first Unionists unwilling to follow the lead of the Round Table, they could find common ground with traditionalist Conservatives in defending the status quo. Thus the hitherto contrasting right-wing preoccupations of Salisbury and Croft became increasingly enmeshed through the language of imperialism.[46] It had an economic aspect also which soon became evident, in the coming together of aristocratic defensiveness about property and aggressive capitalism, which in practice meant protecting the established interests of the upper and middle classes alike.[47] In this sense, the diehards did not endorse or practise the evident distaste of right-wing avant-garde intellectuals for the middling ranks of society.[48] The net result, diehard Conservatism, was not so much a new ideology as a novel consensus shaped and informed by the circumstances of post–1918 politics. It helped to paper over differences of opinion amongst the diehards about tariff reform, which in any case had outgrown the empire-first Unionists. As the committed tariff reformer, William Hewins, noted of the coalition in 1922, its implementation of anti-dumping duties had 'gone ahead of the Die-Hards'.[49]

III

The identity of 'diehard politics' was further sharpened by a common commitment to pursue Unionist first principles and the party's independence. If this distinguished them from the bulk of their party colleagues on the back benches, the sacrifices required by coalition gave the diehards' opposition to coalition a wider and deepening resonance, raising doubts about the political provenance and purpose of certain policies. This was especially marked in the case of the Treasury. Many Unionist MPs had come to regard Austen Chamberlain's policies on income tax, corporation tax, excess capital tax and excess profits duty as oppressive and were anxious about where it all might lead. Banbury brought matters to a head in June 1920 by drawing up a memorial signed by 124 MPs which opposed the imposition of a capital levy.[50] The diehards' claims about the party's independence were likewise lent veracity by months of speculation, following the prime minister's return from the Paris peace conferences, about the possibility of fusing the two parties. The diehards channelled what they believed were the concerns of ordinary party members. Selborne claimed that even the current level of cooperation between the two parties had the effect of obscuring Unionist principles and weakening the party locally. He warned the party chairman, George Younger, in February 1920, that for ordinary party members 'The future looks ... very dark and they want to know under what flag they are going to be led to meet it.'[51] Younger acknowledged Selborne's concerns, but retorted that any unease in the party was aggravated by 'the somewhat querulous tactics of Bob Cecil and others in the House'.[52] Younger was no doubt convinced that Selborne's concerns were out of step with opinion in the parliamentary party when he received a memorial the following day in support of fusion, signed by ninety-five Unionist MPs.[53]

Convinced that the voluntary party was hostile to the coalition, the diehards responded with greater acts of defiance. Salisbury resigned soon after from the party's Reconstruction Committee, owing to 'differences of opinion' about the coalition. With greater consequence, he encouraged Stockport Unionists to stand their own candidate in a forthcoming two-member by-election rather than allow the coalition Liberals to replace their party's deceased MP with a candidate from their own ranks.[54] It did him little good in the short run, however, as a meeting of the 1900 Club 'was dead against' his proposal for an independent party; *The Times* reporting that 'he was only supported by one speaker, a Unionist member of the last Parliament'.[55] For all Salisbury's efforts, it was Lloyd George's inability to carry his own supporters that actually put paid to talk of fusion.

Badly handled meetings with his MPs on 16 and 18 March revealed their resentment with the prime minister's 'strongly Conservative stance'.[56] From this emerged a vague formula of 'closer co-operation' which Unionist leaders now readily adopted, helping them to avoid a potential clash with the voluntary party at the tightly managed annual conference in June.[57] That gathering seemed to confirm that Salisbury did indeed reflect the opinion of a significant number of ordinary party members. Surveying the conference delegates, the party's deputy chairman, Robert Sanders, estimated that 'about five-eighths of the audience were for the Coalition and the rest against'. He added that when Law spoke on 'excess profits, negotiation with Russia, and Ireland[,] [h]is audience was really against him'.[58] Amongst the resolutions not put to the vote was one calling for an independent party, proposed by Basil Peto and the Shrewsbury Unionist Association. The conference was steered instead to a motion denouncing the 'evils of Socialism'.[59] With coalition Liberal MPs and Unionist conference delegates alike demonstrating their reluctance to surrender the respective identities of the two parties, doubts were inevitably raised about the durability of the coalition.

This outcome was not of the diehards making, though it was grist to the mill for their cause. So too with the rise of 'anti-waste' politics. A consequence of the huge increase in income tax since 1914, coupled with wartime inflation lifting much of the lower-middle class into its threshold for the first time, the first Viscount Rothermere's anti-waste mantra harnessed and raised the anxiety of these taxpayers about Lloyd George's reputation for government spending. The issue first made an appearance at the Thanet by-election of November 1919. Local Unionists adopted Rothermere's son, Esmond Harmsworth, as their candidate, in the knowledge of his determination to stand on an explicitly anti-waste ticket.[60] Harmsworth's victory in a safe Unionist seat was not all that remarkable, but his father's pet cause was given a significant boost a year later by the onset of economic depression. Rothermere, to be clear, was not interested in the diehards' fidelity to Edwardian political preoccupations. Amongst his demands were the withdrawal of British forces from France and Russia, naval reduction, and giving up unprofitable overseas possessions in the Caribbean to pay off the wartime debt owed to the United States. He even considered a levy of fortunes made during the war.[61] Nonetheless, Thanet was the first in a series of by-election victories for the anti-waste crusade that diehard critics of the government interpreted as vindicating their calls for independence. The party's front bench drew the opposite lesson, encouraging support among them for a more permanent arrangement with their coalition partners. The diehards' interpretation became the more convincing of the two from January 1921, when Sir Thomas Polson stood as an anti-waste candidate against a coalition Unionist, capturing Dover with a majority of 3,130.[62] Hitching to Rothermere's bandwagon, however, was not without problems for the diehards, for the logic of anti-waste could not be confined to housing and unemployment insurance. The repeal of the Agriculture Act 1920 caused particular upset amongst farmers and protest amongst Unionist knights of the shires.[63] Similarly, the diehards could do little but look on as the drive for economies was brought to bear on the armed forces and imperial affairs.

On the face of it, the Washington conference of 1921–22 was a blow to navalists. But the overwhelming response of Unionists to the demise of the two-power standard preferred instead to celebrate stronger relations with the United States and express relief in the avoidance of a financially ruinous naval race. Even the likes of Gwynne and the NL applauded the resulting treaty, though it provoked a backlash in the latter from a minority of high-profile dissentients, which included the diehard MPs John Gretton and Patrick Hannon, the latter a former secretary of the League.[64] The army's difficulty in maintaining control of Mesopotamia and other newly acquired territories in the Middle East meant that it was forced to succumb to similar pressure.[65] The process of staged withdrawal from Persia and Mesopotamia, overseen initially by Milner at the Colonial Office, met with little overt dissension, the diehards included, excepting complaints within the cabinet by Curzon.[66] Salisbury was even among those calling for withdrawal from Mesopotamia.[67] Croft largely confined himself to warning against a hasty reduction in the size of the army.[68] There was little to be gained, even if the diehards were inclined, by making a stand on Mesopotamia. As a mandate granted by the League of Nations, formally in April 1920, the quasi-independence of 'Iraq' was already widely recognized and accepted; the subsequent outbreak of anti-British violence there seems only to have reinforced the view that Britain must limit its military commitment.[69] With the armed forces under strain, the need to maintain British authority in India and Egypt was a far more pressing concern for the diehards. They were deeply uneasy about developments in Egypt, where the nationalist uprising drew inevitable parallels with Ireland and India.[70] Following a period of coercion, Milner headed a mission despatched in December 1919 which the following year recommended a measure of self-government. His role undoubtedly helped to wrong-foot any attempt at resistance by the diehards. So too with the appointment of Field Marshal the first Viscount Allenby as High Commissioner of Egypt; neither man could be the target of the type of campaign waged against Montagu. Moreover, the issue could not be used to emphasize Unionist–Liberal differences given that Lloyd George came out against Milner. Indeed, Milner's proposals only succeeded in cabinet following Allenby's threat to resign and the conversion of Curzon. Ultimately, the only trace of diehard influence is discernible in the presentation of Allenby's announcement of the settlement in February 1922, a studiously modest affair in recognition of the diehards' hostility to the recent 'Anglo–Irish treaty'.[71]

More immediately, the Dover by-election was followed in February 1921 by ill-tempered scenes in the Commons on the subject of government spending. Chamberlain felt obliged to meet these head-on by reversing his opposition to the re-establishment of the House of Commons Estimates Committee.[72] The diminishing stock of the Chancellor of the Exchequer on the Unionist back benches did not augur well for his unchallenged succession to the party leadership in March, Law and Walter Long having retired around the same time, the former on the grounds of poor health. As the son of Joseph Chamberlain and one-time member of the Halsbury Club, Austen did not want for qualifications that might please the Right of his party. As he boasted to Halsbury, 'I used to tell you that you and I were the only Tories in Balfour's Cabinet. I hear that Lloyd George's comment on hearing the Party's choice was – "Austen! He's an awful Tory"'.[73] For many on the Right, he might never measure up to his father, but he was a figure of significance and one to whom Selborne had looked in March 1918 to lead a revolt against talk of a post-war coalition.[74] To his critics in 1921–22, however, Chamberlain's origins in Liberal Unionism and enthusiasm for fusion looked altogether more suspicious as he now headed the Unionist component of the coalition. His elevation to the party leadership may even have contributed to the timing of Croft's decision in April to wind up the National Party and rededicate its machinery, now labelled the National Constitutional Association (NCA), to the diehard cause.

The National Party had been an unmitigated failure. It returned only two MPs in 1918, Croft and Richard Cooper; the latter, like Croft, the scion of a large family business. Out of its original cohort of MPs, one had died, Carnegie and Hunt retired, and Burgoyne and Duncannon chose to stand as Unionists. Its small membership, overwhelmingly made up of landowners and former military officers, further undermined the party's claims to being 'national'; indeed, the social composition of its membership was less representative of society than that of the Unionist party.[75] Although it opposed the coalition, the party's policies were barely distinguishable from the Unionists, and what little radicalism it did propound was undermined by being carried along with the anti-waste clamour.[76]

The small amount of publicity it managed to attract, beyond the *Morning Post*, typically took the form of ridicule.[77] The only exceptions were the 'passing flurries' of publicity, aided and abetted by Gwynne, over abuses of the honours system.[78] The most significant of these, Croft's motion before the House of Commons on 28 May 1919 – highlighting that out of 155 hereditary peerages created by the prime minister, only one had gone to a member of the armed forces – led several hundred MPs to abstain rather than support their government.[79] A similar motion tabled in July 1922 secured 242 signatures and prompted the government to set up a royal commission.[80] These were high points in the party's otherwise lacklustre performance in Parliament and beyond. Had it remained independent, it is possible that the National Party's especial preoccupation with alien influence and anti-Semitism would have led it into the obscurity of British fascism.[81] Croft's formation of a 'private army' of strike-breakers, to pre-empt any industrial action called by the 'triple alliance', certainly point in this direction.[82] This was undoubtedly the trajectory of one of his party's candidates at the 1918 general election, Harold Wyatt, the co-founder of the Imperial Maritime League, who went on to become involved in October 1921 with 'The Britons'. Addressing its first large public meeting that month at the Caxton Hall, London, Wyatt condemned:

> the appointment of Jews to high Administrative posts in the Home Government, in India, in Palestine and Southern Ireland, etc.; the reception at Downing Street of emissaries of the Jew tyrants and exterminators of Russia, and of the Jew leader of the murder gang in Ireland; the landing in this country of vast numbers of Jew aliens.[83]

But the National Party's defeat at three by-elections led to its decision in January 1921 to no longer contest seats.[84] Unwilling and perhaps unable to simply return to the Unionist fold, Croft reconstituted the party as the NCA in April as an interim measure to boost support for an independent Unionist party.

The NCA's utility to critics of the government was not fully apparent until the November 1921 party crisis over Ireland. As noted already, diehard parliamentarians had in the meantime hitched onto the anti-waste crusade, Salisbury even launched his 'upmarket' version of the Anti-Waste League, the People's Union for Economy, and invited Oswald Mosley to become its secretary.[85] Both the diehards and the Anti-Waste League had secured an important victory at the St George's by-election earlier in the year, on 7 June; not only did the League's victorious candidate, James Erskine, defeat the coalition Unionist candidate, he afterwards joined the diehards in the Commons.[86] A week later, the diehards featured prominently in the 'economy manifesto and pledge' signed by 155 MPs and presented to Chamberlain on 14 June.[87] Days later, the Anti-Waste League again defeated a coalition Unionist candidate at the Hertford by-election called following the sudden retirement of the maverick independent MP, Pemberton Billing.[88] Salisbury interpreted these developments as evidence that the government was 'toppling to its fall'. Selborne disagreed: 'the Unionist Party in every part of the country is practically unanimous in thinking that to-day there ought to be only two parties in the state, those who are in favour of the Labour Party or Socialists, and those who are opposed to them'. He urged Salisbury not to stir up local Unionist associations as it would 'advantage nobody except the Labour Party, and I think our influence with the Party would be destroyed'. Selborne further pleaded that there was little the two peers could do, 'the natural result of our exile in the House of Lords'.[89] Undaunted, Salisbury's appeal to Unionists was subsequently published in the *Morning Post*: 'the duty of every Unionist association in the country', he wrote, 'is to approach its Unionist member or candidate ... and request that henceforth he shall consider himself free from any binding obligation to support the Coalition Government'. Unionist MPs could still vote with the government on issues about which they agreed, but 'the assent would be a clear indication in the name of his constituents that he would prefer a Unionist Government'.[90] Even this was not enough for John Gretton, chairman of both the Unionist Business Committee (UBC) and the Unionist Reconstruction Committee. He hailed, like Croft, from a brewing dynasty, and was a noted yachtsman, having won two gold medals at the 1900 Olympics. Harold Macmillan later described him as 'a man of real kindliness but a somewhat forbidding aspect. His drooping moustache, his heavy spectacles, and his rather sinister appearance made some lover of Sherlock Holmes christen him Professor Moriarty'.[91] With the support of his local party, Gretton resigned the coalition whip in July citing his 'general dissatisfaction with the Government' and specific opposition to the truce recently agreed in Ireland.[92]

Making Ireland the focus of anti-coalition politics proved prescient. The disclosure of draft terms of the truce between Crown forces and the Irish Republican Army (IRA), in the run up to the annual 12 July Orange parades, led to days of rioting in Belfast resulting in the deaths of more than twenty people.[93] As this revealed, preserving the place of 'Northern Ireland' – formally established in June – within the United Kingdom offered a useful pretext for attacking what really troubled the majority of the diehards, the government's decision to negotiate with its sworn enemies.[94] Focusing on Ireland also made up for the declining impact of the anti-waste movement. Two by-elections in August, at

Figure 5 John Gretton

Abbey and West Lewisham, saw coalition Unionist candidates identify themselves as 'anti-waste' and secure narrow victories over their Anti-Waste League rivals.[95] This sleight of hand was lent an air of plausibility by the government's increasing responsiveness to the cry of anti-waste, from the resignation in July of the Liberal minister Dr Christopher Addison, to the formation the following month of a committee of businessmen under Sir Eric Geddes to examine cuts to public expenditure. The 'Geddes axe' duly fell in the months that followed, putting an end to many of the government's ambitious plans for post-war reconstruction.

Not all of those in sympathy with the diehards agreed that Ireland could break the coalition. In correspondence with the eighth Duke of Northumberland (1880–1930), Gwynne acknowledged 'that never since the war – not even over the Dyer case – has there been such a strong feeling', but he expressed doubts about its utility in attacking the government. One unnamed cabinet minister, he claimed, warned him about the dilemma faced by critics of the policy. If the minister informed Lloyd George that he was 'anxious to resign', the prime minister would at once reply: ' "Certainly, if you are opposed to it, we will call it off"', thus preventing his resignation.[96] It did not help the diehards either that

Long had a hand in drafting the fourth home rule bill. In stark contrast to his previous support for southern Irish Unionists and hostility to Ulster exclusion, Long's Better Government of Ireland Act 1920 abandoned the former and acceded to the latter by granting exclusion and limited autonomy to the six north-eastern counties. As such, the legislation that established Northern Ireland had divided the Right of the Unionist party when it came before Parliament in March 1920.[97] Ironically, unity returned following the government's decision to enter discussions with Sinn Féin. But strength of feeling on this issue was still confined to the diehards, at least in Parliament, for an attempt by Gretton and Rupert Gwynne (1873–1924), MP for Eastbourne, to censure the government on 31 October attracted only forty-three MPs, and faced the opposition of ten times that number.[98] Future supporters, such as Gideon Murray (1877–1951), MP for Glasgow St Rollox, were not yet ready to part company with the coalition and risk 'the immediate resumption of bloodshed and murder and very heavy expense'.[99] As *The Times* observed, 'the revolt is admittedly weak in leadership', but it held out the prospect that the diehards' fortunes might soon fare better

Figure 6 'Playthings', *The Star* 8 September 1920

given that some were now 'pointedly asking whether Mr Bonar Law's return to active politics next Session' held out the prospect of a 'change of allegiance'.[100]

A double irony, then. The diehards now adopted the cause of safeguarding Northern Ireland as the most effective means of attacking the government over talks with Sinn Féin. And the diehards looked for deliverance to the man they had long resented for keeping alive the coalition idea. The two positions were related. 'I agree with you that his record is rather feeble', Salisbury confided to Selborne. 'But if Bonar Law comes again into the arena we have at last got a leader in the Commons even if we do not turn the Government out at this moment.'[101] Having interviewed Law, Salisbury knew that only the coercion of 'Ulster' would prompt his intervention. Neville Chamberlain observed that 'much intriguing and colloguing was going on as small groups of Ulster men and die-hards were to be seen in the smokeroom and lobbies at all hours'. He heard rumours that Law was 'taking up the Ulster cause', and learned from Hannon and Robert Horne 'that it was true and that Bonar was "on the warpath"'.[102] Should he be provoked, Law had the opportunity of the forthcoming annual party conference on 17 November to make his views clear.[103]

The NCA swung into action in the days leading up to the conference. Its speakers were not confined to Croft, Cooper and other National Party veterans; most of those taking to the platform were diehard MPs, including Gretton, Oman, Erskine, George Balfour (1872–1941), MP for Hampstead, Charles Foxcroft (1868–1929), MP for Bath, and Rear Admiral Sir Reginald Hall (1870–1943), MP for Liverpool West Derby and a former director of Naval Intelligence. Notably, two rival candidates at the Abbey by-election addressed these meetings, Brigadier General John Nicholson (1863–1924), the victor, and the Anti-Waste League candidate he defeated, Colonel Reginald Applin (1869–1957), formerly of the National Party.[104] They hoped that playing the Ulster card would be especially effective given that the conference was to be held at Liverpool. Salisbury confidently predicted that Gretton's motion condemning the government's Irish policy would 'be carried easily even unanimously'.[105] Such expectations were not confined to the diehards, for Austen Chamberlain believed that he was 'fighting for my political life'.[106] His brother, Neville, was not so sure: 'I sympathise with Ulster ... suddenly finding the tables turned on her and instead of being held up for an example of loyalty[,] courage & patriotism, suddenly pointed out as the obstacle to peace, obstinate stupid & narrow minded.' But with dominion and American opinion strongly in favour of the treaty, 'one must face the question which the Die-hards never will face. What is the alternative?'[107] Alongside the local party chiefs, Archibald Salvidge and

Lord Derby, Neville Chamberlain assisted party managers by bringing into line delegates from Liverpool, Lancashire and Birmingham respectively.[108] It became clear at the conference that sympathy with the diehard view did not necessarily translate into action: as Hewins observed, 'there was general agreement with Gretton' but 'a large number of the delegates did not vote'.[109] Ultimately, however, the potency of the diehards' case was diluted by assurances that the government of Northern Ireland would not face the prospect of coercion despite concurrent negotiations between government ministers and Sinn Féin, allowing Law to remain away from the conference. As a result, Gretton's motion received only seventy votes out of 1,800 delegates. A more strongly worded motion proposed by Northumberland was not even placed before the conference, a reminder that for all his ubiquity in far-Right circles, on account of his patronage and support for various journals and organizations, the enormously wealthy duke never amounted politically to anything more than a county councillor.[110] Appointed president of the National Union at the 1924 party conference held at Newcastle, it was merely the honour typically accorded by the party annually to a local titled magnate and not an endorsement of his political outlook.

The diehards went down to similarly resounding defeats in Parliament. On 16 December, after two days of debate, the House of Commons divided 401–58.[111] On 14 December, Carson, now an appeal court justice and elevated to the peerage, succeeded in rallying only forty-seven peers in the House of Lords. Carson's bitter denunciation of the treaty and its Unionist co-authors overlooked his own record of timely compromise:

> I thought of the last thirty years, during which I was fighting with others whose friendship and comradeship I hope I will lose from tonight, because I do not value any friendship that is not founded upon confidence and trust. I was in earnest. What a fool I was. I was only a puppet, and so was Ulster, and so was Ireland, in the political game that was to get the Conservative Party into power.[112]

For Nicholas Mansergh, the speech was 'the despairing lament of Irish Unionism as Union was finally undone'.[113] However, it is worth remembering that the bulk of Irish peers and those with vested interests in southern Ireland supported the treaty. Carson's first biographer, Edward Marjoribanks, did not live to complete this part of his subject's life, but he foregrounded the episode with a possibly apocryphal anecdote. Carson, he claimed, had been warned in 1892, upon entering the Commons for the first time, that 'sooner or later there is going to be a terrible disillusionment for you: the Conservative Party, mark my word, never yet took up a cause without betraying it in the end; and I don't think you'll betray it with them'.[114] Rather than being merely a backward-looking and parochial *cri de cœur*, Carson's attack on the treaty and Conservative leadership also addressed contemporary diehard anxiety about the fate of the empire, denouncing the treaty as a signal to nationalists in India and Egypt that Westminster lacked the will to stand up for British rule and civilization within twenty miles of its own shore.[115] Within months, Carson visited Gretton's Burton constituency to join publicly with the rebel MP in denouncing the coalition.[116]

IV

The government's success in Parliament led *The Times* to declare that 'The "Diehards" met their Waterloo'.[117] But the episode left the party in a fragile mood and increasingly restless about its identity and independence. Austen Chamberlain was obliged in January 1922 to dismiss coalition Liberal calls for an early general election on account of widespread opposition, not least from the party chairman.[118] There 'is a good deal of dissatisfaction in the Party more or less connected with the Coalition', Neville Chamberlain noted the following month:

> The fact is that they miss anything in the nature of a constructive policy among the Unionist leaders and though the latter are on safe ground when they say that they can't break with Ll.G. unless there is something to break about, there is a sort of feeling, hardly definite enough to be expressed, that if only they had a few ideas of their own there soon would be something to break about, or alternatively that we should be leading the Coalition instead of trailing after the Libs.[119]

In an effort to harness the party's uncertain mood, Gretton wrote to the press in February 1922 complaining of efforts to 'merge' the two parties. He demanded that Unionist leaders state their views on the party's future and, like Salisbury the year before, appealed to 'all Conservatives in the country, who still believe in their principles, not to pledge themselves to support any Coalition candidates until the position of the party and its future policy are made clear'.[120] Gretton afterwards led a back-bench deputation to Austen Chamberlain and received his assurance that the two parties would issue separate manifestos at the next general election.[121] Addressing the party's central council on 21 February, the party leader responded to the increasing tide of criticism by abandoning the label of 'coalition' in favour of an appeal for closer cooperation with the Lloyd George Liberals at the next general election, invoking the earlier example of the Liberal Unionist–Conservative partnership forged by his father.[122] This

modest concession was somewhat undermined the following day when Younger
addressed a meeting of women Unionists on how he looked forward at the next
general election to getting rid of the 'matrimonial alliance' in favour of 'a sort of
co-operation'.[123]

The hesitation of senior figures in the party to respond to its mood only
emboldened the diehards to press harder. *The Times* warned on 3 March that
although diehard numbers amounted to only fifty parliamentarians, the coalition
was 'tottering' and that the Unionist party would 'not tolerate any proscription of
the "Die-hards" by Coalition leaders'.[124] If not pushed out, Neville Chamberlain
expressed the hope that the diehards' 'attitude of general hostility ... must I think
resolve itself ultimately into secession'.[125] The diehards' disproportionate
influence on the executive committee of the National Union troubled his brother,
Austen, but he was not inclined to antagonize them intentionally.[126] The diehards
staked their position on 7 March with a 'manifesto', published after months of
delay, which was not so much a platform as a statement of 'Conservative and
Unionist principles' intended to expose Chamberlain's inability to do the same.[127]
These included loyalty to the throne, the duty of government to protect life and
property, enforcement of law and order, opposition to excessive taxation and
regulation, support for private enterprise, an end to grandiose reconstruction
schemes, peace at home and abroad, and the fulfilment of the 'great duty of firm
and unselfish government in the territories which, as in the case of India, have
long formed part of the Empire'.[128] The list of signatures included the Glasgow
MP, Gideon Murray. A scion of the Lords of Elibank, he had a career as a
colonial administrator before entering the House of Commons in 1918. Having
abandoned the government in the treaty division held on 16 December 1921,
Murray announced on 2 February 1922 that he was abandoning it altogether.
Citing a litany of setbacks to justify his position, in India and Egypt, and in
domestic and diplomatic affairs, he declared that 'the present Coalition has run
its course ... The Conservative party stands for definite principles ... The
Coalition stands for none, but is fitfully and often hopelessly dashed about on
the rocks of opportunism, expediency and vacillation'.[129]

The diehard manifesto went a little way towards countering Archibald
Salvidge's cutting observation that the diehards' position amounted to 'Mr
Balfour must go, or Mr Bonar Law must go. Now it was Mr Chamberlain must
go'.[130] In private, however, Hewins confessed that 'The Die-Hards are men of
excellent will, but there is no one amongst them, except Gretton, with a grip of
policy, and on economic questions which are fundamental they are divided'.[131] A
zealous tariff reformer, Hewins wrote several months later that it was 'unfortunate

that the Die-Hards were so entangled with the Irish question'. He was similarly dismayed that 'they had admitted the peers to their group'; a reference to the greater efforts at coordination between Salisbury's 'independent peers' and Gretton's supporters in the Commons.[132] Carson, despite his public endorsement of Gretton, echoed Hewins's concern in private, lamenting the 'feebleness' of the diehards owing to their lack of 'leaders', and informing Gwynne that Ronald McNeill 'would make the best leader as he is by far the ablest speaker and writer in the group'.[133]

These reservations aside, the diehards were chalking up some noteworthy successes, not the least of which was their growing numbers. According to Murray, about twenty-eight to thirty of them met regularly, three or four times a week, in Committee Room 16 'with doors tightly closed'.[134] As noted in their manifesto, the diehards remained alive to developments in India. The 'Peril of India' was the subject of an NCA meeting in late February, chaired by Lord Sydenham, who joined the diehards around this time, and addressed by the former governor of the Punjab, Sir Michael O'Dwyer, whose fall from grace had accompanied Dyer's.[135] Within days of the publication of the diehard manifesto, a crisis in Indian affairs presented them with another opportunity to strike at the coalition. The mere fact that Montagu and the viceroy, Rufus Isaacs, now first Earl of Reading, were Jews, and that the latter was a friend of Lloyd George, antagonized Unionists.[136] But the diehards were gifted an opportunity to attack both men and the government in March when the India Secretary went public with Reading's concerns about the emerging crisis over Turkey. The diehards responded by scheduling an adjournment debate to reprimand the government. They were only persuaded to stand down after Austen Chamberlain informed Gretton that Montagu had resigned.[137] Sanders noted afterwards, 'A Conservative at the India Office would do a lot to pacify our Die Hards.'[138] A week later, the diehards managed to wreck a large meeting of Unionist MPs convened at Westminster 'with the idea of forming a centre party'. According to Neville Chamberlain, 'the great majority of those present were anxious to support the Coalition', but a revolt 'engineered by "Paddy" Hannon' meant that no resolution was proposed, thereby giving the contrary impression that those gathered had no confidence in the coalition.[139]

As these events demonstrate, Austen Chamberlain's reluctance to challenge the diehards gave them opportunity to organize and strengthened the impression that he would rather bury his head than acknowledge unrest in the party.[140] It was only when the diehards followed through with a direct attack, proposing on 5 April a motion censuring the government for its 'lack of coherent and definite principle', that the Unionist leader responded in kind by attacking their lack of alternative policies and ministers.[141] His brother, Neville, described it as an 'uncharacteristically savage attack', and Sanders noted that Austen was on 'excellent form'.[142] The diehard motion, which was defeated easily, 288–95, was further compromised by its large number of Labour supporters. Still, Austen Chamberlain's success on this occasion was not enough to stem growing unrest in his party over the continuance of the coalition. Lloyd George was sufficiently concerned that he threatened to resign unless a pledge of loyalty was forthcoming from his coalition partners.[143] Already weakened by the failure to hold an early election, the prime minister had good cause to worry given that a series of diplomatic setbacks meant that his stock was falling. Unionists were particularly uneasy about his formal recognition of the Soviet Union and deteriorating relationship with the French. If all that was not bad enough, his support for the Greeks in Anatolia reopened the historic division between Liberals and Conservatives on Near East policy. Worse still, the presence of British troops at Chanak, in the way of Kemal Ataturk's advance on Constantinople, threatened to drag Britain into another war, prompting dominion governments to issue humiliating denials of any strategic interest in the matter. The Chanak crisis was a gift to the diehards by emphasizing the unnecessary compromises required of the coalition; it likewise alarmed other fervent imperialists into believing that the empire was 'only a few steps now to a break-up'.[144] The crisis also highlighted the degree to which Chamberlain's loyalty to the prime minister sustained the diehard campaign and spread disaffection in the party, for it prevented the Unionist leader from airing publicly the expectation that he would succeed to the premiership following a general election.[145] However, just as he protected Lloyd George, Chamberlain was protected in turn by the loyalty of Law, at least in the short term. The former party leader's famous letter to *The Times*, declaring that Britain could not alone be the 'policeman of the world', was not the attack on coalition which it appeared in retrospect, as it also acknowledged that Britain needed to check Turkish expansion.[146] When Gretton met twice with Law in September to persuade him to act, the former party leader refused to oust Chamberlain and expressed his unwillingness to become prime minister.[147]

Even so, the tide seemed to be with the diehards in the summer of 1922. On 2 June Salisbury issued their second manifesto, on this occasion for what he labelled 'the Conservative and Unionist Movement'. Calling on the support of local associations, it drew attention to the social and economic problems facing the country as well as political upheaval in Ireland and the government's faltering foreign policy. Salisbury urged 'the application without delay of a policy based on true national principles ... Our purpose is not to break up the Conservative and Unionist Party, but to rally and revive the true Conservative and Unionist principles'.[148] The letter was signed by ten peers and thirty MPs, including the nominally independent Cooper and Croft. It was augmented by the *Morning Post*'s public appeal for a 'Diehard Fund'. In making preparations for the campaign and fund, Salisbury discussed with Gwynne an alternative name, one 'more suited to the average Conservative mind ... "Old Conservative" sounds reactionary: "New Conservative" connotes a change from tradition which we want specially to avoid'.[149] In reply, Gwynne acknowledged the appeal of the 'pure and simple' name of 'Conservative', but added that by adopting it they 'might keep out of the Party a good many people who were old-fashioned Liberals, and are really good Diehards now'.[150] Gwynne's suggestions, all featuring the word 'party', suggest a measure of confusion or disagreement about the new movement's relationship with the Unionist party, which after a fashion took on the appearance of a cultivated, or at least convenient, ambiguity intended to delegitimize coalition Unionists. At the end of July Salisbury wrote to Gwynne a public letter formally accepting the diehard fund. Declaring that he did not always see eye to eye with the *Morning Post*, the 'leader of the movement' went on to state what they had in common: 'We stand against abortive international conferences; against an unnecessary bureaucracy; against ill-considered and experimental legislation; against concession to crime; for clean government and against the traffic in honours; for principle and against opportunism. In a word, we stand for the spirit of Conservatism and against the spirit of the Coalition'.[151] Their professed concern with the 'traffic in honours' brought about a showdown with Lloyd George on 17 July. Publication in June of the latest honours list renewed the *Morning Post*'s campaign to expose scandals in the award of honours to the prime minister's political and financial backers.[152] The paper's high-minded ethics aside, Unionists were frustrated that their party was disproportionately disadvantaged in raising finance and dispensing patronage by Lloyd George's behaviour. In due course, the prime minister was obliged to give a statement to the House of Commons. Facing a barrage of criticism from Croft, Banbury, McNeill and other diehard MPs, the government readily conceded the royal commission on honours in an effort to diffuse the issue.[153]

Contrary to what might be expected, Hewins was not optimistic about the diehards' recent progress. He regretted in particular their election of Salisbury, a free-trader, as leader. It was an obvious decision given that he was held in higher regard than Gretton, but Hewins deprecated the resulting influence it gave Salisbury over the group's identity.[154] Moreover, he found the diehards 'nervous and unprepared' when Field Marshal Sir Henry Wilson – recently elected MP for North Down and one of the better-known signatories of the diehard manifesto – was assassinated on 22 July outside his home by the IRA.[155] Hewins' judgement, however, was coloured by his passionate commitment to tariff reform and relative indifference to Irish affairs. For if Wilson's death was a setback, it also revived memories of the party crisis over Ireland, which alongside the emerging civil war between pro- and anti-treaty factions, gave the impression of vindicating the diehards' opposition to the 1921 treaty.[156] No doubt Hewins believed that the government was on the ropes and that the diehards had not done enough to press home their advantage. As Lloyd George acknowledged in late August, the 'Coalition is breaking up over the Tory revolt'.[157] If so, Hewins confused effect for agency. The diehards' growing profile was not so much a cause as a symptom of the government's ever-lengthening list of problems, domestic and overseas. Not that the diehards were without influence, even if it was largely indirect. They were a useful foil for party loyalists eager for change; Lord Derby threatened to join them when pleading with Chamberlain to drop Lloyd George; and Long consulted Salisbury as part of his efforts to pacify the party and avoid a split.[158] Even Salisbury employed the tactic, warning Law that 'I would like to keep the Party together, if I can, but every day increases the difficulty'.[159] As this suggests, the very existence of the diehards threatened the unity of the Unionist party ahead of a general election, not least by giving the impression that Chamberlain cared more for the unity of the coalition. Related to this, the diehard campaign lent focus to the otherwise unorganized and incoherent calls by grass-roots Unionists for a return to traditional party identities.

The prospect of such calls at the forthcoming party conference on 15 November contributed to the cabinet's decision in September to go to the polls as soon as possible and as a coalition. Law regarded this line of reasoning as mistaken, but not out of sympathy for the diehards; if a general election were 'rushed', he reasoned, 'the Die Hards would try and call a Conference of the Nat. Union'.[160] In the meantime, *The Times* reported a new development in diehard politics. In 'Diehards join hands', the paper reported the NCA's formal decision to cease maintaining its separate existence and instead cooperate with the 'Conservative and Unionist movement now led by Lord Salisbury'. It was the logical culmination of the National Party's decision in 1921 to no longer contest elections, but it was remarkable all the same that an organization which originated in the Tariff Reform League (TRL) now accepted an opponent of tariff reform, and a Cecil to boot, as its leader. It was still more significant given that the resulting silence of the diehards on economic policy removed one of the issues which clearly separated Unionists from coalition Liberals. Not that diehard MPs were completely subservient to Salisbury; an attempt by the marquess to issue yet another statement of diehard beliefs, this time repudiating the economic resolutions of the 1917 and 1918 imperial conferences, was rejected by them a week prior to the NCA's meeting.[161] It was not this, therefore, which created a minor row at the NCA's final meeting. Rather, it was an amendment to make cooperation conditional on a new Unionist ministry giving no opening to coalitionist Unionists. Described by the chairman, Ampthill, as 'ill advised and silly', the amendment was lost, but another was carried in its place substituting 'closely associated with' for 'co-operation'.[162]

The NCA's decision might have fortified the diehard ranks, but it was a combination of disgruntled junior and middle-ranking ministers, party managers and moderate backbenchers that brought the coalition chapter to a close. Their repeated pleas to Chamberlain that he drop Lloyd George before going to the polls went unheeded and led him to call the famous Carlton Club meeting for 19 October. Chamberlain expected that the result of the previous day's by-election at Newport would strengthen his conviction that Labour could exploit contests between Unionists and Liberals. On the day, however, news came through of the independent Unionist's victory. Amery noted of the meeting's opening, 'the much greater volume of cheering for Bonar than for Austen was an indication which way the wind was blowing'.[163] After lengthy speeches by Chamberlain and Balfour in support of the coalition, it was the long-suffering junior ministers who delivered the fatal blow with a motion calling for an independent party. A meeting of the diehards beforehand had resolved not to speak at the meeting 'except in the last resort', an indication that they were not unaware that their poor reputation on the back-benches might squander a possible victory.[164] This is evident in Law's decisive intervention. Speaking in favour of the motion, Law warned that Chamberlain, like Robert Peel in 1846, risked splitting the party and leaving Conservative identity in the hands of a 'reactionary element'.[165] The result, 187–87, was overwhelming.

V

The Conservative Right was conceived during the post-war coalition and emerged fully formed in its dying days. Its component parts certainly predated this period by some years, and its ideas and outlook can be traced even further back. But its emergence as a distinctive, cohesive and purposive body of politicians was a direct response to the crises that attended the post-war coalition. Quite justifiably, contemporaries and historians have preferred to assess these 'diehards' as agents of the coalition's difficulties and not as one of its effects. Austen Chamberlain, for example, attributed three reasons to the break-up of the coalition, eight years of rule by one government, the diehards and the growth of party feeling.[166] Hewins welcomed the downfall of the coalition, and he too apportioned responsibility to the diehards, or at least one in particular: 'the victory of Conservatism owes more to Gretton than to anybody else.'[167] Historians have been keen to debunk such theses and to distinguish between the diehards and more typical Unionist opposition to the coalition, such as the President of the Board of Trade and future party leader, Stanley Baldwin, and especially amongst junior ministers. But this approach leaves much that requires explanation and overlooks the real significance of 'diehard' politics. It is exacerbated by a tendency to assume that the cohesion in diehard ranks in 1922 pertained also in 1918 or 1919, so that a loosely organized assortment of right-wingers with contrasting and sometimes divergent concerns is judged as if the opposite pertained. Their coming together in 1922 was not preordained. Rather, it was made increasingly likely by structural changes during and after the war. The various vectors of right-wing discontent before the war, with their emphasis on extra-parliamentary activism, gave way during that conflict to a greater focus on harnessing innovative back-bench organization. It was the UBC and Unionist War Committee that delivered conscription, anti-alien measures and the government taking steps towards tariff reform, not the National Service League, NL or TRL, contributing to a broader trend which progressively narrowed the gap between 'high' and 'low' politics.[168] Patriotic opposition, then coalition, encouraged this development, at the same time aggravating right-wing resentment with their own front bench and its determination to work with Liberals. This did not prevent discussions about fashioning new parties which might better embody the Right's obsessions, but when it came to making a reality of such schemes, the National Party and the National Democratic and Labour Party failed spectacularly.

The persistence of the coalition after the Unionists' success at the polls in 1918 perpetuated this unstable dynamic and ensured that right-wing dissidence did not return to the status quo ante bellum. The diehards were well placed to articulate and amplify wider Unionist discontent with the coalition government, such as its repeated failure to fulfil the Unionist party's pledge to 'reform' the House of Lords, and the rift that emerged in relations with France. Crucially, however, the post-war coalition's domestic and overseas policies, and accompanying discussion of fusion, offered the 'other' against which many on the Right of the Unionist party could rally together, sinking their differences into a common defensive front, and lending them both credibility and purpose in the wider party. It took time for their emergence as a cohesive body to be realized organizationally; formally it occurred within days of the Carlton Club meeting. Even then, the diehards were sufficiently aware of their own weakness and confident of larger shifts in party opinion that they resolved to play no prominent part in the proceedings. The diehards' repeated clashes with the Unionist front bench had had the desired effect, stirring up constituency associations and especially the party conferences, and attracting varying levels of sympathy from the Unionist press. Here again, the gravitational force of working within the Unionist party proved decisive, despite the contrary expectations of some diehard supporters and their opponents that the diehards might secede. The Conservative Right was only one of several factors that helped to bring about the demise of the post-war coalition. Its real significance in this period, therefore, is its achievement of a degree of congruity in outlook and identity unparalleled since the days of the Ultra Tories.

Democracy and Empire, 1922–35

I

In contrast to previous phases of right-wing agitation, the post-war diehards did not break up or dissolve following the achievement of their most immediate goal. Lord Salisbury's Conservative and Unionist Movement certainly ceased to operate following the withdrawal of Unionists from the post-war coalition, and his entry to the cabinet, but the 'diehard fund' was kept in reserve, 'ready for action when required'.[1] Attempts to transfer it to the party's coffers were met with strenuous opposition from John Gretton. From the outset, he expressed concern that the Conservative government returned at the November 1922 general election was 'drifting into a mess in every direction'.[2] He might have adopted a different attitude had Andrew Bonar Law accepted his offer to succeed George Younger as party chairman.[3] But Gretton held firm in the years that followed, declaring in 1924, during the first Labour government, that 'None of [our] causes has been won or settled, in fact, they are all in great peril under present conditions.'[4] Possessing a fund but not a formal organization, Gretton summoned meetings of like-minded MPs and peers throughout the 1920s to review political developments.[5] This so-called Gretton Group remained an informal association, however, as the continued growth of back-bench organization and the increasing significance given to the National Union supplied diehards with more effective conduits through which their anxieties could find expression as well as test opinion in the party.

Firmly integrated into the party, the diehards were still defined by being at odds with the perceived moderation of the front bench. The converse also held. On 8 November 1922, Law felt it necessary to reiterate the assurance he had given in 1911 about not presiding over a 'government of reaction'.[6] His successor, Stanley Baldwin, characterized his leadership of the party as steering between the diehards on the one side and the young progressive war veterans on the other, or as he put it, between 'Harold Macmillan and John Gretton'.[7] As Philip Williamson observes, Baldwin's approach to Conservative leadership meant that 'resistance to "revolution" from the Labour left required opposition to "reaction" from the Conservative right'.[8] This was a matter of definition and positioning, not outright exclusion. For all Baldwin's efforts to win over Liberal voters, the diehards still represented a section of opinion in the country which remained important to Conservative success at the polls. He could not afford to ignore them altogether, at least until the landslide general election victory of the National Government in October 1931. This was especially so during spells of opposition when the diehards were at their most testing. Their numbers on the back benches, after all, remained relatively constant, at around forty or so MPs, many representing safe seats; conversely, a significant number of Baldwin's most committed supporters in the Commons held marginal constituencies.

Not unexpectedly, this political contrast is reflected to some extent in the diverging social backgrounds of diehard and 'One-Nation' Conservatives. In his landmark study of Britain's 'political elite', W.L. Guttsman claimed that 'opposition groups among Conservative MPs' correspond 'in some respects more to the traditional image of the Conservative MP than to his modern counterpart'. He found that they contained proportionally more former public school pupils and fewer businessmen, and 'comparatively few of aristocratic descent'; with the armed forces and professions making up the bulk of their number.[9] Guttsman's cohort, however, does not align neatly with the diehards, as it is based on four party rebellions only two of which were exclusively 'diehard' in origin and purpose. Several of the most prominent diehards, including Gretton, Henry Page Croft, Edward Goulding, Patrick Hannon and George Lloyd, hailed from families with strong business interests; Austen Chamberlain was not alone in observing that the diehard cohort overlapped with the British Commonwealth Union, or as he put it, 'the Forty Thieves, hangers on of business, not of the best type'.[10] Further, a significant number of the diehards, including Croft and Lloyd, had familial ties to the gentry, who were, as David Cannadine observes, 'for practical purposes, the equivalent of continental nobles'.[11] The overall thrust of Guttsman's observation still holds, of course, in so far as diehard MPs representing safe seats were less likely to be representative of post-war changes in the social composition of the Conservative back-benches. Even so, it must still be borne in mind that the relative heterogeneity of the pre-war right remained evident in the contrasting backgrounds of the interwar diehard parliamentarians, and that this to some extent helps to account for differences of political emphasis within their ranks.

Ensconced within the party, diehard influence on Conservatism was complex and often indirect. Contemporary critics of the diehards were prone to exaggerate that the very opposite pertained. This had an obvious tactical purpose in the case

Figure 7 'Here they come for the flop final', *The Star* 22 April 1927

of Liberal and Labour opponents. But fear that the diehards wielded enormous influence was evident also from within the Conservative party. Austen Chamberlain, still smarting from the Carlton Club meeting which rejected his leadership, cited the diehards' brooding presence on the back-benches to justify his refusal to return to front-line politics: 'I should have 40 or 50 of them always attacking from behind'.[12] He regarded Law as 'the prisoner of his Die-hard Peers, notably of Salisbury', and described the prime minister's appointment of Sir Reginald Hall as the party's principal agent as 'a definite capitulation to them'.[13] Almost a decade later, Chamberlain still fretted about the diehards, on this occasion, about Baldwin receiving 'barely veiled threats that as the Diehards had made him so they could unmake him.'[14] The menacing presence of the diehards was a theme also of David Low's political cartoons. His most famous creation, 'Colonel Blimp', in many respects embodied the diehard stereotype even if Low denied that it represented any particular party.[15] Jingoistic, chauvinistic and hidebound, Blimp's tanned face and white body suggested military service in the empire. The colonel, of course, was primarily a figure of ridicule; the National

Labour MP, Harold Nicolson, even claimed that the character was so effective in this role that it sapped 'discipline' and would contribute to the 'decline and fall of the British Empire'.[16] It is interesting, therefore, that Michael Powell and Emeric Pressburger's critically acclaimed film, *The Life and Death of Colonel Blimp*, released during the Second World War, subverted Low's original caricature by presenting a sympathetic if still satirical portrait of the main protagonist.[17]

These estimations of diehard influence aside, the reality was more prosaic. Salisbury's appointment as Lord President of the Council was significant politically given his role in the break-up of the coalition, but he was a relatively isolated figure on what the diehards regarded as touchstone issues. Not only did he maintain contact with a broad range of high-minded opinion in the party, but his commitment to free trade meant that he was often at odds with the bulk of diehard MPs. Gretton and Croft even threatened at one point to resign the party whip over the peer's public hostility to tariffs.[18] Salisbury's stock amongst the diehards was only restored when he emerged in 1932 as the leading credible opponent of the government's India policy, having previously stepped down quietly from the front bench.[19] In the meantime, the five other diehards appointed to Law's government – Wilfrid Ashley, William Joynson-Hicks, the second Marquess of Linlithgow (1887–1952), Ronald McNeill and Lord Wolmer – were all promoted to junior offices. As Law no doubt hoped, their loyalty to the government exerted a far greater pull than any allegiance to diehard MPs. When *The Times* published a claim in December 1923 that the 'Diehards [had] obtained absolute control' of the government, the inveterate back-bencher, Sir Frederick Banbury, gave the tart reply that 'there is only one Die-hard in Mr Baldwin's Cabinet, namely, Lord Salisbury, and that as far as I know the Die-hards outside the Cabinet were never consulted as to the policy of the Government'.[20] As for their influence in government, there was a limit to what well-paced diehards could effect. Salisbury was never able to win cabinet support for his quintessentially diehard position on British–Irish relations. The appointment in November 1924 in Baldwin's second government of Joynson-Hicks as Secretary of State for Home Affairs caused more of a stir, and blew a chill wind in certain quarters, including publishers, nightclub owners, and notoriously, the Jewish community. Yet, to take the last of these, Jix's department had for years discriminated against applications made by Russian Jews for naturalization. In truth, the elision of anti-Communism with anti-alienism was widely held amongst Conservatives, including Baldwin, and was not peculiarly diehard. Joynson-Hicks's most significant intervention in this area, an attempt to substitute the annual renewal of the 1919 Aliens Act with a permanent statute, was never realized as the pressure of parliamentary business and his declining standing amongst colleagues took their toll.[21]

What is most striking about the Conservative Right in this period is the lack of a distinct, coherent and active diehard approach to many domestic questions, excepting economic affairs, of course; a reflection, in part, of the declining influence of the peers in diehard ranks. Many peers had become involved in diehard politics through holding strong convictions about the constitutional role of the House of Lords, the sanctity of private property, and the union with Ireland. In contrast, a significant number of interwar diehard MPs were originally activated by empire-first politics, and to this end exhibited a willingness to question traditional Conservative positions on a number of domestic issues. As a result, only a very small number of diehard MPs bothered to oppose the equalization of the franchise in 1928, and although diehard peers and MPs were united in making frequent demands for a stronger House of Lords, this did not amount to anything more than resolutions at annual party conferences. During the prayer-book controversy of 1927–28, the diehards were found on both sides of the argument, underscoring the extent to which religion no longer united let alone defined the Conservative Right.[22] And if there was broad cohesion on agricultural matters, between traditionalists wedded to the defence of the landed interest and advocates of whole-hog protection, it did not amount to a 'country party', nor were the diehards synonymous with the more professional parliamentary lobby on agriculture which emerged in the interwar period.[23] It was imperial and economic affairs, therefore, which more than any other issues defined, activated and unified the diehards. And of the two, it was their zealous imperialism which distinguished them most from the remainder of the parliamentary party. Not that this was without relevance to domestic concerns. After all, upholding the late-Victorian belief in Britain's imperial mission was integral to an idealized conception of conservatism which was held to be under siege at home as well as overseas. The seeming disposition of leading Conservatives to 'scuttle' imperial authority by 'surrendering' to nationalist agitators particularly exercised the diehards, not only for its consequences to British authority and prestige overseas, but for exhibiting a collective failure of nerve at the apex of the party which had implications for Britain as well as its empire. Such unease, even paranoia, about front-bench intentions was hardly new. But in contrast to Arthur Balfour's vacillation towards the empire-first MPs, and Chamberlain's reluctance to square up to his critics, Law and especially Baldwin were more calculated in their respective approaches, both in finding ways of avoiding direct conflict with the diehards as well as demonstrating their willingness to take them head-on.

II

For all its centrality to the post-war diehards' political activism, the importance they attached to empire was not completely out of step with attitudes in the wider party. Empire-mindedness had received a boost during the First World War which continued to be felt in the years that followed. Conservative governments passed the Empire Settlement Act 1922, organized the British Empire exhibition at Wembley two years later, and established in 1926 the Empire Marketing Board.[24] Interwar educational policymakers ensured that empire continued to feature in elementary school curricula, albeit after 1926 with an emphasis on international cooperation.[25] The language of empire was utilized by new representative and advocacy organizations such as the Empire Parliamentary Association, the Empire Industries Association, and even the British Commonwealth Union, the last ostensibly organized to represent the interests of industrialists in Parliament.[26] Imperialism continued to be a conspicuous feature of associational culture, even if the assertive 'masculine' agitation of the pre-war patriotic leagues was succeeded after the war by more 'feminine' organizations such as the Victoria League and the League of the Empire.[27] Most Conservatives took it for granted that theirs was the party of empire, to the extent that members attending the East Midlands provincial area's 1933 annual general meeting discussed changing its name to the 'National Empire Party' or 'Empire Party'.[28] But if these developments suggested increased empire-mindedness, at least among Conservatives, they fell short of the aspirations of empire-first activists.

Not all pre-war empire-first Conservatives found their way into the interwar diehard cohort. Several of the more intellectually minded and politically able – especially those associated with the Compatriots Club – were too wedded to constructive policymaking to become closely entangled with those with a reputation for the opposite. Arthur Steel-Maitland's continued advocacy for tariff reform did not replicate his pre-war enthusiasm for empire, but rather a deepening determination to help domestic industry.[29] Leopold Amery's fervour for imperial unity, in contrast, remained unabated, even if it was compromised in the eyes of the diehards by acceptance of office in the post-war coalition. Yet he was at one with them in remaining convinced that much more had to be done to realize Joseph Chamberlain's dream of empire unity. To their mutual frustration, the means of achieving this outcome, tariff reform, or 'imperial preference', remained stubbornly elusive despite expectations to the contrary. Law omitted tariffs from the Conservatives' 1922 general election manifesto, and compounded the crime by assuring the electorate that his party would make no fundamental change to the fiscal system if returned to office. When Baldwin resolved to free himself from that pledge by going to the polls in December 1923, tariff reformers were pulled up short. Neville Chamberlain could claim plausibly that the diehards had urged Baldwin 'to be more extreme', but a number of them, including Gretton, Joynson-Hicks and Hannon, were anxious about the decision to call a snap election on tariffs and expressed privately their concern that the electorate needed to be better educated on the subject.[30] This made the defeat inflicted on the party at the polls all the more bitter, with 258 MPs returned in place of the 345 returned at the 1922 general election. Given that Baldwin was the first Conservative party leader fully to endorse tariff reform, Croft rushed to defend him and his policy 'without any equivocation', placing blame for the party's defeat instead at the door of the Conservative press. The man who had once harried Balfour and repudiated Law warned that 'To sacrifice Mr Baldwin now to intrigue would be to smash the party for a decade.'[31] Gretton agreed, confiding to Croft months later, after Ramsay MacDonald formed the first Labour government, that 'It would be fatal to abandon Baldwin, for any alternative at the present time would split the Party.'[32]

Croft did not shift from this position when Baldwin abandoned tariffs in the wake of the general election defeat. If the baronetcy awarded to him in Baldwin's resignation honours list was a factor, the general election result still demonstrated that the real problem for tariff reformers was the press and electorate.[33] Never again did he or any other diehard display their former confidence about making empire the central plank of a general election campaign. Winston Churchill's later hyperbole about consulting the electorate over India could only have come from a committed free-trader with no experience of the bitter disappointments long meted out to tariff reformers. As J.C.C. Davidson reputedly said in reply to his threat, 'I thought that the British public was much more interested in the size of their pay-packet on Friday than by great rhetorical appeals to their loyalty to the British Empire.'[34] This would appear to confirm the minimalist assessment of the impact of empire on British working-class culture, or, from a contrasting perspective, that it was 'simply there, not a subject of popular critical consciousness'.[35] Either way, as Richard Whiting observes, imperial policy never became a central issue at general elections, though it was bound up with how party leaders wished to project their party.[36] As such, Baldwin, the master strategist, took great care in crafting his response to the setback of 1923. For their part, Amery and Neville Chamberlain turned to Croft to help revive the tariff reform agitation.[37] What emerged as the Empire Industries Association (EIA) eschewed the militancy and disruptiveness of the old Tariff Reform League (TRL). It aimed instead to build up support in the parliamentary party through persuasion in the hope of coaxing Baldwin back to full-blown tariffs. This was made more not less difficult in the wake of the 1924 general election. Many attributed the party's recovery – 419 MPs were returned – to a manifesto that substituted the cautious policy of industrial safeguarding for tariff reform. Tariff reformers were further frustrated by the surprise appointment afterwards of Churchill as Chancellor of the Exchequer, although some comfort could be drawn from Amery and Neville Chamberlain's cabinet appointments, and that of another tariff reformer, Sir Philip Cunliffe-Lister, as President of the Board of Trade.

In inviting Croft to lead the EIA, Amery and Chamberlain identified one of the cause's most dynamic advocates. But it was also risky given Croft's record of fractiousness. It nearly backfired early on when he resigned over efforts by others in the association to win over 'Socialists'. Persuaded to return, Croft set himself

Figure 8 Sir Henry Page Croft

to the task of building up the EIA with dedication and outward demonstrations of loyalty to Baldwin. There was a structural reason too for not replicating the disruptiveness of the old League. In place of the TRL's local, regional and national structure, which Croft believed had dissipated funds, the EIA's resources were channelled instead into 'active propaganda in the places most needed'. Determined to work with, not against, Baldwin, Croft organized successive deputations to press the prime minister on extending his application of safeguarding to a wider range of industries.[38] The EIA's non-confrontational strategy saw its membership rise steadily in the parliamentary party and encouraged ministers, including Churchill, to treat Croft with a measure of respect.[39] It attracted funding too from businesses with vested interests promoting safeguarding and tariff reform, even if Croft's strategy remained wedded to political calculations rather than the expectations of donors.[40] The voluntary party also responded to Croft's campaign, passing near unanimous votes in favour of his resolutions at annual party conferences in 1926, 1928 and 1929.[41]

Baldwin's persistent resistance to such calls fed into the prevailing sense of apathy amongst Conservatives which attended the final two years of his second government. In particular, his decision to rule out the extension of safeguarding to iron and steel, in response to a campaign orchestrated by the EIA, proved to be highly unpopular and reduced party morale ahead of its defeat at the May 1929 general election. The feeling that Baldwin's timidity on tariffs had squandered his majority became pervasive in Conservative circles, and in the south of England found an outlet in Lord Beaverbrook's 'Empire Crusade'.[42] Against this backdrop, the EIA maintained its outward loyalty to the party leader; Croft's unanimously supported resolution at the 1929 party conference – 'our leaders shall place the policy of Empire development and security for British industry and British wages against unfair foreign competition in the forefront of the Party programme' – was sufficiently vague to elicit Baldwin's acceptance.[43] If anything, Beaverbrook's démarche offered a useful means of applying pressure on Baldwin and a foil for emphasizing the EIA's loyalty. In private, Croft made fitful attempts to engage Beaverbrook, both encouraging him and urging restraint.[44] His diehard colleague, Gretton, took a more direct approach. After summoning several meetings of the diehards in the latter half of January 1930, he secured forty signatures to a letter asking Baldwin to return to the 1923 programme of protection.[45] When Beaverbrook raised the stakes on 17 February, by launching the United Empire Party, the difference in approach between Gretton and Croft became manifest in separate diehard and EIA deputations to Baldwin, even if both urged him to give ground.[46]

Negotiations between Baldwin and Beaverbrook led the former to announce on 4 March that he would be prepared to hold a referendum on food taxes. Croft used the opportunity to make an unsuccessful attempt at recruiting Beaverbrook for the EIA.[47] The uneasy truce that followed was shattered three weeks later when Salisbury, Conservative leader in the House of Lords, published a letter declaring that 'Empire Free Trade' remained an impractical aspiration for the foreseeable future.[48] The diehards were outraged by the behaviour of their former leader, and disappointed too with the equivocal attitude of other senior party figures. But rather than deepen the party crisis, Croft, Hannon and others continued to press restraint on Beaverbrook.[49] Ignoring their pleas, the press baron announced in June that he and Lord Rothermere were prepared to stand candidates in all consistencies where no other candidate was willing to support empire free trade. This provided Baldwin with the pretext to summon on 24 June a special meeting of the parliamentary party and prospective parliamentary candidates. After he had delivered a withering attack on the political pretentions of the press barons, Baldwin's audience responded by passing a motion of support. Now working together, Croft and Gretton tabled an amendment declaring that the referendum pledge was no longer necessary, and that the next Conservative government should have a 'free hand' in tariffs and developing 'empire economic unity'. However, both this and Croft's speech – 'the old tub-thumping Tariff Reform Empire speech that we all know by heart' – misjudged the mood of the meeting and the amendment was defeated by an 'overwhelming majority'.[50]

Baldwin's victory was squandered in the months that followed as critics rounded on his lethargic performance as leader of the opposition. With the EIA remaining outwardly loyal, it was the Empire Economic Union which expressed public appreciation to Beaverbrook and Rothermere 'for having created a new atmosphere by making clear and courageous statements of the policy of the Empire Economic Union'.[51] Recently formed by the Liberal turned Conservative, Sir Alfred Mond, now first Baron Melchett, along with Amery and George Lloyd, now first Baron Lloyd of Dolobran, the Union was primarily occupied with coordinating industrialists throughout the empire. It meant that there were now three major organizations competing for the support of tariff reformers, and, against expectation, Croft headed the only one which continued to stand by Baldwin. With many Conservatives pondering about whether or not their party could survive the crisis, Croft wrote to Beaverbrook in September deploring 'your threat to attack "the safeguarding policy of Baldwin", which is broadly also the policy of every single individual in public life who you can call your friend'.[52] Conversely, in private correspondence with the party chairman, the first Viscount Bridgeman, Croft vented his anxiety that the party was heading for a split and expressed the view that Baldwin should retire.[53]

The seventh Imperial Conference, which convened in London throughout October, supplied a way out of the crisis when the Canadian prime minister, R.B. Bennett, signalled that he would be willing to enter discussions about reciprocal tariffs. Gretton had for several weeks been pressing for a special party meeting to address the crisis. The new party chairman, Neville Chamberlain, now used this demand to isolate the diehards. He persuaded Baldwin to accept Bennett's suggestion and also to schedule a special party meeting for 30 October, in the knowledge that most in attendance would be relieved that the party had stepped back from the brink of self-destruction.[54] The diehards then strengthened Chamberlain's hand through their own inept behaviour. On the day prior to the special party meeting, Gretton organized a meeting of the diehards which issued a declaration to the party whip, purportedly signed by forty-four MPs, calling for a change of leader. To Gretton's embarrassment, a number of those whose names appeared on the declaration subsequently disavowed ever having been in attendance.[55] When MPs, peers and prospective parliamentary candidates gathered the following day for the special meeting, it overwhelmingly gave its approval to Baldwin's new policy. Seemingly oblivious to the party's mood, Gretton and Guy Kindersley (1877–1956), MP for Hitchin since 1923, pressed ahead with a resolution declaring that a change of leadership was in the national interest. Viscount Lymington, MP for Basingstoke, Edward Marjoribanks (1900–32), MP for Eastbourne, and Croft spoke in support. Marjoribanks's speech provoked concerns about his sanity, and was followed six months later by his suicide.[56] As for Croft's contribution, it represented a sudden and remarkable about-turn. Having long stood by Baldwin, Croft now described his leadership as 'flabby and vacillating and changing from day to day', and warned that the party could only win the next general election 'under another leadership.'[57] When the resolution was put to those in attendance, in a secret ballot as a concession to the diehards, it was defeated easily, 462–116. The minority afterwards accepted a unanimous pledge of loyalty to Baldwin and the new policy, which, of note, was seconded by Lord Carson.[58]

Thus chastened, the diehards fell into line on this issue in the months that followed despite lingering unease in the party with Baldwin's leadership and growing restlessness amongst the diehards about his stance on India. In fact,

Croft drew the lesson that any diehard-led campaign on India could not succeed if it openly called into question Baldwin's leadership.[59] He returned to making appeals to Beaverbrook that his 'drive' and 'idealism' would be best served working within the Conservative party, as Baldwin's 'doubtful victory' made 'him amenable to reason'.[60] Increasingly isolated amongst Conservatives, Beaverbrook's candidate nevertheless won a by-election victory at Paddington South in October 1930, and in February 1931, his candidate in Islington East beat the official Conservative into third place. When an independent Conservative candidate at the Westminster St George's by-election looked likely to further embarrass the Conservative front bench, members of the shadow cabinet seriously considered asking Baldwin to step down. However, after briefly deciding to quit on 1 March, he resolved to carry on and stake everything on St George's, a gamble that paid off when the official Conservative candidate secured a convincing victory.[61]

Having strengthened his authority, Baldwin looked to Croft and Gretton in August 1931 to assist him in securing the party's support for participation in the emergency National Government. In response to the global financial crisis, most Conservatives accepted uncritically the advice of the bankers about the need for spending cuts, just as they recognized the utility in spreading responsibility for drastic economies beyond the Conservative party.[62] But it is telling that Baldwin took the precaution of recruiting Croft and Gretton to speak in favour of the new coalition at a specially convened party meeting, to see off right-wing critics such as Lloyd and the young diehard parliamentary candidate for Islington West, Patrick Donner (1904–88).[63] Another young diehard, Lymington, had recently expressed the right-wing's unease by deprecating any move towards 'a so-called national government drawn from all parties. A ministry of all the talents would mean replacing a sodden government with seven devils ... Every party would prostitute its principles'.[64] But with Croft and Gretton's endorsement, Baldwin saw off such criticism. He benefited also by experiencing some temporary relief from dealing with the diehards, for once the new coalition was established, it fell to the prime minister, National Labour's Ramsay MacDonald, to request a meeting with Croft to resolve concerns on the Conservative backbenches about tariffs.[65] Baldwin still had to repay the support given by Croft and Gretton, and so a commitment to the 'ideal of Imperial Economic Unity' was included in the Conservatives' manifesto when the National Government went to the polls on 27 October 1931.[66] Ever vigilant, the EIA took steps to ensure that if Conservatives were asked to stand aside for National Liberal candidates, the latter would be requested to give pledges to the local Conservative constituency association in return for support.[67]

The National Government achieved an overwhelming landslide victory with 554 MPs returned, including 473 Conservatives. It faced a minuscule and weak opposition of fifty-two Labour MPs and nine others. Despite their important role in recent developments, the result allowed Baldwin to marginalize completely the diehards and avoid appointing any of their number to the cabinet, a task made easier by the fact that places in the National Government had to be shared with the other two participating parties. The EIA, however, could not so easily be ignored given that it had the nominal support of over 300 Conservative backbenchers, and Croft was only too willing to issue veiled threats about the conditionality of its support.[68] Fortunately for Baldwin and the EIA, the former was satisfied that the recent economic and political upheaval meant that the time was now right for initiating some move towards imperial preference. The National Government duly introduced the Abnormal Imports bill in November 1931 and the Import Duties bill in February 1932. Months later it agreed a series of bilateral agreements at Ottawa which empire-first Conservatives hailed as the beginning of further steps towards empire free trade. The diehards amongst them took an understandable measure of personal satisfaction in this outcome. It supplied a rare instance of achievement in marked contrast to the diehards' failure in so many other areas of policy. Yet it was not a specifically 'diehard' campaign, and success tended to come when the diehards did not behave in the confrontational manner they adopted on other imperial questions, working instead through larger groups and organizations and remaining outwardly loyal to the party leader. Similarly, the party crisis of 1929–31 was not brought on by the diehards or even empire-first Conservatives, but Baldwin's protracted deliberations on when and how opinion in the country might align with opinion in his party. Throughout, he would shore up his position amongst Conservatives by exploiting the culture of loyalty to the party leader, and with the active assistance of Neville Chamberlain, he was able also to make timely concessions and isolate his critics. The diehards in turn had no reason or interest in breaking with the party over tariffs: they were given a hearing throughout and always with the tantalizing prospect of success on the horizon.

III

The diehards' integral if peculiar role in the Conservative party's debates about tariff reform is at odds with historiography that emphasizes instead links between the Conservative Right and the extreme right. There is a tendency in these works to give undue prominence to exceptional cases, such as Lymington's abandonment of conventional party politics, to draw inferences from speeches given by the diehards which appear to defend or excuse Nazi Germany and the British Union of Fascists (BUF), or to give attention to individuals, especially peers, with little or no political standing in the Conservative party let alone influence over Conservative governments.[69] Martin Pugh, for example, argues that 'so far from fascism being repudiated and marginalised by the conventional politicians, there was a flourishing traffic in ideas and in personnel between fascism and the Conservative Right throughout the inter-war period'.[70] Amongst Conservative parliamentarians, there were without doubt a handful who held positions in groups such as the Britons and the Imperial Fascist League, including Patrick Hannon, Lord Sydenham, Charles Burn, Robert Bower and Sir Burton Chadwick. Only two of these, Sydenham and Hannon, were regarded in the 1920s as belonging to the diehards. The pronounced anti-Semitism of Sydenham certainly conforms to the expectations of fascist beliefs. His hostility to the Jews disposed him in 1917, like others on the right, including Croft, Joynson-Hicks and Herbert Nield (1862–1932), MP for Ealing, to supporting the Balfour declaration as a means of diverting Jews uprooted by the war to Palestine.[71] Yet within a few years he opposed the cause of Zionism, now under the supervision of the post-war coalition, and gave a favourable hearing to the predicament of Palestinian Arabs.[72] The latter is likely to have complemented rather than stemmed from Sydenham's anti-Semitism; his general esteem for Muslims and use of high-level back channels to secure assistance for refugees from the Turkish Republic seem more in keeping with the traditional Conservative regard for the Ottoman Empire and India's Muslims.[73] Lord Lloyd, a former Governor of Bombay, likewise supported the building of a mosque in London to shore up the country's influence in the Islamic world.[74] Hannon too was demonstrably sympathetic towards Muslims. He considered A.R. Dard, imam of London's first mosque, a 'wonderful friend'.[75] But the contrast between Sydenham's conspiracy-obsessed hysteria about Jewish influence and Hannon is stark. For on 7 April 1933, the latter addressed a meeting of Birmingham Conservatives on the plight of 'Jews in Germany'.[76] This raises some doubt about the importance attached by historians to Sydenham and Hannon's membership of both the Conservative party and fascist groups, especially when considered alongside their diametrically opposed positions on two of the most controversial questions of the interwar period: Indian self-government and British–Soviet relations. Sydenham's hostility to the former is outlined in Chapter 3. Around the same time, in early 1920, he was a leading member of Lord Northcliffe's short-lived Liberty League, alongside Sir Rider Haggard and Rudyard Kipling. In March 1920 the League caused controversy by calling publicly for a fight in Russia, before collapsing shortly afterwards owing to financial mismanagement.[77] Hannon, in contrast, backed the White Paper that became the 1935 India Act, and his business interests placed him among a number of Conservative MPs keen to ratify the trade agreement reached between the first Labour government and the Soviet Union.[78] If common membership of both diehard and fascist groups could not bring congruity to the politics of these two men, then the same applies to the journalism, of Conservatives and fascists alike, that appeared in the Duke of Northumberland's stable of publications and Lady Houston's *Saturday Review*. In practice, there was only one recognized 'diehard' journal in this period, the *Morning Post*, and it remained hostile to Nazi Germany through to its demise and acquisition in 1937 by the *Daily Telegraph*.[79]

Caution too is required when considering the evidence for Pugh's assertion that an undemocratic 'militarist element' entered the calculations of the diehards who opposed the installation of the first Labour government. He cites by way of example Croft's call on 11 October 1924 for a 'platoon' to be raised in every constituency.[80] Published in the *Morning Post*, Croft explicitly used the term as a metaphor to call for bottom-up mobilization in the Conservative party's electioneering strategy, as opposed to waiting for a lead from the 'generals' at Central Office: 'seats can only be won and held if the fighting unit, that is, the constituency organization, is effective'.[81] Croft's belief in the need for local initiative chimes with David Thackeray's observation that the party's electoral recovery and widening appeal after 1918 were 'rooted in the efforts of local activists', whereas the reputation of Central Office was that of 'an incubus to modernisation'.[82] Another example of the 'militarist element' presented by Pugh was an address by Frederick Banbury to the National Citizens Union (NCU). In this Banbury declared that he would save the constitution from a Labour government by leading the Coldstream Guards in occupying the House of Commons.[83] The NCU began life after the First World War as the Middle Classes Union. Its self-depiction as a moderating force was belied by pronounced anti-waste and anti-socialist positions, and its members readily adopted reactionary outlooks on the franchise and income tax. With its strength concentrated in the south of England, the NCU fed off and amplified the post-war backlash against local government spending, not least in the London borough of Poplar where a rates rebellion led by Labour councillors conjured the spectre of 'Poplarism'.[84] In this vein, the NCU declared its willingness to provide essential services in the event of a general strike. It is hardly surprising that Banbury should address such a group, nor for that matter, that its membership overlapped with that of other right-wing and extremist organizations. Indeed, its chairman from 1928, Colonel A.H. Lane, was a prominent figure in the Britons, Imperial Fascist League and similar fringe groups, and under his leadership the NCU later became markedly anti-Semitic.[85] What weight, therefore, should be placed on Banbury's purported threat?

In its coverage of Banbury's address to the Union, *The Times* made no reference to the Coldstream Guards. The speech was merely presented as a warning about the damage an incoming Labour government would inflict on business interests.[86] The *Manchester Guardian*, in contrast, gave the guards comment prominent attention: 'Ready to be a second Cromwell' declared its headline. It recorded that Banbury's threat followed the spurious suggestion that MacDonald might refuse to relinquish power if his minority ministry were to be defeated by the Commons, and that he could use the armed forces and police to this end. Just as the lord protector had dissolved the 'Long Parliament' with the aid of the Coldstream Guards, so Banbury 'should have great pleasure in leading the Coldstream Guards into the House of Commons if Mr MacDonald attempted anything of that sort'.[87] He was playing to the gallery, for the eighty-one-year-old's ability to lead an occupation of the House of Commons was compromised by both his age and acceptance of a peerage. Indeed, the latter resulted from long-standing efforts to remove him from the House of Commons, to find a better representative of City opinion, and also rid the chamber of a notorious 'champion obstructionist'.[88] More significantly, Pugh's concentration on Banbury's bluster at the NCU overlooks the MP's better-known and unambiguous proposal about the prospect of Labour taking office. In December 1923, Banbury called on Baldwin to ask his Liberal counterpart, Herbert Asquith, to support a minority Conservative government on an 'undertaking not to bring in any contentious legislation'. If Asquith declined, Banbury cited the precedent of Conservative support for Viscount Palmerston to suggest that 'we tell him that we will support him if he forms a Government and gives a similar undertaking. If he refuses the country will see which party is the most patriotic'.[89] Banbury moved a resolution to this effect during his address to the NCU which was carried unanimously.[90] What is really significant here is how far a diehard MP was prepared to go in cooperating with Asquith, even if it fell short of Lord Derby's hope that the threat of a Labour government would lead the diehards to relent in their opposition to the principle of coalition.[91] Not unexpectedly, Baldwin did not follow Banbury's advice. He still managed, however, to shift the burden of responsibility for installing a Labour ministry onto the Liberals, thus presenting the Conservatives as the only effective anti-socialist party ahead of an imminent return to the polls.[92]

Croft's call for local political activism and Banbury's suggestion of a Liberal–Conservative pact both demonstrate their commitment to parliamentary democracy and not its overthrow. As a hostile observer could note, 'Most of the opponents of democracy ... have lost their fear of it ... they have become some of its most stalwart supporters'.[93] This is not to deny any overlap in personnel or outlook between the Conservative Right and British fascism. However, even Pugh concedes that the latter in the 1920s was not so much fascist in an Italian or German understanding of the term, but distinctly British and Conservative in its support for the established constitution and the Conservative party. Its 'fascistic' quality was instead expressed through pronounced and interrelated anti-communist, anti-socialist and anti-alien preoccupations. Fascist groups in the 1920s were not perceived by Conservatives as political rivals so much as something akin to the patriotic leagues. The offer of stewards by fascists to keep order at Conservative gatherings was consistent with this relationship. It helped to facilitate the desire of Conservatives after 1918 to project orderliness at their platform meetings in contrast to the apparent rowdiness of Labour gatherings.[94] Likewise, fascist groups volunteering their services in the event of a national strike was consistent with Conservative views about the unconstitutionality of this type of stoppage. Even so, Joynson-Hicks, as Home Secretary in the months leading up to the 1926 General Strike, was only prepared to accept such help if it came from individual fascists and not fascist organizations.

As Philip Williamson cautions, none of this amounted 'to "ideological" approval for fascism; nor do such attitudes towards nominal "fascists" in the 1920s necessarily indicate sympathy for genuine fascists in the 1930s'.[95] The racial slurs employed by the diehards, to oppose alien immigration and self-government in the empire, reflected in most cases their unashamed 'cultural provincialism' rather than any systematized racist doctrine.[96] Lord Sydenham and Howell Gwynne's preoccupation with anti-Semitic conspiracy theories was unusual and not taken seriously by others, and in the case of Gwynne, it did not prevent his open dislike of Nazi Germany. A similar attitude was evident in the *National Review*, under the editorship of Violet Milner, née Maxse.[97] Diehard MPs displayed no interest in the eugenics movement, despite its growing international profile in the late 1920s and early 1930s, nor did the Eugenics Society seek to win diehard MPs over to its cause.[98] As Chapter 5 demonstrates, all diehards regarded Adolf Hitler's regime as a potential threat to Britain and its empire, even if they were divided on the efficacy of Neville Chamberlain's policy of appeasement. It is noteworthy, then, that historiography remains drawn to assessing Conservative Right attitudes to the Third Reich through the lens of ideology.[99] Dan Stone, for example, argues that Nazi Germany was 'a "sounding board" that the British right neither could nor wanted to ignore'.[100] But in the case of the majority of diehard MPs, it is important to note that public commentary on Nazi ideology, let alone expressions of admiration, are conspicuous by their relative absence. The role of Wilfrid Ashley, created first Baron Mount Temple in 1932, in founding the Anglo–German Fellowship three years later, and his visits to Germany, including meeting Hitler, were atypical for a diehard. The fellowship included only two other diehard MPs, and the practise of amateur diplomacy was taken up across the political spectrum.[101] The diehards' profound anxiety about British decline meant that most of them were indifferent to the Nazis' internal policy, except when they used its racism or autocracy to condemn particular deals with Hitler's government. This is not to rule out the possibility that diehard ranks contained some Nazi sympathizers, admirers and crypto-fascists, or that the ambiguity of some diehard assessments of Nazism could be read as a threat as well as a warning, such as Croft's claim that 'but for Communism there would be no Nazi rule in Germany ... let the British people who love this dear land of ours say that Communism shall not be allowed to drop its poison here amongst our children and our youth'.[102] But the overriding political concern of the diehard cohort in Parliament, which had animated its component parts since the Edwardian period, was with internal and external threats to Britain's position as a global power.

None of the seventy-nine Conservative MPs who voted against the 1935 India bill joined the pro-Nazi Right Club. Conversely, its founder, Archibald Ramsay, MP for Peebles and Southern Midlothian, and a well-known anti-Semite, sided with the National Government. According to Richard Griffiths, the Right Club was overwhelmingly Scottish with a sprinkling of National Labour and National Liberal MPs.[103] No diehard appears to have been involved with the pro-Nazi 'Link'.[104] As noted already, only two diehard opponents of the India bill in the House of Commons were members of the Anglo–German Fellowship, Sir Alfred Knox (1870–1964) and Charles Taylor (1910–89), MP for Eastbourne.[105] That many more Conservative MPs and peers belonged to the fellowship underlines the problem with placing too much emphasis on the supposed traffic in personnel and ideas between the 'Conservative Right' and fascism. Whereas the diehards were divided fundamentally from the extreme right by their adherence to anti-statist capitalism, many progressive Conservatives, in common with British fascists, were favourably disposed to statist approaches to capitalism; indeed, several were associated with Mosley and his New Party before he abandoned that project to found the BUF.[106] A number of diehard MPs, such as the young MP for Mid-Bedfordshire, Alan Lennox-Boyd (1904–1983), were involved with Mosley's January Club, which arranged dinners to bring British fascists into contact with the political establishment, but the club also included National Labour and centrist Conservative MPs, as well as Zionists, with an interest in or admiration for Italian fascism. The club was careful to distance itself from Nazism and did not survive Mosley's fall from grace. Like many Conservatives, Lennox-Boyd regarded Germany as a bulwark against the Soviet Union, but the most youthful of diehard MPs was no less typical for being 'repelled by the brutality of the Nazis'.[107] Even outside of Parliament, among right-wing pressmen, opinion was not necessarily dictated by ideological affinity.[108] Douglas Reed resigned in 1938 as *The Times*'s Central European correspondent over its support for appeasement, despite a 'background and life history' which Richard Thurlow describes as 'the classic facsimile of the alleged fascist'.[109] As noted above, the anti-Semitism of Gwynne at *Morning Post* did not preclude the paper's strong line against Germany throughout the interwar period.[110] As he explained in February 1937: 'I, a high old Tory, loathe, with equal strength, both Fascism and Communism, each of which is alien to our character and political education. I cannot get the thick-headed Germans to understand this, and some equally thick-headed English politicians seem to think that you must be in favour of one or the other.'[111]

Dissatisfaction with Baldwinite Conservatism, and by extension, post-war democracy, is used often to explain the supposed 'traffic' between the Conservative party and fascist parties. Here too the diehards do not fit neatly the role expected of them. As detailed above, even at the height of Conservative unrest over Baldwin's leadership, the public loyalty of the diehards faltered only once and was immediately corrected by a demonstration of party unanimity. The enthusiasm of the majority of the diehards for imperial preference, even after the formation of the coalition National Government, was a significant factor, as was its apparent contribution to economic recovery in the mid-1930s, which in turn undercut the potential appeal of Mosley's alternative economic remedy. In Scotland, middle-class disenchantment with Scottish Unionism – which nevertheless remained hegemonic in the 1930s – was far more likely to find expression in nationalist calls for home rule than in support for fascism, especially as concerns increased about the southern English focus of the National Government's approach to economic recovery.[112] In Northern Ireland too, local conditions – the deep-rooted sectarian cleavage – meant that growing criticism of the Ulster Unionist government there and the National Government at Westminster did not translate into electoral support for the BUF.[113] In fact, for all the supposed dissatisfaction with Baldwin, membership of the BUF remained stubbornly low, albeit with a significant turnover as the initial enthusiasm of new members quickly dissipated. When this is contrasted with the Conservative party's membership of somewhere between 1.2 million and 1.6 million, it becomes plain that the movement of Conservatives to the fascists was numerically insignificant.[114]

Whilst it is important not to equate party membership simplistically with tacit support for fascism, natural curiosity about possible links between the diehards and the fascists too often comes at the expense of acknowledging the integral place of the former within the Conservative party, and by extension, parliamentary democracy. The diehards enjoyed significant levels of support amongst the party's grass roots, a feature that was regularly displayed at the National Union's annual conferences. In 1926, Gretton was elected vice chairman of the council of the National Union.[115] Croft, in addition to leading the EIA, was appointed in 1927 vice chairman of the Primrose League and the following year was elevated to chancellor.[116] Cunliffe-Lister even advocated his appointment as a junior minister at the Board of Trade.[117] At the height of the party controversy over India, Victor Raikes (1901–86), MP for South East Essex, was elected secretary of the 1922 Committee, which represented Conservative backbenchers.[118] Campaigning in the 1929 general election, Lord Wolmer's address to the electors of Aldershot summarized the successes of 'Mr Baldwin's government' and asked that the prime minister be allowed to 'continue the good work'.[119] Even in the wake of the party's defeat, Wolmer criticized the Duke of Northumberland for claiming that Baldwin's government had abandoned the 'principle of authority'.[120] At the following general election, however, Wolmer's address made no mention of Baldwin.[121] And within a few years, Wolmer was damning his party leader's position on India as 'a sort of sloppy, bastard Liberalism, a sort of half-baked notion that because the British people enjoyed self-government it is our duty to give it to these other races and gradually clear out'.[122] What accounts for this dramatic change in the attitude of the diehards to Baldwin, or, conversely, what explains their apparent quiescence throughout the 1920s, only to turn on him the following decade?

The protracted campaign for tariff reform, examined above, was clearly a factor; its partial realization in 1931–32 in effect removed the diehards' reliance on Baldwin's goodwill. So too was the long shadow cast by the fall of the post-war coalition. If the party managed to avoid a public feud between coalitionists and anti-coalitionists, and any temptation to purge the parliamentary or voluntary party, then, according to Stuart Ball, 'It was never forgotten on which side anyone had taken their stand, and the victors were always unsure about the permanence of the outcome and unconvinced of the reliability of the losers.'[123] As the diehards knew from bitter personal experience, taking up the banner of 'Baldwin Must Go' risked the possibility of him being replaced by unwelcome alternatives, such as Lord Derby, or even the despised coalitionists.[124] Defeat in 1923 and the landslide victory the following year also brought home to all Conservatives their reliance on former Liberal voters. An in-house analysis of the Conservatives' performance put it more bluntly, 'in general the Liberal Party has been merged into the Conservative Party, and that the Socialist gains have been chiefly from the latter Party'.[125] The denominational antagonism which had long reinforced the Liberal–Conservative cleavage might have held out in Wales, limiting the progress there of the Conservatives' post–1918 revival, but the opposite pertained in England. The advantage this gave to them was further assisted by what Ross McKibbin describes as the abandonment of 'older, rhetorically aggressive traditions … in favour of a more reticent and sanctimonious style', a style personified by Baldwin, and even, he claims, Joynson-Hicks.[126] Nonconformist and secular middle-class associational culture alike seemed to align with their projection of English national identity, including organizations which were ostensibly apolitical. In Scotland, where electoral cooperation between Scottish Unionists and Liberals outlived the post-war coalition, the former's increasing electoral success at the expense of the latter owed much to the party gradually distancing itself from old sectarian appeals.[127] Little wonder then that Lord Lloyd admitted in 1931 that Baldwin's 'Left-hand position had, in general affairs, been useful four or five years ago, and had conduced to an easier settlement of industrial troubles than an extreme Right attitude would have done'.[128]

Not that this should be taken to mean that Baldwin had failed to offer any comfort to diehard sentiment. At the very least, he substantiated his claim to be steering a course between Gretton and Macmillan by giving little satisfaction to those younger Conservative MPs promoting planning and the 'middle way'.[129] Despite his omission of tariffs from the 1924 party manifesto, Baldwin's approach to that general election campaign was avowedly partisan, contrasting his personal commitment to the empire and naval expenditure with that of the other party leaders, and whipping up a red scare to traduce the Labour party as unwitting tools of Soviet foreign policy.[130] This type of demonization could not last, of course, not only because of the moderation of the first Labour government and the collapse of the General Strike on 12 May 1926, but because Baldwin himself was never comfortable as a class warrior. He preferred, as Williamson notes, to educate the electorate through rhetoric which was socially inclusive and 'sympathetic towards the legitimate aspirations of all classes, and as such it presented trades unions, even the Labour party, as having positive places in society'.[131] Even the diehards seemed capable of being reined in by this message. When the Scottish Unionist MP, Frederick Macquisten, sponsored a private member's bill in 1925, which would have resulted in trades unionists having to contract in to the political levy rather than contract out, the diehards and many other Conservatives were sympathetic. Baldwin, however, successfully urged his party to stay its hand and substitute it instead with a resolution approving of the bill in principle but declaring that a measure of such far-reaching importance should not be introduced as a private member's bill. His concluding appeal, 'Give peace in our time, O Lord', was tested within months by mounting unrest between coal owners and miners over hours and wages.[132]

Baldwin's decision to give a nine-month subsidy to the industry, during which a royal commission would draw up recommendations, was a difficult pill for the diehards to swallow. The Home Secretary, Joynson-Hicks, expressed his frustration in public, declaring that the subsidy would have to end once the commission reported.[133] Gretton also sounded off when Parliament debated the White Paper, complaining that 'there was some very loose thinking and very loose estimating in this matter'. Discomfort, certainly, but hardly the stuff of back-bench rebellions. Indeed, although Gretton and a number of other diehard MPs declined to take part in the subsequent division on the subsidy, others, including Croft and Wolmer, supported the government, contributing to its overwhelming victory, 351–16.[134] Neville Chamberlain observed 'only two die-hards in the [no] division lobby'.[135] After the subsidy ran its course, the nine-day General Strike that began on 3 May 1926 appeared at first to undermine Baldwinite moderation and satisfy those on the Right quietly relishing a showdown with the trades unions. However, the government's reaction united the Right by depicting the strike as a political challenge to the constitution and state. Revealingly, the government's organ during the strike, the *British Gazette*, was to all intents and purposes the *Morning Post*. As Gwynne informed his then proprietor, the Duke of Northumberland, a major coal owner in the north-east of England:

> It was a voluntary act on our part, as you know, inviting commandeering, and we
> are now a Government office ... It was no small achievement to turn from the

Morning Post into the *British Gazette* in twenty-four hours and to produce nearly a quarter of a million the first night ... My own staff were splendid ... Since the beginning of the strike I sit in my office with the Treasury telephone at my elbow and am a kind of liaison officer between the Government and the paper. Winston [Churchill] has been my most frequent visitor ... he has been a bit of a nuisance, for he is constantly coming in and dictating articles, some of which I have to cut out.[136]

The maintenance of the miners' strike following the collapse of the General Strike was met with calls from mine owners, diehards and other Conservatives for a tough legislative response. The grass roots added their voices in October, at the annual party conference convened at Scarborough, by passing a series of resolutions critical of the trades unions and calling for curbs on their organization and activities.[137] 'Contracting in' and other restrictive measures were duly included in the Trades Disputes Act 1927. If this represented the high point of a distinctly diehard approach to the crisis, Gwynne was keen to pull back Northumberland from developing a wider attack on the government:

Figure 9 Howell Arthur Gwynne

I do not think that English politics has ever been in such a curious position as it is now. In Baldwin we do possess a man, who, whatever his faults, is not a trickster or a professional. Behind him are some of the biggest scoundrels – I am speaking politically – that we know, and if anything happens to him we shall have a combination of weaklings and traitors.[138]

Baldwin himself regarded the 1927 Act as a symbolic measure to satisfy his party's right wing, at a time when their stock had risen briefly causing ministers to be cautious in a number of policy directions.[139] After its passage, both he and the Minister for Labour, Arthur Steel-Maitland, worked around the legislation by deliberately positioning the Ministry of Labour as the 'arbiter of "good" industrial relations, with the aim of integrating unions and employers into a consultative process'.[140] Steel-Maitland's contribution nearly twenty years before to the Confederacy's *New Order* indicates that his approach to this question had its roots in the Edwardian crisis of conservatism, just as it demonstrates the considerable gulf that emerged after the war between him and other contributors to that volume, most of whom were now counted as diehards.[141]

Baldwin was better placed to ignore revived calls for a strengthened House of Lords. Along with trades union reform, it was one of the most popular subjects for resolutions passed by constituency associations throughout the 1920s.[142] As Selborne declared at the first National Union conference held following the General Strike, in October 1926, 'What was the use of amending trades union law until they amended the Parliament Act? A Socialist Government could undo all the Conservative Government's work in two years.' Several other prominent diehards lent their support to a carefully worded resolution which welcomed the 'assurance of the Prime Minister that it is the intention of the Government to deal in the present Parliament with the question of Second Chamber reform'. It received the unanimous support of delegates.[143] From the partisan perspective of its advocates, reform was rooted in a commitment to democracy but with the intention of making it 'safe'.[144] Many senior party figures, however, were anxious about going down a route that opponents could present as anti-democratic and thereby risked further inflaming class politics.[145] Another stumbling block was the continued difference of opinion amongst peers about what reform meant in practice. This had plagued the question since the constitutional crisis of 1911, and did so again in 1927, when it was considered by the Lord Chancellor, the first Viscount Cave, in response to the previous year's party conference resolution.[146] Regardless, the 1927 conference once again heard calls for the issue to be addressed by the government and a resolution to this effect was supported 'by an overwhelming majority', thus ignoring an appeal from Lord Londonderry, a major coal owner, and signatory of the March 1922 diehard 'manifesto', that the constitution had been vindicated during the General Strike.[147] Ignored by the grass roots, Londonderry still represented the outlook of the more active peers in believing that it was better to leave the matter well alone. It was their view that prevailed in 1927, and again in 1934, when Salisbury attempted to force the issue by introducing a bill to the House of Lords, and yet again in 1935, when it was omitted from the party's general election manifesto.[148]

If the diehards barely put up any fight over the House of Lords, most went along with the Conservative government's unanticipated support for a fifth reform act. Baldwin was closely associated with the several decisive steps taken by the party to increase its appeal to women voters and to encourage women party members.[149] It was against expectation, therefore, that when the question of an equal franchise was revived in February 1925, it was the result of an intervention by the diehard Home Secretary, Joynson-Hicks.[150] Regarded initially as symptomatic of Jix's erratic behaviour, embarrassment and upset amongst ministerial colleagues and party opinion alike gradually gave way to cautious support as it became clearer that equalization was likely to benefit Conservatives.[151] When he first laid the bill before the House of Commons in March 1927, a motion rejecting it – for endowing 'women with permanent political supremacy' – received support from just four Conservative MPs, only two of whom, Reginald Applin and Guy Kindersley, had track records as diehards.[152] Opposition increased to ten when the bill received its second reading, most of whom, on this occasion, were diehards: Charles Craig (1869–1960), George Balfour, Esmond Harmsworth, Sir Joseph Nall (1887–1958), Sir Charles Oman and Sir Archibald Boyd-Carpenter (1873–1937).[153] Harmsworth's inclusion is noteworthy, for he either disregarded or failed to recall the role of women in his 1919 Thanet by-election victory and the anti-waste campaign generally.[154] Many diehard MPs, however, including Gretton and Lymington, preferred to signal their opposition to the franchise bill by making up the 135 Conservative abstentions.[155] Lymington afterwards lamented that his party had 'confused democracy with leadership' by giving 'the franchise to girls instead of educating them to tend the hearth'.[156] But these abstentions did not represent a diehard revolt. A third and sizeable category of diehard MPs voted with the government, including Croft, Knox, William Carver (1868–1961), John Courtauld (1880–1942), Sir William Davison (1872–1953), Lindsay Everard (1891–1949), Sir John Ganzoni (1882–1958), Gordon Hall-Caine (1884–1962), Sir George Hamilton (1877–1947), R.R. Henderson (1876–1932), Thomas Moore (1888–1971), W.G. Nicholson (1862–1942), John Remer (1883–1948) and Sir William Wayland (1869–1950).[157]

The behaviour of the diehards in the mid- to late 1920s is striking given their reputation before and after for divisiveness. To the explanation given above must be added a structural factor that firmly integrated them into the parliamentary party. The Unionist Business Committee and Unionist War Committee had withered since the war, but a new intake of MPs in 1923 were determined to revive back-bench organization by establishing the 1922 Committee. Unlike its wartime predecessors, the new committee was founded as an educative group for new members elected in 1922, and opened its membership four years later to all back-bench Conservative MPs. It deliberately tried to avoid controversy, devoting its meetings to visiting speakers on a range of domestic, foreign and imperial questions.[158] It nevertheless helped to improve communication between the back and front benches, even if this particular function was better fulfilled by the further development of parliamentary party subject committees. Instituted shortly after Baldwin's resignation as prime minister in January 1924, fifteen were established to help prepare the next party manifesto. In this way, MPs were implicated in a consultative policymaking process under the supervision of the party hierarchy.[159] These committees were set on a permanent footing following the Conservatives' return to office in November 1924. Given the dearth of talented parliamentary speakers in diehard ranks, the party committees provided a reasonably friendly and safe alternative to the combative atmosphere of the House of Commons. Conversely, participation served to blunt reflexive diehard claims about a remote party leadership, and confront them with a realistic grasp of the limited influence of their outlook in the parliamentary party. This was exemplified by the first fruits of the new subject committees, *Looking Ahead*. Published in June 1924, it signalled that many Conservative MPs were prepared to moderate the party's approach to questions such as social services, local government, unemployment and taxation.[160] Undoubtedly discomfited, the diehards could find a measure of solace from the party remaining united around the core belief that the primary role of the state was to be ameliorative of capitalism and not its ultimate replacement.[161] At a fundamental level, after all, the party remained committed, in a modified form, to the increasingly anachronistic ideal that property had the function of marking off a zone into which the authority of the state could not enter.[162] Just as the party committees helped to contain the diehards in the mid- to late 1920s, Baldwin's failure to give them the same profile and role during the 1929–31 spell in opposition contributed to the leadership crisis which then gripped the party. The apparent revival in electoral support for the Liberals is also likely to have revived diehard concern with the direction of Conservative party policy.[163] Above all, however, it was the return of imperial constitutional reform to the political agenda that pushed the diehards into open revolt in the early 1930s, not least because it took place in the context of a new coalition, the National Government.

IV

The latent potential of imperial questions to upset diehard–front bench relations was evident from the outset. Just as the collapse of the post-war coalition cast a long shadow, so the diehards remained aggrieved with the Irish settlement of 1921–22. The passage of the Irish Free State (Agreement) Act 1922 was particularly resented as a deal reached with the 'murder gang', yet the diehards found themselves in the strange position in the years that followed of defending key elements of the legislation, above all, a particular reading of its provisions concerning the Irish border, the payment to Britain of land annuities, and the continued British sovereignty of naval bases at Berehaven, Queenstown and Lough Swilly. In a further ironic twist, the 1922 settlement also helped to remove a long-standing tension amongst the diehards between those who sympathized primarily with southern Irish Unionists and those who favoured the Ulster Unionists. With partition and dominion status for southern Ireland accomplished facts, the diehards could now unite around protecting Northern Ireland's territorial integrity and constitutional status. This was in keeping with wider opinion in the Conservative party, but in the case of the diehards, it was bound up also with their resistance to the shift in Conservative rhetoric away from territorial-unionism to one-nation conservatism.[164] Not that the diehards completely abandoned the loyalist community still resident in the Irish Free State. In 1923, Salisbury tried unsuccessfully to persuade cabinet colleagues to object to the Land bill laid before Dáil Éireann on the basis that it expropriated private property.[165] The diehards enjoyed greater success in 1929, in the guise of the Southern Irish Loyalists Relief Association, which secured funding from the Treasury to extend compensation to loyalists adversely affected by Britain's withdrawal.[166] Such interventions revealed that old passions lingered, informing diehard attitudes even as the context of British–Irish relations changed dramatically.

The diehards' determination to oppose any alteration of the border was first aired in parliamentary debates on the 1922 Free State bill and its provisions for a Boundary Commission. No doubt, some were genuinely concerned about the integrity of Northern Ireland, but this sensitive question had the additional utility of undermining the entire bill and raising doubts amongst Conservatives about its sponsor, the post-war coalition government.[167] Responsibility for the legislation fell to the Secretary of State for the Colonies, Winston Churchill, who attempted to see off the diehards by privately assuring the prime minister of Northern Ireland, Sir James Craig, of his goodwill.[168] In Parliament, Churchill's skilful defence of the bill dismissed any significant adjustment to the border and emphasized the need to support the treaty *in toto*, routing the diehard revolt 295–52.[169] In the months that followed, Churchill gave the diehards little opportunity to fault his handling of the Belfast government in the crucial matters of finance, security and franchise reform.[170] When rumours circulated that the Lord President of the Council, Arthur Balfour, was concerned about the impermanence of the existing border, the Lord Chancellor, Lord Birkenhead, set aside his personal preference for unification – itself a dramatic turnaround from his pre-war enthusiasm for the Ulster cause – to reassure his colleague that there was no possibility of Northern Ireland losing counties to its southern neighbour.[171]

Following a hiatus caused by civil war in the Irish Free State and Baldwin's decision to hold a general election in December 1923, the boundary question returned in May 1924 when the first Labour government put in place mechanisms for the establishment of the Boundary Commission. The crisis emerged when the government of Northern Ireland responded defiantly by declining to nominate its commissioner.[172] The Judicial Committee of the Privy Council afterwards determined that new legislation was required to permit the British government to make the necessary appointment on behalf of Northern Ireland. To Baldwin's considerable discomfort, this drew attention to his party's majority in the House of Lords; the bill could be delayed there in the reasonable expectation that the minority Labour government could not long remain in office. Having made careful preparations for an imminent poll, Baldwin had no wish to see his efforts undermined by Labour calling a general election on the issue of the peers versus the people.[173] In addition, he understood that failing to uphold the 1922 Act would weaken British–Irish relations and undermine the pro-treaty faction which emerged victorious in the recent civil war. Nevertheless, he had to balance this with the careful management of his party, especially in the wake of his recent rapprochement with Birkenhead and Austen Chamberlain, two of the 1921 treaty's Conservative signatories, and the implacable support given to Ulster Unionists by the Conservative press. Baldwin therefore worked behind the scenes with the prime minister, MacDonald, in trying to persuade the Ulster Unionists to adopt a less confrontational posture. The futility of this expectation became evident at the intergovernmental conference convened in London in early August. Indisposed by ill health, Craig sent the Leader of the

Senate, Lord Londonderry, in his stead, provoking suspicions amongst the diehards that the peer might buckle under pressure.[174] These were not without foundation, for in contrast to most Ulster Unionists, Londonderry favoured some sort of concession.[175] The Ulsterman and diehard MP for Canterbury, Ronald McNeill, took the precaution of pressuring Londonderry to declare publicly that he would not shift position.[176]

Attention now turned to what the House of Lords might do when presented with MacDonald's bill to grant his government the authority to appoint Northern Ireland's commissioner. Baldwin outwardly maintained his party's commitment to the Ulster Unionists, but behind the scenes he pressed Craig to instruct the Conservative peers not to block the bill.[177] After consulting with Salisbury, Londonderry informed Baldwin that the peers would not stand in the way of a bill on condition of 'a direct intimation being received from Northern Ireland that there will be no misunderstanding between the Conservative Party and Ulster on this particular point'.[178] Ministers at Belfast subsequently agreed but indicated also that they expected Conservative peers to pass amendments in their favour.[179] Crucially, Salisbury decided to disregard this advice when the bill came before the House of Lords on 8 October. He warned peers instead about the constitutional and electoral consequences of passing amendments, adding that Ulster Unionists had no interest in becoming the subject of a general election. Carson too cautioned the House against amendments, albeit damning his own party in the process: 'if a Conservative government were returned to power', he argued, 'the Conservative Party would propose and insist upon the very Bill that is now before your Lordships' House. And why? Because all the eminent men of the Conservative Party are up to the neck in the original Treaty which, through its ambiguities, has led to the present situation'. Whichever speech was more effective, opposition in the House of Lords was confined to thirty-eight peers.[180] Carson threw a spanner in the works the following day, however, with an amendment proposing that the bill should require confirmation by the parliament of Northern Ireland, but was persuaded to withdraw before it was put to peers.[181] The bill thereafter cleared Parliament weeks in advance of the general election held on 29 October, thus allowing Baldwin to concentrate instead on the supposed relationship between Labour and the Soviet Union. Returned to office, Baldwin's second government did not interfere with the Boundary Commission but took steps that undoubtedly assisted the Ulster Unionists, including the appointment of one of their number, J.R. Fisher, to represent Northern Ireland. Fisher secretly kept Craig informed of developments via an intermediary, and was probably responsible for the commission's findings being leaked to the *Morning Post* which it published on 7 November 1925.[182] In doing so the newspaper precipitated a crisis which led the three governments to reach a new agreement leaving the border untouched. It also made provisions about restructuring the outstanding debt owed by the Free State. The last provoked a complaint from Salisbury, but with further Treasury assistance to Northern Ireland, there was no row or division called in the House of Commons when it debated the agreement on 8 December.[183]

The question of debt was at the heart of the new phase in British–Irish relations inaugurated in 1932 by Fianna Fáil's assumption of power. The British government responded to Eamon de Valera's decision to suspend the payment of land annuities by raising duties on agricultural imports from the Free State, which in turn led to the imposition of retaliatory tariffs on British imports. All this was conducted in the wake of the recently passed Statute of Westminster. Meant to settle the constitutional relationship between Britain and the dominions, it gave formal recognition to their legislative and political independence. Ministers regarded the legislation as troublesome but necessary in view of the demands of South Africa and the Irish Free State. But it was open to criticism for undermining the 'safeguards' enshrined in the Irish Free State Act 1922, and had obvious implications for any scheme of federal self-government drawn up for India. As John Darwin notes, unease amongst Conservatives was not confined to the diehards; requiring ministers to pull out all the stops to avoid an embarrassing retreat.[184] As a result of their efforts, Gretton's attempt to exclude the Irish Free State from the Statute of Westminster went down to a dramatic defeat, 360–50; as did an attempt by the diehards the following week to rule out the Statute's definition of 'dominion status' to any scheme devised for India.[185] These were serious setbacks, but the diehards felt vindicated afterward by the unfriendly behaviour of the Fianna Fáil government. All the same, what followed brought little satisfaction. For although the National Government's determination to implement a new constitution for India meant that it was all but impossible to reach a settlement with Dublin which might end the 'economic war', the resulting stalemate did nothing to abate the latter's step-by-step progress towards realizing the ideal of an independent republic.[186]

Seemingly oblivious to their role in this dynamic, the diehard's unity in Irish matters held until the summer of 1935 when the passage of India bill looked secure. Thereafter, a number of differences of opinion emerged or re-emerged, reflecting how Ireland, at least for the diehards, had become entangled in the question of armaments and the National Government's position on Germany. These were first exposed in July 1935 during the course of an adjournment debate about a recent ruling of the Judicial Committee of the Privy Council which found that the Free State had the power to abrogate the 1921 treaty. Churchill's characterization of the government's relations with Ireland, as part of the 'perpetual progress of British degeneration', was wholly in keeping with the diehard tone he had come to adopt on India. But on this occasion two other diehard MPs, Gretton and Croft, corrected their colleague's assertion that the blame lay with the Statute of Westminster, preferring instead to locate it with the 1921 treaty and the subsequent legislation which Churchill piloted through Parliament.[187] Even Gretton and Croft parted company on Ireland as it became tangled up in the wider diplomatic initiatives of the late 1930s. Neville Chamberlain, as both Chancellor of the Exchequer and then prime minister, was particularly keen to resolve the economic war, especially in the light of escalating tensions in Europe. Overruling opposition within his cabinet and on the back benches, he reached an agreement with de Valera in April 1938 which several diehard MPs afterwards condemned in the strongest terms. Their principal objection concerned the prime minister's decision to hand over the 'treaty ports'. Croft and Gretton were vice presidents of the Irish Loyalist Imperial Federation, pledged to 'safeguard the constitutional rights and liberties of South-Irish born Loyalists'. After Hitler's assumption of power in 1933, the federation had revived the pre–1914 spectre of Germany using Ireland as a launch pad to invade Great Britain.[188] Yet Croft's support for Chamberlain's handling of Berlin now determined his attitude to the return of the treaty ports. He therefore pressed Churchill in private to avoid a division on the 1938 agreement as it 'would result in a very small minority', and that a 'long and sustained fight' would only distract from the 'real danger' posed by Germany.[189] As the author of the provision on the 'treaty ports', Churchill disregarded Croft's advice by leading the attack on the 1938 agreement. Gretton too denounced it unreservedly. Croft, in contrast, hailed it as part of the 'wide scope of the peace promotion of the Government in Europe at the present time', and urged its critics to direct their anger instead to the 1921 treaty.[190] If Paul Canning is correct to describe the diehards as the 'most effective pressure group influencing the British Government's Irish policy during the 1920s and 1930s', this clearly did not pertain in the late 1930s, when division in their ranks over foreign policy leaked into Irish affairs and weakened their coherence as a parliamentary grouping.[191]

V

The diehards were not alone in believing that the fate of Ireland should inform Conservative thinking on India. Baldwin attributed the loss of southern Ireland to decades of party warfare at Westminster. In failing to satisfy the nationalist demand for home rule, and substituting in its place a mixture of coercion and concession, the question had become so embittered that in the end it was reduced to a choice between war and surrender. If India was not to go the same way, then it was essential to work in partnership with Indian representatives, and substitute shared beliefs in place of the historic emphasis on racial difference. From this perspective, it was essential that India should be elevated above party politics. And like the diehards, Baldwin did not see Ireland and India in isolation. He regarded his India policy in particular as a means of liberalizing his party, and demonstrating its 'progressive' credentials to a domestic electorate which many assumed had little interest in the fine points of Britain's constitutional relationship with South Asia.[192] Possessing an overwhelming majority, the National Government might reasonably expect to repeat the routing delivered to the diehards in 1931 over the Statute of Westminster. But when it came to the future of India, the diehards were given a field of opportunity to win over others in the party. Questions remained about the effectiveness of constitutional safeguards given that the Statute of Westminster granted dominions legislative independence.[193] There was also Baldwin's marked departure from steering a course between 'Harold Macmillan and John Gretton', traversing instead what Philip Williamson calls 'the long hard road of leading the party towards the "advanced" perspective'.[194] Baldwin's boldness over India had the effect of revealing the presence of a large middle ground of opinion in the party, at Westminster and beyond, uncommitted either way, which duly became the focus of rival ministerial and diehard campaigns. The diehards did not need to win over a majority of MPs, merely a sufficient minority, including abstentions, to undermine front-bench claims to represent settled Conservative opinion. As Churchill assured Croft, even if they did not save 'the ship', their efforts might still 'save much from the wreck'.[195]

The breach between the diehards and Baldwin over India first emerged when the latter gave qualified support to the viceroy, Lord Irwin, who had announced on 31 October 1929 that dominion status was the ultimate goal of British policy in India and that a round-table conference of British and Indian politicians would be convened in London to discuss how it might be implemented. In doing so, Baldwin had not only failed to consult his shadow cabinet, but in effect jettisoned the reform process he had initiated when still in government. The India Act 1919 had provided that a statutory commission should review its progress within a decade; whilst still in government, Baldwin had seized the initiative by establishing it in 1927 to avoid the risk of a Labour ministry taking charge. The then Secretary of State for India, Lord Birkenhead, appointed the Liberal MP, Sir John Simon, as its chair, and confined the commission's membership to Westminster parliamentarians. The latter caused uproar in India and near unanimity amongst its politicians about the need for their inclusion. Irwin's declaration two years later, an idea he proposed to the second Labour government, was an attempt to heal these wounds. Yet this very act, by a Conservative-appointed viceroy, epitomized long-held anxiety amongst the diehards about collaboration between front benches. As such, even after the formation of the National Government, the diehards persisted in arguing that its stewardship of Indian constitutional reform was 'socialist' in provenance.[196] Its legitimacy was further questioned by the diehards as it overlooked the Simon Commission. Conveniently, the commission's report, published in May–June 1930, recommended full provincial self-government but ruled out federal self-government unless it overcame the hurdle of being acceptable to all minorities and the princely states. Little wonder then that the *Indian Daily Mail* referred to it as a 'badly cooked rice pudding, strongly flavoured with the cinnamon of die-hardism'.[197] Inconveniently for the diehards, however, Simon and his commissioners sought to reduce the political temperature by avoiding a direct conflict with the government.[198] Moreover, for all the diehards' fixation with the legitimacy of the Simon Commission, they still took issue with some of its recommendations; for example, they could not countenance the transfer of law and order or any infringement on gubernatorial involvement in ministerial appointments.[199]

The House of Commons division on India during its consideration of the Statute of Westminster was the first real test of diehard strength in Parliament. Despite that setback, a majority of the diehards were initially content to confine their activity to Parliament, perhaps confident that the parliamentary subject committee on India provided an ample opportunity to press their case. As Amery recorded of one of its meetings, the 'preponderant Die-Hard element' required careful handling if it was not to sow the seeds of wider disaffection.[200] But a minority, led by Lords Sydenham and Salisbury, felt that it was necessary to organize a pressure group to coordinate opposition within and outside Parliament. With the exception of Salisbury and the first Viscount Sumner (1859–1934), a former law lord, these diehards were distinguished from the wider cohort by close personal connections to the Raj.[201] The Ulsterman, Alfred Knox, was a retired major-general in the Indian Army; Reginald Craddock (1864–1937), MP for the Combined English Universities, had a career in the Indian Civil Service (ICS) which culminated in his appointment as Lieutenant Governor of Burma; and the Oxford academic and MP, Charles Oman, was the

Indian-born son of an indigo planter in Bihar.[202] They were joined by a number of retired governors, including Sir Michael O'Dwyer, as well as retired officers of the Indian civil, military and medical services. Established on 4 July 1930, the Indian Empire Society (IES) published propaganda and a monthly periodical, the *Indian Empire Review*, which included contributions from old India hands as well as a number of figures connected with fascist organizations.[203]

The most significant addition to the IES, however, was that of Churchill. It followed the announcement on 26 January 1931, by the Conservative's India spokesman, Samuel Hoare, that His Majesty's Opposition gave its backing to all-India federation. When Churchill responded by expressing his opposition, Baldwin rose to reply and used the opportunity to declare that a future Conservative government would continue the present government's course of action.[204] Churchill's fellow 'coalitionists', Birkenhead and Austen Chamberlain, were also uneasy about Hoare's declaration; indeed, Churchill's position was to some extent influenced by Birkenhead; but neither followed Churchill into the diehard camp.[205] It was a surprising move, after all. Churchill's stance on free trade, his early departure from the Conservative party over fiscal policy, denunciation of Brigadier Dyer and reputation for political opportunism all identified Churchill as a major opponent of the diehards. Not that Churchill shied away from or denied his past; his speech on Dyer's actions at Amritsar was reprinted along with others on India in a book published in May 1931.[206] More covertly, he appears not to have regarded this as a break with the coalitionists, for he privately assured Austen Chamberlain in 1933 that the former party leader would head a reconstructed government should the diehards succeed in inflicting sufficient damage on the National Government.[207] At the same time, Churchill was not a complete stranger to the diehards' point of view. Whilst he and Edwin Montagu had worked together in drumming Dyer out of the army, Churchill had created a rift between them in January 1922 by publicly opposing the grant of equality between white and Indian settlers in Kenya.[208] It not only reflected his new brief at the Colonial Office, but as Cowling suggests, it was part of a more reactionary turn in his politics in the early months of 1922, evident also in Churchill's combative positions on Russia, Ireland and Labour.[209] In fact, however much the diehards a decade later might speculate about Churchill's sincerity in joining their cause, what actually distinguished him from them, as Richard Toye observes, was his preparedness to use India to break the government.[210] With the exception of Gretton, whose hostility to the Conservatives' adherence to the National Government was grudging at best, the diehards did not display any obvious determination to follow Churchill to such lengths. Yet, in a cohort singularly bereft of former ministers, let alone great parliamentary performers, Churchill's involvement could hardly be spurned. He was not the only high-profile Conservative to shift positions vis-à-vis the diehards. Samuel Hoare and Lord Irwin had also fundamentally revised their relationship with them, albeit travelling in the opposite direction. Hoare had been an opponent of Welsh disestablishment in 1919, and cooperated initially with the diehards two years later in opposing the Anglo–Irish treaty, before falling into line with the post-war coalition government.[211] Irwin had been 'a minor Die Hard hero' in the early 1920s, abandoning that afterwards to become closely associated with the politics of conciliation.[212]

Lord Lloyd was another significant addition to the diehard cause. He quickly became the key figure in the organization of the House of Lords India Group, amongst whose number were veterans of previous right-wing campaigns, including Lords Ampthill, Mount Temple, Banbury of Southam and Malmesbury.[213] Ampthill was regarded with especial symbolic importance as his earlier tenure as Governor of Madras had required him to serve briefly as acting viceroy of India. But it was Lloyd's adherence to the cause which was more

Figure 10 Lord Lloyd

significant politically. After a brief career in the House of Commons, during which time he distinguished himself as an ardent tariff reformer and proponent of war against Germany, Lloyd left the Commons in 1918 to take up the post of Governor of Bombay. A supporter of the India Act 1919, he took what his biographer describes as 'an eminently liberal line' over Amritsar, and enjoyed a reasonably good working relationship with Montagu at the India Office. Lloyd's ambition to become viceroy caused him to stand apart from the diehards in the early 1920s, a particular strain when Lord Milner's 1920 report on the future of Egypt seemed to contradict the lessons of his own youthful experience of the Middle East. What was suppressed then came to the fore after his appointment in 1925 as Britain's High Commissioner to Cairo. In that post, he struggled to accept the direction of the Foreign Office, especially in his dealings with Egyptian nationalists.[214] Labour's victory at the polls in 1929 not only signalled the end of Lloyd's tenure at Cairo, but Baldwin's refusal to defend the outgoing High Commissioner's record ensured that Lloyd emerged from the episode as a diehard martyr.[215] Lloyd's background helped to ensure that the lesson of Egypt stood alongside that of Ireland in diehard rhetoric about India.[216] He recanted for his previous aloofness from Irish affairs by becoming a vice president of the Irish Loyalist Imperial Federation alongside Croft and Gretton.[217] Michael Bloch suggests that Lloyd was the inspiration for a fictional character, Henry Fortescue MP, the main protagonist of Compton Mackenzie's novel about suppressed homosexuality, *Thin Ice*.[218] Apparently drawing on their time together at Cairo, Fortescue certainly bears some resemblance to Lloyd, not least in his fastidious appearance and zealous imperialism. But there are important differences, and the mention of Lloyd's name in the novel – his appointment to Bombay depriving Fortescue of that opportunity, thus sending his career on the downward trajectory which is at the heart of the story – raises some doubt about it being a straightforward *roman-á-clef*.[219]

The adhesion of Churchill and Lloyd to diehard ranks lent the group a measure of significance in the party which it previously lacked. But their appeal on the back benches was limited. As the erstwhile diehard, Patrick Hannon, conceded, 'It is true that an intense interest is felt in [*sic*] the Indian outlook by most of our thoughtful Conservatives, but they are very reluctant to be led by either Winston or Lloyd.'[220] The diary of Cuthbert Headlam, MP for the marginal seat of Barnard Castle, notes something similar about 'the Right wing to which I ought to belong – and should, I think, if it were not lead by Winston, Page Croft, etc.'[221] The diehards' reputation was clearly a problem in trying to win over significant numbers of MPs, especially given that a large number attributed their ability to hold marginal seats to Baldwin. In due course the diehards ended up resorting to reviving the old TRL tactic of encouraging dissent in the constituencies, in the hope that MPs might respond to pressure from below, but this tended to confirm rather than rebut their reputation for disruptiveness and divisiveness.[222]

The voluntary party had been content to leave the subject of India well alone throughout the deliberations of the first, second and third round-table conferences, which stretched from November 1930 to December 1932. It applied even to Conservatives in Lancashire, where there was growing anxiety about the effect of Indian tariffs on manufactured cotton exports to the subcontinent.[223] This changed with the publication of the India White Paper in the spring of 1933, as proponents and opponents alike could turn their attention to a definite statement of intent which would inevitably attract the attention of the Conservative grass roots. The diehards duly initiated a new campaign in March 1933 by organizing themselves as the India Defence Committee, and four months later establishing the India Defence League (IDL).[224] The name of the latter evoked the TRL and other patriotic leagues. And like them, the IDL hid its internal difficulties behind exaggerated claims to have 10,000 subscribing members in sixty branches across the country.[225] Patrick Donner was appointed its honorary secretary. Born into Finland's Swedish-speaking minority, he acquired a life-long hatred of communism having witnessed at first hand the Bolshevik revolution. Scottish on his mother's side, his father's diplomatic appointment to London after the war meant that he was schooled in Britain, where he developed a distinctly British sense of patriotism despite receiving taunts at school for being a 'foreigner', and experiencing in 1927 the bitter disappointment of having his application for citizenship declined by Joynson-Hicks.[226] When the latter was subsequently granted, Donner embarked on a parliamentary career which quickly took him into the orbit of the diehards.

The IES continued to produce pamphlets and the *Indian Empire Review*, but the leadership and organization of agitation shifted decisively to the IDL. The new league was partly financed with the £4,500 which remained of the 'diehard fund', vindicating Gretton's prediction in 1923 that it would one day come in useful, as well as a membership fee of £50 for parliamentarians.[227] It opened a secretariat at 48 Broadway, Westminster, to service an executive committee, and published pamphlets, organized speaking tours, and coordinated campaigning amongst grass-roots Conservatives. Around the same time, supporters of the White Paper organized themselves as the Union of Britain and India. Like the IES, most of its members were ex-ICS. However, it failed to excite the rank and file in the same way as the IDL, especially as the latter benefited from several years of dissatisfaction in certain quarters with Baldwin's leadership. Despite this, the contrasting fortunes of the two organizations mattered less in the long run given that the National Government worked hard at confining deliberations to Parliament. As Wolmer lamented privately, the IDL faced 'a vastly superior Organisation, built mainly on the Conservative Party Organisation, which is the work of generations, and, with the very limited amount of our resources, it has been impossible for the IDL to build up a comparable organisation'.[228] Yet the very existence of the IDL created considerable nervousness amongst ministers, especially in advance of party caucuses, and as a result had a bearing on their presentation of the White Paper to Conservative MPs and party members alike.

The press played a vital role in assisting the diehards to communicate with the party membership, appeal for funds, organize meetings and recruit to the IDL. As Gretton informed Churchill, 'It is very necessary that the Harmsworth press should begin to push the Albert Hall meeting ... we are relying very much on them to make a meeting'.[229] Both the *Daily Mail* and its regional titles took a strong line on India, the former publishing articles by Churchill as well as pieces by Sydenham, O'Dwyer and Craddock. In addition, Rothermere's agents lent expertise to the IDL in press management.[230] The *Daily Express* was not so obliging.[231] Beaverbrook was close to Hoare, whose brother was an investor in the *Express*, and India mattered less to the Canadian than the dominions, save for when it had a direct bearing on his pet project of empire free trade.[232] The press barons therefore did not present the same united front on India that had appeared to threaten Baldwin's leadership in 1930, even if his Bewdley constituency association still complained in 1934 about 'the unjustifiable attacks on our Member which appear from time to time in some sections of the Press supposed to be friendly to the Unionist Party'.[233]

Before returning to the organization of the IDL campaign, it is instructive to examine first how the diehards presented their case. As with previous campaigns, the diehards could only increase their support amongst backbenchers by cultivating a crisis of conservatism. The peculiar circumstances of the National Government's overwhelming majority made this an onerous task. Moreover, appealing to hearts rather than heads was more challenging than it had been in the early 1920s, owing to the Conservative party's establishment of a research department and a training college at Ashridge, and at the local level, the proliferation of weekend political schools.[234] Merely reiterating impractical Conservative ideals would not do. Most histories which deal with this episode, however, are content to assume that diehard arguments were purely reactionary and not worth investigation, with the notable exception of two studies which identify them as part of an 'extreme right-wing community' and 'orthodox' Anglicanism respectively.[235]

It is widely accepted that Nazi thinking combined elements of modernism with romanticism in what Jeffery Herf calls 'reactionary modernism'.[236] Patrick Zander discerns something similar in Britain. Citing David Egerton's challenge to the conventional view that science did not penetrate 'English culture', Zander goes further by representing Egerton's summary of assorted Conservative, pro-fascist, and fascist enthusiasts for air power as a single 'community'.[237] Set alongside the commonplace acceptance of the importance of air technology to interwar imperial communication, Zander transforms Lady Houston's sponsorship of the 1933 Mount Everest aerial expedition into 'an opportunity to use modern technology as a metaphor for national regeneration', and a means of making 'a strong statement to the indigenous people of that region'. Perhaps, at least in the mind of Houston and other backers, but the claim that it was 'rich with political significance' goes too far.[238] The pilot, Lord Clydesdale, was reluctant to attack the India White Paper.[239] The expedition barely received any attention in Parliament; when it was remarked upon, it was not by a diehard, but that quintessential moderate, R.A.B. Butler, addressing the Commons as Under-Secretary of State for India.[240] And if some 'modernist' fascists in Britain were drawn to the supposedly 'modern' technology of the aeroplane, then it is worth remembering that political air-mindedness had been around for several decades, first emerging as part of the turn-of-the-century national efficiency movement.[241] Far from highlighting the existence of an 'extreme right political community', the involvement of Houston, the enormously wealthy widow of the former Conservative MP and shipping magnate, Robert Houston, can be taken as a reminder of the fundamental divisions on the Right. For she also funded the IDL, but her call for it to evolve into a separate diehard-led party was resisted by two of her favoured diehards, Lords Lloyd and Wolmer, the former even severing his connection with her and returning her money.[242] When Houston at the height of the India controversy attacked the prime minister as a 'traitor', Wolmer stuck with parliamentary convention by defending MacDonald's personal integrity and encouraged her to concentrate instead on his 'fallacious' policies.[243]

Gerald Studdert-Kennedy finds that the diehard–front bench cleavage is observable in both politics and Anglicanism. Religion certainly mattered to the diehards, and in the case of several, including Croft and Lloyd, it informed their belief in Britain's providential duty to rule over other peoples. As such, they were not shy of invoking religious themes in their speeches, especially to the party faithful.[244] But this was not a straightforward matter of upholding Tory orthodoxy in both religious and secular spheres. Religion, after all, was as likely to divide as define the diehards. The prayer-book debates confirmed that there was no consensus among them about the Protestant character of the Church of England. Even the most openly reactionary of their number, Lord Lymington, argued that 'as it has ceased to be the religion of the people as it was four hundred years ago, [the Church of England] should share its representation [in the House of Lords] with those great bodies of religion whose leaders will take the oath to the Crown'.[245] There were unusual cases too; the former MP and diehard peer, Gideon Murray, second Viscount Elibank, became a follower of Christian Science; and Donner hinted in his memoirs at a belief in reincarnation.[246] More significant was the changing relationship between the Conservative Right and Catholicism. Recusant and convert Catholics had long been drawn to Conservative politics, but what is more remarkable is that the two most prominent Catholic diehards hailed from Irish families, Patrick Hannon and Brendan Bracken (1901–58), the MP for North Paddington.[247] The former's faithful adherence to the Church contrasted markedly with Bracken's abandonment of it in his teens, but the presence of both in diehard ranks underscored the distance travelled from older notions of Tory orthodoxy.[248] Lord Lloyd's adherence to Anglo-Catholicism even encouraged him to flirt with the idea of converting to Roman Catholicism.[249] This reflected a broader trend. The leading right-wing periodical of the 1930s, Houston's *English Review*, was edited by the Anglo-Catholic intellectual, Douglas Jerrold, and two of the most prominent right-wing public intellectuals of the period were both Catholics, G.K. Chesterton and Hilaire Belloc.[250] As G.C. Webber observes: 'the politically timid Protestant Right were replaced as the leading exponents of religious conservatism during the inter-war years by a group of right-wing Catholics'.[251] The pronounced anti-socialism of the diehards was an obvious factor, especially when it led them to highlight the violence inflicted upon Catholic clergy and property during the Spanish Civil War. But the declining importance of religion to the Conservative Right meant that the diehards' attitude to Catholicism, and the presence of Catholics in diehard ranks, did not add up to anything significant politically; indeed, when it came to Northern Ireland, old sectarian attitudes prevailed.

The more noteworthy feature of diehard arguments against the White Paper was their employment of what appeared to be humanitarian objections about the plight of the poor, minorities and women. These would be the principal victims, they argued, of a caste-bound system overseen by self-interested Brahman politicians.[252] They had good cause to pursue this line of argument. Not only did the Indian Medical Service (IMS) express similar concerns about all-India government, but the welfare of Indian peasants attracted considerable attention worldwide following the publication of Katherine Mayo's controversial exposé, *Mother India*.[253] For the diehards, the American campaigner provided a modern gloss to long-standing stereotypes about Hinduism's effeminacy, unrestrained sexuality, manifestation as physical and moral weakness, and numerous other vices and character flaws. Two women MPs, the Duchess of Atholl and Eleanor Rathbone, helpfully echoed Mayo's observations in Parliament. Both were primarily motivated by humanitarian considerations, but in the case of Atholl it extended to actively working alongside the IDL.[254] She was the only woman in the diehards' ranks, which was all the more remarkable given that she had been a Baldwinite loyalist in the 1920s and the first Conservative woman MP to hold ministerial office.[255] Croft recommended that his parliamentary opponents read Mayo.[256] The IES, through its secretary, Sir Mark Martin, maintained correspondence with her, as did a number of individual diehards including Churchill.[257] Mayo even contributed an article to the *Indian Empire Review* encouraging readers to propagandize in the United States.[258] At root, of course, the diehards' apparent concern for the welfare of India's masses was a barely concealed excuse to employ the essential vocabulary and paradigm of savagery–barbarism–civilization, to argue that however ready Indian politicians might be for all-India federation, the majority of Indians had not acquired European habits of political and social organization.[259] Nevertheless, by questioning the ability of the Indian National Congress politicians to run India fairly, the diehards tapped into widespread unease on the Conservative benches, and even amongst Labour MPs, about its disruptive and sometimes violent campaigns in 1920–22 and 1930–34.[260] As such, the emphasis given to humanitarian arguments complemented more typically diehard objections to the violence, or 'terrorism', of such campaigns for national self-determination and their disregard for British conceptions of peaceful and constitutional government.[261]

The diehards' emphasis on the welfare of the Indian people may also have been intended to rebut their easy caricature as racist reactionaries, especially given Baldwin's willingness to inform MPs of letters he received from retired colonels labelling him a 'negrophile'.[262] But repackaging anachronistic ideas about civilizational development in the language of contemporary global humanitarianism was in practice rarely consistent, successful or convincing. The most obvious weakness was that the Raj had singularly failed to tackle these very same social problems. If Sydenham could write that 'The real truth in many matters connected with Indian public life is so revolting that no decent periodical would publish it', what did this say about seventy years of British direct rule and a far longer period of contact between the peoples of Britain and India?[263] The poor regard in which the white domiciled community in India was held by the more transient ranks of white professionals, businessmen and military personnel did not hold out much hope either.[264] Likewise, the diehards' soft spot for the Indian princes, and Indian village life, sat at odds with the idea of the British administration as a representative and agent of political and economic modernization.[265] Most diehards, of course, realized that the Raj was about railways, telegraphs, the production of commodities and consumption of British manufactures. But in attempting to derail the White Paper and subsequent bill through tactics that emphasized the need to safeguard the interests of the princely states, and to prevent the exploitation of village peasants, the diehards set their faces against the reality that it was the commercial forces of the empire, and not the prospect of 'Brahman politicians' taking power at the centre, which undermined the very things they now claimed to be protecting. An international scrutiny of Indian welfare would have revealed as much, which explains perhaps why the diehards declined to advocate such a course of action. In the minds of the diehards, it might have been consistent to denounce unrepresentative Brahmin politicians, and at the same time write off the proposed mass electorate as 'incredibly illiterate, ignorant and inexperienced', in so far as the former could exploit the latter.[266] But in reality, the diehards had little enthusiasm about handing over powers to the same politicians, regardless of the scope of the franchise, and high-handed dismissals of the political and social capacity of the masses did not sit well with declarations of having their best interests at heart. All of which underlines the fact that the diehards' engagement with humanitarianism was partial and self-serving, not least because it ignored the growing body of contemporary humanitarian opinion which argued that greater self-government and economic modernization should be the precondition and not the reward for social and cultural improvement.[267]

This explains why Hoare, appointed India Secretary in the National Government, believed that his White Paper was both progressive and intellectually superior to criticisms levelled by the diehards: the 'trouble is that our case is a complicated case of detail, whilst the [diehard] attack is an attack of headlines and platform slogans'.[268] Yet, front-bench claims to represent informed and progressive opinion on India were often accompanied behind closed doors by quiet reassurances to

Conservatives that they all held common views on India's problems. Turning diehard arguments on their head, Hoare could argue that Indian politicians were best left to deal with some of the subcontinent's most intractable problems. His reforms would allow British-appointed officials to concentrate instead on the economic and strategic issues that mattered most to Britain. Similarly, the diehards' preoccupation with the weaknesses of 'Hindu character' was implicitly acknowledged by ministers with suggestions that it could be exploited to undermine nationalism.[269] This did not go unnoticed by the diehards and their supporters: 'they cannot but agree, albeit reluctantly, with us "die-hards." Or rather, they will agree with us, privately, in a friendly and whole-hearted manner, but only very reluctantly in public, in the presence of the warm-hearted and fickle, and generally completely ignorant voters.'[270] Another noted 'that facts asserted by so-called "Diehards" are ignored till they are repeated by a member of the Government or one of its officials. Then they are admitted without demur.'[271] Neville Chamberlain reveals something of this in his private correspondence. Referring to the diehards' cultivation of the Indian princes, he noted Hoare's observation that this explained the princes' extremely bad behaviour, alongside 'the usual oriental habit of blackmail.'[272] On India more generally, Chamberlain remarked: 'the problem is ... how to give the Indian child the knife which it is demanding and at the same time to contrive that the knife wont [sic] open till the child is old enough to use it without danger to itself and other people.'[273] The reluctance of ministers openly to affirm such prejudices, more usually found in the mouths of diehards, finally dissolved once the India bill was laid before the House of Commons. As Baldwin admitted frankly in February 1935, when commending the bill to MPs, 'the problems were rooted in the religious life of India and they were being transferred to Indians to deal with.'[274]

Shared prejudices aside, the contrasting outlooks and purposes which divided the diehards from the front bench remained significant. Whatever doubts there were about the contemporary relevance and veracity of the *Indian Empire Review*, it provided a window into the diehards' minds. If like other Conservatives, the diehards regarded the Raj as a force for civilization amidst backwardness, then their belief in the durability of its social, religious and cultural problems all too easily slid into fatalism, and even catastrophism, which tended to undermine the rationale of Britain's imperial mission.[275] A related tendency cast all Indian politicians as extremist, even Liberals and well-known moderates.[276] There was little appreciation of tensions between Mohandas Gandhi and the so-called 'young hooligans' unprepared to settle for dominion status, let alone the unwitting role of diehard utterances in uniting Indian opinion in condemnation. Then there were the revealing complaints about the indifference of the British public to their empire, something blamed on foreigners, and the *Indian Empire Review*'s regular advertisement for A.H. Lane's *Alien Menace*, on the fallacy of 'admitting [to Britain] shoals of undesirables'.[277]

The front bench also drew on established patterns of Conservative thought about imperial development, but with markedly greater success in promoting a coherent vision which still managed to accommodate change. The Round Table group of intellectuals, and in particular, Geoffrey Dawson, editor of *The Times*, were especially prominent in this endeavour. To the frustration of the diehards, the newspaper assisted the case advanced by Conservative ministers through journalism which promoted progress towards an all-India responsible government as consistent with Britain's overriding imperial mission.[278] Whereas the diehards' arguments about maintaining the status quo were often inconsistent and contradictory, the thrust of the arguments advanced by the Round Table and *The Times* acknowledged and prized the importance of consistency. Change, therefore, could be promoted as consistency; as George Boyce observes, it was 'necessary for the British to be flexible in their handling of imperial issues; yet they could draw upon a notion that there was some over-riding plan or purpose in all this; that, in retrospect, it could be seen as fitting into a pattern'.[279]

These contrasting strategies led to mutual accusations of ignorance. Writing to the Chancellor of the Chamber of Princes, the Maharajah of Patiala, Gwynne dismissed Baldwin's capacity to fight the diehards as he knew 'nothing of India' and 'is content to drift along the current, pushed by Sir Samuel Hoare and the Prime Minister'. Yet, in the same letter, Gwynne admitted that he had only ever been in India for three days.[280] And if the *Morning Post* sought to challenge or correct *The Times*'s dominant position in Indian reportage, and the government's control over those currently employed in the ICS, it chose an odd way of doing it in focusing its resources so heavily on what Gwynne regarded as the White Paper's weakest point: the attitude of the Indian princes. Still, under the direction of Gwynne, the *Post*'s India correspondent, Madhava Rao, was instrumental in encouraging opposition to the measure amongst the princes.[281] The *Indian Empire Review*, in contrast, liked to present itself as a periodical on Indian current affairs. Its contributors were typically former India civil servants and all too willing to invoke personal expertise. In ordinary circumstances, these were not people to be dismissed lightly; the 'Heaven born', after all, were recruited from among high educational achievers. However, contributors to the *Review* were by definition retired and many explicitly denounced the post–1919 turn in Raj policy, typically by lamenting declining administrative standards and increasing bureaucracy, and associating these with the Indianization of the civil service.[282] Evelyn Waugh helped to make such people figures of fun, characterizing their post-retirement domicile in Britain as the occupants of small manor houses and large rectories, jealously guarding the rural character of their neighbourhoods, and subsisting on the tribute of pensions from imperial service.[283] The outlay on those pensions, it should be noted, rivalled New Delhi's expenditure on welfare and development, a fact which escaped the attention of contributors to the *India Empire Review*.[284] More generally, the topicality of commentary in the *Review* gradually gave way over time to articles that were repetitive, banal and anonymous. This made it relatively straightforward for ministers to argue that only those currently employed by the government of India properly understood the rapidly changing situation. If ICS rules ensured no public contradiction from that quarter, then Churchill's claim that the government suppressed criticism and coerced compliance amongst ICS officers brought only criticism that the 'outstanding men in the Civil Service are the begetters of the policies they publicly defend'.[285]

It is possible to chart the ebb and flow of the struggle between the diehards and the front bench for wavering Conservative MPs through successive parliamentary divisions and party caucuses. The India division in December 1931 has already been noted. The following year's party conference, in October 1932, also saw the diehards go down to a defeat, but to Hoare's alarm, their resolution, denouncing the attempt to 'force a democratic system upon a great and mainly primitive and illiterate electorate', received what he described as a 'surprisingly good reception'.[286] When the House of Commons divided on a diehard amendment on 22 February 1933, binding the India White Paper's joint select committee to examine only the Simon report, the diehards mustered only forty-two in support, but, crucially, 245 Conservative MPs abstained or otherwise absented themselves.[287] A week later the diehards scored a further spectacular result at a meeting of the National Union's Central Council, securing a large majority in favour of safeguarding Lancashire's declining cotton trade with India, and narrowly losing 189–165, after 151 abstentions, a motion opposing all-India government.[288] If these developments pointed to the diehards inflicting further embarrassments on the front bench, the latter were moved to place India policy out of the reach of the voluntary party by confining discussion to Parliament.

This was achieved through the establishment in March 1933 of the parliamentary Joint Select Committee (JSC) on India. A decisive turning point, it wrong-footed the diehards in a number of ways. Hoare met diehard demands for greater representation on the thirty-two man committee with an offer of five of the eleven places reserved for Conservatives, an ostensibly generous quota which made the diehards' initial claim for more places appear foolish.[289] The JSC committed its members, the diehards included, to a protracted deliberative process, ensuring that the IDL did not submit its most able spokesmen, Churchill, Croft and Lloyd, for membership.[290] Their exclusion in turn played to ministerial claims that the diehards sought only to pursue divisive ends. So too did Churchill's valiant if ultimately doomed attempt to expose a breach of procedure on the JSC concerning Hoare's dealings with the Manchester Chamber of Commerce.[291] Similarly, the cultivation by the diehards on the JSC of opposition in the Chamber of Princes seemed to enhance the former's reputation for disruptiveness without properly repaying the investment in time and effort.[292] The diehards' attempt to harness the princes also exposed divisions and shortcomings in their own ranks. Salisbury, the most prominent diehard on the JSC, was reluctant to call before it the Maharajah of Patiala. In a blunt exchange of letters with Gwynne, he overrode the editor by pressing the opinion that Patiala did not have the 'nerve' to reject the White Paper.[293] When Gwynne afterwards attempted to buttress his newspaper's contacts with the Chamber of Princes by organizing a delegation of diehard parliamentarians to visit its standing committee, it backfired when no prominent diehard was willing to make the journey; only John Courtauld, Viscount Clive (1904–43) and Lord Lymington stepped forward.[294]

Further embarrassment was caused when, within a week of this being arranged, Lymington signalled his intention to resign his seat, with the explanation 'that to be uncompromising on principle, whether over India, defence, or home politics, is to be unable to adapt oneself to party politics'.[295] There was some indication of his growing malaise three years previously in his declaration that 'Toryism is not and cannot be democratic in the political sense of the word'.[296] It is, he argued, a 'relic of feudalism', and Disraeli had been wrong to think 'that the proletariat vote would correct the selfishness of the moneyed vote'.[297] He therefore echoed Baldwin's recent denunciation of the press barons – 'One man without service or responsibility to the Crown can inflame the passions or debauch the minds of the people' – but used it instead to advocate press censorship.[298] The solution, he concluded, was not 'Fascism', or the 'Socialist faith' which characterized Mosley's BUF, but a 'powerful House of Lords'.[299] After resigning his seat in 1934, Lymington drifted into the relative obscurity of esoteric, 'back to the land', and extreme Right politics, along the way inheriting his father's peerage in 1943 as the ninth Earl of Portsmouth, and later sitting, from 1957 to 1960, on Kenya's legislative council.[300]

These setbacks were of the diehards' own making. The most devastating impact of the JSC, however, was Hoare's ability to secure the agreement of the voluntary party to gag itself until the committee submitted its final report. Both the women's and youth sections objected, but a sufficient majority in most grassroots organizations, including the Primrose League, acquiesced in their own marginalization.[301] It not only cut dead the diehards' strategy of harnessing the voluntary party, it also had a financial toll on the IDL, for its leaders reluctantly yielded to the process by agreeing that it was 'unwise to make a public appeal for funds through the *Morning Post* until after the Joint Select Committee had reported'. When they were finally released from this bind in the autumn of 1934, it was too late, for their appeal 'brought in only about 1/3rd of the amount the *Morning Post* was able to raise for the Irish Campaign in 1920'; the resulting deficit obliged the IDL afterwards to consider reconstituting itself in order to pay off its debts.[302]

Two Commons divisions, on 10 April 1933, demonstrated the immediate effect of the JSC on the diehards' campaign. Although the first, allowing six government ministers to serve on the JSC, prompted a diehard-led rebellion of seventy-nine Conservatives, the second, opposing the JSC's constitution, reduced them to forty-three.[303] This helped to establish a new momentum which extended also to the party's main caucuses, the Central Council and the annual party conference. It was a gathering of the former, on 28 June 1933, which voted 838–356 in favour of gagging itself until the JSC reported.[304] The diehards therefore steeled themselves for the party conference in October.[305] As the conference gathered at Birmingham, the *Morning Post* 'had rows of sandwichmen walking round with legends about surrender and betrayal and a pamphlet with wide black borders was handed to the delegates at the doors'.[306] The diehards' motion on India was presented by Wolmer, who took care to express confidence in the National Government, before signalling 'apprehension' with the White Paper's proposals on 'finance, defence, police, the welfare of the Indian peoples, and trade discrimination in India'. The result of the vote was 737–344 in favour of the government.[307] A decisive result, but one which still revealed considerable unease in the party. Regardless of this, Neville Chamberlain was typical amongst ministers in interpreting it as 'a definite approval of the general lines of the Government's policy'.[308]

The Central Council and conference votes in 1933 curtailed diehard hopes of marshalling the grass roots in advance of the bill. However, the protracted nature of the JSC's deliberations inevitably aroused frustration in sections of the party. This was evident at the October 1934 party conference, when a diehard motion criticizing the muzzle placed on the party lost narrowly, 543–520.[309] Even so, success on this specific issue did not have the opportunity of developing into support for the case advanced by the IDL. Not only was the party pacified to some extent by the publication soon after of the JSC's report, but it provided the occasion for the most prominent waverer, Austen Chamberlain, to signal his support, as well as allow the government to make much of its safeguards on terrorism and trade. The diehards' complaint of insufficient time to consider the report met with little sympathy when the House of Commons debated it on 1 November. According to Amery, Churchill's plea to this effect produced only mockery; and the 'House very nearly tittered at Winston's championship of the rights of Indian democracy'.[310] When the party's Central Council considered the report in the first week of December, the diehards' motion went down to a convincing defeat, 1102–390.[311] Among the former was Peter Agnew (1900–90), a member of the IDL and MP for Camborne; his decision influenced, it appears, by the prospect of being appointed parliamentary private secretary to the President of the Board of Trade, Walter Runciman.[312] Neville Chamberlain recorded that neither Baldwin nor his opponents acquitted themselves well in the debate, but that Croft was particularly poor, 'rhetorical & absurd with his "lonely white men"... he made a personal attack on Austen over the Irish Treaty which fairly opened his flank'.[313] When the House of Commons divided over the JSC report on 12 December 1934, it revealed that diehard support stood at seventy-five, and a humiliating sixty-two in the House of Lords.[314]

The front bench approached the imminent introduction of the India bill with confidence. Much was made of the inclusion of safeguards and the exclusion of any reference to India as a dominion. In a broadcast on 2 January 1935, Hoare called on the diehards to desist in pursuing their 'active opposition' in the Commons.[315] The IDL was never likely to heed such advice, but the embarrassment of calling off their campaign would not have been much worse than the desperation and disorder which marked its final stage. The diehards attempted to emphasize the measure's impracticality given opposition from significant sections of Indian opinion, but it was a potentially self-defeating tactic given that it could just as likely convince wavering backbenchers to support the bill in the knowledge that its provisions would not see the light of day.[316] More spectacularly, the IDL was humiliated by the sudden decision of Randolph Churchill to run against the official Conservative candidate selected to fight a by-election at Liverpool Wavertree. Lancashire should have been an asset to the diehard cause given anxiety there about Indian politicians securing control over tariffs and using this to further protect their domestic textile industry at Lancashire's expense.[317] But

Wavertree proved to be the latest in a series of unexpected setbacks for the diehards in the county. Lancashire had confounded their conviction that grass-roots pressure might be exerted on MPs, for although a majority of delegates to the National Union's Northwest Area Council defied their leaders by calling for safeguards on trade, only a dozen of its MPs were prepared to carry this through to opposing the bill.[318] Even amongst this minority, few were prepared to engage with the diehards' wider critique of the reforms, and several distanced themselves from the IDL following Winston Churchill's attempt to expose Hoare's clandestine dealings with the Manchester Chamber of Commerce.[319] Against this backdrop, it is hardly surprising that Randolph Churchill's candidacy at Wavertree attracted the visible support of only one local MP, Reginald Purbrick (1877–1950); a stance which earned the Australian-born diehard the rebuke of his Walton constituency association.[320] Nor did the IDL relish Churchill's unannounced candidacy, and it quickly exposed marked divisions in their ranks, from the enthusiastic endorsements and combative rhetoric of Lords Carson and Lloyd on the one hand, to the resignation of two IDL parliamentarians – A.W. Goodman (1880–1937), MP for North Islington, and William Craven-Ellis (1880–1959), MP for Southampton – from the organization on the other.[321] Locally, the preparedness of constituency associations to support MPs opposed to the India bill did not extend automatically to endorsing Churchill at Wavertree.[322] And it quickly became clear that his hope of triggering a wider movement in the party, or a revival in the diehards' case against the India bill, could not be fulfilled. Not only did Churchill's candidacy split the Conservative vote and hand victory to Labour, but his reasonably good showing at the poll reflected a campaign which of necessity focused on local concerns about Westminster's neglect of Liverpool's industrial decline.[323] Undiminished, Churchill lingered on in Merseyside, harassing local party chiefs until Lord Derby intervened to secure him the candidacy in West Toxteth.[324] Further afield, and encouraged by Lady Houston, Churchill became involved in another by-election, this time at Norwood, in support of an extreme right-wing candidate and against the official Conservative and sometime IDL member, Duncan Sandys (1908–1987).[325]

Shortly after Wavertree, on 11 February 1935, the House of Commons witnessed its first major division on the India bill. Diehard support increased slightly to eighty-four Conservative MPs, one of the party's largest recorded rebellions against a three-line whip.[326] It was far from sufficient, however, if they intended to wound the government. Anticipation amongst them that the Chamber of Princes might render the whole process redundant was only partially met, as it merely signalled the expectation that the India Office accept its fundamental demands in return for support. The diehards attributed the unhelpful ambiguity of the chamber's pronouncement on the Government of India's ready use of bribery and coercion.[327] By April Gwynne despaired that in 'the House of Commons a steam-roller majority moves on ruthlessly and clause after clause is passed without amendment'.[328] Symbolic but empty gestures followed. On 1 May five MPs – Atholl, Frederick Astbury (1872–1954), Nall, Linton Thorp (1884–1950) and Alfred Todd (1890–1970) – complained to Baldwin about the government's 'socialist' tendency on India and domestic issues; when no satisfactory reassurance was forthcoming all resigned the 'National Government whip'.[329] A fortnight later, Hoare confidently sent Wolmer a breakdown of the government's timetable for dealing with the remaining clauses, asking him to pass on the details to 'your friends'.[330] In the final House of Commons division, on 5 June, diehard numbers were reduced slightly to seventy-nine.[331] The result led Wolmer to label Baldwin 'Peel II', but having succeeded MacDonald as prime minister in June, the Conservative leader presided over a party which remained united if battered.[332] Crucially, unlike Peel and his band of followers, the front bench was in the majority. Defeated in Parliament, the diehards afterwards declaimed their fight to be victorious when it became clear that the princely states and Congress rejected the resulting India Act.[333] The latter was hardly what the diehards expected or intended, though they had some responsibility for the outcome. Their campaign, after all, had from the outset helped to stimulate wavering MPs into demanding clarifications from ministers, impressing upon the latter the need for a slow and cautious attitude that did not overstep the limits set by their backbenchers.[334] If this dynamic ultimately served to undermine the diehards' critique, it encouraged disillusion in India with the National Government. As J.A. Spender observed shrewdly, the diehards 'played into the hands of the Nationalist Die-Hards of India who thought, or pretended to think, that it revealed the real intentions behind the false facade of the constitutional scheme'.[335] If the diehards presented this as a victory, Spender and others recognized that it did little to preserve the Raj in the face of the challenge posed by Congress. Sowing doubts among the princes about federation did little good either, for it helped to undermine their place in Indian society and eventual disappearance as a political order.[336]

VI

The diehards had a complex relationship with Britain's post-war democracy. Instinctively hostile to the electoral consequences of the 1918 Representation of the People Act, diehard rhetoric, communication and strategy nevertheless continued to draw on pre–1914 democratic forms of organization and agitation to check the authority of their own party leadership. This might have brought them close in practice and ideas to British fascist organizations and personnel in the 1920s, but the overwhelming majority of the diehards were demonstrably committed to their party and the democracy in which it operated. Wariness of the dead end offered by faction and the attendant risk of giving an advantage to Labour were important factors, as was Baldwin's instrumental role in ensuring that the 1924 general election established the Conservatives as the main party of resistance to socialism.[337] Consequently, the diehards struggled to articulate or even cohere on a number of important domestic questions, from women's franchise and the Church of England prayer book to the House of Lords.

This did not extend to imperial affairs. The inevitable tension between empire and liberty, which had once distinguished Conservatives from Liberals, gradually shifted Rightwards after the First World War to define a fault line *within* the Conservative party. The post-war diehards therefore cast themselves in the role of true believers, though it did not follow that theirs was the politics of straightforward reaction. They were prominent in the EIA and other initiatives to promote imperial preference, integrated into a wider campaign that boasted a social dimension which was not entirely at odds with Baldwin's one-nation conservatism, even if the diehards looked to imperial preference as a means of strengthening an empire which they saw undermined in other directions. The corollary was strong opposition to any constitutional, strategic or economic concessions to nationalists seeking self-government or independence. This went deeper than an obsession with maintaining Britain's global prestige and authority, important as these were in animating the diehards, for it fulfilled in the case of India the old Tory ideal of maintaining a hierarchical society which had long been besieged at home.

Approaching the diehards as integral to conservatism, playing a part alongside other internal and external influences, produces a complex picture of their influence on the party and Conservative or Conservative-led governments. It is demonstrated in their malign impact on British–Irish relations in the 1920s and early 1930s, and the consequential effect of this on the National Government's India policy. The 1935 Act's omission of the term 'dominion' and any reference to dominion status was symptomatic of ministers taking more heed of the diehards at home than opinion in India, satisfying neither but with far greater consequences for Britain's authority on the subcontinent.[338] Even when diehard influence was not the decisive factor in shifting policy, most notably in the development of the Ottawa trade agreements, the outcome seemed to vindicate years of diehard agitation and offer a sense of personal triumph in its realization.[339] As these examples underscore, the articulation of diehard politics was not so much an aberration from conservatism, or an example of latent fascism, but a product of their integral place and role in the party. Contrary to expectation, the diehards' zealous imperialism allowed right-wing Conservatives to work-off their frustrations within a specific context, ensuring that they did not expand their critique of society in the way that similar movements, lacking a foil, did on continental Europe. The diehards thereby provided a consistent strain of loyal opposition within a party with little effective internal accountability. Given that Conservatives relied on appealing to a relatively heterogeneous base of support across the country, it was a feature that, contrary to popular image, promoted Conservative unity during a period when Britain came to terms with full democracy, and which contributed also to the party's remarkable electoral success between the wars.

Consensus and Disunity, 1935–40

I

Foreign policy assumed a central place in British politics following the Conservative party crisis over India.[1] It featured prominently in the general election held in November 1935, with Labour's manifesto accusing the National Government of bearing a 'terrible responsibility' for the worsening international situation, and, in particular, for 'wrecking' the prospect of international disarmament, restarting an arms race and failing to uphold the principle of collective security through the League of Nations.[2] It referred to the recent failure of the World Disarmament Conference, the Italian invasion of Abyssinia, and the claim by Adolf Hitler that Germany's air force had reached parity with the Royal Air Force (RAF). As might be expected, the diehards reacted to these events very differently. Yet they lacked the unity of purpose and coherence of previous campaigns on overseas affairs. In particular, there was no single 'diehard' position on the most important foreign policy question of the late 1930s: how to deal with Nazi Germany. Paul Addison, in his essay on Lord Rothermere and appeasement, represented this as the 'classic dilemma of the die-hard Right'; individuals could simultaneously admire 'Fascism as a bulwark against Bolshevism', but also fear 'that Hitler would undermine Britain's [global] position'.[3] The assumption that Rothermere was a diehard seems to be based on his support for several diehard causes, but he was never formally a Conservative or recognized as such by the party leadership and most MPs. His random support for specific diehard campaigns did not add up to him being a diehard, but was regarded as symptomatic of his reputation for erratic and unpredictable political affiliations, to David Lloyd George in the early 1920s, Oswald Mosley and his British Union of Fascists (BUF) a decade later, and the Hungarian government in the 1930s, the latter influencing his attitude to Germany.

Rather than the dilemma identified by Addison, the public statements of diehard MPs reveal a different predicament. Like most Conservatives, the diehards believed that Great Britain needed to rearm to more adequate levels and that Germany posed a direct threat. The problem arose from how to respond to these bare facts. For a sizeable minority, Britain could only preserve its great-power status by checking German aggrandizement in Europe. This drew on a strain of anti-Germanism which predated the First World War. It found expression immediately after that conflict in calls for the restoration of the Anglo–French alliance, and survived in attenuated form into the 1930s as German revanchism seemed increasingly likely.[4] A majority, however, went along with Neville Chamberlain's policy of appeasement, on the assumption that conflict with Germany, even if Britain emerged victorious, would weaken British power to the advantage of other rivals. This dilemma was hardly specific to the diehards, for it was the same quandary faced by all Conservatives and foreign policymakers.[5] But the division in diehard ranks is particularly noteworthy given that they were otherwise united in opposition to the 'international' turn in post-war diplomacy. In fact, this lay at the root of their contrasting positions over how to address the revisionist claims of Nazi Germany. Whereas a minority adopted a posture of opposition that differed little in sentiment from the 1910s, the majority drew the lesson that years of weak Conservative leadership and two Labour governments had left Britain unable and unwilling to fight.

As the 1935 rebellion on India doubled the size of those labelled 'diehards', it is useful when examining diehard attitudes to foreign policy in the late 1930s to distinguish between 'core diehards' and 'India diehards'. The former is based on the parliamentary division on India held on 3 December 1931, when diehard MPs made a futile attempt to exclude any scheme devised for India from the Statute of Westminster's definition of dominion status. The India diehards are those who opposed the 1935 bill. The analysis presented in this chapter relies on examining the voting behaviour of diehard MPs, as well as the speeches of those who identified themselves to, and were called by, the speaker of the House of Commons. As with other topics, most diehard MPs did not contribute to parliamentary debates. Lack of ability, confidence or inclination, or a preference for the more encouraging atmosphere of parliamentary committees, are all likely explanations.[6] These observations aside, it is noteworthy that both cohorts exhibit similar voting patterns in key parliamentary divisions on appeasement. The larger cohort of India diehards shrank by twenty-six MPs by the time of the 'Norway vote' in 1940, which toppled Chamberlain from the premiership; the smaller core diehard cohort was also reduced by a third after the 1935 general election. Amongst the India diehards, nine abstained on the 1938 Anglo–Italian Agreement; eleven abstained on Munich, fourteen abstained on Norway, and four voted against the government in that landmark division. Of the core diehards, two abstained on the Anglo–Italian Agreement, six abstained on Munich, the same figure abstained on Norway, and two voted against Chamberlain. The remainder in each cohort supported the government. In both cases, a quarter defied the government on Munich, and dissentients increased noticeably between the parliamentary divisions on Munich and Norway.

II

Diehard dismay with the liberal approach to imperialism adopted by the Conservative front bench had a counterpart in the latter's apparent connivance in post-war multilateralism as a substitute for bilateralism and great-power pacts. The League of Nations was especially reviled. Leopold Maxse described its foundation as a 'front-bench affair hurriedly adopted and recklessly advocated simply and solely to please President [Woodrow] Wilson'.[7] Looking back on the interwar period, Croft relayed how involvement in the League had led Britain to proceed:

> under a long spell of effete leadership, to go 'international' and our great country, which had been saved by the valour and patriotism of our people, was deliberately encouraged to rely for its safety upon a hotch-potch collection of small states embodied in what was never a world League of Nations but a League of some nations based not on defensive force but on pious resolutions which were endorsed by ceaseless chatter at many conferences.[8]

Not that scepticism about the League's purpose and effectiveness was confined to the diehards. Conservative statesmen, including Stanley Baldwin and Austen Chamberlain, were also prone to pay lip service to the League while continuing to rely on so-called old diplomacy.[9] The diehards, however, were not required to hide their true feelings behind diplomatic niceties, nor did they share the front bench's wariness of alienating liberal public opinion. Responding to Germany's withdrawal from the League of Nations in October 1933, three young diehard MPs, Patrick Donner, Alan Lennox-Boyd and Victor Raikes, signed a letter to *The Times* deprecating arguments that peace could only be secured through the League, and the accompanying notion that Germany's withdrawal meant that it had withdrawn from the councils of Europe. The letter pressed instead for a 'non-Genevan' four-power pact and took care to disavow appearing to support 'Nazi policies, internal or external'.[10]

The letter affirmed that the diehards were not immune to the reorientation of Conservative opinion about Germany which had gathered pace since 1918. It revealed something more profound, however, than sympathy for the plight of a former foe. In contrast to the pronounced militarism of the Edwardian Right, the diehards no longer clung on to a belief in the redemptive quality of waging war against a rival European power. The likely character of such a conflict, of course, had changed since 1914, so that it was impossible politically to equate the valour and sacrifice of a citizen soldier with the large number of civilian casualties expected to result from aerial bombing.[11] But the shift in opinion was bound up also with a fundamentally diehard reading of recent history. Whereas right-wing militarists before 1918 supposed that conflict with Germany would serve as a necessary corrective to Britain's internal problems, the majority of the diehards in the 1930s felt that these would be exacerbated by the very same. For the diehards, the course of domestic politics since the war had served to weaken Britain, internally and externally, and as such supplied no end of a lesson on the unintended consequences of global conflict. As Raikes informed a meeting of women Conservatives in his South East Essex constituency, 'To accept the doctrine of war every 20 years was so ghastly that one might just as well look forward to the end of civilisation.'[12] This did not mean that the diehards abandoned or repudiated their strong support for the Great War. Croft decried how the war literature of the late 1920s portrayed 'the spirit of British troops in such a libellous manner ... I could only come to the conclusion that the writers were all shell-shock cases'.[13] And Lord Selborne continued to be preoccupied well into the 1930s with the 'danger' of conscientious objectors. Yet it was clear that both men were out of step with prevailing public opinion. In the case of Selborne, his political and social standing required the Cabinet Secretary, Maurice Hankey, to politely rebuff the former First Lord of the Admiralty's suggestion of relocating 'conscies' to an 'island', as it was 'a delicate matter to raise formally' and likely be 'pooh-poohed'.[14]

There was, of course, the remarkable and peculiar case of Lord Robert Cecil. In many respects the epitome of traditionalist Conservatism, Cecil played a significant role in the establishment the League of Nations in 1918–19, and served in Baldwin's first and second cabinets as minister with responsibility for League of Nations affairs until his resignation over policy in 1927. Cecil's deepening commitment to the League and its ideals, and particularly his position as president from 1923 of the supportive pressure group, the League of Nations Union, placed him increasingly at odds with colleagues in government, let alone the Right of the Conservative party. It led eventually to his resignation from the government, and over a decade later, to him considering defection to the Labour party.[15] Cecil aside, the diehards could not understand or agree with the League's especial preoccupation with promoting disarmament. Even disarmament initiatives outside of the League were deprecated. In contrast to the broad support given by most of the diehards to the 1922 Washington Naval Treaty, they were considerably more hostile towards its successor, the 1930 London Naval Treaty. Lord Lymington was particularly blunt, describing the agreement as whittling 'down the needs for our defence to please the self-importance of America'.[16] Political opportunism was certainly a factor given that the 1930 treaty was the product of a Labour government. After all, the charge laid in Parliament by Lord Carson, one-time First Lord of the Admiralty, that it ended Britain's naval supremacy on the unreliable pretext of improving relations with the United States, could just as easily have been levelled at the 1922 Treaty.[17] But such criticism was hardly an isolated occurrence. The following year, Lord Lloyd took up the presidency of the Navy League (NL). In this role he became a high-profile advocate for its long-running campaign to raise awareness of the vulnerability of food imports in the event of war.[18] The NL was not alone in advocating rearmament. It was joined in the late 1930s by the Army League, which recalled the activities of the National Service League, albeit on a considerably smaller scale, and the Air League of the British Empire, founded in 1909, which experienced enhanced relevance as the 'peril' of aerial warfare became increasingly apparent. The diehards were inevitably drawn to these leagues, alongside other Conservatives, and even MPs from other parties. If this raised the spectre of a 'war party', it was compromised in several ways: isolationists and interventionists alike were attracted to the leagues, each league remained divided in purpose and marked by inter-service rivalry for scarce funding, and all singularly failed to attract significant levels of public support.[19]

Rather than pursing rearmament through extra-parliamentary vehicles, the diehards looked instead to harnessing the voluntary party. Against the backdrop of the World Disarmament Conference, the 1933 annual conference at Birmingham heard Lloyd present 'his Defence debate', as Neville Chamberlain recalled, 'and the Conference which was exceedingly jingo and anti-foreign cheered every sentence of a speech which was really a very vicious attack on the Government'.[20] Disagreement amongst ministers about the line to take at the disarmament conference meant that Lloyd's efforts on this occasion were not entirely in vain, not least by strengthening the hand of service ministers in resisting pressure to make significant concessions.[21] If the collapse of the disarmament conference the following year meant that this was never put to the test, then diehard anxiety about armaments remained unabated. The 'pacifist' interpretation of the Conservatives' defeat at the East Fulham by-election, held on 25 October 1933, gave the diehards grounds for concern, especially when endorsed by senior party figures.[22] Lloyd duly reappeared at the 1934 party conference and proposed the same motion carried at Birmingham. When Arthur Steel-Maitland responded by moving an amendment which drew attention to increased air estimates, Neville Chamberlain persuaded him to withdraw it in favour of one that acknowledged the government's willingness to take up the financial burdens of rearmament. Intended in part to highlight the absence that year of Winston Churchill, who had made this point at the previous annual conference, it succeeded in securing an overwhelming majority with only two dissentients.[23] As this suggests, Conservatives were wary of turning on one another over armaments in a manner similar to the party crisis over India, even if the latter found expression on the same occasions through resolutions specific to India. The reason for this, ironically, was the very cause of the government's public cautiousness on rearmament: the Labour party's constant attacks on its record of disarmament. These encouraged Conservatives of all shades to rally behind condemnations of Labour's irresponsible attitude to armaments, even if the defensive declarations of ministers contrasted with the bullish demands of the diehards.[24] The latter were easily provoked, something anti-war protestors sought to harness to their advantage. During a House of Commons debate on 24 October 1935, Croft and Raikes expressed deep frustration when Labour MPs turned a debate on the 'world crisis' to one on unemployment. It prompted protestors seated in the strangers' gallery to throw down leaflets into the chamber and shout: 'Never again. Those who speak for peace also prepare for war.'[25]

The diehards remained persistent in their demands and suspicious about government intentions even as the tide of opinion turned in favour of rearmament. Winston Churchill was the most prominent diehard voice on this particular issue.[26] His continued warnings about German air strength played an important part in changing public opinion, at least among Conservatives, but only after these appeared to be vindicated by Hitler's misleading claim in March 1935 that the Luftwaffe had reached parity with the RAF. Although the government revised upwards its defence estimates in response, the diehards were alarmed at the Air Ministry's apparent lack of urgency and ambition.[27] This absence of faith in their own party leadership, and conviction that years of neglect in defence spending had taken its toll, helps to account for the division in diehard ranks about how to respond to German expansionism in central and eastern Europe. John Gretton spoke for a significant minority in depicting Nazi

Germany as an existential threat to Britain and its empire. He regarded attempts to appease its government as the product of the same weakness and poor leadership which had presided over years of enervating disarmament. The political impossibility of advocating a preventative war, alongside his deep concerns about armaments, inhibited him from pushing this publicly to its logical conclusion. Croft, in contrast, argued that because Britain did not possess adequate armaments, it could not challenge the revision of Germany's eastern borders. The diehards were not the only well-defined body of Conservative MPs to be divided over the policy of appeasement. Mirroring them on the left of the party, younger, progressive war veterans also found their solidarity undermined by conflicting responses to a succession of foreign policy crises.[28] A crucial difference, however, was that the diehards remained united on imperial questions, even when these intruded on appeasement. If the 'restitution' of former colonies ever did offer a means of deflecting German expansionism outside of Europe, Gretton and Croft were at one in resolutely opposing any transfer of territories administered by Britain and the dominions, intimating that it would provoke a backlash in the party similar to that over India.

III

Diehard opposition to colonial restitution was not only consistent with their objection to any perceived diminution of Britain's global power and prestige, it reflected long-held strategic concerns about German access to African ports and the potential for its submarines to interfere with shipping.[29] Successive post-war German governments had expressed resentment at the loss of their colonies, and, encouraged by their settler lobby, Berlin continued to make demands for equal access to the League of Nations mandates in the face of resistance from the British and other colonial powers, as well as those dominions that received mandates. Hitler first raised the colonies with the British at his meeting in March 1935 with Sir John Simon. The Foreign Secretary's cool response on that occasion contrasted with the preparedness of other European governments to discuss the matter. Hitler's first public pronouncement on the colonies came in the wake of the remilitarization of the Rhineland, on 7 March 1936, and was reiterated months later in his Nuremburg speech of 9 September. As the Nazis moved towards demanding restitution as of right, the British government indicated that it could only consider the matter as part of a general settlement.[30] Not unexpectedly, the diehards objected from the outset to such demands.

In the wake of the 1935 India Act, the India Defence League (IDL) expanded its horizons and title to become the Empire and India Defence League, and several of its bulletins in the spring of 1936 made clear the League's opposition to the transfer of any colonies to Germany.[31] Gretton had high hopes for the League, particularly in maintaining 'the group of upwards of 70 Members who have acted together on the Indian question' ahead of the imminent general election:

> as a strong Conservative line is very badly needed on foreign policy to insure
> [sic] security and peace for the British Empire; to secure adequate National
> defences; to resist attempts for further disintegration of the Empire or to
> surrender British territories to foreign powers; to watch legislation in the British
> Parliament and to oppose administrative action of a definitely Socialist
> character.[32]

Contrary to his expectation, however, Conservative losses at the November 1935 general election were not on a sufficient scale to transform the diehard rump into anything that might wield direct influence over Baldwin. In any case, holding together Conservative opponents of the India Act was never going to be an easy task given that many had not previously counted themselves as active or committed diehards. When the opportunity arose to attack Baldwin's handling of the 1936 abdication crisis, not one of them rallied to Churchill's side, nor for that matter was the diehard cohort equated in public speculation with the alternative 'Cavalier' government he might lead.[33] Only Esmond Harmsworth, now out of the House of Commons, appears to have been actively involved in the constitutional crisis and merely as an enthusiast for morganatic marriage.[34] At first glance, it is striking that the abdication failed to produce a 'diehard' response; yet even in the case of Churchill, his support for Edward VIII was largely motivated by personal regard for the king and his plight.[35] Moreover, in the long view, even the Ultra Tories did not equate devotion to the Crown with piety towards individual sovereigns and members of the royal family.[36] In their own lifetimes, the diehards looked on as the king's father, George V, acceded to a slew of unwelcome legislation and constitutional developments. Perhaps some even knew of or sensed his disdain for the malign effects of the 'retired die-hards from India'.[37] However, silence on the abdication is one thing; their inability to agree a common position on a major area of foreign policy is quite another. It was, indeed, unprecedented, and inevitably leaked into related matters such as the Spanish Civil War. The contrasting positions of Gretton and Croft on foreign policy also coloured their attitudes to the National Government. This was manifested in the former's complaint in 1936 about Conservative party funds being used for 'National' propaganda, part of 'an insidious and persistent attempt being made to water down the Conservative Party and to change its name'.[38] Croft in reply did not repudiate directly his colleague's concerns, but he urged instead that they should press for certain conditions on how the funds were spent, and pointedly warned against adopting the posture of a 'blank negative' which would 'achieve nothing'.[39]

Policy disagreements and the resulting tensions dashed Gretton's hope that the Empire and India Defence League might evolve into a diehard vehicle. Its financial difficulties worsened as a result, forcing its amalgamation in July 1936 with the Indian Empire Society.[40] The League's fate perhaps accounts for the wishful hope of Geoffrey Dawson, editor of *The Times*, that reactionary conservatism no longer existed.[41] In reality, the diehards simply eschewed the compromised League as the means of advancing their case on colonial restitution. Working instead alongside other Conservatives similarly opposed to the German demand, the diehards focused on despatching speakers to constituency associations, annual party caucuses and public meetings, and tabling early day motions in the House of Commons.[42] If the diehards participated in the 'Mandates Committee' formed in April 1936, it was more of a meeting place than an executive in the manner of the old leagues. Similarly, the committee's transformation two years later into a Colonial Defence Committee, or 'Colonial League', was largely a paper exercise; its greater efforts at coordinating with settlers in the mandates amounted to little in practice given that the government continually denied that there were any proposals for the surrender of the territories.[43] This was not the only potential problem faced by the anti-restitution campaign. It was not altogether certain, at least in spring 1936, that the party would rally to the cause of the mandates. Still reeling from the recent crisis over India, few wished to revisit the bitterness of those debates.[44] Moreover, if the diehards had failed to save the jewel in the crown, what hope had they in drumming up opposition to the restitution of recently acquired mandates such as Tanganyika and South-West Africa, the latter administered by South Africa?[45] Could the diehards even rely on their own number given that several had supported withdrawal from the mandate of Mesopotamia in the early 1920s, and only a handful in 1936 appeared to be exercised by the prospect of withdrawing British troops from Cairo?[46] The grass roots were not unresponsive, it must be said, but it was not on the scale of the revolt whipped up by the diehards over India.[47] The North-West Area Council, which had been galvanized into expressing its dissent on that issue, declined to take any position on colonial restitution.[48]

It follows that an exclusively diehard campaign on the mandates would probably have met with indifference and even hostility in some quarters. But significant weight to the cause was lent by Austen Chamberlain, and Churchill too remained at one with diehard MPs on this issue. Croft was only one of its three leading spokesmen, alongside Leopold Amery and Duncan Sandys; a triumvirate which was prominent also in the Chamberlain Centenary Committee. Founded in 1936 to commemorate Joseph Chamberlain's birth, its 'Empire Unity Campaign' supplied a useful foil to give renewed attention to imperial unity and accord a new place in his original vision to the importance of the mandates. The committee's invitation to the prime minister in 1938 to address a rally at London's Central Hall was therefore more than a mere gesture to Joe's son.[49] The prominence of the youthful Sandys in both the committee and the anti-restitution campaign is noteworthy given that he had only recently entered Parliament. His father, George Sandys, had been MP for Wells, during which time he was connected to Croft's Imperial Mission. Duncan Sandys had a brief career in diplomacy, including a posting to Berlin, before his own election in 1935 to the House of Commons. In between, he lacked a settled view on party political affiliation and dallied with fascist and corporatist ideas, joining the January Club and Anglo–German Fellowship. His short-lived 'British Movement', formed in 1934, in several respects replicated the outlook of the BUF, in particular, its combination of imperialism and concern for distressed areas.[50] He regarded it as an alternative to fascism; right-wing preoccupation with these topics was not unique to the BUF, given that they featured also in contrasting Conservative Right and Baldwinite discourses, and they were even historicized around this time by Conservative historians associated with the party's training college at Ashridge.[51] There was a bridge to cross, therefore, and Sandys soon moved on from his British Movement to throw his lot in with the Conservatives. Having been briefly associated with the IDL, he took the opportunity of his candidacy at the Norwood by-election to repudiate both it and its opposition to the India bill. He was further helped in this cause by facing an extreme right-wing candidate backed by Randolph Churchill. The by-election delivered other political developments too. Sandys came into contact with Churchill's sister, Diana, and their marriage soon after helped to ensure that Sandys abandoned his favourable disposition to German revisionism in eastern Europe by moving closer to the position articulated by his father-in-law.[52]

The campaign of opposition to colonial restitution was launched in the wake of a Commons debate held on 5 February 1936. It heard the former Labour leader, George Lansbury, argue for an international conference to arbitrate on opening access more equally to the mandates. He reasoned that this would lessen international tension by providing a fairer distribution of raw materials and destinations for emigration. In the same debate, David Lloyd George questioned the right of Britain to treat its mandates as if they were British territory, and argued that the government should reconsider its attitude for the sake of peace.[53] On 10 February, Sandys tabled an early day motion, signed by forty-seven other MPs, which opposed the transfer of any mandates.[54] Two days later, Croft challenged the Secretary of State for the Colonies, National Labour's J.H. Thomas, to give an assurance that the government 'had not considered, and was not considering, the handing over of any of the British Colonies, either under mandate or otherwise to a foreign power, and that they were not prepared to make British Colonies the subject of barter in any world conference'.[55] Satisfied with Thomas's response, Sandys subsequently withdrew the motion, though the episode failed to quell anxiety among British settlers in East Africa.[56] On 9 March, following the German reoccupation of the Rhineland, the British government secretly commissioned the second Earl of Plymouth to investigate the mandate question. His report considered it likely that the several thousand British settlers in Tanganyika would mount an armed resistance to the transfer of their territory to German authority, an unwelcome prospect which no doubt conjured memories of the pre-war Ulster crisis.[57] In any case, Plymouth concluded that it would be impractical and worthless to transfer mandates to Germany. But the secrecy surrounding the issue encouraged continued unrest amongst Conservatives. On 6 April, Sandys and Lennox-Boyd questioned the prime minister, Stanley Baldwin, about a recent speech given by a junior minister, which indicated that the government had become favourable to colonial restitution.[58] Baldwin flatly denied the suggestion. Weeks later, Herbert Williams (1884–1954), MP for Croydon, again raised the subject on the floor of the Commons with the prime minister. Baldwin patiently explained that the League covenant contained no provisions for the transfer of mandates from one power to another, that any such transfer would require the approval of the League Council, and repeated 'once more in the most categorical terms that we have not considered and are not considering the transfer of any mandated territories to any other Power'.[59]

Unconvinced, Amery afterwards chaired an ad hoc committee on mandates attended by Colonel Charles Ponsonby (1879–1976), MP for Sevenoaks; J.J. Stourton (1899–1992), MP for South Salford; Alfred Wise (1901–1974); John Grimston, MP for St Albans (1912–1973); Sir John Sandeman-Allen (1865–1935), MP for West Derby; Edward Grigg (1879–1955), MP for Altrincham;

Frederick Guest (1875–1937), MP for Plymouth; Charles Emmott (1898–1953), MP for Glasgow Springburn, and Herbert Williams, Sandys and Donner. Those in attendance agreed that whilst Baldwin's answer had been 'more satisfactory in tone than his previous replies, it was still not a sufficient assurance'. Resolving to continue to ask questions of the front bench, Foreign Office and Colonial Office, the committee also agreed that its membership would not be extended to 'Socialists and Liberals', 'though their co-operation would be sought'.[60] On 1 May the *Morning Post* published a letter from several MPs demanding an unequivocal pledge from the front bench, adding that it 'would be nothing less than a dereliction of duty for us to contemplate the transference of our obligations to a Power whose political, religious and racial standards do not conform with our own'.[61] A week later, Baldwin was again pressed, this time by a delegation from his party's Imperial Affairs Committee.[62] Austen Chamberlain took his brother to task on the issue, prompting Neville to confide to their sister, Ida, that it 'was really impossible to declare that in no circumstances and at no time would we ever consider the surrender of our mandate over any territory that we hold now ... it would have certainly caused embarrassment to some Govt in the future & would probably have had to be repudiated'. Revealingly, he concluded that he did not believe that 'we could purchase peace and a lasting settlement by handing over Tanganyika to the Germans, but if I did I would not hesitate for a moment to do so. It would be of no more value to them than it is to us'.[63]

At the Conservatives Central Council on 24 June, Croft moved, on behalf of his Bournemouth constituency association, a motion seconded by Sandys, which 'called upon the Government to resist any proposals which might tend to weaken the integrity of the Empire and urged that all possible steps should be taken to promote the lasting unity of all its component parts'. Croft went on to refer to 'dictators with expansionist tendencies', and 'war tyrants of the world ... out to grab territories'.[64] Further, he repudiated the suggestion 'in some quarters ... that we might placate Hitler by making sacrifices of mandated territories: as if the appetite of the tiger to-morrow will be appeased by throwing him chunks of meat to-day'.[65] But rather than condemn Hitler's demand, Croft instead attacked 'Socialist leaders' who proposed handing over the mandates to the League. Two speakers queried Britain's right to hold on to mandates indefinitely, but the mood of the meeting was clear when Croft's motion was passed 'by an overwhelming majority'.[66] On 3 July Croft signed a letter to the press, along with Amery, Sandys, and nine other MPs, demanding that their government follow the example of the dominion governments, by giving an assurance of their 'unwillingness to consider any such cession'.[67] On 16 July Baldwin was obliged to dampen concerns in the Commons. These were raised following an interview given by a visiting South African defence minister, in which he suggested that 'influential persons' in Britain were in favour of 'colonial compensation'. Baldwin denied that this referred to British ministers, but declined to 'amplify' his views on the subject despite interventions by Croft and Churchill.[68] On the same day, Baldwin received another delegation on the mandates; he informed them that the difficulties of returning colonies meant it was 'almost impossible'.[69]

After a meeting of the party's Foreign Affairs Committee, also on 16 July, Sandys indicated to Amery that he had drawn up a new 'memorial demanding a clear assurance on the mandated territories question'.[70] Tabled as an early day motion a week later, it secured 117 signatures, the first four of which were Sandys, Croft, Austen Chamberlain and Churchill.[71] Diehard names were conspicuous; only one of the India diehards, who later abstained on Munich, John Courtauld, did not add his name. The Foreign Secretary, Anthony Eden, responded with the government's position when he addressed the Commons on 27 July. Acknowledging that access to the mandates' raw materials might be open to discussion, he repeated previous ministerial statements about the 'grave difficulties, moral, political and legal, of which His Majesty's Government must frankly say that they have been unable to find any solution'.[72] Prior to Eden's statement, Neville Chamberlain, Lord Irwin, now the first Viscount Halifax, and Samuel Hoare, who all favoured territorial concessions, had insisted that it should 'convince Hitler that the door was open to future negotiations'.[73] Privately, the Foreign Secretary was disposed to considering South-West Africa for transfer.[74] These ministers appear to have believed that Hitler was genuinely concerned about Germany's former colonies, and assumed that their contact, Hjalmar Schacht, a veteran campaigner on the question, exercised greater influence over the Nazi government than was actually the case.[75] The minutes of 1922 Committee meeting held after Eden's statement reveal the resulting confusion and concern on the Conservative backbenches.[76]

In advance of the party conference of 1–3 October, Sandys and Croft maintained their pressure by giving notice of a motion. This sought assurance from the government that its position had not changed since Simon's March 1935 statement. A compromise amendment was also touted, described by Amery in his diary as 'feeble', and 'put forward at Government instigation'.[77] It stated that any decision on mandates rested with the League Council and the relevant mandatory powers, that the British government would not initiate this process, and that it would not take any action without full discussion in Parliament. At the party conference in Margate, Sandys proposed his motion and was seconded by Croft. Hoare, as First Lord of the Admiralty, replied on behalf of the government, claiming that its position had not changed, but indicating also that ministers could not elaborate further due to the 'present delicate international situation'. Hoare's conclusion, that the 'passing of the resolution ... could not make them any more cautious than they were already', was ignored by delegates, who on a show of hands defeated the amendment and carried Sandys and Croft's resolution 'by a large majority, amid cheers'.[78]

Government assurances aside, in February 1937, the British held secret conversations with the French on the possibility of Schacht's ideas on economic access to colonies as part of a peace deal.[79] The diehards and others remained suspicious about their government's intention, especially as Nazi speeches continued to mention colonial restitution.[80] In an early day motion dated 15 February, ninety-seven signatories – including Croft, Gretton and other diehards – pointedly noted 'with satisfaction the assurance given by His Majesty's Government that they are not considering the cession of any colonial or mandated territory'.[81] A week later, Croft addressed an empire unity meeting at Swindon, declaring that Germany could only re-enter Africa if it abandoned submarines, ended conscription, and reduced its air power by 75 per cent, 'to prove once and for all that she stands with the British Empire for a new world order of non-aggression'.[82] A meeting the following month, between Eden and Joachim von Ribbentrop, produced a shrill reaction in Germany to the British Foreign Secretary's public refusal to countenance the transfer of mandates.[83] Indeed, Nazi demands for restitution, as of right, effectively ended Franco–British hopes of colonial appeasement as part of a peace deal. Even Hitler let the issue rest, realizing that it might mean compromising on Austria and Czechoslovakia, although it continued to feature in his public speeches.[84] As prime minister from May 1937, Neville Chamberlain nevertheless remained open to the possibility of a deal on colonies if the Germans were forthcoming, though he looked to other governments to make the necessary sacrifices.[85] The United Kingdom's representatives duly informed the eighth Imperial Conference at London, on 2 June, that transferring British mandates would create a crisis which might bring down the government, a position which implicitly shifted the burden of responsibility to the dominion governments in possession of mandates.[86]

Chamberlain was not alone in remaining disposed to a peace deal which included the return of colonies.[87] Sections of Liberal and Labour opinion, prominent peers and clergymen, and the Anglo–German Fellowship, all promoted the scheme to varying degrees.[88] In the final three months of 1937, *The Times* carried letters on the subject in which proponents outnumbered opponents, and the latter mustered only Amery and Croft as significant advocates.[89] Not all of the former took as radical a position as the journalist and educationalist, Leonard Barnes, who argued that 'the impulses which drive Hitlerism … spring from the same economic and psychological sources as the impulses that drive the rulers of Britain to maintain dominance over 400 millions of Asiatics and Africans', and that 'Indian independence would be the answer, the only decisive answer, to Hitler's demand for the return of ex-German colonies'.[90] But Croft's responses to the policy's more considered advocates simply expressed his impatience and anger that the idea was being discussed at all.[91] He blamed sections of the press for encouraging German demands, repeated Jan Smuts's claim that returning Germany's former African colonies would give it submarine bases that would affect the security of all nations, and effectively revived what Germans labelled the 'colonial guilt lie', which the British government had abandoned in 1925.[92] Focusing on South-West Africa, Croft cited a report on the 'merciless destruction of the Hereros', whose population had decreased by more than two-thirds: 'It may be that the Nazi regime would be far more enlightened in its treatment of blacks – let us all hope so; but the most vital test of all is the safety of the British Empire in Africa and the ultimate peace of the world'.[93] These arguments reiterated those of interest groups representing the British settlers, as well as assumptions deeply held amongst Conservatives about the inherent paternalism and superiority of British imperialism.[94] Given the Nazis' admiration for the British empire, and in particular, its subjugation of indigenous peoples, such statements encouraged growing resentment among them about British hypocrisy.[95] It exposed also the inherent contradiction of Croft's attitude to Nazi Germany, for his vehement opposition to colonial restitution inevitably undermined the broader policy of appeasement which he supported.

In Croft's February address to Swindon Conservatives, he had claimed to speak for 'non-official Conservative opinion'.[96] By the time of his October letter to *The Times*, he confidently asserted that he spoke 'for the great mass of the British people as well as the unanimous National Union of Conservative Associations'.[97] This change of self-appointed status probably reflected the support he had received several weeks beforehand, at the party conference, alongside his frustration with the lack of allies making their views clear in the press. At that conference, on behalf of the Wessex Provincial Area, Croft moved, and Lennox-Boyd seconded, a motion which, in strong language, returned to the idea of associating the surrender of colonies with Labour and Liberal 'sentimentalist' intellectuals, and which bitterly condemned the idea as economically disastrous and a 'treacherous betrayal' of the settlers.[98] The party conference carried the motion 'without opposition'.[99] *The Times*'s Berlin correspondent subsequently reported that it 'naturally caused disappointment here and provoked some abusive comment in the Press', adding that it would lead to further demands for the return of German colonies.[100] Croft continued to be exercised by British supporters of restitution, even chiding Labour MPs in December 1937 for sending out the wrong signal to Germany by raising the subject in Parliament.[101] It is surprising therefore, that days later his party leader, Chamberlain, believed that he had slipped a 'complete new departure in Colonial Policy' past hearers in the Commons, 'namely that the French and we were prepared to discuss the question of colonies provided it were part of a general settlement'. To his delight, 'not a dog barks', though he acknowledged that there were further hurdles ahead.[102]

The prime minister's determination to purse this line followed Halifax's unofficial visit to Germany in November 1937.[103] Chamberlain relayed Halifax's findings to his sister: Hitler and Hermann Göring 'want Togoland & Kameruns. I am not quite sure where they stand about SW Africa, but they will not insist on Tanganyika if they can be given some reasonably equivalent territory on the W. coast possibly to be carved out of Belgian Congo and Angola'.[104] In January 1938, Chamberlain indicated his support for a new scheme, at a cabinet subcommittee on foreign affairs, which placed the burden of transfer on other colonial powers, especially Belgium and Portugal, with minimal territorial effect on British possessions: 'a new regime of colonial administration ... roughly corresponding to the conventional zone of the Congo Basin Treaties, acceptable and applicable to all the Powers concerned on exactly equal terms'.[105] This was communicated to Hitler by the British ambassador to Berlin on 3 March 1938.[106] As with Halifax's efforts months earlier, Hitler had no interest in this latest scheme, insisting instead on the simple return of colonies. In the weeks and months that followed, diplomatic attention moved decisively away from colonies to the *Anschluss* with Austria and the Sudeten crisis, developments which Chamberlain believed had 'made it quite impossible for us in present circumstances to continue talking over colonies'.[107] As a result, the colonial question largely disappeared, but rather than reassure Croft and others, the silence encouraged their anxiety. Having supported the Munich agreement, which did not deal with the colonies, Croft subsequently delivered a speech in his Bournemouth constituency which distinguished the annexation of the Sudetenland from colonial restitution:

Because Germany has succeeded by strong measures in embracing Germanic peoples under the rule of the Reich, this is no reason why we should contemplate paying her Danegeld or handing over territories which in her hands would prove a strategic menace to the British Empire and the peace of the world. On the contrary, the very principle which concedes that people of German race ... should be included, if they wish, in the Reich, must deny any such right to coerce native or European peoples in the colonies into the Germanic system against their wish.[108]

If Croft believed that he had delivered the definitive diehard position, then a discordant note was sounded days later, when Lord Selborne wrote to *The Times* claiming that colonies could only be discussed as part of a general settlement of all outstanding issues between Germany and 'the Commonwealth of British Nations'.[109] In a further contrast to the behaviour of his fellow diehards, Selborne shortly afterwards became involved prominently in church schemes to shelter Jewish child refugees from Germany.[110]

On 14 November, Churchill's close friend and fellow India diehard, Brendan Bracken, reopened the controversy by calling on the prime minister to end the 'discouragement to development and employment caused by uncertainty regarding the future Government of Tanganyika and other African mandates formerly under German rule'. Chamberlain's response to this, and other questions, was to refer to Baldwin's statements to the Commons in 1936. This encouraged further questions: on whether the prime minister was aware of 'Nazi propaganda' in Tanganyika, or a planned visit by a South African minister to Berlin, and asking if he had received representations from the colonies concerned.[111] Afterwards, at the 1922 Committee, the press reported that those who had supported Chamberlain's foreign policy, including Croft, were puzzled and disconcerted by the prime minister's statements on the mandates.[112] The minutes of the meeting indicate that the India diehard, Annesley Somerville, vice chairman of the committee, who had supported Chamberlain on Munich, was the first of eight to speak against the return of any colonies.[113] The result was another early day motion, containing twenty-nine signatures, mostly ordinary Conservative MPs, which stated that 'no British colony or mandated territory should be transferred to Germany without the consent of the people of Great Britain'.[114] The issue thereafter sank below the surface of political debate.[115] If Chamberlain remained disposed to considering it as part of a general settlement, he was continually surprised that the German government did not again make it an important demand.[116]

It is perhaps no coincidence that the disappearance of the controversy occurred around the same time as the organization of a private dinner between

ministers and former members of the IDL. Intended 'to heal the wounds within
the Conservative Party caused by the years of internecine warfare over India', it
resulted in an 'olive branch'; a request from Hoare, now Home Secretary, to
Donner, that the young diehard serve as his parliamentary private secretary.[117]
Donner's selection no doubt reflected his enthusiastic support for Chamberlain's
policy of appeasing Germany in Europe, but he still took counsel from Churchill,
Gretton and Lord Wolmer before accepting Hoare's offer. The honeymoon was
short-lived, for a number of the diehards – and in particular, Thomas Moore and
William Wayland – featured prominently in a chorus of back-bench objections
to a clause in Hoare's Criminal Justice bill which abolished the use of corporal
punishment.[118] The resulting delays to the bill's progress in the spring of 1939 led
ministers initially to concede a free vote on the clause, but its delay until after the
summer recess proved fatal given the outbreak of war in September.[119] Donner
later recalled that in communicating back-bench concerns to Hoare, the Home
Secretary rightly 'supposed that I agreed with the motion'. At the time, Donner
dismissed provocatively the need for his resignation on account of the
overwhelming opposition it aroused. Not surprisingly, this turned their
relationship 'glacial' through to the termination of Donner's appointment
following Britain's declaration of war on Germany.[120]

IV

The end of the party row over colonial restitution coincided with declining
enthusiasm for the broader policy of appeasement. Diehard divisions on the
latter had been slow to emerge as early attempts to present a coherent diehard
position were studiously ambiguous. The March 1936 bulletin of the Empire and
India Defence League, for example, cast 'the European situation' as the result of
'Franco-German difficulties', arguing that both countries had justifiable concerns
about the other, and that British statesmen should avoid 'an attitude either pro-
French or pro-German'. It claimed that a succession of international agreements
'have been honoured in the breach as well as in the observance', singling out
Britain's suspension of payments in settlement of the American debt accrued
during the First World War, and its controversial bilateral naval agreement
reached with Germany in 1935. The bulletin's editorial strayed onto more secure
ground with the well-worn conviction that Britain had been 'the only nation' to
implement 'practical measures of disarmament', before swiftly implying that this
had been somehow responsible for Europe's current tensions: 'Is not the most

important lesson for Great Britain to learn that a strong Britain is the surest means of maintaining the peace of Europe?'[121] As a base line of diehard opinion, the bulletin was reasonably sure-footed. But it was woefully inadequate as a means of maintaining the coherence of diehard opinion in response to the crises caused by Germany's successive breaches of the Versailles settlement. Rearmament and colonial restitution aside, the integrity of the diehard cohort, like that of other parliamentary groupings, would succumb to the shifting cross-party combinations which marked Parliament's handling of foreign policy in the late 1930s.

If the Italian invasion of Abyssinia in October 1935 led Croft, Churchill, Wolmer and others on the right, to ally calls for rearmament with support for the League of Nations, then Croft's espousal of the League was tepid and intended to signal his support for the government.[122] He inevitably broke with Churchill in the months and years that followed, especially as the latter's advocacy of the League intensified in the late 1930s, when the USSR enhanced its role on the League Council, bringing Churchill into contact with more progressive elements of his own party as well as MPs in other parties.[123] In the wake of the Munich agreement, Churchill wrote to Croft lamenting that it was 'difficult for me to believe that we can be so far apart' given their 'association in the long fight about India'.[124] Croft replied that Churchill's success in convincing him of Britain's 'hopeless disparity' in the air, alongside the need to build up the army, meant that he could not substitute the 'arbitrament of war' in place of the agreement reached at Munich.[125] Croft's poor regard for the League, like that of most diehard parliamentarians, meant that a majority of their calls for rearmament remained unallied to institutions or agreements which promoted multilateralism. Not that Churchill reaped any obvious benefit from the distance which now lay between him and Croft. Anthony Crossley, MP for Stretford, and one of the younger anti-appeasers on the left of the party, recorded that 'we did not wish to align ourselves with the Cabal who were notorious for plots against the Government'.[126] The resulting lack of clarity about the position adopted by the diehards is captured in David Low's 1937 cartoon, 'Foreign Policy Vaudeville Act', which places Croft alongside Amery and 'Colonel Blimp' as opponents of concessions to Germany.[127] Likewise, that searing indictment of appeasement, *Guilty Men*, produced by 'Cato' in the wake of the 1940 Dunkirk evacuation, lauds Churchill, Lloyd, Wolmer and Salisbury; other diehards are not mentioned, though presumably they suffered from what the authors describe as the 'miasma of acquiescence' which 'settled upon our parliamentary institutions and over a considerable section of the Press'.[128] From a different angle, the eclecticism of the anti-appeasement camp is treated to derision in Evelyn Waugh's paean to the aristocracy, *Brideshead Revisited*.[129]

Churchill might have been considered by some as a leading plotter and critic of appeasement, but Gretton had a greater claim to the appellation of 'diehard'. Two years before Chamberlain's policy of seeking bilateral agreements with Germany, the MP for Burton launched a scathing attack in the Commons on the 1935 Anglo–German Naval Agreement.

> It ties our hands, but it does not necessarily tie the hands of Germany ... Germany is governed by an autocracy and has all the elements of secrecy in the carrying out of her naval policy. What is to bind Germany to this Agreement? ... What Treaty or engagement has Germany kept since the War? Germany has become almost a professional treaty-breaker. Yet you have nothing but the word of the German Government to guarantee the fulfilment of this Agreement ... if you say, 'We believe the German Government has not kept its engagements, and we must have an increased programme,' you will immediately cause diplomatic repercussions.[130]

The Admiralty, Gretton argued, 'had been quite reckless' in allowing Germany a submarine fleet, 'which would give her a power in submarines far greater than anything possessed by other naval powers'.[131] Despite speaking frequently on the subject of armaments, Croft was conspicuously quiet in this debate. Labour MPs also criticized the agreement, from a different perspective to that of Gretton, though such concurrences of opposition encouraged him to believe, or claim to believe, that some in the Labour movement supported strong rearmament, and he expressed this in private to Chamberlain in January 1937.[132] Gretton's objection to the naval agreement was not the first occasion on which he voiced apprehension about the existential threat posed by Germany. A fortnight before, he claimed that a recent declaration by Eamon de Valera, that no foreign power could use Irish aerodromes, was made in response to statements emanating from Germany.[133] In his contribution, Croft declined to echo Gretton's concerns.[134] As noted in Chapter 4, Croft and Gretton's responses to the 1938 agreement between London and Dublin on the treaty ports differed markedly. The latter implicitly referenced its implications for mounting tensions in Europe, describing it as an 'indefensible bargain and arrangement ... As regards Defence, we are admittedly giving up everything, and there is nothing to be set on paper or even an assurance given to this House that we are getting anything in exchange'.[135]

The contrasting positions adopted by the diehards on relations with Spain and Italy were also connected to concern about Germany, in as much as neither side wanted to encourage alliances between Berlin, Madrid and Rome. Unlike British–Irish relations, however, these were differences of emphasis rather than outright disagreement. Whereas Croft was General Franco's 'noisiest supporter', Gretton chose not to endorse him.[136] In a House of Commons division on 25 June 1937, called by Labour to challenge the government's controversial approach to non-intervention, Croft backed the government. Gretton, in contrast, abstained, distinguishing himself from Labour by criticizing the League and demanding a policy of active neutrality on the part of the British government: 'We have not tried the orthodox, regular, clear policy of recognising both sides as belligerents and acting as a neutral Power ... We should then be able to play our part even in restraining supplies of munitions of war. Our policy would be clearly understood by every nation and every Government in the world.'[137] Like most British observers, Gretton understood that neutrality undermined Franco's opponents, but like his attitude to Europe more generally, he rationalized his stance in the language of British self-interest rather than support for another regime.

The division between Croft and Gretton on Italy was more subtle again. Only two of the 'core diehards', Churchill and Courtauld, opposed the 1938 Anglo-Italian Agreement, which acknowledged the conquest of Abyssinia, though they were joined by seven additional 'India diehards', including the Duchess of Atholl.[138] A supporter of the republicans in Spain, Atholl's opposition to the agreement, and appeasement generally, became so pronounced that it led her to resign the Conservative whip and even call a by-election at which she was defeated by the official Scottish Unionist candidate.[139] One of Gretton's criticisms of the Anglo–German Naval Agreement was that it undermined the Stresa Front, also signed in 1935, though in keeping with his focus on British self-interest, he failed to comment on Italian and French concerns.[140] Speaking in a Commons debate in the middle of the Abyssinian crisis, Gretton criticized both the opposition and government for basing their policies on the League, and claimed that the burden of responding to Italy would fall on the British and French navies.[141] Churchill's otherwise brief interventions are notable for his challenge to Croft's claim that the Italian conquest of Abyssinia was an established fact. The latter brushed this aside, saying that he could not sympathize with a country which allowed the killing of British subjects in Kenya and that practised the slave trade.[142] Croft supported the government during the crisis, and took this further than others by actively refuting widespread claims that the British public had bombarded their MPs with letters of protest.[143] Wolmer felt that 'if Mussolini gets away with it ... he has smashed the League of Nations, and that I should regard as a disaster – although I never believed it would stand any real strain ...

what chance has it of standing up against Hitler?'[144] For his part, Donner expressed frustration with the government for putting 'themselves into a position whereby [Oswald] Mosley's men can claim that they are the only Peace Party in the country', his response also to news that the BUF intended to put up a candidate against him at the general election.[145]

From the remilitarization of the Rhineland through to the Munich agreement, diehard MPs were preoccupied with opposing colonial restitution. With the exception of the debates outlined above, they did not publicly address developments in Germany. Throughout this period, few observers would have doubted the diehards' patriotism, but as war with Germany appeared increasingly likely towards the end of 1938, and the pressure to appease Germany in directions other than the colonies mounted, Croft and his supporters had to tread carefully in justifying agreements with Hitler.[146] Like the government, Croft felt obliged to denounce the brutality of the *Anschluss*, although he accompanied this, characteristically, with condemnation of Labour's support for disarmament.[147] The Commons had no extensive opportunity to discuss British–German relations until the start of October 1938, when, in a dramatic reversal, it debated the Munich Agreement over four days. Churchill, Croft and Raikes were the only diehards from the core cohort to speak. Churchill's contribution, on the third day of the debate, is well known. Croft's first contribution came on the first day, when his interruption of Duff Cooper's resignation speech expressed the irritation of many at the consequent delay to Chamberlain's statement.[148] Croft's more substantial contribution came on the third day, and immediately followed Churchill. He began by regretting that the two men should disagree, having worked together 'on so many causes'. Croft rejected the charge that Britain had 'suffered total and unmitigated defeat'. He broke also with Chamberlain by expressing regret at the pledge given to Czechoslovakia: 'I have always felt that we have burdens enough in our present commitments, and ought not to go meddling in the distant parts of Central Europe.' But his speech was essentially supportive of the prime minister's policy. Croft argued that there were now two schools of thought. The first says that 'We cannot have any conversations or intercourse, and certainly no agreement, with dictators; we differ from them, their form of government and their methods.' The second realizes 'that the dictatorial form of Government has now existed in a great many countries for many years'. He went on to justify the latter:

> there is no evidence of any great uprising of the people in those countries where they are subject to dictatorships, and, since you cannot wait for all this great range of countries to eliminate their firmly-established dictators, if the

machinery of civilisation is still to work you have got to understand their mentality, you have got to work with them, and, if possible, you have got to reach agreement ... or we have to fight them ultimately.

Croft believed that Germany was ready to invade the Sudetenland, and that Britain's inability to prevent this militarily meant that it had no alternative but to reach an agreement. Conscription would take half a year to implement properly, and a naval blockade would require a 'long time' to bring about the necessary conditions of 'starvation'. An air war, he reasoned, based on Churchill's figures for the British and German air forces, would not result in immediate victory. In response to an interruption, which suggested assistance from the USSR, Croft made the uncharacteristic admission that 'I am the last person to want in any way to criticise a country which might have come to our common aid at that time', before expressing his doubts that it could mobilize fast enough, and highlighting problems within the Soviet Union's armed forces.[149]

Raikes's speech, two days before Churchill and Croft, was the first from the Conservative back benches. He pre-empted Croft's argument by remarking that

Figure 11　Victor Raikes

'War might have been waged in revenge for Czechoslovakia's dismemberment, but Czechoslovakia knew well that the brunt of that war would tear their State to pieces before a single step could be taken to stop it.' He then brusquely dismissed concerns about the shortness of the time limit for Jews and Social Democrats to leave the Sudetenland, contending that they had 'known for weeks ... that they were in danger from a German occupation and that they would have been wiped out when that occupation took place'. Raikes placed blame upon the Czechoslovakian government, for annexing the Sudetenland before it was ratified by the Paris peace conferences, and for taking twenty years to grant rights to the Sudeten Germans. He compared criticisms of Chamberlain to those which greeted Benjamin Disraeli following the 1878 Treaty of Berlin, and concluded that 'our leader will go down to history as the greatest European statesman of this or any other time'.[150] Little wonder that Amery noted ruefully in his diary that Raikes had 'blessed' the government position.[151] It is noteworthy therefore that Raikes abstained or otherwise absented himself from one of the divisions called on 6 October on the Munich Agreement. As no explanation was offered, it is not clear if his consistent support for Chamberlain momentarily faltered.[152] He was certainly present for the division which voted against a Labour amendment. Whatever the explanation, Raikes joined Gretton and nine other 'India diehards' in abstaining on one of the crucial divisions in support of the government.[153] The diehard peer, Selborne, responded to the debate by pressing Halifax on Britain's commitments to what remained of the Czechoslovak state, and publicly expressed his support for a 'free conference' to settle all 'outstanding differences', including disarmament and the colonies.[154]

In the months that followed, Raikes returned to defending the government, against the criticism made by Churchill and others that it should enter into an alliance with the Soviet Union.[155] When the House of Commons debated the Czechoslovakian crisis of March 1939, Selborne's son, Lord Wolmer, was the only diehard called to address the Commons. The MP for Aldershot acknowledged that he was a critic of the government, and censured Chamberlain for his claim that 'he was not going to relax his efforts to preserve the peace of Europe ... Is it proper, legitimate, right and sensible to describe the state of Europe to-day as one of peace'. Wolmer supported Anthony Eden's calls for all parties to set aside their differences, but went further than the timid dissidence of the former Foreign Secretary by recommending the formation of 'a real National Government' committed to national service. Wolmer believed that this was the only message capable of being understood by a 'dictator state'.[156]

Figure 12   Viscount Wolmer

Croft responded to the crisis by writing to *The Times*, associating himself with calls by former service chiefs that the country should concentrate its 'main purpose on producing the maximum punching power against an aggressor'. He took the opportunity to blame the crisis on 'the whole psychology of political leadership of all parties during the last few years', and singled out Baldwin's famous claim in 1935 that there was no defence against air attack, accusing the former prime minister of playing the game of the enemy by preferring flight to fight.[157] On 31 March, *The Times* published another letter from Croft, condemning critics of Chamberlain, in particular Eden, for issuing calls for national unity whilst tabling a motion critical of the government. Chamberlain, Croft boasted, had brought about a 'miraculous change' in the 'defence and spirit of the people', when three years previously 'we were suffering from a poisonous attitude of pacifism and a yielding to a complete psychology of defeat'.[158] In the weeks that followed he announced that 'Hitler had broken faith with Great Britain ... and no nation was now safe unless a halt was called to violence'. He supported 'national service' as a result, and signalled also that he had been 'reluctantly converted to widening our obligation in partnership with any nation which would join us in resisting an attempt to dominate and dictate to the world'.[159] When Parliament was recalled after the summer recess in 1939, to hear the prime minister's announcement on 3 September that war had been declared on Germany, Croft was the only diehard to address the House. He declared that he spoke on behalf of the 'old Tories', and signalled his peace with Churchill, who had just been brought into the government as First Lord of the Admiralty. Briefly reflecting on a political career promoting imperial unity, Croft sidestepped recent divisions by expressing his pride that in the 'great Dominions overseas to-day hearts are pulsating for liberty and freedom in precisely the same way as in the old land'.[160]

Despite calls for unity between the parties, rifts in the Conservative party, and even in diehard ranks, widened and fractured again, exacerbated by the uncertainty and pessimism about war aims and strategy generated by the 'bore war', and the failure of Chamberlain to meet these by restructuring his cabinet. The chief whip, David Margesson, had considered offering Croft an office in the government as an undersecretary of state: the diehard's reply, expressing a preference for 'definite war work' and not 'Education, Health, Labour, Mines, etc.', brought that line of discussion to an end.[161] At the party Central Council on 4 April 1940, Sir Adam Maitland (1885–1949), an 'India diehard' and supporter of appeasement, proposed a measure calling for national unity that others regarded as an attempt to curb criticism of the government. Prominent critics of appeasement, Vyvyan Adams and Richard Law, ensured a less restrictive motion was passed instead.[162] That same day, the so-called Watching Committee held its first meeting. Established by Salisbury over the preceding months, as a body containing the necessary experience and responsibility to watch over the government's handling of the war, the committee contained several diehards, including Joseph Nall and Lord Wolmer in the House of Commons and FitzAlan and Lloyd in the House of Lords. It also included Lords Londonderry and Moyne, both associated briefly with Conservative Right groups in the 1910s and early 1920s respectively. Wolmer's suggestion that Salisbury invite also Croft and Admiral of the Fleet Sir Roger Keyes (1872–1945), MP for Portsmouth North and one of the India diehards, appears not to have been acted upon.[163] Its lack of specific policy goals meant that it was not quite the equivalent of the Unionist War Committee, which Salisbury had headed in 1918, nor for that matter the Conservative and Unionist Movement of 1922; it was, rather, as Londonderry observed, akin to the 'independent Peers' headed also by

Salisbury.[164] Yet the concerns of members soon found expression in a common belief that the cabinet had to be reconstructed, and, in due course, in the need for Chamberlain's resignation as prime minister.

The Watching Committee's critique of Chamberlain was merely one channel of wider dissatisfaction in Conservative ranks. This blew into the open following the debacle of the Norway expedition. During the famous two-day Norway debate of 7–8 May 1940, division amongst the diehards was again on show. Early on, Admiral Keyes condemned his government, comparing the withdrawal of the expeditionary force sent to Norway with the disastrous assault on Gallipoli during the First World War. As one of the few India diehards to stick with Churchill in the late 1930s, it is significant that he criticized naval policy in this manner.[165] It is often remarked that the scale of the Norway rebellion was 'inflated', yet the episode demonstrated plainly Chamberlain's inadequacy as a war leader just as it confirmed the indispensability of Churchill's 'fighting spirit'.[166] It was this profound shift in the mood of the party and Parliament, and not scheming by the Watching Committee or other groups of Chamberlain's critics, that sealed the prime minister's fate.[167] As a member of the government, Churchill was obviously not among the diehards who defied the party whips on the crucial vote of confidence held on 8 May. Another diehard, Courtauld, also ended his record of abstentions by supporting Chamberlain, without indicating why his position had changed since Munich. Of the core diehard cohorts, six abstained and two went further by voting against their government, Alfred Wise and Lord Wolmer.[168] In the larger cohort of India diehards, fourteen abstained and four voted against the government, the additional two being Admiral Keyes and Charles Taylor.[169]

The core diehard MP, Sir William Davison, who abstained on Munich and did so again on Norway, made a number of interruptions during the two-day debate, all directed at Labour speakers. But the only substantial diehard contribution came from Croft.[170] He defended the government at great length; indeed, Amery suggests that calling Croft to speak was intended to kill the debate.[171] The Bournemouth MP caused considerable controversy by blaming the present crisis on articles in the press, for encouraging 'despondency among our people because of some temporary setbacks', and criticized MPs for devoting too much of their energies to 'social problems' rather than fostering the 'offensive spirit' which was necessary to win the war.[172] These provocative remarks prompted several Labour MPs to leave the chamber.[173] Croft's speech went on, for some duration, to deal with the problems faced by the British army. In the wake of Chamberlain's resignation on 10 May, and his replacement with Churchill, Croft was rewarded for his service to both men by his appointment to the government post he had preferred months earlier: Under-Secretary of State for War. The new prime minister, it appears, simply ignored Croft's general support for appeasement. Churchill's memoirs certainly avoid any mention of this, preferring instead to cast Croft as an ally in the cause of rearmament.[174] Other diehard parliamentarians invited to join Churchill's government included Lord Lloyd, as Colonial Secretary, and junior appointments went to Bracken and Wolmer.[175] After years of marginalization under the leadership of Baldwin and Chamberlain, it is a striking irony that the need to include Labour in the National Government supplied the pretext which heralded the return of the diehards to ministerial office.

V

Preserving Britain's status as an imperial and global power were central preoccupations of the diehards. These defined and gave meaning to the diehard group in Parliament in a manner which seemed to be no longer possible on the great domestic questions tackled by Conservative and Conservative-led governments. The long campaign for tariffs and especially the campaign over Indian responsible government disposed the diehards to mobilize against any surrender or dilution of British authority in British or dominion-administered mandates. Along with their constant demands for rearmament, the diehards added to the peculiar difficulties that bedevilled the delicate and complex diplomatic calculations of British ministers when handling Nazi Germany. But unlike the 1910s, the Conservative Right did not rally around a bombastic and resolutely anti-German position. Some, of course, remained faithful to old prejudices. Gretton's attacks on the 1935 naval agreement recalled the hysteria of the pre-war naval race. Croft too was willing to resuscitate the idea of the characteristic barbarity of German colonialism if it aided his opposition to the 'return' of the mandates. And if the diehards' calls for rapid rearmament were reluctant to identify the likely enemy or enemies, perhaps out of concern for provoking unfavourable comparisons to the Edwardian Right, most understood, at least from 1933, that a revanchist Germany was top of the list. Old prejudices account also for why a majority of diehards supported Chamberlain's emphasis on active appeasement, for it was welcomed as a contrast to years of reactive appeasement under Baldwin, Simon and Hoare. His determination to seek bilateral deals or great-power pacts likewise signalled an end to the era of League of Nations diplomacy. Even if Chamberlain disliked the diehards, he hid it well and was not without appeal to them. Not only was he Joseph's son, but as Chancellor of the Exchequer in 1932, he took the decisive steps which brought to an end almost a century of free trade. He was also, importantly, not Baldwin, and appeared, at least on the surface, to lack his predecessor's overt hostility to the diehards. This was most apparent in his attitude to armaments. Chamberlain had not been prominent or committed in cabinet debates about Britain's position at the World Disarmament Conference, whilst his record at the Treasury, and subsequent reputation as prime minister, presented him as a proponent of rearmament.[176]

Chamberlain's supporters and detractors amongst the diehards were alike informed by similar long-standing assumptions and prejudices. The dilemma which split their ranks, between challenging Germany before it was too late, and a conviction that Britain lacked the means to do so, was predicated in a belief that Britain needed to accelerate rearmament, and that Germany posed a direct threat to British power. If a division on this scale was unprecedented, it underlined both the diehards' integration into the wider Conservative party as well as the instability of their parliamentary grouping. As a cohort, the diehards had since the early to mid–1920s come to see the benefit of remaining an integral element of the party. However misguided about the likely influence this might yield, they believed that on appeasement, as on other issues, they could contribute to the shape of Chamberlain's foreign policy. This appeared to be vindicated by the seeming refusal of ministers to acknowledge the likelihood of colonial restitution as well as its eventual abandonment by the British and German governments. Moreover, it was the diehards' very integration into the Conservative party that provided a safe space in which divisions could emerge amongst them about German revisionism in Europe. At the same time, the challenge posed by Nazi Germany struck at the very heart of the zealous imperialism which brought them together, revealing that diehard conservatism had not developed fully a political philosophy which was more than the sum of its parts.

Retrospect and Prospect

Reactionary conservatism has been a feature of Britain's parliamentary politics for several centuries. Fundamentally relational, in so far as it is bound up with and defined by the position adopted by moderate and pragmatic politicians on the Right, it is striking that this dynamic has nevertheless exhibited enduring preoccupations with nativism and xenophobia, the political and moral corruption of progressive politicians, great-power status, and the unreliability of their own party leaders. Throughout, these have often been expressed in doom-laden prognostications which reveal an inherent defensiveness and paranoia. If this suggests continuity then it is worth recalling Karl Mannheim's distinction between 'universal traditionalism', an instinctive aversion to change found in most societies, and 'conservatism', which, although tied to traditionalism, articulated an aspiration on the part of its proponents to locate themselves politically in the course of profound social, economic and political change.[1] His dichotomy is not simply another expression of the binary division outlined in the Introduction, between positional and doctrinaire conservatism, as it applies to both of these. Old Tories, Ultra Tories, ditchers and diehard Conservatives alike might have invoked the notion that they stood for Conservative principles, but the articulation of what this meant in practice was inevitably bound up with and changed over time by the dynamic processes unleashed by modernization.

The key elements of Ultra politics, its Protestant constitutionalism, patriotism, pastoralism, protectionism and philanthropy, changed considerably in meaning and varying intensity in the hands of later generations on the Conservative Right. Even something as specific as anti-Semitism, a seemingly abiding feature – in old Tory, Ultra, empire-first Unionist and diehard politics – underwent change, from being bound up with anti-Catholicism and anti-latitudinarianism in the eighteenth and early nineteenth centuries, to being associated with socialism and communism in the twentieth. This applies also to the hostility towards democracy which is a prominent characteristic of reactionary conservatism from its emergence, and which in certain forms has survived through to the present day. Whereas most Ultras were reluctant to utilize democratic forces against democracy, diehard MPs in the twentieth century relied almost completely on such tactics to make their influence felt in the Conservative party. Anglican exclusivism could not survive this transition, at least as the means of embodying and rallying elements committed to Conservative principles, and so from the last quarter of the nineteenth century the union and overseas empire increasingly stood in its stead. The defence of property remained a marked feature throughout, yet it too underwent significant change in response to the growth of democracy, from Ultra hostility to the bourgeoisie and its political pretensions, to actively working together with the middle class in opposition to 'socialism', even to the extent of cultivating local political alliances with ratepayers.

If anything, the substantive continuities between Ultra and diehard politics are overwhelmingly negative: the inability of both to offer a viable prospect or programme for government and, related to this, their lack of any suitable leader of national standing. The Ultras and the diehards alike were reluctant and unable to articulate a coherent and distinct political philosophy, viewing their roles as ultimately subordinate to the very same front bench they held in suspicion. What came closest to this, the spontaneous, aggressive right-wing journalism practised by the likes of Henry Bate Dudley in the early nineteenth century, and that of Leopold Maxse and Howell Gwynne a century later, was greeted with indifference by ministerial opinion and a measure of wariness by otherwise sympathetic parliamentarians. The Ultras and the diehards, therefore, were most identifiable by and visible in their acts of defiance, which tended to cluster around certain highly sensitive issues, such as anti-Catholicism in the case of the former, and for the latter, opposition to any measure deemed to weaken British imperial power and prestige.

The three distinct vectors of right-wing dissent within the Edwardian Unionist party, the empire-first Unionists, the legion of leagues, and the ditcher peers, were all attempts to articulate approaches to conservatism which could meet the challenge of resurgent radicalism at home and economic, imperial and military rivalry abroad. As Mannheim suggests, all were tied to traditionalism, even if it was more explicit and existential in the case of the ditcher peers. This seemingly pressing need to change certain modes of Conservative politics helps to explain the overlapping personnel and ideas of the three vectors. These still remained distinct, however, as they disagreed with one another on tactics and emphasis, even, for that matter, within their own ranks. Collectively, they were a product of and contributor to the Edwardian 'crisis of conservatism', but the differences between and amongst them ultimately weakened their particular remedies.

Yet, their capacity to whip up a party crisis was not without consequences. It contributed to the removal of a party leader, Arthur Balfour, the more aggressive political style of his successor, Andrew Bonar Law, and triggered the long overdue reform of the Unionist party machine.

Against expectation, the political upheaval wrought by the First World War did not bring about a more coherent and united Conservative Right. Crucial steps, nevertheless, were taken along that road – in particular, the spontaneous establishment of back-bench organization. This encouraged right-wing MPs to focus their activism in Parliament and in coordination with other backbenchers, rather than relying on applying pressure to ministers and MPs through external leagues and associations. Increasingly vocal and willing to challenge their party leader directly, and under the pretext of patriotic necessity, it had the effect of producing significant changes in wartime government, from the establishment of a coalition in 1915 to the restructuring of that coalition in favour of the Unionists the following year. These were not necessarily what the government's critics desired, but such changes were the result of the destabilizing effects of growing back-bench influence. The responsiveness of the front bench produced two contrasting reactions among right-wing discontents. For a majority, it demonstrated the utility of working within the Unionist parliamentary party. For a small minority, however, the restraining consequences of this signalled the need for a breakaway National Party more committed to Conservative principles, albeit in the guise of supposedly 'national' politics.

The split amongst right-wingers over political strategy gradually healed in the years immediately following the Armistice, spurred on by the continuance of the Unionist–Liberal coalition. The attendant risks of some sort of fusion between the two parties, and the accompanying loss of a distinctive Conservative identity, produced the increasingly coherent 'diehard' reaction within the Unionist party that was committed to avoiding this outcome, and which had a magnetic effect on erstwhile allies in the National Party. These diehards' efforts also struck a chord among Unionists in the voluntary party, creating alarm amongst the party leadership about what it could mean in practice if left unchecked. It was this which ultimately convinced important sections of the parliamentary party in 1922 to withdraw from the coalition and return to the pre-war party system. Pursuing this outcome went a long way to promoting a measure of unity on the Right, symbolized by the abandonment of the National Party. But it was also lent greater coherence and distinctiveness through a number of other questions. These included the right-wing's support for protectionism, particularly whole-hog food taxes, both for the sake of imperial unity and for the depressed home agricultural sector, pronounced hostility to government spending, and strident opposition to post-war imperial constitutional reform, which drew upon and now explicitly included the delicate question of Great Britain's relationship with the Irish Free State. Rather than churchly affairs and parliamentary reform, which still mattered to some high-profile diehards, the epithet became more readily identified by contemporaries with strong opposition to nationalist demands in Ireland and the empire.

Having achieved this measure of unity and sense of purpose, the diehards had an ambiguous relationship with interwar parliamentary democracy, deeply hostile to the rise of Labour but still willing and able to work within the constitutional bounds of Conservative party politics. The indigenous forms of fascism which emerged in the 1920s were attractive to some; these were, after all, ultra-Conservative rather than fascist on continental lines, but the overwhelming majority were convinced of the need to work within their own party. The resulting acquiescence with Stanley Baldwin's leadership was cultivated deliberately by the further development of back-bench organization. This to some extent satisfied the diehards' desire for an enhanced place in party policymaking, but it also exposed them to the limited appeal of their viewpoint on the back benches. As a result, most of the diehards toed the line on domestic reforms, however reluctantly, finding some satisfaction that Conservative policies were necessary and fundamentally Conservative in intention. As a result, it became clear that subjects that had once defined the Conservative Right no longer aroused the same level of concern and passion, including the sanctity of monarchy, the Protestant constitution, extending the franchise and defending the agricultural interest. In contrast, it was in Irish and imperial affairs, and to some extent also in economic matters, that the diehards felt able to demonstrate to the wider party that Conservative principles were under attack, from without and within. Rumblings about Irish policy in the early to mid–1920s hinted at what was to come a decade later over India, and throughout the diehards were prominent in the campaign for greater imperial unity through trade.

The spectacular series of party battles over India orchestrated by the diehards in the early 1930s proved to be the highpoint of their organizational capacity and common purpose. Thereafter, they remained united on most imperial questions, in particular, opposing the restitution of former German colonies, and were highly prominent in the rearmament campaign. However, the broader policy of appeasing the Nazi government divided diehard ranks. For a sizeable minority, Britain could only preserve its great-power status by opposing German aggrandizement in Europe. The majority, however, assumed that risking conflict with Germany, even if Britain could emerge victorious, would exacerbate its weakness at home and abroad. These contrasting positions were both grounded in peculiarly diehard readings of recent history. Opponents of appeasement regarded it as further evidence of Britain's decline, and a dangerous departure from the country's decades-old hostility to German territorial expansion. Supporters believed that appeasement was rendered necessary because of years of weak Conservative leadership and two Labour governments, the result of which left Britain unable and unwilling to fight.

The Second World War and the Conservatives' defeat at the 1945 general election brought to a close the first phase in the forging of the Conservative Right, by removing from the House of Commons the generation of diehard MPs which included Henry Page Croft and John Gretton. A small number of the younger generation survived, of course, and as the Conservatives recovered electorally in the 1950s, they were joined by others in Parliament, and the constituency associations once again became a reliable prop in right-wing campaigns against the front bench. Like the Edwardian inter-party conferences, the 1916–18 and 1918–22 coalitions, and the National Government, the post-1945 'political consensus' provided a context in which calls for a return to Conservative principles thrived. What this meant in practice reflected very contemporary concerns, just as it did for previous generations of Tories, Ultras, Unionists and Conservatives. Yet, as noted above, enduring themes remained, and in the case of anxiety about national and imperial decline, and the accompanying rhetoric on race, in an intensified form which left an indelible mark on late-modern British conservatism. Indeed, in the late 1960s and early 1970s the Conservative Right achieved an unprecedented measure of organizational unity and congruity, in the form of the Monday Club, only for it to decline just as rapidly after succumbing to infighting and public controversy over links with the extreme Right. Even so, its preoccupations with Britain's place in the world, non-white immigration, left-wing disorder, moral and economic decline, all of which long predated the Monday Club, also survived it, albeit below the surface for much of the 1970s and 1980s as the breakdown of the post-war consensus, and the accompanying ascendancy of the 'New Right', brought a qualified measure of satisfaction to the imperialist Conservative Right.[2] Thus incubated, these concerns resurfaced with vigour at the turn of the twenty-first century, encouraged by three successive general election defeats in a row, and expressed, very often, through strong resentment at the United Kingdom's continued membership of the European Union. It even led a sizeable

number of Conservatives to join the first electorally significant challenger party
on the right, the United Kingdom Independence Party. The 2016 referendum on
EU membership, called by the Conservative prime minister, David Cameron,
was meant to arrest this development. Against expectation, it brought about
what is arguably the Conservative Right's greatest triumph.

Notes

Introduction

1 Rodney Barker, *Political Ideas in Modern Britain: In and After the Twentieth Century* (2nd edition, London: Routledge, 1997), p. 7.

2 G.C. Webber, *The Ideology of the British Right, 1918–1939* (London: Croom Helm, 1986), p. 1.

3 For relationship between the latter two, and how 'conservatives' have an advantage over 'liberals', see, Jonathan Haidt, *The Righteous Mind: Why Good People Are Divided by Politics and Religion* (London: Allen Lane, 2012).

4 Michael Kinnear, *The Fall of Lloyd George: The Political Crisis of 1922* (London: Macmillan, 1973), pp. 79–82; Gillian Peele, 'Revolt over India', in Chris Cook and Gillian Peele (eds), *The Politics of Reappraisal, 1918–1939* (London: Macmillan, 1975), pp. 114–145; John Ramsden, *The Age of Balfour and Baldwin, 1902–1940* (London: Longman, 1978), *passim*; Stuart Ball, *Baldwin and the Conservative Party: The Crisis of 1929–1931* (London: Yale University Press, 1988), *passim*; David Dutton, *'His Majesty's Loyal Opposition': The Unionist Party in Opposition 1905–1915* (Liverpool: Liverpool University Press, 1992), pp. 98–103, 152–156; Alan Clark, *The Tories: Conservatives and the Nation State 1922–1997* (London: Weidenfeld and Nicolson, 1998), pp. 75–76; Graham Stewart, *Burying Caesar: Churchill, Chamberlain and the Battle for the Tory Party* (London: Weidenfeld and Nicolson, 1999) *passim*; Jeremy Smith, *The Tories and Ireland 1910–1914: Conservative Party Politics and the Home Rule Crisis* (Dublin: Irish Academic Press, 2000), *passim*; Nigel Keohane, *The Party of Patriotism: The Conservative Party and the First World War* (Aldershot: Ashgate, 2010), *passim*; Stuart Ball, *Portrait of a Party: The Conservative Party in Britain 1918–1945* (Oxford: Oxford University Press, 2013), pp. 342–348; N.C. Fleming, 'Diehard Conservatism, Mass Democracy, and Indian Constitutional Reform, c.1918–1935', *Parliamentary History*, 32, 2 (2013), pp. 337–360; N.C. Fleming, 'Diehard Conservatives and the Appeasement of Nazi Germany, 1935–1940', *History*, 100, 441 (2015), pp. 412–435.

5 Rodney Barker, *Politics, Peoples and Government: Themes in British Political Thought Since the Nineteenth Century* (Basingstoke: Palgrave Macmillan, 1994), pp. 24–25.

6 For a similar argument about Conservatism generally see, Harvey Glickman, 'The Toryness of English Conservatism', *Journal of British Studies*, 1 (1961), pp. 114–115.

7   For similar observation see, Andrew Gamble, 'Europe and America', in Ben Jackson
    and Robert Saunders (eds), *Making Thatcher's Britain* (Cambridge: Cambridge
    University Press, 2012), p. 229.

8   A notable exception, though it only hints at the author's politics, is the commentary
    of John Biggs-Davison, a leading figure in the Monday Club, formed in 1961, on the
    Halsbury Club, formed in 1911: 'Wyndham belonged to a farseeing minority ... The
    Halsbury Club was an excellent start for a ginger group', see, John Biggs-Davison,
    George Wyndham: A Study in Toryism (London: Hodder and Stoughton, 1951),
    p. 215.

9   Ian Colvin, *The Life of Lord Carson, Volume II* (London: Victor Gollancz, 1934), p. 39.

10 Selborne to Violet Milner, 25 April 1935, Bodleian Library, Oxford, Violet Milner
    Papers 26; Richard A. Gaunt, 'From Country Party to Conservative Party: The
    Ultra-Tories and Foreign Policy', in Jeremy Black (ed.), *The Tory World: Deep History
    and the Tory Theme in British Foreign Policy, 1679–2014* (Farnham: Ashgate, 2015),
    p. 165.

11 Bruce Coleman, *Conservatism and the Conservative Party in Nineteenth-Century
    Britain* (London: Edward Arnold, 1988), pp. 3–5.

12 D.R. Shackleton Bailey, *Cicero, Letters to Friends, Volume I: Letters 1–113*
    (Cambridge, MA: Harvard University Press, 2001), p. 145.

13 Maurice Cowling, *The Impact of Labour 1920–1924: The Beginning of Modern British
    Politics* (Cambridge: Cambridge University Press, 1971), p. 3.

14 Ball, *Portrait*, p. 79.

15 E.H.H. Green, *The Crisis of Conservatism: The Politics, Economics and Ideology of the
    British Conservative Party, 1880–1914* (reprinted edition, London, 1996), pp. 319–
    333. See also, Martin Blinkhorn, *Fascism and the Right in Europe, 1919–1945*
    (London: Routledge, 2000), pp. 8–15.

16 Robert Stewart, *The Foundation of the Conservative Party, 1830–1867* (London:
    Longman, 1978), pp. 103–104.

17 Ball, *Portrait*, pp. 71–72, 79–80.

18 Bill Schwarz, 'The Language of Constitutionalism: Baldwinite Conservatism', in
    Martin Langan and Bill Schwarz (eds), *Formations of Nation and People* (London:
    Hutchinson, 1984), pp. 1–18.

19 Ross McKibbin, *Parties and People: England 1914–1951* (Oxford: Oxford University
    Press, 2010), pp. 62–63, 195.

20 Brian Girvin, 'The Party in Comparative and International Context', in Anthony
    Seldon and Stuart Ball (eds), *Conservative Century: The Conservative Party Since
    1900* (Oxford: Oxford University Press, 1990), pp. 695–725.

21 Martin Blinkhorn (ed.), *Fascists and Conservatives: The Radical Right and the
    Establishment in Twentieth Century Europe* (London: Routledge, 1990), pp. 1–14.
    Similarly, Roger Griffin distinguishes the 'non-fascist radical right' and 'parafascists'

from fully fledged fascists. The non-fascist radical right were groups who, 'although undoubtedly anti-liberal and anti-communist, sought to fulfil goals which were insufficiently palingenetic or ultranationalist in their inspiration'. These include 'anti-communist right-wing movements of the interwar period which, although often associated with fascism, never committed themselves unequivocally to the overthrow of liberalism, and acted in practice as right wing pressure groups'. See, Roger Griffin, *The Nature of Fascism* (London: Routledge, 1993), pp. 117–118.

22 Brian Girvin, *The Right in the Twentieth Century: Conservatism and Democracy* (London: Pinter, 1994), pp. 3, 20, 48, 80.

23 Martin Daunton and Bernard Rieger, 'Introduction', in Martin Daunton and Bernard Rieger (eds), *Meanings of Modernity: Britain from the Late-Victorian Era to World War II* (Oxford: Berg, 2001), pp. 1–7.

24 Maurice Cowling, *The Impact of Hitler: British Politics and British Policy, 1933–1940* (Chicago: University of Chicago Press, 1977), pp. 84–87.

25 Ibid., pp. 45–46.

26 Cowling, *Labour*, pp. 84–87; John Darwin, 'Fear of Falling: British Politics and Imperial Decline Since 1800', *Transactions of the Royal Historical Society*, fifth series (1986), pp. 27–43; Andrew S. Thompson, *Imperial Britain: The Empire in British Politics, c.1880–1932* (London: Longman, 2000), pp. 163–164; Philip Williamson, *National Crisis and National Government: British Politics, the Economy and the Empire, 1926–1932* (Cambridge: Cambridge University Press, 1992), p. 124.

27 Bill Schwarz, 'Politics and Rhetoric in the Age of Mass Culture', *History Workshop Journal*, 46 (1998), pp. 131, 154.

28 Ball, *Baldwin*, p. 23.

29 Philip Norton and Arthur Aughey, *Conservatives and Conservatism* (London: Temple Smith, 1981), p. 258.

30 Green, *Crisis*, p. 23. For 'Radical Tories' see, C.P. Kowol, 'The Lost World of British Conservatism: The Radical Tory Tradition, 1939–1951', DPhil, University of Oxford (2013).

31 Alan Sykes, *The Radical Right in Britain: Social Imperialism to the BNP* (Basingstoke: Palgrave Macmillan, 2005), pp. 1–10.

32 Robert Blake, *The Conservative Party from Peel to Churchill* (London: Fontana, 1972), pp. 56–57, 71, 179, 194, 275.

33 Alan Sykes, 'The Radical Right and the Crisis of Conservatism Before the First World War', *Historical Journal*, 26, 3 (1983), p. 665.

34 Glickman, 'Toryness', pp. 111–143.

35 Coleman, *Conservatism*, p. 6.

36 Barker, *Politics*, p. 20.

37 T.F. Lindsay and Michael Harrington, *The Conservative Party, 1918–1970* (London: Macmillan, 1974), pp. 2–5.

38 Viscount Lymington, *Ich Dien: The Tory Path* (London: Constable, 1931), p. 117.

39 Lord Butler (ed.), *The Conservatives: A History from Their Origins to 1965* (London: George Allen and Unwin, 1977), p. 12.

40 Norton and Aughey, *Conservatives*, pp. 62–68.

41 Salisbury to the Earl of Selborne, 10 Aug. 1904, cited in Gregory D. Phillips, 'Lord Willoughby de Broke and the Politics of Radical Toryism, 1909–1914', *Journal of British Studies*, 20, 1 (1980), p. 206.

42 Earl Winterton, *Orders of the Day* (London: Cassell 1953), pp. 60, 80.

43 Blinkhorn, *Fascists*, p. 2 (original italics).

44 Coleman, *Conservatism*, pp. 200–201.

45 Gregory D. Phillips, *The Diehards: Aristocratic Society and Politics in Edwardian England* (Cambridge, MA: Harvard University Press, 1979), p. 156.

46 John Charmley, *A History of Conservative Politics Since 1830* (2nd edition, Basingstoke: Palgrave Macmillan, 2008), p. 121.

47 Anthony Trollope, *The Eustace Diamonds* ([1871–73] London: Folio Society, 1990), pp. 29–30.

48 Benjamin Disraeli, *Sybil, or the Two Nations* ([1845] Oxford: Oxford University Press, 1998), pp. 9–25.

49 James J. Sack, *From Jacobite to Conservative: Reaction and Orthodoxy in Britain, c.1760–1832* (Cambridge: Cambridge University Press, 1993), pp. 49–50.

50 Gaunt, 'Country', p. 160.

51 *The Times*, 14 July 1830, p. 3.

52 Stewart, *Foundation*, p. 104.

53 Gaunt, 'Country', p. 156.

54 Jeremy Black, 'Introduction', in Jeremy Black (ed.), *The Tory World: Deep History and the Tory Theme in British Foreign Policy, 1679–2014* (Farnham: Ashgate, 2015), pp. 3–4, 10.

55 D.G.S. Simes, 'A Long and Difficult Association: The Ultra Tories and "the Great Apostate"', *Wellington Studies*, 3 (1999), pp. 56–87.

56 Sack, *Jacobite*, pp. 11, 23–24.

57 Coleman, *Conservatism*, p. 22.

58 Sack, *Jacobite*, pp. 40–41.

59 Patrick McNally, *Parties, Patriots and Undertakers: Parliamentary Politics in Early Hanoverian Ireland* (Dublin: Four Courts Press, 1997), pp. 60–61.

60 Sections of the Ultra- and Orange-leaning press had been supportive of a measure of reform following the decline of radicalism in the 1810s, although it never became an issue of importance, see, Sack, *Jacobite*, pp. 95, 149–152.

61 Donald M. MacRaild, *Faith, Fraternity and Fighting: The Orange Order and Irish Migrants in Northern England, c.1850–1920* (Liverpool: Liverpool University Press, 2005).

62 Edwin Jaggard, 'Lord Falmouth and the Parallel Political Worlds of Ultra-Toryism, 1826–32', *Parliamentary History*, 33, 2 (2014), pp. 300–320.

63 Simes, 'Long', p. 74.

64 Arthur Balfour to Salisbury, 17 Sept. 1889, in Robin Harcourt Williams (ed.), *Salisbury–Balfour Correspondence: Letters Exchanged Between the Third Marquess of Salisbury and His Nephew, Arthur James Balfour 1869–1892* (Ware: Hertfordshire Record Society, 1988), pp. 293–294.

65 Norman Gash, *Aristocracy and People: Britain, 1815–1865* (Cambridge MA: Harvard University Press, 1979), pp. 175–176.

66 Stewart, *Foundation*, pp. 102–103.

67 Coleman, *Conservatism*, pp. 69, 107.

68 John Ramsden, *An Appetite for Power: A History of the Conservative Party Since 1830* (London: Harper Collins, 1999), p. 89.

69 I.G.C. Hutchison, *A Political History of Scotland 1832–1924: Parties, Elections, Issues* (Edinburgh: John Donald, 1986), p. 59.

70 Andrew Shields, *The Irish Conservative Party, 1852–1868: Land, Politics and Religion* (Dublin: Irish Academic Press, 2007), pp. 209–210.

71 Walter L. Arnstein, *Protestant Versus Catholic in Mid-Victorian England* (Columbia, MO: University of Missouri Press, 1982), p. 3.

72 H.J. Hanham, *Elections and Party Management: Politics in the Times of Disraeli and Gladstone* (Hassocks: Harvester Press, 1978), pp. 284–322.

73 Gathorne Hardy, diary, 16 and 18 July 1874, in Nancy E. Johnson (ed.), *The Diary of Gathorne Hardy, later Lord Cranbrook, 1866–1892: Political Selections* (Oxford: Clarendon Press, 1981), p. 214.

74 Coleman, *Conservatism*, pp. 137–138.

75 Alan Warren, 'Disraeli, the Conservatives and the National Church, 1837–1881', *Parliamentary History*, 19, 1 (2000), pp. 96–117.

76 Anthony Trollope, *Phineas Redux* ([1873–74] London: Folio Society, 1990), see Chapter 8 in particular.

77 Coleman, *Conservatism*, p. 144.

78 E.J. Feuchtwanger, *Disraeli, Democracy and the Tory Party: Conservative Leadership and Organization after the Second Reform Bill* (Oxford: Clarendon Press, 1968), pp. 99–101.

79 Matthew Roberts, 'Popular Conservatism in Britain, 1832–1914', *Parliamentary History*, 26, 3 (2007), p. 399.

80 Henry W. Lucy, *A Diary of the Unionist Parliament 1895–1900* (Bristol: J.W. Arrowsmith, 1901), p. 354.

81 See, Balfour to Salisbury, Jan. 1892, in Williams (ed.), *Salisbury–Balfour*, p. 388; Sir Edward Hamilton, diary, 2 April 1895, in David Brooks (ed.), *The Destruction of Lord Rosebery: From the Diary of Sir Edward Hamilton, 1894–1895* (Gloucester:

Historians' Press, 1986), p. 235; Viscount Wolmer [afterwards second Earl of Selborne] to Salisbury, 7 April 1895, in D. George Boyce (ed.), *The Crisis of British Unionism: Lord Selborne's Domestic Political Papers, 1885–1922* (London: Historians' Press, 1987), pp. 22–24.

82 Sanders, diary, 26 July 1910, in John Ramsden (ed.), *Real Old Tory Politics: The Political Diaries of Sir Robert Sanders, Lord Bayford 1910–1935* (London: Historians' Press, 1984), p. 22.

83 David Thackeray, 'Rethinking the Edwardian Crisis of Conservatism', *Historical Journal*, 54, 1 (2011), pp. 208–209.

84 Gaunt, 'Country', pp. 162–163.

85 Simes, 'Long', p. 67.

86 Cited in Eveline Cruickshanks, *Political Untouchables: The Tories and the '45* (London: Duckworth, 1979), pp. 47–48.

87 Black, 'Introduction', p. 14; Tony Claydon, 'Toryism and the World in the Later Stuart Era, 1679–1714', in Jeremy Black (ed.), *The Tory World: Deep History and the Tory Theme in British Foreign Policy, 1679–2014* (Farnham: Ashgate, 2015), p. 26; Nigel Aston, 'The Tories and France, 1714–60: Faith and Foreign Policy', in Jeremy Black (ed.), *The Tory World: Deep History and the Tory Theme in British Foreign Policy, 1679–2014* (Farnham: Ashgate, 2015), pp. 72–73. The Confederate, Thomas Comyn-Platt, had a poor opinion of the Stuarts in his survey of foreign policy, and correspondingly admired the 'Protestant' focus of Elizabeth I and Oliver Cromwell, see, Thomas Comyn-Platt, 'Foreign Policy', in the Earl of Malmesbury (ed.), *The New Order: Studies in Unionist Policy* (London: Francis Griffiths, 1908), p. 152.

88 Claydon, 'Toryism', p. 30.

89 Cited in Cruickshanks, *Untouchables*, pp. 47–48.

90 Frank O'Gorman, *British Conservatism: Conservative Thought from Burke to Thatcher* (London: Longman, 1986), p. 10.

91 For Burke's transformation into the founder of modern British conservatism see, Emily Jones, 'Conservatism, Edmund Burke and the Invention of a Political Tradition, c.1885–1914', *Historical Journal*, 58, 4 (2015), pp. 1115–1139.

92 Linda Colley, *Britons: Forging the Nation 1707–1837* (reprinted edition, London: Yale University Press, 2005), pp. 130–131.

93 Coleman, *Conservatism*, p. 35.

94 T.G. Otte, ' "We are Part of the Community of Europe": The Tories, Empire and Foreign Policy, 1874–1914', in Jeremy Black (ed.), *The Tory World: Deep History and the Tory Theme in British Foreign Policy, 1679–2014* (Farnham: Ashgate, 2015), p. 214.

95 C.C. Eldridge, *Disraeli and the Rise of a New Imperialism* (Cardiff: University of Wales Press, 1996), p. 7; Adrian Brettle, '1864: The Genesis of a New Conservative World?', in Jeremy Black (ed.), *The Tory World: Deep History and the Tory Theme in British Foreign Policy, 1679–2014* (Farnham: Ashgate, 2015), pp. 197–198.

96 Bernard Porter, *Empire Ways: Aspects of British Imperialism* (London: I.B.Tauris, 2016), p. 166.

97 Andrew Roberts, *Salisbury: Victorian Titan* (London: Weidenfeld and Nicolson, 1999), p. 349. On Peel as a lesson to subsequent leaders see, Donald Southgate, 'Introduction', in Donald Southgate (ed.), *The Conservative Leadership 1832–1932* (London: Macmillan, 1974), p. 14.

98 Catriona Burness, 'The Making of Scottish Unionism, 1886–1914', in Stuart Ball and Ian Holliday (eds), *Mass Conservatism: The Conservatives and the Public Since the 1880s* (Abingdon: Routledge, 2002), pp. 16–35.

99 Ian Cawood, *The Liberal Unionist Party: A History* (London: I.B.Tauris, 2012); Peter Fraser, 'The Liberal Unionist Alliance: Chamberlain, Hartington, and the Conservatives 1886–1904', *English Historical Review*, 77, 302 (1962), pp. 53–78; John France, 'Salisbury and the Unionist Alliance', in Lord Blake and Hugh Cecil (eds), *Salisbury: The Man and His Policies* (London: Palgrave Macmillan, 1987), pp. 219–251.

100 Lucy, *Diary*, pp. 236–237.

101 Robert Rhodes James, *Lord Randolph Churchill* (reprinted edition, London: Phoenix, 1994), pp. 281–283.

102 John Darwin, *After Tamerlane: The Rise and Fall of Global Empires, 1400–2000* (London: Allen Lane, 2007), p. 494.

103 Andrew S. Thompson, 'The Language of Imperialism and the Meanings of Empire: Imperial Discourse in British Politics, 1895–1914', *Journal of British Studies*, 36, 2 (1997), p. 148.

104 Richard Shannon, *The Age of Salisbury 1881–1902: Unionism and Empire* (London: Longman, 1996), p. 110; Roberts, *Salisbury*, pp. 666–667.

105 John Benyon, ' "Intermediate" Imperialism and the Test of Empire: Milner's "Excentric" High Commission in South Africa', in Donal Lowry (ed.), *The South African War Reappraised* (Manchester: Manchester University Press, 2000), pp. 84–103.

106 A.V. Dicey, *Lectures on the Relation between Law and Public Opinion in England during the Nineteenth Century* (London: Macmillan, 1905), pp. 454–455.

107 Michael Heffernan, 'The French Right and the Overseas Empire', in Nicholas Atkin and Frank Talbot (eds), *The Right in France, 1789–1997* (London: I.B.Tauris, 1998), pp. 89–113.

108 J.A. Froude, *Oceana, or England and Her Colonies* (London: Longmans, 1886).

109 Kennedy Jones, *Fleet Street and Downing Street* (London: Hutchinson, 1920), pp. 144–151; Colley, *Britons*.

110 Duncan Bell, 'Empire and International Relations in Victorian Political Thought', *Historical Journal*, 49, 1 (2006), pp. 284, 287.

111 Anne Summers, 'Militarism in Britain before the Great War', *History Workshop Journal*, 21 (1976), pp. 118–119; Thompson, *Imperial*, p. 22. For the Tariff Reform League's use of religious imagery see, Frans Coetzee, *For Party or Country:*

Nationalism and the Dilemmas of Popular Conservatism in Edwardian England (Oxford: Oxford University Press, 1990), pp. 97–98.

112 Coleman, *Conservatism*, p. 73.

113 Ibid., p. 76.

114 Anna Gambles, *Protection and Politics: Conservative Economic Discourse 1815–1852* (Woodbridge: Boydell and Brewer, 1999), pp. 205–206.

115 Angus Hawkins, *Parliament, Party and the Art of Politics in Britain, 1855–1859* (Stanford, CA: Stanford University Press, 1987), p. 123.

116 Roland Quinault, *British Prime Ministers and Democracy: From Disraeli to Blair* (London: Bloomsbury Academic, 2011), p. 24.

117 Robert Blake, *Disraeli* (New York: St Martin's Press, 1967), p. 516.

118 See Chapter 1.

119 Andrew Adonis, *Making Aristocracy Work: The Peerage and the Political System in Britain 1884–1914* (reprinted edition, Oxford: Clarendon Press, 2002), pp. 129–133.

120 Landed participation in the National Union was not insignificant, see, Phillips, *Diehards*, pp. 10–11.

121 One-fifth of Conservative MPs in 1820s had a 'colonial connection', see, Black, 'Introduction', p. 15.

122 Salisbury to Balfour, 31 Dec. 1892, in Williams (ed.), *Salisbury–Balfour*, p. 442; Cawood, *Liberal*, pp. 77–105.

123 Paul Readman, 'Conservatives and the Politics of Land: Lord Winchelsea's National Agricultural Union, 1893–1901', *English Historical Review*, 121, 490 (2006), pp. 25–69.

124 Martin Pugh, *The Tories and the People, 1880–1935* (Oxford: Blackwell, 1985), p. 24.

125 Adonis, *Making*, p. 113. See also, Corinne C. Weston, 'Salisbury and the Lords 1868–1895', *Historical Journal*, 25, 1 (1982), pp. 103–129; *The House of Lords and Ideological Politics: Lord Salisbury's Referendal Theory and the Conservative Party, 1846–1922* (Philadelphia, PA: American Philosophical Society, 1995).

126 Stephen Constantine, 'Amateur Gardening and Popular Recreation in the 19th and 20th Centuries', *Journal of Social History*, 14, 3 (1981), p. 392.

127 Sack, *Jacobite*, pp. 156–187.

128 Phillips, *Diehards*, pp. 58–60.

129 Paul Smith, *Disraeli: A Brief Life* (Cambridge: Cambridge University Press, 1996), p. 161; *Disraelian Conservatism and Social Reform* (London: Routledge and Keegan Paul, 1967), pp. 158–60.

130 Michael Bentley, *Lord Salisbury's World: Conservative Environments in Late Victorian Britain* (Cambridge: Cambridge University Press, 2001), p. 178.

131 Avner Offer, *Property and Politics 1870–1914: Landownership, Law, Ideology and Urban Development in England* (Cambridge: Cambridge University Press, 1981), pp. 297–301.

132 Green, *Crisis*, pp. 78–119.

133 Peter Marsh, *Joseph Chamberlain: Entrepreneur in Politics* (London: Yale University Press, 1994), p. 399. Londonderry was known for 'occasionally brighten[ing] proceedings by at least the promise of a revolt', and for saying things about the Liberal Unionists 'that sent a cheerful chuckle through the Carlton Club', see, Lucy, *Diary*, pp. 353–354.

134 Peter Cain, 'Empire and the Language of Character and Virtue in Later Victorian and Edwardian Britain', *Modern Intellectual History*, 4, 2 (2007), pp. 252–253.

135 Peter Marsh, *The Discipline of Popular Government: Lord Salisbury's Domestic Statecraft, 1881–1902* (Hassocks: Harvester Press, 1978), pp. 289–330.

Chapter 1   Edwardian crisis, 1900–14

1 Frans Coetzee, 'Faction and Failure: 1905–1910', in Stuart Ball and Anthony Seldon (eds), *Recovering Power: The Conservatives in Opposition Since 1867* (Basingstoke: Palgrave Macmillan, 2005), pp. 92–112.

2 This might be suggestive of the 'gentlemanly capitalists' thesis advanced by Professors Cain and Hopkins but the tariff reformers' critique of free trade and high finance places them outside this category. However, Cain and Hopkins note that the stark choices offered by the 1909 People's Budget led even City opinion to perceive the virtue of indirect taxes, see, Peter Cain and A.G. Hopkins, *British Imperialism: Crisis and Decolonisation, 1914–1990* (2nd edition, London: Longman, 2002), pp. 184–185, 646–647.

3 A.J. Mayer, 'Internal Crisis and War since 1870', in Charles L. Bertrand (ed.), *Revolutionary Situations in Europe, 1917–1922: Germany, Italy, Austria-Hungary* (Montreal: Centre interuniversitaire d'études européennes, 1977), pp. 206–211.

4 G.R. Searle, *The Quest for National Efficiency: A Study in British Politics and Political Thought, 1899–1914* (Oxford: Wiley Blackwell, 1971); 'Critics of Edwardian Society: The Case of the Radical Right', in Alan O'Day (ed.), *The Edwardian Age: Conflict and Stability 1900–1914* (London: Macmillan, 1979), pp. 79–96. Searle abandons the distinction in an essay which directly takes on the Mayer thesis, see, G.R. Searle, 'The "Revolt from the Right" in Edwardian Britain', in Paul Kennedy and Anthony Nicholls (eds), *Nationalist and Racialist Movements in Britain and Germany Before 1914* (London: Macmillan, 1981), pp. 21–39.

5 Searle, 'Critics', p. 82.

6 Ibid., pp. 84–85 (original emphasis).

7 A near identical schema is used in Brendan Evans and Andrew Taylor, *From Salisbury to Major: Continuity and Change in Conservative Politics* (Manchester: Manchester University Press, 1996), pp. 14–17.

8   Alan Sykes, 'The Radical Right and the Crisis of Conservatism Before the First World War', *Historical Journal*, 26, 3 (1983), pp. 674–675.

9   E.H.H. Green, *The Crisis of Conservatism: The Politics, Economics and Ideology of the British Conservative Party, 1880–1914* (reprinted edition, London: Routledge, 1996), pp. 23, 331; Peter Cain, 'The Conservative Party and "Radical Conservatism", 1880–1914: Incubus or Necessity?' *Twentieth Century British History*, 7, 3 (1996), p. 377.

10 Alan Sykes, *The Radical Right in Britain: Social Imperialism to the BNP* (Basingstoke: Palgrave Macmillan, 2005); Richard Thurlow, *Fascism in Britain: From Oswald Mosley's Blackshirts to the National Front* (London: I.B.Tauris, 1998), pp. 2–13.

11 Searle, 'Critics', pp. 83–96.

12 This is ironic given that Sykes was a prominent critic of the approach adopted by Searle in 'Crisis'.

13 Sykes, *Radical*, pp. 2–33.

14 Earl Winterton, *Pre-War* (London: Macmillan, 1932), p. 211.

15 Lord Willoughby de Broke, 'The Tory Tradition', *National Review*, 57 (1911), p. 211. See also his 'National Toryism', *National Review*, 58 (1912), pp. 420–421; 'The Restoration of the Constitution', *National Review*, 58 (1912), p. 866.

16 Richard A. Soloway, *Demography and Degeneration: Eugenics and the Declining Birth Rate in Twentieth Century Britain* (Chapel Hill, NC: University of North Carolina Press, 1995), pp. xxiv, 35; Mark Mazower, *Dark Continent: Europe's Twentieth Century* (London: Allen Lane, 1998), p. 92–97.

17 Alex Windscheffel, *Popular Conservatism in Imperial London 1868–1906* (Woodbridge: Boydell and Brewer, 2007), pp. 75–78.

18 James Belich, *Replenishing the Earth: The Settler Revolution and the Rise of the Anglo-World, 1783–1939* (Oxford: Oxford University Press, 2009), p. 153; Bill Schwarz, *Memories of Empire, Volume I: The White Man's World* (Oxford: Oxford University Press, 2011), pp. 165–167.

19 Hugh Cunningham, 'The Conservative Party and Patriotism', in Robert Colls and Philip Dodd (eds), *Englishness: Politics and Culture 1880–1920* (London: Croom Helm, 1986), pp. 283–307.

20 Peter Cain, 'Empire and the Language of Character and Virtue in Later Victorian and Edwardian Britain', *Modern Intellectual History*, 4, 2 (2007), pp. 252–253.

21 Wolfgang Mock, 'The Function of "Race" in Imperialist Ideologies: The Example of Joseph Chamberlain', in Paul Kennedy and Anthony Nicholls (eds), *Nationalist and Racialist Movements in Britain and Germany Before 1914* (London: Macmillan, 1981), pp. 190–203.

22 *Navy League Journal*, 10, 10 (1905), p. 258.

23 *Bournemouth Observer and Chronicle*, 7 Dec. 1907, cited in Larry L. Witherell, *Rebel on the Right: Henry Page Croft and the Crisis of British Conservatism, 1903–1914* (London: Associated University Presses, 1997), p. 79.

24 Winterton, *Pre-War*, p. 13.

25 *House of Commons Debates*, 20 Feb. 1911, vol. 21, cols 1699–700W; 1 March 1911, vol. 22, cols 516–7W; 12 April 1911, vol. 24, cols 566–567; 28 April 1911, vol. 24, cols 2106–2185. Sir Robert Houston MP also expressed concern about aliens in advance of the 1911 bill, referring to 'wretched aliens from the Eastern part of Europe' mingling with 'British blood'. He was not an empire-first Unionist but his wife, Lady Houston, as his widow, financially supported the patriotic press in the 1920s, providing platforms for both diehard Conservatives as well as British fascists, see, *House of Commons Debates*, 9 Feb. 1911, vol. 21, col. 533. Rowland Hunt went on to become associated with the National League for Clean Government, established by G.K. Chesterton and Hilaire Belloc, and endorsed by Leopold Maxse, in the wake of the Marconi scandal, and complained about Jewish 'influence', see, Colin Holmes, *Anti-Semitism in British Society, 1876–1939* (reprinted edition, Abingdon: Routledge, 2016), p. 102.

26 Harry Defries, *Conservative Party Attitudes to Jews, 1900–1950* (London: Routledge, 2001), pp. 1–14.

27 Dilwyn Porter, ' "A Trusted Guide of the Investing Public": Harry Marks and the *Financial News* 1884–1916', *Business History*, 28, 1 (1986), pp. 1–17.

28 Wilfried Fest, 'Jingoism and Xenophobia in the Electioneering Strategies of British Ruling Elites Before 1914', in Paul Kennedy and Anthony Nicholls (eds), *Nationalist and Racialist Movements in Britain and Germany Before 1914* (London: Macmillan, 1981), pp. 171–189; J.A. Hobson, *Imperialism: A Study* (New York: James Pott, 1902); Bernard Porter, *Critics of Empire: British Radicals and the Imperial Challenge* (London: I.B.Tauris, 2008), p. 202.

29 Richard Soloway, 'Counting the Degenerates: The Statistics of Race Deterioration in Edwardian England', *Journal of Contemporary History*, 17, 1 (1982), pp. 137–164.

30 David Glover, *Literature, Immigration, and Diaspora in Fin-de-Siècle England: A Cultural History of the 1905 Aliens Act* (Cambridge: Cambridge University Press, 2012), pp. 1–14.

31 See, White correspondence on eugenics, 1912–14, National Maritime Museum, Greenwich, Arnold White Papers [hereafter WHI/] 55; Arnold White, *The Views of 'Vanoc': An Englishman's Outlook* (London: Keegan Paul, Trench, Trübner, 1910), pp. 273–306; Daniel Gorman, *Imperial Citizenship: Empire and the Question of Belonging* (Manchester: Manchester University Press, 2006), pp. 115–140.

32 See, correspondence between White and Lionel Yexley, 1902–03, WHI/202.

33 Arnold White, *Society, Smart Society, and Bad Smart Society: Their Influence on Empire, Being Seven Letters Written to the Editor of the 'Daily Chronicle'* (London: Daily Chronicle, 1900).

34 See, correspondence between White and Rothschild, 9–21 May 1902, WHI/166.

35 White, *Views*, pp. 82–86.

36 *Star*, 24 Aug. 1921; 'Mr Arnold White not Anti-Semitic!', *Jewish Chronicle*, 2 Sept. 1921.

37 Panikos Panayi, 'Anti-Immigrant Riots in Nineteenth- and Twentieth-Century Britain', in Panikos Panayi (ed.), *Racial Violence in Britain, 1840–1950* (Leicester: Leicester University Press, 1993), pp. 1–25.

38 Gisela C. Lebzelter, 'Anti-Semitism: A Focal Point for the British Radical Right', in Paul Kennedy and Anthony Nicholls (eds), *Nationalist and Racialist Movements in Britain and Germany Before 1914* (London: Macmillan, 1981), pp. 88–105.

39 Belloc and Cecil Chesterton's *The Party System* (London: Stephen Swift, 1911) was published in the wake of the 1910 inter-party conferences. Its observations about front bench collaboration and the slowness of reform coincided with the attitudes of some Unionist MPs, but their distributionist politics, and a number of other positions, opposed the landed interest, highlighting the unconventionality of their particular right-wing politics.

40 John A. Hutcheson, *Leopold Maxse and the* National Review, *1893–1914* (New York: Garland, 1989); *National Review*, 33 (June 1899), pp. 31–37.

41 Jim English, 'Empire Day in Britain, 1904–1958', *Historical Journal*, 49, 1 (2006), pp. 247–276.

42 James Loughlin, *Ulster Unionism and British National Identity Since 1885* (London: Pinter, 1995), p. 67.

43 Dilwyn Porter, 'The Unionist Tariff Reformers, 1903–1914', PhD, University of Manchester (1976), p. iii; Alan Sykes, *Tariff Reform in British Politics 1903–1913* (Oxford: Clarendon Press, 1979), pp. 5–6.

44 Richard A. Rempel, *Unionists Divided: Arthur Balfour, Joseph Chamberlain and the Unionist Free Traders* (Newton Abbot: David and Charles, 1972), p. 181.

45 Anon., *Who's Who, 1933* (London: A. & C. Black, 1933); Michael Stenton and Stephen Lees (eds), *Who's Who of British Members of Parliament, Volume III, 1919–1845* (Hassocks: Harvester, 1979); Witherell, *Rebel*, appendix 1 and 2; Cameron Hazlehurst, Sally Whitehead and Christine Woodland (eds), *A Guide to the Papers of British Cabinet Ministers 1900–1964* (Cambridge: Cambridge University Press, 1996).

46 Maurice Cowling, *The Impact of Labour 1920–1924: The Beginning of Modern British Politics* (Cambridge: Cambridge University Press, 1971), p. 414.

47 E.H.H. Green, *Ideologies of Conservatism: Conservative Political Ideas in the Twentieth Century* (Oxford: Oxford University Press, 2002), pp. 74–75.

48 Marchioness of Londonderry, *Henry Chaplin: A Memoir* (London: Macmillan, 1926), p. 180. Chaplin was an early advocate of linking protectionism with old age pensions, see, Alfred M. Gollin, *Balfour's Burden: Arthur Balfour and Imperial Preference* (London: Anthony Blond, 1965), p. 45.

49 *The Times*, 11 Feb. 1909, p. 10.

50 For a detailed account of these campaigns see, Witherell, *Rebel*, Chapters 2–5.

51 A. Susan Williams, *Ladies of Influence: Women of the Elite in Interwar Britain* (London: Allen Lane, 2000), pp. 62–83.

52 Leo Maxse to Lady Edward Cecil [Violet Maxse], 17 August 1900, Bodleian Library, Oxford, Violet Milner Papers 19.

53 Hutcheson, *Maxse, passim.*

54 Gregory D. Phillips, *The Diehards: Aristocratic Society and Politics in Edwardian England* (Cambridge, MA: Harvard University Press, 1979), p. 134.

55 Willoughby de Broke, 'Toryism', p. 423; 'Tradition', pp. 201–213.

56 Lord Willoughby de Broke, *The Passing Years* (London: Constable, 1924), p. 255.

57 Gregory D. Phillips, 'Lord Willoughby de Broke and the Politics of Radical Toryism, 1909–1914', *Journal of British Studies*, 20, 1 (1980), p. 205; Roland Quinault, 'Portrait of a "Diehard": Greville Verney, nineteenth Lord Willoughby de Broke', in Robert Bearman (ed.), *Compton Verney: A History of the House and Its Owners* (Stratford-upon-Avon: Shakespeare Birthplace Trust, 2000), pp. 157–174.

58 Anon., *Who's Who, 1933*, p. 2145.

59 Alan Sykes, 'Goulding, Edward Alfred, Baron Wargrave (1862–1936)', *Oxford Dictionary of National Biography* (Oxford: Oxford University Press, 2004); online edition [accessed 29 Feb. 2016].

60 Alan Sykes, 'The Confederacy and the Purge of the Unionist Free Traders, 1906–1910', *Historical Journal*, 18, 2 (1975), pp. 349–366.

61 Croft described himself as 'one of Mr Chamberlain's purging brigade', see, Lord Croft, *My Life of Strife* (London: Hutchinson, 1948), p. 70; Chamberlain to Edward Goulding, 21 June 1909, Parliamentary Archive, Westminster, Lord Wargrave Papers [hereafter WAR] 2/29.

62 Winterton, *Pre-War*, p. 76. In a later volume of his memoirs, Winterton was more defensive about the Confederacy:

> I am convinced ... that it did good. We were no more rebellious or critical in general of the official hierarchy than the '22 or Conservative Committee [1922 Committee] has been on occasion in recent years; unlike the Conservative committee, ours was not representative of the whole party, but, like it, it provided a useful, vigorous and entirely confidential method of discussing and, if necessary, differing from official policy

See, Earl Winterton, *Orders of the Day* (London: Cassell 1953), p. 66.

63 Maxse to Croft, 7 Feb. 1908, Churchill Archives Centre, Cambridge, Croft Papers [hereafter CRFT] 1/16.

64 *The Times*, 12 Dec. 1903, p. 12; Bernard Holland, *The Life of Spencer Compton, Eighth Duke of Devonshire, Volume II* (London: Longmans, Green and Co., 1911), p. 379.

65 Devonshire to the fifth Earl Spencer, 2 Jan. 1904, in Peter Gordon (ed.), *The Red Earl: The Papers of the Fifth Earl Spencer 1835–1910, Volume II: 1885–1910* (Northampton: Northamptonshire Record Society, 1986), pp. 321–322.

66 Peter Marsh, *Joseph Chamberlain: Entrepreneur in Politics* (London: Yale University Press, 1994), p. 633.

67 Croft, *Life*, p. 43; L.S. Amery, *My Political Life, Volume I: England Before the Storm 1896–1914* (London: Hutchinson, 1953), pp. 273–274.

68 Leopold Amery, Sir George Elliot Armstrong, Viscount Duncannon, Sir Henry Ferryman Bowles, Alan Burgoyne, Commander Warren Frederick Caborne, Viscount Morpeth, George Courthope, John Ratcliffe Cousins, Henry Page Croft, Ronald McNeill, Viscount Hardinge, Frederick Leverton Harris, Earl of Harrowby, Claude Hay, 'Mr Herman', William A.S. Hewins, John W. Hills, Sir Charles Roderick Hunter, Sir Arthur Lee, George Ambrose Lloyd, Henry Lygon, the Earl of Malmesbury, Harry Marks, Leopold Maxse, Wilfred W. Ashley, Lord Oranmore and Brown, Sir Horatio Gilbert Parker, Sir Basil Peto, Sir Thomas Comyn-Platt, James Fitzalan Hope, Sir Hugh O'Neill, Sir James Remnant, Samuel Fforde Ridley, Sir John Rolleston, Sir Leslie Scott, Sir William Mitchell-Thomson, Geoffrey Skeffington Smyth, Sir Harold Smith, Edward George Spencer-Churchill, Sir Arthur Steel-Maitland, Vivian Stewart, Michael Temple, George Clement Tyron, Arnold Ward, Sir Fabian Ware, Edward Goulding, Henry Spenser Wilkinson, Sir Spencer Pocklington Maryon Maryon-Wilson, Lord Winterton and Bernhard Wise, see, Witherell, *Rebel*, pp. 214–220.

69 Ibid., pp. 66–67.

70 Sykes, *Tariff*, p. 125.

71 *The Times*, 2 Feb. 1907, p. 13.

72 Witherell, *Rebel*, p. 73.

73 *Daily Telegraph*, 21 Feb. 1907, cited in Witherell, *Rebel*, p. 74.

74 *The Times*, 26 March 1907, p. 10. See also, David Dutton, *Austen Chamberlain: Gentleman in Politics* (Bolton: Ross Anderson, 1985), pp. 60–61.

75 David Dutton, *'His Majesty's Loyal Opposition': The Unionist Party in Opposition 1905–1915* (Liverpool: Liverpool University Press, 1992), p. 56.

76 *House of Commons Debates*, 15 July 1907, vol. 178, cols 363–464.

77 *The Times*, 15 Nov. 1907, pp. 10, 11.

78 Rempel, *Unionists*, pp. 178–186, 228.

79 Earl of Malmesbury (ed.), *The New Order: Studies in Unionist Policy* (London: Francis Griffiths, 1908).

80 Sykes claims that Thomas Comyn-Platt was the real editor, see, Sykes, 'Confederacy', p. 355. Comyn-Platt also completed the final chapter of Willoughby de Broke's memoir, following the latter's death, *Passing*, p. xvi. James Fitzalan Hope, J.L. Garvin, W. Mitchell-Thomson, and W.A.S. Hewins appear as additional names on an earlier draft of contributors, see, Witherell, *Rebel*, p. 63.

81 Malmesbury, *New*, p. 4. For the *New Order*'s place in the development of Conservative thought see John D. Fair and John A. Hutcheson, 'British Conservatism in the Twentieth Century: An Emerging Ideological Tradition', *Albion*, 19, 4 (1987), pp. 549–578.

82 T.G. Otte, ' "We are Part of the Community of Europe": The Tories, Empire and Foreign Policy, 1874–1914', in Jeremy Black (ed.), *The Tory World: Deep History and the Tory Theme in British Foreign Policy, 1679–2014* (Farnham: Ashgate, 2015), p. 225.

83 Malmesbury, *New*, p. 129.

84 Ian Packer, 'The Conservatives and the Ideology of Landownership, 1910–1914', in Martin Francis and Ina Zweiniger-Bargielowska (eds), *The Conservatives and British Society, 1880–1990* (Cardiff: University of Wales Press, 1995), pp. 39–57.

85 Malmesbury, *New*, pp. 321, 331, 334. McNeill prefigures Friedrich Hayek's warnings about planning, though the two held contrasting attitudes to nineteenth-century liberalism, see, F.A. Hayek, *The Road to Serfdom: Text and Documents [The Collected Works of F.A. Hayek, Volume II, ed. Bruce Caldwell]* (London: University of Chicago Press, 2007), pp. 65–75.

86 See, Lord Crawford, diary, 29 June 1907, John Vincent (ed.), *The Crawford Papers: The Journals of David Lindsay Twenty-Seventh Earl of Crawford and Tenth Earl of Balcarres, 1871–1940, During the Years 1892 to 1940* (Manchester: Manchester University Press, 1984), p. 102.

87 David Thackeray, 'Rethinking the Edwardian Crisis of Conservatism', *Historical Journal*, 54, 1 (2011), p. 206.

88 Sykes, *Tariff*, p. 179.

89 *Daily Mail*, 19 Jan. 1909, cited in Witherell, *Rebel*, pp. 94–95.

90 *The Times*, 28 Jan. 1909, p. 10; 29 Jan. 1909, p. 10.

91 Frans Coetzee, *For Party or Country: Nationalism and the Dilemmas of Popular Conservatism in Edwardian England* (Oxford: Oxford University Press, 1990), pp. 101–106.

92 Neal Blewett, *The Peers, the Parties and the People: The General Elections of 1910* (London: Macmillan, 1972), pp. 106–107, 114–123.

93 Croft, *Life*, p. 50.

94 Lord Willoughby de Broke, 'The Coming Campaign', *National Review*, 56 (1910), p. 63.

95 Willoughby de Broke, *Passing*, p. 271.

96 Cited in Croft, *Life*, pp. 53–54.

97 *The Times*, 8 Oct. 1910, p. 10.

98 Gerald Arbuthnot MP, Sir Martin Archer-Shee MP, A.E. Beck, Sir Alfred Frederick Bird MP, R.D. Blumenfeld, William Orde-Powlett MP, afterwards fifth Baron Bolton, Henry Brackenbury MP, Sir William Bull MP, Sir Alan Burgoyne, Henry Page Croft MP, the ninth Earl of Denbigh, Edward Algernon Fitzroy MP, Philip Steveley Foster MP, James Galbraith, Richard Chaloner, afterwards first Baron Gisborough, Ralph

Glyn, Charles Sydney Goldman MP, Patrick Hannon, the third Viscount Hardinge, William Ormsby-Gore MP, afterwards fourth Baron Harlech, John W. Hills MP, Rowland Hunt MP, Louis Stanley Johnson, Henry Seymour King MP, John Hendley Kirkwood MP, the third Baron Leconfield, Oliver Locker-Lampson MP, the second Earl of Londesborough, Sir Halford John Mackinder MP, the fifth Earl of Malmesbury, Leopold Maxse, G.V.A. Monkton-Arundel, William Arthur Mount MP, John Norton-Griffiths MP, Basil Peto MP, John Rolleston MP, Edmund Royds MP, Edward Goulding MP, Vaughn Williams, Lord Willoughby de Broke, Leslie Orme Wilson, and Laming Worthington-Evans MP, see, Witherell, *Rebel*, pp. 221–225.

99 Maxse to Croft, 19 Oct. 1910; 22 Oct. 1910, CRFT 1/16.

100 *The Times*, 20 Oct. 1910, p. 7.

101 *The Times*, 10 Nov. 1910, p. 12.

102 Sykes, *Tariff Reform*, p. 228. Blumenfeld resigned from the Reveille following the publication of its manifesto, see, Witherell, *Rebel*, p. 138. Blumenfeld's membership of the Confederacy is not recounted in his published diaries, see, R.D. Blumenfeld, *R.D.B.'s Diary, 1887–1914* (London: Heinemann, 1930).

103 John D. Fair, *British Interparty Conferences: A Study of the Procedure of Conciliation in British Politics, 1867–1921* (Oxford: Clarendon Press, 1980), pp. 98–102.

104 *The Times*, 19 Oct. 1910, p. 10; 20 Oct. 1910, p. 7. For the Reveille's second manifesto, see, *The Times*, 22 Dec. 1910, p. 6.

105 *The Times*, 18 Nov. 1910, p. 8; 25 Nov. 1910, p. 15; Blewett, *Peers*, pp. 177–178.

106 *The Times*, 22 Dec. 1910, p. 6.

107 Witherell, *Rebel*, pp. 147–150; see, Andrew S. Thompson, *Imperial Britain: The Empire in British Politics, c.1880–1932* (London: Longman, 2000), pp. 133–156.

108 *The Times*, 10 Feb. 1911, p. 9.

109 *The Times*, 26 Oct. 1911, p. 7.

110 Witherell, *Rebel*, p. 168.

111 *House of Commons Debates*, 20 Feb. 1911, vol. 21, cols 1518–1522; 31 May 1911, vol. 26, cols 1111–1119.

112 Croft, *Life*, pp. 57–61.

113 Witherell, *Rebel*, p. 115.

114 Croft, *Life*, pp. 58–59. See, Michael Humphries, ' "The Eyes of an Empire": The Legion of Frontiersmen, 1904–14', *Historical Research*, 85, 227 (2012), pp. 133–158.

115 The parliamentary group initially consisted of Croft, Leopold Amery, Ion Hamilton Benn, Martin Archer-Shee, John Norton-Griffiths, Alan Burgoyne, Basil Peto, George Sandys, Arthur Shirley Benn and Ronald McNeill, see, *The Times*, 16 Nov. 1911, p. 7.

116 *Morning Post*, 18 October 1911, CRFT 3/2.

117 Not all peers on the grandly titled executive branch of the Imperial Mission's central council were diehard peers, for example, the Earl of Dundonald, Lord Tennyson and Lord Wolverton, see, Witherell, *Rebel*, p. 172.

118 Croft, *Life*, pp. 60–61; *The Times*, 20 Oct. 1911, p. 6.

119 Croft to Max Aitkin, 1 Dec. 1911, Parliamentary Archive, Westminster, Beaverbrook Papers, C/101.

120 Thompson, *Imperial*, pp. 42, 46.

121 R.J.Q. Adams, 'The National Service League and Mandatory Service in Edwardian Britain', *Armed Forces and Society*, 12, 1 (1985), p. 62.

122 N.C. Fleming, 'The Imperial Maritime League: British Navalism, Conflict and the Radical Right, *c.*1907–1920', *War in History*, 23, 3 (2016), p. 320.

123 Coetzee, *Party*, p. 7; Thompson, *Imperial*, pp. 38–41; Searle, 'Critics', pp. 85, 95.

124 Frank McDonough, *The Conservative Party and Anglo–German Relations, 1905–1914* (Basingstoke: Palgrave Macmillan, 2007), p. 113.

125 Lord George Hamilton, *Parliamentary Reminiscences and Reflections 1886–1906* (London: John Murray, 1922), pp. 324–326.

126 Matthew Johnson, *Militarism and the British Left, 1902–1914* (Basingstoke: Palgrave Macmillan, 2013).

127 Harold Frazer Wyatt and L. Graham H. Horton-Smith to press, 7 Jan. 1910, reprinted in Wyatt and Horton-Smith, *The Imperial Maritime League: The Secret of Its Success* (London: Imperial Maritime League, 1910), pp. 11–13; Henry Tero to editor, *Fleet* (March 1908), p. 78, reprinted in Harold Frazer Wyatt and L. Graham H. Horton-Smith, *The Passing of the Great Fleet* (London: Sampson Low, Marston, 1909), pp. 336–337.

128 A.J.A. Morris, *The Scaremongers: The Advocacy of War and Rearmament, 1896–1914* (London: Routledge and Keegan Paul, 1984).

129 Anne Summers, 'The Character of Edwardian Nationalism: Three Popular Leagues', in Paul Kennedy and Anthony Nicholls (eds), *Nationalist and Racialist Movements in Britain and Germany Before 1914* (London: Macmillan, 1981), pp. 68–87.

130 Frans and Marilyn S. Coetzee, 'Rethinking the Radical Right in Germany and Britain Before 1914', *Journal of Contemporary History*, 21, 4 (1986), pp. 515–537.

131 John Barnes, 'Ideology and Factions', in Anthony Seldon and Stuart Ball (eds), *Conservative Century: The Conservative Party Since 1900* (Oxford: Oxford University Press, 1990), pp. 339–340; Lord Willoughby de Broke, 'Toryism', p. 414.

132 D.A. Hamer, *The Politics of Electoral Pressure: A Study in the History of Victorian Reform Agitations* (Hassocks: Harvester Press, 1977), pp. viii–ix.

133 Rhodri Williams, *Defending the Empire: The Conservative Party and British Defence Policy 1899–1915* (London: Yale University Press, 1991), p. 150.

134 McDonough, *Conservative*, pp. 14, 83.

135 Despite his role as a founding member of the NSL, Seely's career demonstrates the difficulty of pigeonholing politicians into labels such as radical right or even Conservative Right. Seely resigned the Unionist whip and his seat in 1904 over the fiscal question and Chinese labour. Subsequently returned unopposed, he

afterwards took the Liberal whip and represented Liverpool Abercromby, 1906–10, and Ilkeston, 1910–18, serving also as a minister in the Liberal government until his resignation in 1914 as Secretary of State for War.

136 Anne Summers, 'Militarism in Britain Before the Great War', *History Workshop Journal*, 21 (1976), p. 116.

137 Ibid., pp. 120–121. The patriotic leagues, of course, took this a step further than church brigades by undertaking regular rifle and combat training, see National Maritime Museum, Greenwich, Imperial Maritime League: Junior Branch, Lionel Graham Horton Horton-Smith Papers 16.

138 Adams, 'National', pp. 53–74.

139 Matthew Hendley, ' "Help us to Secure a Strong, Healthy, Prosperous and Peaceful Britain": The Social Arguments of the Campaign for Compulsory Military Service in Britain, 1899–1914', *Canadian Journal of History*, 30, 2 (1995), pp. 261–288.

140 McDonough, *Conservative*, p. 81.

141 *House of Lords Debates*, 12 July 1909, vol. 2, cols 255–352; 13 July 1909, vol. 2, cols 356–470; Phillips, *Diehards*, p. 101.

142 *House of Lords Debates*, 12 March 1914, vol. 15, cols 461–499; 18 March 1914, vol. 15, cols 518–560; 19 March 1914, vol. 15, cols 562–608. See, Lord Willoughby de Broke, 'The Comfortable Classes and National Defence', *National Review*, 63 (1914), pp. 419–442.

143 Matthew Hendley, *Organized Patriotism and the Crucible of War: Popular Imperialism in Britain, 1914–1932* (Montreal and Kingston: McGill-Queen's University Press, 2012), pp. 12–13.

144 W. Mark Hamilton, 'The "New Navalism" and the British Navy League, 1895–1914', *Mariner's Mirror*, 64, 1 (1978), pp. 37–44.

145 A.J. Marder, *From the Dreadnought to Scapa Flow: The Royal Navy in the Fisher Era, 1904–1919, Volume I: The Road to War, 1904–1914* (London: Oxford University Press, 1961), p. 140.

146 Harold Frazer Wyatt, 'The Ethics of Empire', *Nineteenth Century* (April 1897), pp. 516–530; 'War as the Supreme Test of National Value', *Nineteenth Century* (Feb. 1899), pp. 216–225; 'The Army and the Empire', *Idler* (June 1900), pp. 55–62. Wyatt won a song competition on the theme of war, see, 'Peace and War', *Boy's Own Paper*, 26 Dec. 1885, p. 207.

147 Wyatt to editor, *Morning Post*, 3 Feb. 1898, p. 3; 1 Jan. 1900, p. 7.

148 MPs: Sir Arthur Bignold, W. Clive Bridgeman, Viscount Castlereagh, afterwards seventh Marquess of Londonderry, G.L. Courthope, Arthur du Cros, Walter Faber, H.C. Gooch, Claude G.D. Hay, Rowland Hunt, Sir Henry Kimber, G.R. Lane-Fox, Francis W. Lowe, James McCalmont, John Middlemore, William R.L. Peel, J.F.P. Rawlinson, Thomas Sloan, F.E. Smith, H.S. Staveley-Hill, Colonel W. Hall Walker, Earl Winterton, George Wyndham. Peers: Earl of Altamont, Lord Ampthill, Earl of

Denbigh, Lord Dunboyne, Earl of Dundonald, Lord Ebury, Viscount Hardinge, Lord Kesteven, Earl of Kinnoull, Earl of Kintore, Lord Leconfield, Earl of Lovelace, Earl of Malmesbury, Earl of Mar, Lord Mostyn, Lord Muskerry, Duke of Newcastle, Earl of Norbury, Marquess of Ormonde, Earl of Pembroke, Earl of Romney, Earl of Rosslyn, Earl of Seafield, Lord Sherborne, Viscount Sidmouth, Lord Sinclair, Marquess of Sligo, Duke of Sutherland, Lord Teynham, and the Marquess of Waterford. See, Wyatt and Horton-Smith, *Passing*, pp. 529–534.

149 According to Winterton, Hunt was known as 'Boadicea' and had once briefly lost the party whip for 'some alleged Party misdemeanour', see, Winterton, *Pre-War*, p. 59.

150 Before the First World War Burgoyne and Wyatt clashed swords on naval questions, see, 'The Anomalous Position and Curious Inconsistency of Mr Alan Burgoyne... Exposed by the Imperial Maritime League', 8 Jan. 1912, British Library, St Pancras, Imperial Maritime League: History: Volume IV, 1912; *Navy*, 17, 2 (1912), p. 43; 17, 5 (1912), p. 131.

151 Fleming, 'Imperial', p. 315.

152 L. Graham H. Horton-Smith, *Perils of the Sea: How We Kept the Flag Flying: A Short History of a Long Fight* (London: Imperial Maritime League, 1920), pp. 201a–x.

153 *The Times*, 22 June 1909, p. 12.

154 Harold Frazer Wyatt, 'The Navy and the Unionist Party', *Outlook*, 10 Aug. 1912.

155 See for example, J.A. Pease, diary, 23 March 1909, in Cameron Hazlehurst and Christine Woodland (ed.), *A Liberal Chronicle: Journals and Papers of J.A. Pease, 1908 to 1910* (London: Historians' Press, 1994), pp. 108–109.

156 Wyatt and Horton-Smith to editor, *Daily Express*, 7 May 1908, p. 4.

157 Wyatt to the editor, *Daily Express*, 8 Aug. 1908, p. 4. Notably, Wyatt and Horton-Smith looked to Oliver Cromwell, a figure more typically associated with Liberals, as the historical exemplar of patriotism, see, Harold Frazer Wyatt and L.G.H. Horton-Smith, *The True Truth About the Navy* (London: Imperial Maritime League, 1909), pp. 5–11.

158 Earl of Midleton, *Records and Reactions 1856–1939* (London: John Murray, 1939), pp. 270.

159 *The Times*, 16 Jan. 1906, p. 6.

160 Andrew Adonis, *Making Aristocracy Work: The Peerage and the Political System in Britain 1884–1914* (reprinted edition, Oxford: Clarendon Press, 2002), pp. 112–116.

161 Ibid., pp. 138–140.

162 *House of Commons Debates*, 24 June 1907, vol. 176, cols 925–926.

163 Willoughby de Broke, *Passing*, p. 245.

164 Phillips, *Diehards*, pp. 114–115.

165 *House of Lords Debates*, 31 July 1908, vol. 193 cols 1910–1939.

166 *The Times*, 25 Nov. 1908, p. 13. Milner was amongst the small number of dissentients, see, Lord Newton, *Lord Lansdowne: A Biography* (London: Macmillan, 1929), p. 370.

167 Adonis, *Making*, p. 27; Willoughby de Broke, *Passing*, p. 246.

168 Viscount Long of Wraxall, *Memories* (London: Hutchinson, 1923), p. 184.

169 *House of Lords Debates*, 30 Nov. 1909, vol. 4, cols 1233–1346.

170 Willoughby de Broke, *Passing*, p. 251.

171 Blewett, *Peers*, pp. 106–107.

172 Phillips, *Diehards*, pp. 127–129; *House of Lords Debates*, 22 March 1910, vol. 5, cols 459–494; *The Times*, 24 March 1910, p. 9.

173 Somerset to Halsbury, 8 May 1911, British Library, St Pancras, Halsbury Papers [hereafter Hals.], vol. 9, ff. 1–2.

174 *House of Lords Debates*, 15 May 1911, vol. 8, cols 369–434; 22 May 1911, vol. 8, cols 635–694. Willoughby de Broke afterwards became convinced that it was necessary to oppose the bill completely rather than tack on amendments, see, Willoughby de Broke to Halsbury, 11 June 1911, Hals., vol. 9, f. 9; Lord Willoughby de Broke, 'A Plea for an Unreformed House of Lords', *National Review*, 49 (1907), pp. 770–771; 'The House of Lords and After', *National Review*, 57 (1911), pp. 394–404; 'Restoration', p. 865.

175 Dicey cited in Balfour to Salisbury, 11 Nov. 1892, in Robin Harcourt Williams (ed.), *Salisbury–Balfour Correspondence: Letters Exchanged Between the Third Marquess of Salisbury and His Nephew, Arthur James Balfour 1869–1892* (Ware: Hertfordshire Record Society, 1988), p. 439. See exchange of letters between F.S. Oliver and Selborne in March 1911, in D. George Boyce (ed.), *The Crisis of British Unionism: Lord Selborne's Domestic Political Papers, 1885–1922* (London: Historians' Press, 1987), pp. 51–54; *House of Lords Debates*, 2 March 1911, vol. 7, cols 253–288.

176 Midleton, *Records*, 274. See, Selborne to Halsbury, 6 July 1911, Hals., vol. 9, f. 13.

177 Chris Ballinger, 'Hedging and Ditching: The Parliament Act 1911', *Parliamentary History*, 30, 1 (2011), pp. 19–32; Philip Norton, 'Resisting the Inevitable? The Parliament Act 1911', *Parliamentary History*, 31, 3 (2012), pp. 444–459.

178 Ronan Fanning, '"Rats" versus "Ditchers": The Die-hard Revolt and the Parliament Bill of 1911', in Art Cosgrove and J.I. Maguire (eds), *Parliament and Community: Historical Studies XIV* (Belfast: Appletree Press, 1983), p. 196.

179 Alfred M. Gollin, *The* Observer *and J.L. Garvin 1908–1914: A Study in a Great Editorship* (London: Oxford University Press, 1960), pp. 311–312; J. Lee Thompson, *Northcliffe: Press Baron in Politics, 1865–1922* (London: John Murray, 2000), pp. 201–203.

180 *National Review* (July 1911), pp. 732–733, cited in Witherell, *Rebel*, p. 155.

181 *Daily News*, 13 July 1911, cited in Witherell, *Rebel*, p. 156.

182 Sanders, diary, 18 July 1911, in John Ramsden (ed.), *Real Old Tory Politics: The Political Diaries of Sir Robert Sanders, Lord Bayford 1910–1935* (London: Historians' Press, 1984), p. 28.

183 'Meeting of Peers', 12 July 1911, Hals., vol. 9, f. 20.

184 *The Times*, 22 July 1911, p. 8.

185 Manifesto, 21 July 1911, Hals., vol. 9, ff. 25–26.

186 Balfour, memorandum, 22 July 1911, cited in Blanche E.C. Dugdale, *Arthur James Balfour, First Earl of Balfour, KG, OM, FRS, Volume II: 1906–1930* (London: Hutchinson, 1936), pp. 69–70.

187 Witherell, *Rebel*, p. 156.

188 *House of Commons Debates*, 24 July 1911, vol. 28, cols 1467–1484; Amery, diary, 24 July 1911, in John Barnes and David Nicholson (eds), *The Leo Amery Diaries, Volume I: 1896–1929* (London: Hutchinson, 1980), p. 80; Amery, *Life*, I, pp. 379–380. Lord Hugh Cecil once argued that tariff reform repelled 'inheritors of the ancient Conservative tradition'. His joining forces with Croft in the ditcher camp was therefore consistent with his politics. Cited in Gollin, *Balfour's*, p. 249; see also, Kevin Manton, 'Edwardian Conservatism and the Constitution: The Thought of Lord Hugh Cecil', *Parliamentary History*, 34, 3 (2015), pp. 365–382.

189 Sanders, diary, 16 July 1911; 24 July 1911, Ramsden, *Real*, pp. 30–31.

190 *The Times*, 27 July 1911, pp. 6, 7, 8, 9; George Wyndham to Wilfrid Ward, 30 July 1911, in J.W. Mackail and Guy Wyndham, *Life and Letters of George Wyndham, Volume II* (London: Hutchinson, 1925), p. 697.

191 For contrasting views see, David Cannadine, *The Decline and Fall of the British Aristocracy* (reprinted edition, London: Papermac, 1996), p. 517; Phillips, *Diehards*, pp. 1–12, 21, 25, 83.

192 Willoughby de Broke, *Passing*, pp. 283–285.

193 See letters of support to Lord Halsbury, Hals., vol. 9, ff. 68–73, 76–89, 98, 101, 105.

194 Amery, *Life*, I, p. 381.

195 Third Baron Templemore to Halsbury, 28 July 1911, Hals., vol. 9, ff. 49–50. Notably, the Irish peer and empire-first Unionist, Lord Oranmore, also indicated that he disagreed with the ditchers, Oranmore to Halsbury, 30 July 1911, Hals., vol. 9, ff. 58–59.

196 *House of Commons Debates*, 7 Aug. 1911, vol. 29, cols 795–921.

197 Willoughby de Broke, *Passing*, p. 286.

198 Maxse to Goulding, 19 Dec. 1910, WAR 2/75.

199 Willoughby de Broke, *Passing*, pp. 284–285.

200 David Southern, 'Lord Newton, the Conservative Peers and the Parliament Act of 1911', in Clyve Jones and David Lewis Jones (eds), *Peers, Politics and Power: The House of Lords, 1603–1911* (London: Hambledon Press, 1986), pp. 519–525.

201 Corinne Comstock Weston and Patricia Kelvin, 'The "Judas Group" and the Parliament Bill of 1911', in Clyve Jones and David Lewis Jones (eds), *Peers, Politics and Power: The House of Lords, 1603–1911* (London: Hambledon Press, 1986), pp. 533–534.

202 Carson to J.S. Sandars, 2 Aug. 1911, British Library, St Pancras, Balfour Papers, vol. 27, ff. 136–137.

203 Sixteenth Marquess of Winchester to Halsbury, 11 Aug. 1911, Hals., vol. 9, ff. 91–93.

204 Sandars to Balfour, 11 Aug. 1911, cited in Fanning, ' "Rats" ', p. 192.

205 Willoughby de Broke, *Passing*, p. 301. By way of contrast, Law, a Scot, attacked Asquith's difficulty over mobilizing the army on Ulster in 1913 by comparing the prime minister to James II; it flew in the face of Tory identity but complied with the historical worldview of Orangemen, see, R.J.Q. Adams, *Bonar Law* (London: John Murray, 1999), pp. 153–154.

206 Selborne to Wyndham, 22 Aug. 1911, in Boyce, *Crisis*, pp. 65–66.

207 See correspondence from Steel-Maitland to Halsbury, 11 Sept.–2 Oct. 1911, Hals., vol. 9, ff. 106–115.

208 Maxse to Croft, 18 October 1911, CRFT 1/16.

209 Memorandum, n.d., Hals., vol. 9, f. 129; Lord Willoughby de Broke, 'The Unionist Position', *National Review*, 62 (1913), pp. 212–224.

210 *The Times*, 13 Oct. 1911, p. 6.

211 The executive committee included Leopold Amery, Waldorf Astor, Edward Carson, Hugh Cecil, Robert Cecil, Austen Chamberlain, George Lloyd, Lord Lovat, Lord Milner, William Ormsby-Gore, E.G. Pretyman, F.E. Smith, Lord Willoughby de Broke, Lord Winterton and George Wyndham, see, Willoughby de Broke to Selborne, 7 November 1911 [copy of Halsbury Club minutes], Bodleian Library, Oxford, Second Earl of Selborne Papers [hereafter MS. Selborne] 75.

212 Crawford, diary, 22 Oct. 1911, Vincent, *Crawford*, p. 234.

213 Winterton, *Pre-War*, pp. 230–231; *The Times*, 9 Nov. 1911, p. 8.

214 Maurice V. Brett (ed.), *Journals and Letters of Reginald, Viscount Esher, Volume III: 1910–1915* (London: Nicholson and Watson, 1938), p. 30.

215 Sandars memo., 8 Nov. 1911, cited in Fanning, ' "Rats" ', pp. 200–201. See also, Amery, *Life, I*, p. 385.

216 Crawford, diary, 1 Oct. 1911, Vincent, *Crawford*, p. 226.

217 Crawford, diary, 30 Sept. 1911, ibid., p. 224.

218 Sanders, diary, 12 Nov. 1911, Ramsden, *Real*, pp. 34–35.

219 Adams, *Law*, pp. 64, 67, 71.

220 Law to Willoughby de Broke, 26 Jan. 1914, Parliamentary Archive, Westminster, Willoughby de Broke Papers [hereafter WB] 7/13.

221 Richard Murphy, 'Faction in the Conservative Party and the Home Rule Crisis, 1912–14', *History*, 71, 232 (1986), pp. 222–234.

222 Daniel Jackson, *Popular Opposition to Irish Home Rule in Britain* (Liverpool: Liverpool University Press, 2009), pp. 1–28.

223 Lord Willoughby de Broke, 'Unionist Position', p. 218. He extended this to all supposedly unpopular Unionist policies, see, Lord Willoughby de Broke, 'The Unionist Party and the General Election', *National Review*, 63 (1914), p. 784.

224 *The Times*, 27 March 1913, p. 8.

225 Timothy Bowman, *Carson's Army: The Ulster Volunteer Force, 1910–22* (Manchester: Manchester University Press, 2007), pp. 17–18.

226 Jeremy Smith, *The Tories and Ireland 1910–1914: Conservative Party Politics and the Home Rule Crisis* (Dublin: Irish Academic Press, 2000), pp. 136–137; Jackson, *Popular*, p. 232.

227 The figures are given by Long, see, Long, *Memories*, p. 203.

228 William S. Rodner, 'Leaguers, Covenanters, Moderates: British Support for Ulster, 1913–1914', *Éire-Ireland*, 17, 3 (1982), pp. 68–85.

229 Sanders, diary, 13 Feb., 19 March 1914, Ramsden, *Real*, pp. 72, 74.

230 Loughlin, *Ulster*, p. 68.

231 Willoughby de Broke to Halsbury, 5 July 1914, Hals., vol. 9, ff. 159–160.

232 F.S. Oliver to Milner, 3 March 1911, Bodleian Library, Oxford, Viscount Milner Papers, deposit 13.

233 John Kendle, *Ireland and the Federal Solution: The Debate over the United Kingdom Constitution, 1870–1921* (Kingston and Montreal: McGill-Queen's University Press, 1989), pp. 117–120, 169–174; Witherell, *Rebel*, pp. 204–205.

234 Thomas C. Kennedy, 'Troubled Tories: Dissent and Confusion Concerning the Party's Ulster Policy, 1910–1914', *Journal of British Studies*, 46, 3 (2007), pp. 570–593.

235 Ian Colvin, *The Life of Lord Carson, Volume II* (London: Victor Gollancz, 1934), p. 304.

236 Jeremy Smith, *Tories*, pp. 188–190; Lord Ampthill to Willoughby de Broke, 4 Jan. 1914, WB/7/1.

237 Henry W. Lucy, *The Balfourian Parliament 1900–1905* (London: Hodder and Stoughton, 1906), p. 362.

238 Alvin Jackson, *The Ulster Party: Irish Unionists in the House of Commons, 1884–1911* (Oxford: Oxford University Press, 1989), pp. 243–283; Wyndham to Philip Hanson, 19 Dec. 1907, in Mackail and Wyndham (eds), *Life*, pp. 594–596. Wyndham and Carson also found themselves on opposing sides over Oscar Wilde's failed libel case against the Marquess of Queensbury. As the defending barrister, Carson implicated Wilde in illegal acts, which encouraged Wyndham, a cousin of Lord Alfred Douglas, to urge Wilde to flee the country, see, Edward Marjoribanks, *The Life of Lord Carson, Volume I* (London: Victor Gollancz, 1932), p. 227.

239 Marjoribanks, *Carson*, pp. 352–355.

240 *The Times*, 30 Jan. 1909, 12. See also, Gaynor Johnson, *Lord Robert Cecil: Politician and Internationalist* (Farnham: Ashgate, 2013), p. 35.

241 Colvin, *Carson*, pp. 171–185.

242 G.R. Searle, *Corruption in British Politics, 1895–1930* (Oxford: Clarendon Press, 1987), p. 190. See also, Bryan Cheyette, 'Racism and Revision: Hilaire Belloc and the "Marconi Scandal" 1900–1914: A Reassessment of the Interactionist Model of Racial Hatred', in Tony Kushner and Kenneth Lunn (eds), *The Politics of*

Marginality: Race, the Radical Right and Minorities in Twentieth Century Britain (London: Routledge, 1990), pp. 131–142. One organ which made much of the scandal, the *Outlook*, was owned by the Unionist M P, Walter Guinness, see Ramsden, *Real*, p. 69.

243 P.F. Clarke, *Lancashire and the New Liberalism* (Cambridge: Cambridge University Press, 1971), p. vii.

244 Sykes, *Tariff Reform*, pp. 256–265. The Anti-Socialist Union had been in decline since 1911, Coetzee, *Party*, pp. 155–158.

245 Witherell, *Rebel*, pp. 177–178.

246 Sanders, diary, 12, 19, Jan. 1913, Ramsden, *Real*, p. 59; W.A.S. Hewins, *The Apologia of an Imperialist: Forty Years of Empire Policy, Volume I* (London: Constable, 1929), pp. 294–295.

247 Crawford, note, Dec. 1912–Jan. 1913, in Vincent, *Crawford*, p. 305. Those who refused to sign included Leopold Amery, Martin Archer-Shee, Allen Bathurst, Charles Bathurst, William Burdett-Coutts, George Lloyd, George Touche and Lord Winterton, see, Adams, *Law*, p. 91; Amery, diary, 7 Jan. 1913, Barnes and Nicholson, *Diaries, I*, p. 91.

248 David Thackeray, 'The Crisis of the Tariff Reform League and the Division of "Radical Conservatism", *c*.1913–1922', *History*, 91, 301 (2006), p. 54.

249 *The Times*, 3 April 1913, p. 12; 14 April 1913, p. 10.

250 For minutes and memoranda of Halsbury Club see, Hals., vol. 9, ff. 131–141; and MS. Selborne 75 and 76.

251 Jon Lawrence, *Electing Our Masters: The Hustings in British Politics from Hogarth to Blair* (Oxford: Oxford University Press, 2009), pp. 71–95; David Thackeray, 'Building a Peaceable Party: Masculine Identities in British Conservative Politics, *c*.1903–24', *Historical Research*, 85, 230 (2012), pp. 651–673.

Chapter 2   Patriotism strained, 1914–18

1 Lloyd to Leopold Amery, 31 March 1916, quoted in John Charmley, *Lord Lloyd and the Decline of the British Empire* (London: Weidenfeld and Nicolson, 1987), p. 51.

2 Amery, diary, 31 July 1914, 1–2 Aug. 1914, in John Barnes and David Nicholson (eds), *The Leo Amery Diaries, Volume I: 1896–1929* (London: Hutchinson, 1980), pp. 103–106.

3 Charmley, *Lloyd*, pp. 33–35.

4 Blanche E.C. Dugdale, *Arthur James Balfour, First Earl of Balfour, KG, OM, FRS, Volume II: 1906–1930* (London: Hutchinson, 1936), pp. 113–114; John W. Young, 'Conservative Leaders, Coalition, and Britain's Decision for War in 1914', *Diplomacy and Statecraft*, 25, 2 (2014), pp. 214–239.

5 Long to Law, 9 Aug. 1914, Parliamentary Archive, Westminster, Bonar Law Papers [hereafter BL] 34/3/28; Robert Cecil to Lord Selborne, 18 Aug. 1914 [copy], BL 34/4/54.

6 Cited in R.J.Q. Adams, *Bonar Law* (London: John Murray, 1999), p. 173.

7 *House of Commons Debates*, 15 Sept. 1914, vol. 66, col. 905.

8 Younger to Law, 5 Sept. 1914, BL 34/5/16.

9 John Stubbs, 'The Impact of the Great War on the Conservative Party', in Chris Cook and Gillian Peele (eds), *The Politics of Reappraisal, 1918–1939* (London: Macmillan, 1975), p. 19.

10 H.A. Gwynne to John Sandars, 21 Oct. 1915, Bodleian Library, Oxford, John Sandars Papers, MS.. Eng. hist. c. 769.

11 C.P. Scott to L.T. Hobhouse, 2 Nov. 1914, in Trevor Wilson (ed.), *The Political Diaries of C.P. Scott 1911–1928* (London: Collins, 1970), p. 109.

12 J. Lee Thompson, *Northcliffe: Press Baron in Politics, 1865–1922* (London: John Murray, 2000), p. 230.

13 Stephen Koss, *The Rise and Fall of the Political Press in Britain* (London: Fontana, 1990), p. 694.

14 Panikos Panayi, 'Anti-German Riots in Britain During the First World War', in Panikos Panayi (ed.), *Racial Violence in Britain in the Nineteenth and Twentieth Centuries* (Leicester: Leicester University Press, 1993), pp. 65–91.

15 Richard Burdon Haldane, *An Autobiography* (London: Hodder and Stoughton, 1929), pp. 282–285; Koss, *Rise*, pp. 694–695.

16 *House of Lords Debates*, 6 Jan. 1915, vol. 18, cols 237–262; Robert Blake, *The Unknown Prime Minister: The Life and Times of Andrew Bonar Law 1858–1923* (London: Eyre and Spottiswoode, 1955), p. 238.

17 David Gilmour, *Curzon: Imperial Statesman, 1855–1925* (reprinted edition, London: John Murray, 2003), pp. 436–437.

18 W.A.S. Hewins, *The Apologia of an Imperialist: Forty Years of Empire Policy, Volume II* (London: Constable, 1929), pp. 11–12; Viscount Long of Wraxall, *Memories* (London: Hutchinson, 1923), p. 219.

19 Blake, *Unknown*, p. 239.

20 Stubbs, 'Impact', p. 25.

21 *House of Commons Debates*, 21 April 1915, vol. 71, col. 277.

22 Ibid., cols 324–325.

23 Earl of Oxford and Asquith, *Memories and Reflections 1852–1927, Volume II* (London: Cassell, 1928), p. 75.

24 *House of Commons Debates*, 6 May 1915, vol. 71, cols 1295–1310.

25 Blake, *Unknown*, p. 243.

26 John Turner, *British Politics and the Great War: Coalition and Conflict 1915–1918* (London: Yale University Press, 1992), p. 439.

27 Sanders, diary, 13 Sept. 1915, in John Ramsden (ed.), *Real Old Tory Politics: The Political Diaries of Sir Robert Sanders, Lord Bayford 1910–1935* (London: Historians' Press, 1984), p. 82.

28 Maxse to Violet Cecil, 29 June 1915, Bodleian Library, Oxford, Violet Milner Papers [hereafter VM] 19.

29 Maxse to Croft, 13 Jan. 1916, Churchill Archives Centre, Cambridge, Croft Papers [hereafter CRFT] 1/16.

30 *House of Commons Debates*, 16 July 1896, vol. 42, cols 1649–1684; Edward Marjoribanks, *The Life of Lord Carson, Volume I* (London: Gollancz, 1932), pp. 261–270. He remained friends with Arthur Balfour, see Balfour to Carson, 24 July 1896, British Library, St Pancras, Balfour Papers [hereafter Balf.] vol. 27, f. 96; Marjoribanks, *Carson*, pp. 365–368.

31 Ibid., pp. 14, 68, 99, 133, 274, 278.

32 *The Times*, 14 Jan. 1916, p. 9.

33 *House of Commons Debates*, 6 Jan. 1916, vol. 77, cols 1133–1256; *The Times*, 17 March 1916, p. 9. Notably, Lord Sydenham of Combe dissented on the basis of what was required by the economy, see, Nigel Keohane, *The Party of Patriotism: The Conservative Party and the First World War* (Aldershot: Ashgate, 2010), p. 27.

34 Keohane, *Party*, pp. 30–31.

35 Ibid., p. 48; Adams, *Law*, p. 209–212; *House of Commons Debates*, 4 May 1916, vol. 82, cols 142–267.

36 *The Times*, 5 May 1916, p. 5.

37 A.M. Gollin, *Proconsul in Politics: A Study of Lord Milner in Opposition and Power* (London: Anthony Blond, 1964), pp. 323–344.

38 Gwynne to Carson, 16 March 1916, Bodleian Library, Oxford, H.A. Gwynne Papers, deposit 17.

39 Amery to Violet Cecil [afterwards Lady Milner], 25 April 1916, VM 31.

40 John D. Fair, *British Interparty Conferences: A Study of the Procedure of Conciliation in British Politics, 1867–1921* (Oxford: Clarendon Press, 1980), pp. 125–126.

41 Major Somerset Saunderson to Carson, 15 June 1916, Public Record Office of Northern Ireland, Carson Papers, D/1507/A/17/17.

42 Long to Edith, Lady Londonderry, 1 June 1916, Public Record Office of Northern Ireland, Londonderry Papers [hereafter D/3099] D/3099/8/3; Gwynne to Long, 7 June 1916, in Keith Wilson (ed.), *The Rasp of War: The Letters of H.A. Gwynne to the Countess Bathurst, 1914–1918* (London: Sidgwick and Jackson, 1988), pp. 172–174.

43 *The Times*, 8 July 1916, p. 9; McNeill to Edith, Lady Londonderry, 1 July 1916, D/3099/8/3.

44 Selborne to Asquith, 16 June 1916, in D. George Boyce (ed.), *The Crisis of British Unionism: Lord Selborne's Domestic Political Papers, 1885–1922* (London: Historians' Press, 1987), pp. 177–178; Patrick Buckland, *Irish Unionism: One: The Anglo–Irish and the New Ireland 1885–1922* (Dublin: Gill and Macmillan, 1972), p. 71.

45 *The Times*, 8 July 1916, p. 9.

46 Keohane, *Party*, p. 79.

47 Guinness, diary, June–July 1914, in Brian Bond and Simon Robbins (eds), *Staff Officer: The Diaries of Walter Guinness (First Lord Moyne) 1914–1918* (London: Leo Cooper, 1987), p. 99.

48 Cited in Stubbs, 'Impact', p. 31.

49 Cornelius O'Leary and Patrick Maume, *Controversial Issues in Anglo–Irish Relations, 1910–1921* (Dublin: Four Courts Press, 2004), p. 54.

50 Salisbury to Violet Cecil, 1 Sept. 1916, VM 66.

51 *House of Commons Debates*, 8 Nov. 1916, vol. 87, cols 249–368.

52 Alan Clark (ed.), *A Good Innings: The Private Papers of Viscount Lee of Fareham* (London: John Murray, 1974), pp. 159–163.

53 Alvin Jackson, *Sir Edward Carson* (Dundalk: Dundalgan Press, 1993), pp. 45–47.

54 Lloyd George's Liberal backers shared such concerns. C.P. Scott acknowledged that the country needed to pull 'itself together' and submit 'to something not unlike a Prussian organization for the period of the war', see, Scott to Hobhouse, 7 May 1915, in Trevor Wilson (ed.), *Political*, p. 123.

55 Adams, *Law*, p. 247.

56 R.B. McDowell, *The Irish Convention, 1917–18* (London: Routledge and Keegan Paul, 1970), pp. 77–78; Carson to Dawson Bates, 23 May 1917, D/3099/2/7/7.

57 J.C. Beckett, *The Anglo–Irish Tradition* (London: Faber and Faber, 1976), p. 127.

58 H.C. Plunkett, *The Irish Convention: Confidential Report to His Majesty The King by the Chairman* (Dublin: HMSO, 1918), p. 51; Londonderry to Theresa, Lady Londonderry, 23 Sept. 1917, Durham County Record Office, Londonderry Papers, D/Lo/C/682 (245)); Adam Duffin to Londonderry, 16 Nov. 1917, in Patrick Buckland (ed.), *Irish Unionism 1885–1923: A Documentary History* (Belfast: HMSO, 1973), pp. 422–423; Carson to Lloyd George, 14 Feb. 1918 [copy], Balf., vol. 27, f. 163–165.

59 Lloyd George to H.T. Barrie, 21 Feb. 1918, cited in McDowell, *Irish*, p. 163; Minutes of the Ulster Unionist delegation to the Irish Convention, 25 Feb. 1918, Public Record Office of Northern Ireland, Ulster Unionist Council Papers, D/1327/3/17.

60 Plunkett, *Confidential*, pp. 134–137.

61 *The Times*, 4 March 1918, p. 9.

62 Ibid., 18 April 1918, p. 7; Selborne to Salisbury, 17 June 1918, Boyce, *Crisis*, pp. 218–221.

63 Alan O'Day, *Irish Home Rule 1867–1921* (Manchester: Manchester University Press, 1998), 290–300.

64 Keohane, *Party*, p. 148.

65 Martin Pugh, *Electoral Reform in War and Peace 1906–1918* (London: Routledge and Keegan Paul, 1978), pp. 103–118.

66 Sascha Auerbach, 'Negotiating Nationalism: Jewish Conscription and Russian Repatriation in London's East End, 1916–1918', *Journal of British Studies*, 46, 3 (2007), pp. 594–620.

67 Pugh, *Electoral*, pp. 94, 113–114, 125–126.

68 Keohane, *Party*, p. 144.

69 Northumberland to Halsbury, 30 March 1917, British Library, St Pancras, Halsbury Papers [hereafter Hals.], vol. 9, f. 181.

70 Long to Halsbury, 21 Jan. 1918, Hals., vol. 9, ff. 182–183.

71 Sanders, diary, 1 Dec. 1917, Ramsden (ed.), *Real*, pp. 92–93.

72 Neville Chamberlain to Hilda Chamberlain, 1 Dec. 1917, in Robert C. Self (ed.), *The Neville Chamberlain Diary Letters, Volume I: The Making of a Politician, 1915–1920* (Aldershot: Ashgate, 2000), pp. 236–237.

73 Cited in Keohane, *Party*, p. 144.

74 Pugh, *Electoral*, p. 118.

75 Selborne to Law, 13 March 1912, BL 25/3/26; Selborne to Salisbury, 25 Aug. 1916, Boyce, *Crisis*, pp. 194–195.

76 Matthew C. Hendley, *Organized Patriotism and the Crucible of War: Popular Imperialism in Britain, 1914–1932* (Montreal and Kingston: McGill-Queen's University Press, 2012), p. 63.

77 Roy Douglas, 'The National Democratic Party and the British Workers' League', *Historical Journal*, 15, 3 (1972), pp. 533–552; J.O. Stubbs, 'Lord Milner and Patriotic Labour, 1914–1918', *English Historical Review*, 87, 345 (1972), pp. 717–754.

78 Gwynne to Lloyd George, 8 Nov. 1915, Keith Wilson, *Rasp*, pp. 151–152.

79 Gwynne to Law, 5 Nov. 1915, Keith Wilson, *Rasp*, pp. 148–150.

80 Keith M. Wilson, 'National Party Spirits: Backing into the Future', in Matthew Hughes and Matthew Seligmann (eds), *Leadership in Conflict 1914–1918* (Barnsley: Leo Cooper, 2000), p. 210.

81 *The Times*, 13 Jan. 1916, p. 5.

82 Gwynne to Derby, 20 Jan. 1916; 21 Jan. 1916, Keith Wilson, *Rasp*, pp. 159–160, 162; Gwynne to Lady Carson, 12 March 1916, Ibid., p. 165.

83 Ibid., p. 205.

84 Wilson, 'National', p. 216.

85 Ibid., pp. 216–217; Gregory D. Phillips, *The Diehards: Aristocratic Society and Politics in Edwardian England* (Cambridge, MA: Harvard University Press, 1979), p. 155.

86 Stubbs, 'Impact', p. 33; Turner, *British*, p. 85.

87 David A. Thackeray, 'The Crisis of the Tariff Reform League and the Division of "Radical Conservatism", c.1913–1922', *History*, 91, 301 (2006), pp. 50–51.

88 Lord Croft, *My Life of Strife* (London: Hutchinson, 1948), p. 130.

89 The fifteenth Duke of Somerset, seventh Earl of Bathurst, tenth Earl of Northesk, second Baron Ampthill, and the first Baron Leith of Fyvie had been ditcher peers in

1911. The eleventh Earl of Galloway and fourth Baron Sherborne were listed on the IML's general council. The remaining peers included the eighth Earl of Bessborough, ninth Earl of Egmont, sixth Baron Erskine, second Baron Dunleath, second Baron Montagu of Beaulieu, first Baron Beresford, first Baron Hollenden, fifth Baron Rossmore, eleventh Baron Sherard, twelfth Baron Stafford and the fourth Baron Strathspey.

90 *The Times*, 12 Sept. 1917, p. 5.

91 Thackeray, 'Crisis', pp. 55–60.

92 Hendley, *Organized*, pp. 11–66.

93 N.C. Fleming, 'The Imperial Maritime League: British Navalism, Conflict and the Radical Right, c.1907–1920', *War in History*, 23, 3 (2016), pp. 320–321.

94 The final and most significant output of this nature was Lionel Graham Horton Horton-Smith, *Perils of the Sea: How We Kept the Flag Flying: A Short History of a Long Fight* (London: Imperial Maritime League, 1920).

95 *The Times*, 4 April 1921, p. 7.

96 *Navy*, 20, 9 (Sept. 1915), pp. 274–275; 20, 10 (Oct. 1915), p. 326; 20, 11 (Nov. 1915), p. 360; 22, 2 (Feb. 1917), p. 31; 22, 5 (Aug. 1917), p. 115; 23, 2 (April 1918), p. 27; 23, 5 (Oct. 1918), pp. 90, 102.

97 Long to Law, 4 Sept. 1917, cited in Keith Wilson, 'National', p. 221.

98 Long to Law, 19 Sept. 1917, BL 82/4/19.

99 Wilson, 'National', p. 218.

100 Lloyd to Puss Gaskell, c. Aug. 1917, cited in Charmley, *Lloyd*, pp. 63–64.

101 Gwynne to Lady Bathurst, 27 Aug. 1917, Wilson, *Rasp*, pp. 227–229. For National Party's declared aims, see, *The Times*, 30 Aug. 1917, p. 8.

102 Oliver to Lord Selborne, 5 Sept. 1917, Bodleian Library, Oxford, Selborne Papers [hereafter MS. Selborne] 87.

103 Adrian Gregory, *The Last Great War: British Society and the First World War* (Cambridge: Cambridge University Press, 2008), pp. 234–235.

104 It is worth noting that the National Party was the subject of a raid following its efforts to expose a ministerial scandal, see, Croft, *Life*, pp. 133–138.

105 David Monger, *Patriotism and Propaganda in First World War Britain: The National War Aims Committee and Civilian Morale* (Liverpool: Liverpool University Press, 2012), pp. 244–245; Lawrence James, *Warrior Race: A History of the British at War from Roman Times to the Present* (London: Abacus, 2001), p. 528.

106 *The Times*, 14 Nov. 1917, p. 3; David A. Thackeray, 'Building a Peaceable Party: Masculine Identities in British Conservative Politics, c.1903–24', *Historical Research*, 85, 230 (2012), pp. 661–662.

107 Selborne to Violet Cecil, 5 May 1918, VM 66.

108 Hewins, diary, 11 April 1917, *Apologia*, II, pp. 132–135.

109 *The Times*, 20 July 1917, p. 7; 21 July 1917, p. 7.

110 Hewins, diary, 4 Aug. 1917, *Apologia, II*, pp. 158–159.

111 *The Times*, 20 June 1917, p. 7.

112 David Dutton, *Austen Chamberlain: Gentleman in Politics* (Bolton: Ross Anderson, 1985), p. 140.

113 *The Times*, 7 March 1918, p. 8.

114 J.M. McEwen, ' "Brass-Hats" and the British Press During the First World War', *Canadian Journal of History*, 18, 1 (1983), pp. 60, 63.

115 *The Times*, 9 May 1918, p. 7.

116 Crawford, diary, 18 Aug. 1916, John Vincent (ed.), *The Crawford Papers: The Journals of David Lindsay Twenty-Seventh Earl of Crawford and Tenth Earl of Balcarres, 1871–1940, During the Years 1892 to 1940* (Manchester: Manchester University Press, 1984), p. 360.

117 Jackson, *Carson*, p. 52.

118 Frans Coetzee, *For Party or Country: Nationalism and the Dilemmas of Popular Conservatism in Edwardian England* (Oxford: Oxford University Press, 1990), pp. 158–159.

119 Sanders, diary, 9 Aug. 1918, Ramsden, *Real*, pp. 107–108.

120 Keohane, *Party*, p. 58.

121 *The Times*, 13 Aug. 1917, p. 7.

122 Neville Chamberlain to Hilda Chamberlain, 1 Dec. 1917, Self, *Diary Letters, I*, pp. 236–237; *The Times*, 1 Dec. 1917, p. 9.

123 Sanders, diary, 20 Jan. 1918, Ramsden, *Real*, p. 98.

124 Adams, *Law*, pp. 254–255.

125 Keohane, *Party*, pp. 188–189, 200, 204.

126 George Lloyd and Edward Wood, *The Great Opportunity* (London: John Murray, 1919), p. 79.

127 Keohane, *Party*, pp. 179–180, 200.

128 Selborne to Lord Hugh Cecil, 11 March 1918, MS. Selborne 87.

Chapter 3   Breaking the Coalition, 1918–22

1 Nigel Keohane, *The Party of Patriotism: The Conservative Party and the First World War* (Aldershot: Ashgate, 2010), pp. 164–165.

2 *The Times*, 9 April 1919, p. 13; 14 April 1919, p. 13. The seven others included Sir Edward Coates, Angus Hambro, Percy Hurd, Kennedy Jones, James Lonsdale, Claude Lowther and Archibald Weigall.

3 *House of Commons Debates*, 16 April 1919, vol. 114, cols 2951–2953; Kennedy Jones, *Fleet Street and Downing Street* (London: Hutchinson, 1920).

4 *The Times*, 2 June 1920, p. 18; 12 June 1920, p. 18.

5   *The Times*, 14 June 1920, p. 15.

6   David Thackeray, 'Rethinking the Edwardian Crisis of Conservatism', *Historical Journal*, 54, 1 (2011), pp. 208–209.

7   Keohane, *Party*, pp. 62–63.

8   Sanders, diary, 10 Nov. 1918, in John Ramsden (ed.), *Real Old Tory Politics: The Political Diaries of Sir Robert Sanders, 1910–1935* (London: Historians' Press, 1984), p. 112.

9   Sanders, diary, 19 Aug. 1919, ibid., p. 129.

10 Salisbury cited in Kenneth O. Morgan, *Wales in British Politics, 1868–1922* (Cardiff: University of Wales Press, 1980), p. 289; *House of Commons Debates*, 11 Aug. 1919, vol. 119 col. 1039.

11 Viscount Cecil of Chelwood, *All the Way* (London: Hodder and Stoughton, 1949), p. 146.

12 In the longer term the Association of Independent Unionist Peers evolved into something like the Upper House's equivalent of the 1922 Committee, see, Philip Norton, 'The Parliamentary Party and Party Committees', in Anthony Seldon and Stuart Ball (eds), *Conservative Century: The Conservative Party Since 1900* (Oxford: Oxford University Press, 1990), p. 136.

13 Felix Aubel, 'The Conservatives in Wales, 1880–1935', in Martin Francis and Ina Zweiniger-Bargielowska (eds), *The Conservatives and British Society, 1880–1990* (Cardiff: University of Wales Press, 1995), pp. 96–110; Geraint Thomas, 'The Conservative Party and Welsh Politics in the Inter-War Years', *English Historical Review*, 128, 533 (2013), pp. 877–913.

14 *The Times*, 10 July 1918, p. 3.

15 *House of Commons Debates*, 23 Oct. 1919, vol. 120, cols 235–236.

16 *The Times*, 25 Oct. 1919, p. 12. The delegation included Sir John Butcher, Edward Carson, Sir William Joynson-Hicks, Sir Herbert Nield, Sir Ernest Wild, Sir Thomas Whittaker, Kennedy Jones, John Hinds and the maverick Liberal, Horatio Bottomley.

17 Chandrika Kaul, *Reporting the Raj: The British Press and India, c.1880–1922* (Manchester: Manchester University Press, 2003), pp. 201–202.

18 *The Times*, 27 Nov. 1919, p. 14.

19 *The Times*, 13 Dec. 1919, p. 14; Lord Sydenham of Combe, *My Working Life* (London: John Murray, 1927), pp. 369–372. Selborne chaired the joint select committee.

20 *The Times*, 25 Nov. 1919, p. 12.

21 Kipling to Oman, 18 Nov. 1919, Bodleian Library, Oxford, Charles Oman Papers [hereafter MS. Eng. c. 8182], MS. Eng. c. 8182.

22 Robert McCalmont (1881–1953) [former Unionist MP for East Antrim] to Gwynne, 26 May 1920; Dyer to Gwynne, 28 May 1920; Carson to Gwynne, 31 May 1920; McCalmont to Gwynne, 1 June 1920; Gwynne to McCalmont, 2 June 1920; Gwynne to Carson, 2 June 1920, Gwynne to Carson, 7 June 1920, Bodleian Library, Oxford, H.A. Gwynne Papers [hereafter MS. Gwynne], deposit 8 (B).

23 *House of Commons Debates*, 8 July 1920, vol. 131, cols 1705–1819.

24 *House of Lords Debates*, 19 July 1920, vol. 41, cols 222–307.

25 Sanders, diary, 10 July 1920, Ramsden, *Real*, pp. 139–140.

26 Neville Chamberlain to Hilda Chamberlain, 11 July 1920, in Robert C. Self (ed.), *The Neville Chamberlain Diary Letters, Volume I: The Making of a Politician, 1915–1920* (Aldershot: Ashgate, 2000), pp. 280–281.

27 Colin Holmes, *John Bull's Island: Immigration and British Society, 1871–1971* (Basingstoke: Macmillan, 1988), p. 113.

28 Harry Defries, *Conservative Party Attitudes to Jews, 1900–1950* (London: Routledge, 2001), p. 87.

29 Jacqueline Jenkinson, 'The 1919 Riots', in Panikos Panayi (ed.), *Racial Violence in Britain, 1840–1950* (Leicester: Leicester University Press, 1993), pp. 92–111.

30 Ross McKibbin, *Classes and Cultures: England 1918–1951* (Oxford: Oxford University Press, 1998), pp. 54–55.

31 Keith M. Wilson, *A Study in the History and Politics of the* Morning Post *1905–1926* (Lampeter: Edwin Mellon, 1991), pp. 169–191.

32 Gwynne to Dyer, 14 Dec. 1920; Gwynne arranged the appeal in response to Mrs Dyer's request for financial assistance, see, Gwynne to Mrs Dyer, 17 June 1920, MS. Gwynne, deposit 8 (B).

33 Oman to Gwynne, 24 Feb. 1920; Gwynne to Oman, 25 Feb. 1920, MS. Gwynne deposit 7 (1–2).

34 H. Peacock to Lord Bathurst, n.d. [Spring 1920], MS. Gwynne deposit 7 (1–2).

35 Gwynne to Lady Bathurst [enclosing 'Memorandum on the Jewish Question'], 27 Jan. 1920, MS. Gwynne dep. 7 (1–2).

36 Defries, *Conservative*, 206.

37 McKibbin, *Classes*, pp. 55–57. This is consistent with research conducted in the 2000s, which demonstrated that polling data that revealed widespread authoritarianism and anti-Muslim feeling in British society did not translate into 'demand' for extremist parties; it was checked by the salience of other political issues and the ability of mainstream parties to shift tactically to the right on immigration and law and order. See, Robert Ford, 'Who Might Vote for the BNP? Survey Evidence on the Electoral Potential of the Extreme Right in Britain', in Roger Eatwell and Matthew J. Goodwin (eds), *The New Extremism in 21st Century Britain* (Abingdon: Routledge, 2010), pp. 145–168.

38 Andrew S. Thompson, *Imperial Britain: The Empire in British Politics, c.1880–1932* (London: Longman, 2000), p. 164.

39 Derek Sayer, 'British Reaction to the Amritsar Massacre, 1919–1920', *Past and Present*, 131 (1991), pp. 130–164.

40 Not all pre-war ditchers went along with this development. Lord Winterton's appointment in March 1922 as Under Secretary of State for India placed him firmly

on the side of reformers in the post-war period, see, Winterton, *Pre-War* (London: Macmillan, 1932), pp. 278–279; and his *Orders of the Day* (London: Cassell 1953), p. 112.

41 John M. Mackenzie, *Propaganda and Empire: The Manipulation of British Public Opinion, 1880–1960* (Manchester: Manchester University Press, 1984), pp. 166–168; Philip Woods, 'Lionel Curtis, the Round Table Movement and the Montagu–Chelmsford Reforms (1919)', in Andrea Bosco and Alex May (eds), *The Round Table, the Empire/Commonwealth and British Foreign Policy* (London: Lothian Foundation Press, 1997), pp. 369–379; Duncan Bell, *The Idea of Greater Britain: Empire and the Future of World Order, 1860–1900* (Princeton, NJ: Princeton University Press, 2007), pp. 269–270.

42 Bernard Porter, *Empire Ways: Aspects of British Imperialism* (London: I.B.Tauris, 2016), p. 166.

43 G.K. Peatling, *British Opinion and Irish Self-Government, 1865–1925: From Unionism to Liberal Commonwealth* (Dublin: Irish Academic Press, 2001), pp. 155–165.

44 Ronald Hyam, 'The British Empire in the Edwardian Era', in Judith M. Brown and Wm. Roger Louis (eds), *The Oxford History of the British Empire, Volume IV: The Twentieth Century* (Oxford: Oxford University Press, 1999), pp. 52–53.

45 David Cannadine, *Ornamentalism: How the British Saw Their Empire* (London: Allen Lane, 2001), p. 57.

46 Despite their difference of opinion over tariff reform, Croft later wrote of Salisbury, 'he always appeared to me, like his illustrious father, to represent more nearly than anyone the true Conservative faith', Lord Croft, *My Life of Strife* (London: Hutchinson, 1948), p. 126.

47 G.C. Webber, *The Ideology of the British Right, 1918–1939* (London: Croom Helm, 1986), p. 107.

48 John Carey, *The Intellectuals and the Masses: Pride and Prejudice Among the Literary Intelligentsia, 1880–1939* (London: Faber and Faber, 1992).

49 Hewins, diary, 26 June 1922, in W.A.S. Hewins, *The Apologia of an Imperialist: Forty Years of Empire Policy, Volume II* (London: Constable, 1929), p. 251.

50 *The Times*, 4 June 1920, p. 16.

51 Selborne to Younger, 27 Feb. 1920, in D. George Boyce (ed.), *The Crisis of British Unionism: Lord Selborne's Domestic Political Papers, 1885–1922* (London: Historians Press, 1987), pp. 224–225.

52 Younger to Selborne, 1 March 1920, ibid., p. 226.

53 Robert Blake, *The Unknown Prime Minister: The Life and Times of Andrew Bonar Law 1858–1923* (London: Eyre and Spottiswoode, 1955), p. 416.

54 *The Times*, 9 March 1920, p. 16.

55 *The Times*, 15 March 1920, p. 16.

56 Kenneth O. Morgan, *Consensus and Disunity: The Lloyd George Coalition Government 1918–1922* (Oxford: Clarendon Press, 1979), p. 185; *The Times*, 17 March 1920, p. 16.

57 R.J.Q. Adams, *Bonar Law* (London: John Murray, 1999), p. 290.

58 Sanders, diary, 23 June 1920, Ramsden, *Real*, p. 139.

59 *The Times*, 2 June 1920, p. 18; 11 June 1920, p. 18.

60 *The Times*, 29 Nov. 1919, p. 13.

61 Maurice Cowling, *The Impact of Labour 1920–1924: The Beginning of Modern British Politics* (Cambridge: Cambridge University Press, 1971), pp. 49–50.

62 *The Times*, 14 Jan. 1921, p. 10.

63 Simon Moore, 'The Agrarian Conservative Party in Parliament, 1920–1929', *Parliamentary History*, 10, 2 (1991), pp. 342–362.

64 Morgan, *Consensus*, pp. 264–267; Duncan Redford, 'Collective Security and Internal Dissent: The Navy League's Attempts to Develop a New Policy Towards British Naval Power Between 1919 and the 1922 Washington Naval Treaty', *History*, 96, 321 (2011), pp. 48–67.

65 Christopher Catherwood, *Winston's Folly: Imperialism and the Creation of Modern Iraq* (London: Constable, 2004), pp. 187–188.

66 Morgan, *Consensus*, pp. 118–119.

67 Cowling, *Labour*, p. 71.

68 *House of Commons Debates*, 22 March 1922, vol. 152, cols 543–548.

69 Daniel Silverfarb, *Britain's Informal Empire in the Middle East: A Case Study of Iraq, 1929–1941* (Oxford: Oxford University Press, 1986), pp. 6–8.

70 Kipling to Oman, 18 Nov. 1919, MS. Eng. c. 8182.

71 Thompson, *Imperial*, pp. 163–164.

72 *The Times*, 26 Feb. 1921, p. 10.

73 Chamberlain to Halsbury, 28 March 1921, British Library, St Pancras, Halsbury Papers, vol. 9, f. 197.

74 Selborne to Chamberlain, 18 March 1918, Bodleian Library, Selborne Papers, 87.

75 William D. Rubenstein, 'Henry Page Croft and the National Party 1917–22', *Journal of Contemporary History*, 9, 1 (1974), pp. 137–139.

76 Keohane, *Party*, p. 197.

77 Rubenstein, 'Croft', pp. 136–137. Lord Bathurst, proprietor of the *Morning Post*, sat on the party's grand council.

78 Ibid., p. 137; Croft to Gwynne, 1 March 1921, MS. Gwynne deposit 8 (A).

79 *House of Commons Debates*, 28 May 1919, vol. 116, cols 1334–1382. The motion was defeated, 50–112. The ayes included Labour MPs.

80 Rubenstein, 'Croft', p. 146.

81 Croft, *Life*, pp. 130, 139.

82 Ibid., p. 151.

83 Cited in Nick Toczek, *Haters, Baiters and Would-Be Dictators: Anti-Semitism and the UK Far Right* (Abingdon: Routledge, 2016), pp. 88–89.

84 Croft, *Life*, p. 152.

85 Webber, *Ideology*, p. 20; Oswald Mosley, *My Life* (London: Thomas Nelson and Sons, 1968), p. 20.

86 *The Times*, 8 June 1921, p. 12.

87 Ibid., 15 June 1921, p. 10.

88 Ibid., 18 June 1921, p. 10. Billing suffered a sudden decline in health beforehand, bringing to a close a notorious parliamentary career, independent of the Unionists, distinguished by his promotion of conspiracy theories about the hidden influence of Jews and homosexuals. He continued to promote his ideas outside of Parliament.

89 Selborne to Salisbury, 13 June 1921, Boyce, *Crisis*, pp. 228–229.

90 *Morning Post*, 20 June 1921, cited in R.T. McKenzie, *British Political Parties: The Distribution of Power Within the Conservative and Labour Parties* (2nd edition, London: Heinemann, 1967), p. 84.

91 Harold Macmillan, *Winds of Change 1914–1939* (London: Macmillan, 1966), p. 178.

92 *The Times*, 21 July 1921, p. 10.

93 *The Times*, 11 July 1921, p. 12; 12 July 1921, p. 12; 14 July 1921, p. 10; 15 July 1921, p. 10.

94 D. George Boyce, *Englishmen and Irish Troubles: British Public Opinion and the Making of Irish Policy 1918–22* (Cambridge, MA: Massachusetts Institute of Technology Press, 1972), p. 164; Gwynne to Austen Chamberlain, 23 July 1921, MS. Gwynne deposit 17.

95 *The Times*, 22 Aug. 1921, p. 9.

96 Gwynne to Northumberland, 24 Oct. 1921, MS. Gwynne deposit 21.

97 *House of Commons Debates*, 31 March 1920, vol. 127, cols 1287–1339.

98 *House of Commons Debates*, 31 Oct. 1921, vol. 147, cols 1367–1484.

99 Gideon Murray [Viscount Elibank], *A Man's Life: Reflections and Reminiscences of Experiences in Many Lands* (London: Hutchinson, 1934), pp. 255–256.

100 *The Times*, 28 Oct. 1921, p. 10.

101 Salisbury to Selborne, 15 Nov. 1921, Boyce, *Crisis*, pp. 232–233.

102 Neville Chamberlain to Ida Chamberlain, 12 Nov. 1921, Robert C. Self (ed.), *The Neville Chamberlain Diary Letters, Volume II: The Reform Years, 1921–1927* (Aldershot: Ashgate, 2000), p. 83.

103 Blake, *Unknown*, pp. 430–433.

104 *The Times*, 15 Nov. 1921, p. 10; 22 Nov. 1921, p. 12; see also, Croft, *Life*, p. 160.

105 Salisbury to Selborne, 15 Nov. 1921, Boyce, *Crisis*, pp. 232–233.

106 Austen Chamberlain to Hilda Chamberlain, 13 Nov. 1921, in Robert C. Self (ed.), *The Austen Chamberlain Diary Letters: The Correspondence of Sir Austen Chamberlain with His Sisters, Hilda and Ida, 1916–1937* (Cambridge: Cambridge University Press, 1995), p. 171.

107 Neville Chamberlain to unknown, n.d. (probably 17 Nov. 1921), Self, *Diary Letters, II*, p. 87.

108 Neville Chamberlain to Ida Chamberlain, 19 Nov. 1921, ibid., pp. 83–84.

109 Hewins, diary, 8 Dec. 1921, *Apologia, II*, pp. 244–245.

110 *The Times*, 18 Nov. 1921, p. 10.

111 *House of Commons Debates*, 16 Dec. 1921, vol. 149, cols 305–363.

112 *House of Lords Debates*, 14 Dec. 1921, vol. 48, cols 5–56. Field Marshal Henry Wilson suggested that he would have made a 'much more vehement speech myself', see, Wilson to Sir Walter Congreve, 16 Dec. 1921, in Keith Jeffery (ed.), *The Military Correspondence of Field Marshal Sir Henry Wilson, 1918–1922* (London: Bodley Head for the Army Records Society, 1985), p. 320.

113 Nicholas Mansergh, *The Unresolved Question: The Anglo–Irish Settlement and Its Undoing 1912–72* (London: Yale University Press, 1991), p. 197; Paul Canning, *British Policy Towards Ireland, 1921–1941* (Oxford: Clarendon Press, 1985), p. 24.

114 Edward Marjoribanks, *The Life of Lord Carson, Volume I* (London: Gollancz, 1932), pp. 163–164. Marjoribanks was elected the Conservative MP for Eastbourne from May 1929 until his suicide in April 1932.

115 D.G. Boyce, 'Edward Carson (1845–1935) and Irish Unionism', in Ciaran Brady (ed.), *Worsted in the Game: Losers in Irish History* (Dublin: Lilliput Press, 1989), p. 155.

116 *The Times*, 27 March 1922, p. 7.

117 Ibid., 18 Nov. 1921, p. 10.

118 Gwynne to Northumberland, 5 Jan, 1922, MS. Gwynne deposit 21.

119 Neville Chamberlain to Hilda Chamberlain, 12 Feb. 1922, Self, *Diary Letters, II*, p. 95.

120 *The Times*, 3 Feb. 1922, p. 12.

121 T.F. Lindsay and Michael Harrington, *The Conservative Party, 1918–1970* (London: Macmillan, 1974), p. 36.

122 *The Times*, 22 Feb. 1922, p. 6.

123 Ibid., 23 Feb. 1922, p. 9.

124 Ibid., 3 March 1922, p. 12.

125 Neville Chamberlain to Ida Chamberlain, 4 March 1922, Self, *Diary Letters, II*, p. 99.

126 Austen Chamberlain to Ida Chamberlain, 11 March 1922, Self, *Correspondence*, p. 184; Stuart Ball, *Portrait of a Party: The Conservative Party in Britain, 1918–1945* (Oxford: Oxford University Press, 2013), p. 265.

127 Hewins, diary, 6 March 1922, *Apologia, II*, p. 248.

128 *The Times*, 8 March 1922, p. 14. As this was not intended as a diehard manifesto, its signatories included Lord Londonderry and Esmond Harmsworth, both of whom did not sign the explicit diehard manifesto issued on 2 June 1922. The remaining

signatories included the peers: Salisbury, Carson, Finlay, Linlithgow, Northumberland, Sumner and Sydenham; and the MPs: John Gretton, Frederick Banbury, C.T. Foxcroft, Rupert Gwynne, William Joynson-Hicks, Ronald McNeill, and A. Sprot. Additional names were publicized subsequently, see, *The Times*, 18 March 1922, p. 12.

129 Cited in Murray, *Man's*, pp. 256–258.

130 *The Times*, 18 Nov. 1921, p. 14.

131 Hewins, diary, 8 March 1922, *Apologia, II*, pp. 248–249.

132 Hewins, diary, 13 Aug. 1922, ibid., p. 253.

133 Carson to Gwynne, 18 Feb. 1922, MS. Gwynne deposit 17.

134 Murray, *Man's*, p. 260.

135 Sydenham, *Working*, p. 421. Other NCA meetings at this time included 'The need for a Conservative government', and 'The peril of government extravagance', the latter addressed by the Anti-Waste League MP, Edward Harmsworth, see, *The Times*, 16 Feb. 1922, p. 10; 22 March 1922, p. 9.

136 Winterton, *Orders*, p. 112.

137 Hewins, diary, 10 March 1922, *Apologia, II*, p. 249.

138 Sanders, diary, 10 March 1922, Ramsden, *Real*, p. 174.

139 Neville Chamberlain to Ida Chamberlain, 18 March 1922, Self, *Diary Letters, II*, pp. 101–102; Hewins, diary, 15 March 1922, *Apologia, II*, p. 249.

140 David Dutton, *Austen Chamberlain: Gentleman in Politics* (Bolton: Ross Anderson, 1985), pp. 177–178. This did not mean that he was always insensitive to press reports which he deemed misleading, see, Chamberlain to Gwynne, 22 July 1921, MS. Gwynne 17.

141 *House of Commons Debates*, 5 April 1922, vol. 152, cols 2344–2391; Austen Chamberlain to Ida Chamberlain, 8 April 1922, Self, *Correspondence*, p. 186.

142 Neville Chamberlain to Hilda Chamberlain, 8 April 1922, Self, *Diary Letters, II*, p. 106; Sanders, diary, 12 April 1922, Ramsden, *Real*, p. 176.

143 Morgan, *Consensus*, p. 252.

144 Hewins, diary, 24 Sept. 1922, *Apologia, II*, p. 255.

145 Dutton, *Chamberlain*, p. 189.

146 *The Times*, 7 Oct. 1922, p. 11.

147 Hewins, diary, 24 Sept. 1922; 26 Sept. 1922, *Apologia, II*, pp. 255, 257.

148 *The Times*, 3 June 1922, p. 8. The thirty MPs listed include: Gretton, Wilfrid Ashley, Thomas Adair, M. Archer-Shee, George Balfour, F.G. Banbury, A. Boyd-Carpenter, J.S. Harmood-Banner, Viscount Curzon, Cooper, Croft, William Davison, J.M.M. Erskine, Charles Foxcroft, W.G. Howard Gritten, Rupert Gwynne, Reginald Hall, William Joynson-Hicks, Cuthbert James, J.A.R. Marriott, Ronald McNeill, Gideon Murray, J.S. Nicholson, Herbert Nield, Charles Oman, De F. Pennefather, Alexander Sprot, Wolmer, Field Marshal Henry Wilson, and Charles Yate. A smaller number of peers signed the second manifesto and Selborne was an addition.

149 Salisbury to Gwynne, 21 July 1922, MS. Gwynne deposit 8 (C). Salisbury touted 'True Conservative' and 'National Conservative' though he was wary of the latter being confused with the National Party.

150 Gwynne to Salisbury, 24 July 1922, MS. Gwynne deposit 8 (C).

151 *The Times*, 31 July 1922, p. 6.

152 Charles V. Sale to Gwynne, 26 June 1922, MS. Gwynne deposit 8 (A).

153 *House of Commons Debates*, 17 July 1922, vol. 156, cols 1745–1862.

154 Hewins, diary, 13 Aug. 1922; 15 Oct. 1922, *Apologia, II*, pp. 253, 258.

155 Hewins, diary, 26 June 1922, ibid., p. 251. Bernard Ash argues that had Wilson lived, he would have provided right-wing Conservatives, 'the crowd of vociferous reactionaries', with the leadership they lacked and that this would somehow have allowed them to quickly gain control of the party, see, Bernard Ash, *The Lost Dictator: A Biography of Field-Marshal Sir Henry Wilson Bart GCB DSO MP* (London: Cassell, 1968), pp. 258, 271, 278. This is rebutted, convincingly, in Keith Jeffery, *Field Marshal Sir Henry Wilson: A Political Soldier* (Oxford: Oxford University Press, 2006), pp. 294–295.

156 Pre-empting the civil war by a month, Milner's dismay with the government's Irish policy led him to assert that 'It may be best for both parties [in the coalition] that the Southern Irish should cut one another's throats, instead of ours', Milner to Mr Craven, 10 Jan. 1922, Bodleian Library, Oxford, first Viscount Milner Papers deposit 50.

157 David Lloyd George to Margaret Lloyd George, 29 Aug. 1922, in Kenneth O. Morgan, *Lloyd George Family Letters 1885–1936* (Cardiff: University of Wales Press, 1973), pp. 195–196.

158 Dutton, *Chamberlain*, p. 190; Hewins, diary, 15 Oct. 1922, *Apologia, II*, p. 259.

159 Salisbury to Law, 23 Sept. 1922, Parliamentary Archive, Westminster, Bonar Law Papers 107/2/61.

160 Malcolm Fraser (Central Office) to Sanders, 22 Sept. 1922, Ramsden, *Real*, p. 182.

161 Hewins, diary, 15 Oct. 1922, *Apologia, II*, p. 258.

162 *The Times*, 17 Oct. 1922, p. 14. In his autobiography Croft claims that the original resolution was passed with only four dissentients, see, Croft, *Life*, pp. 163.

163 Amery, diary, 19 Oct. 1922, in John Barnes and David Nicholson (eds), *The Leo Amery Diaries, Volume I: 1896–1929* (London: Hutchinson, 1980), pp. 299–301.

164 Hewins, diary, 22 Oct. 1922, *Apologia, II*, p. 260. Henry Craik was one of the four MPs to propose the motion. Labelled a 'diehard' for his opposition to constitutional reforms in India, Ireland and Egypt, he was not a signatory of the two manifestos used by the diehards in March and June 1922, see, *The Times*, 9 March 1922, p. 8.

165 Adams, *Law*, p. 328.

166 Austen Chamberlain to Ida Chamberlain, 21 Nov. 1922, Self, *Correspondence*, p. 206. See also, Neville Chamberlain to Hilda Chamberlain, 24 Oct. 1922, Self, *Diary Letters, II*, p. 126.

167 Hewins, diary, 22 Oct. 1922, *Apologia, II*, p. 261.

168 Brendan Evans and Andrew Taylor, *From Salisbury to Major: Continuity and Change in Conservative Politics* (Manchester: Manchester University Press, 1996), p. 27.

Chapter 4   Democracy and Empire, 1922–35

1 John Gretton to H.A. Gwynne, 23 Oct. 1923, Bodleian Library, Oxford, H.A. Gwynne Papers [hereafter MS. Gwynne] deposit 8.

2 Ibid.; Gwynne to Sir Reginald Hall, 28 Dec. 1922; Hall to Gwynne, 29 Dec. 1922, MS. Gwynne deposit 8.

3 Maurice Cowling, *The Impact of Labour, 1920–1924: The Beginning of Modern British Politics* (Cambridge: Cambridge University Press, 1971), p. 239.

4 Gretton to Gwynne, 8 Aug. 1924, MS. Gwynne deposit 8.

5 Gretton Group private papers provided to Stuart Ball, University of Leicester, by Mrs Elizabeth Meynell, grand-daughter of the first Baron Gretton, in the late 1990s. The author thanks Professor Ball for allowing him to view copies of the documents.

6 *The Times*, 9 Nov. 1922, p. 13.

7 R.A.B. Butler, memo., 19–21 July 1935, in Philip Williamson and Edward Baldwin (eds), *Baldwin Papers: A Conservative Statesman 1908–1947* (Cambridge: Cambridge University Press, 2004), p. 343.

8 Philip Williamson, *Stanley Baldwin: Conservative Leadership and National Values* (Cambridge: Cambridge University Press, 1999), p. 204.

9 W.L. Guttsman, *The British Political Elite* (London: MacGibbon and Kee, 1965), pp. 307–308.

10 Austen Chamberlain to Ida Chamberlain, 2 Nov. 1930, in Robert C. Self (ed.), *The Austen Chamberlain Diary Letters: The Correspondence of Sir Austen Chamberlain with His Sisters, Hilda and Ida, 1916–1937* (Cambridge: Cambridge University Press, 1995), p. 358; Stuart Ball, *Portrait of a Party: The Conservative Party in Britain, 1918–1945* (Oxford: Oxford University Press, 2013), p. 343.

11 David Cannadine, *The Decline and Fall of the British Aristocracy* (reprinted edition, London: Papermac, 1996), pp. 12, 207.

12 Austen Chamberlain to Hilda Chamberlain, 14 April 1923, Self, *Correspondence*, p. 227; see also, Austen Chamberlain to Ida Chamberlain, 10 March 1923, ibid., p. 223.

13 Austen Chamberlain to Hilda Chamberlain, 18 March 1923, ibid., p. 224. It was Hall's appointment that provoked the debate amongst diehards about what to do with the 'diehard fund'. Gwynne wrote to Hall and the Duke of Bedford, both trustees of the fund, about an earlier agreement that it 'should be handed over to the Central Office

provided the right people were appointed', which in turn provoked objections from Gretton, whose claim to be a third trustee Gwynne had overlooked, see, Gwynne to Gretton, 24 Oct. 1923; Bedford to Gwynne, 26 Oct. 1923; Hall to Gwynne, 27 Oct. 1923; Gwynne to Gretton, 6 Aug. 1924, MS. Gwynne deposit 8.

14 Austen Chamberlain to Ida Chamberlain, 31 Oct. 1931, Self, *Correspondence*, p. 234.

15 David Low, *Low's Autobiography* (London: Michael Joseph, 1956), pp. 265–276. Evelyn Waugh created a similar character, 'General Connolly', a caste-conscious, déclassé Irish veteran in the service of 'Emperor Seth of Azania', in his *Black Mischief* ([1932] London: Penguin, 2000), pp. 37, 132.

16 Harold Nicolson, diary, 24 Feb. 1942, in Nigel Nicolson (ed.), *Harold Nicolson: Diaries and Letters, 1939–1945* (London: Collins, 1967), pp. 213–214.

17 It should be noted that in the film 'Blimp' was in fact the character Clive Wynne-Candy, a career soldier and not a politician. See, Michael Powell and Emeric Pressburger (dir.), *The Life and Death of Colonel Blimp* (1943).

18 Cowling, *Labour*, pp. 70–90; G.C. Webber, *The Ideology of the British Right, 1918–1939* (London: Croom Helm, 1986), p. 39.

19 Ball, *Portrait*, pp. 416, 438–439.

20 *The Times*, 31 Dec. 1923, p. 11. Banbury was incorrect on the number as Joynson-Hicks had joined the cabinet in May 1923 as Financial Secretary to the Treasury, and since October that year had been Minister for Health.

21 David Cesarani, 'The Anti-Jewish Career of Sir William Joynson-Hicks, Cabinet Minister', *Journal of Contemporary History*, 24, 3 (1989), pp. 461–482.

22 *House of Commons Debates*, 15 Dec. 1927, vol. 211, cols 2531–2655; Peter Catterall, 'The Party and Religion', in Anthony Seldon and Stuart Ball (eds), *Conservative Century: The Conservative Party Since 1900* (Oxford: Oxford University Press, 1990), p. 645.

23 Simon Moore, 'The Agrarian Conservative Party in Parliament, 1920–1929', *Parliamentary History*, 10, 2 (1991), pp. 342–362.

24 Andrew S. Thompson, *Imperial Britain: The Empire in British Politics, c.1880–1932* (London: Longman, 2000), pp. 157–185.

25 J.L. Crutchley, 'E is for Empire? Imperialism and British Public Elementary School Curricula, 1902–1931', PhD, University of Worcester (2016), pp. 123–186.

26 Nigel Keohane, *The Party of Patriotism: The Conservative Party and the First World War* (Aldershot: Ashgate, 2010), pp. 111–112; Barbara Storm Farr, *The Development and Impact of Right-Wing Politics in Britain, 1903–1932* (London: Garland, 1987), pp. 43–52.

27 Matthew C. Hendley, *Organized Patriotism and the Crucible of War: Popular Imperialism in Britain, 1914–1932* (Montreal and Kingston: McGill-Queen's University Press, 2012), pp. 173–224.

28 East Midlands Provincial Area Council, minutes of annual general meeting, 21 Jan. 1933, Bodleian Library, Oxford, Conservative Party Archive, ARE 5/1/1.

29 E.H.H. Green, *Ideologies of Conservatism: Conservative Political Ideas in the Twentieth Century* (Oxford: Oxford University Press, 2002), pp. 94, 109.

30 Neville Chamberlain to Ida Chamberlain, 11 Nov. 1923, in Robert C. Self (ed.), *The Neville Chamberlain Diary Letters, Volume II: The Reform Years, 1921-1927* (Aldershot: Ashgate, 2000), p. 193; Hannon to Baldwin, 9 Nov. 1923, cited in Larry L. Witherell, 'Sir Henry Page Croft and Conservative Backbench Campaigns for Empire, 1903-1932', *Parliamentary History*, 25, 3 (2006), p. 367; Cowling, *Labour*, p. 311.

31 Lord Croft, *My Life of Strife* (London: Hutchinson, 1948), pp. 173-174; *The Times*, 11 Dec. 1923, p. 15.

32 Gretton to Croft, 4 Feb. 1924, Churchill Archives Centre, Cambridge, Croft Papers [hereafter CRFT] 1/12.

33 *The Times*, 9 Feb. 1924, p. 10.

34 Robert Rhodes James (ed.), *Memoirs of a Conservative: J.C.C. Davidson's Memoirs and Papers 1910-37* (London: Weidenfeld and Nicolson, 1969), p. 385.

35 Bernard Porter, *The Absented-Minded Imperialists: Empire, Society and Culture in Britain* (Oxford: Oxford University Press, 2004), pp. 194-226; Catherine Hall and Sonya Rose (eds), *At Home with the Empire: Metropolitan Culture and the Imperial World* (Cambridge: Cambridge University Press, 2006), p. 2.

36 Richard Whiting, 'The Empire and British Politics', in Andrew Thompson (ed.), *Britain's Experience of Empire in the Twentieth Century* (Oxford: Oxford University Press, 2012), pp. 161-210.

37 Robert Self, *Neville Chamberlain: A Biography* (Aldershot: Ashgate, 2006), p. 79.

38 Croft, *Life*, pp. 179-182.

39 Churchill to Croft, 25 July 1928, Churchill Archives Centre, Cambridge, Winston Churchill Papers [hereafter CHAR] 2/158/63-67; Churchill to Croft, 24 Nov. 1928, CRFT 1/8.

40 John Turner, 'The Politics of Business', in John Turner (ed.), *Businessmen and Politics: Studies of Business Activity in British Politics, 1900-1945* (London: Heinemann, 1984), p. 16.

41 Croft, *Life*, p. 180.

42 Ball, *Portrait*, p. 230.

43 Witherell, 'Croft', p. 374.

44 Croft to Beaverbrook, 3 Jan. 1930, Parliamentary Archive, Westminster, Beaverbrook Papers [hereafter BBK] C/101.

45 Stuart Ball, *Baldwin and the Conservative Party: The Crisis of 1929-1931* (New Haven: Yale University Press, 1988), pp. 55-56.

46 Ibid., pp. 59-60.

47 Croft to Beaverbrook, 5 March 1930, BBK C/101.

48 *The Times*, 25 March 1930, p. 17.

49 Croft to Beaverbrook, 8 April 1930, 6 June 1930, 10 June 1930, BBK C/101; Hannon to Beaverbrook, 28 July 1930, Parliamentary Archive, Westminster, Patrick Hannon Papers [hereafter HNN] 17/1.

50 George Lane-Fox to Lord Irwin, 25 June 1930, in Stuart Ball (ed.), *Conservative Politics in National and Imperial Crisis: Letters from Britain to the Viceroy of India 1926–31* (Aldershot: Ashgate, 2014), pp. 335–336; *The Times*, 25 June 1930, p. 10.

51 *The Times*, 27 June 1930, p. 16. The Empire Economic Union's original aim had been to 'get into touch with similar bodies of industrialists throughout the Empire with a view to seeing how far agreement can be arranged between manufacturers and producers', see, *The Times*, 19 Dec. 1929, p. 14.

52 Croft to Beaverbrook, 9 Sept. 1930, BBK C/101.

53 Bridgeman to Croft, 8 Oct. 1930; 11 Oct. 1930, CRFT 1/5.

54 *The Times*, 18 Oct. 1930, p. 8; 24 Oct. 1930, p. 14; 25 Oct. 1930, p. 12; Neville Chamberlain to Ida Chamberlain, 26 Oct. 1930, in Robert C. Self (ed.), *The Neville Chamberlain Diary Letters, Volume III: The Heir Apparent, 1918–1933* (Aldershot: Ashgate, 2002), pp. 215–216.

55 *The Times*, 30 Oct. 1930, pp. 14–15.

56 Ball, *Portrait*, p. 345.

57 *The Times*, 31 Oct. 1930, pp. 14, 19.

58 Ibid.

59 Croft to Churchill, 21 Nov. 1934, CHAR 2/225/71.

60 Croft to Beaverbrook, 5 Nov. 1930, BBK C/101.

61 Gillian Peele, 'St George's and the Empire Crusade', in Chris Cook and John Ramsden (eds), *By-Elections in British Politics* (London: Macmillan, 1973), pp. 79–108; Ball, *Baldwin*, pp. 130–150; Hannon to Beaverbrook, 1 April 1931, BBK C/155.

62 Ball, *Conservative*, pp. 86–87.

63 Croft, *Life*, pp. 190–192; Patrick Donner, *Crusade: A Life Against the Calamitous Twentieth Century* (London: Sherwood, 1984), p. 76.

64 Viscount Lymington, *Ich Dien: The Tory Path* (London: Constable, 1931), p. 124.

65 MacDonald to Croft, 28 Sept. 1931, CRFT 1/16.

66 'The Nation's Duty: Mr Stanley Baldwin's General Election Message', in F.W.S. Craig (ed.), *British General Election Manifestos 1918–1966* (Chichester: Political Reference Publications, 1970), pp. 64–65.

67 Croft, *Life*, pp. 195–196.

68 Witherell, 'Croft', p. 379.

69 For example, Richard Griffiths, *Fellow Travellers of the Right: British Enthusiasts for Nazi Germany 1933–9* (London: Constable, 1980); Dan Stone, *Responses to Nazism in Britain, 1933–1939: Before War and Holocaust* (Basingstoke: Palgrave Macmillan,

2003); Karina Urbach, 'Age of No Extremes? The British Aristocracy Torn Between the House of Lords and the Mosley Movement', in Karina Urbach (ed.), *European Aristocracies and the Radical Right, 1918–1939* (Oxford: Oxford University Press, 2007), pp. 53–71.

70 Martin Pugh, *'Hurrah for the Blackshirts!' Fascists and Fascism in Britain Between the Wars* (London: Jonathan Cape, 2005), p. 5.

71 Harry Defries, *Conservative Party Attitudes to Jews, 1900–1950* (London: Routledge, 2001), p. 64.

72 Ibid., pp. 103, 107.

73 Lord Sydenham of Combe, *My Working Life* (London: John Murray, 1927), pp. 437–438; Alexander Maxwell [Home Office] to Sydenham, 8 Aug. 1922; 9 Aug. 1922, British Library, St Pancras, Sydenham Papers [hereafter Syd.], vol. X (ff. 295), large folio 1, ff. 47–49.

74 John Charmley, *Lord Lloyd and the Decline of the British Empire* (London: Weidenfeld and Nicolson, 1987), p. 237. See, Francis Robinson, 'The British Empire and the Muslim World', in Judith M. Brown and Wm. Roger Louis (eds), *The Oxford History of the British Empire, Volume IV: The Twentieth Century* (Oxford: Oxford University Press, 1999), pp. 398–420.

75 Dard to Hannon, 1 March 1934; Hannon to Dard, 2 March 1934, HNN/89.

76 Amery, diary, 7 April 1933, in John Barnes and David Nicholson (eds), *The Empire at Bay: The Leo Amery Diaries 1929–1945* (London: Hutchinson, 1988), p. 292.

77 W.J. Randall to Sydenham, 4 May 1920, Syd., vol. X, large folio 1, ff. 34–36.

78 Hannon to Sir George Armstrong, 10 June 1926, HNN/85/1. Hannon was unusual amongst the diehards in this respect. Croft claimed to have made contact with German anti-communists after the First World War, Croft, *Life*, pp. 124–125. In November 1940, when Britain was the only power to face Nazi Germany, Selborne persisted in expressing concern about ministers attempting to woo Moscow, see, Halifax to Selborne, 22 Nov. 1940, Bodleian Library, Oxford, second Earl of Selborne Papers [hereafter MS. Selborne] 87.

79 Keith M. Wilson, *A Study in the History and Politics of the* Morning Post *1905–1926* (Lampeter: Edwin Mellon, 1991), pp. 229–251. Gwynne received a request to consider giving part of the diehard fund to assist the *Patriot*, Northumberland's avowedly right-wing weekly, which he responded to by saying that he had to consult the trustees. There is no further correspondence in the archive on this matter, see, Philip Farrer to Gwynne, 15 June 1925; Gwynne to Farrer, 16 June 1925, MS. Gwynne deposit 17.

80 Pugh, *'Hurrah'*, p. 86.

81 *Morning Post*, 11 Oct. 1924; *Bournemouth Echo*, 6 Dec. 1924, CRFT 3/8.

82 David Thackeray, *Conservatism for the Democratic Age: Conservative Cultures and the Challenge of Mass Politics in Early Twentieth-Century England* (Manchester: Manchester University Press, 2013), pp. 194–195.

83 Pugh, 'Hurrah', p. 86, cites David Jarvis, 'Stanley Baldwin and the Ideology of the
    Conservative Response to Socialism, 1918-1931', PhD, Lancaster University (1991),
    p. 139, which in turn cites the New Vote, 4 Feb. 1924. Information on the New Vote
    supplied by Dr Jarvis.

84 Thackeray, Conservatism, pp. 155-157.

85 Webber, Ideology, pp. 156-157; Nick Toczek, Haters, Baiters and Would-Be Dictators:
    Anti-Semitism and the UK Far Right (Abingdon: Routledge, 2016), p. 200.

86 The Times, 9 Jan. 1924, p. 14.

87 Manchester Guardian, 9 Jan. 1924, p. 8.

88 Dundee Courier, 14 Aug. 1936, p. 7; The Times, 8 Jan. 1924, p. 12; 9 Jan. 1924, p. 14;
    George Lansbury, My Life ([1928] London: Constable, 1931), p. 116.

89 The Times, 12 Dec. 1923, p. 13.

90 Manchester Guardian, 9 Jan. 1924, p. 8.

91 Derby to Lord Birkenhead, 7 Dec. 1923, in Randolph S. Churchill, Lord Derby 'King
    of Lancashire': The Official Life of Edward, Seventeenth Earl of Derby 1865-1948
    (London: Heinemann, 1959), p. 541.

92 John Ramsden, An Appetite for Power: A History of the Conservative Party Since 1830
    (London: Harper Collins, 1999), pp. 262-263.

93 Leonard Woolf, After the Deluge: A Study of Communal Psychology (Harmondsworth:
    Pelican, 1937), pp. 140-141.

94 David A. Thackeray, 'Building a Peaceable Party: Masculine Identities in British
    Conservative Politics, c.1903-24', Historical Research, 85, 230 (2012), pp. 651-673.

95 Philip Williamson, 'The Conservative Party, Fascism and Anti-Fascism 1918-1939',
    in Nigel Copsey and Andrzej Olechnowicz (eds), Varieties of Anti-Fascism: Britain in
    the Inter-war Period (Basingstoke: Palgrave, 2010), pp. 76-77.

96 Paul B. Rich, Race and Empire in British Politics (2nd edition, Cambridge: Cambridge
    University Press, 1990), p. 5.

97 A. Susan Williams, Ladies of Influence: Women of the Elite in Interwar Britain
    (London: Allen Lane, 2000), pp. 80-81.

98 Bradley W. Hart and Richard Carr, 'Sterilization and the British Conservative Party:
    Rethinking the Failure of the Eugenics Society's Political Strategy in the Nineteen-
    Thirties', Historical Research, 88, 242 (2015), pp. 716-739.

99 See, W.A. Rudlin, The Growth of Fascism in Great Britain (London: George Allen and
    Unwin, 1935), pp. 115-117, 131-132; David Baker, 'The Extreme Right in the 1920s:
    Fascism in a Cold Climate, or "Conservatism with Knobs On"?', in Mike Cronin
    (ed.), The Failure of British Fascism: The Far Right and the Fight for Political
    Recognition (Basingstoke: Palgrave Macmillan, 1996), p. 18; Pugh, 'Hurrah', pp. 3-5,
    32-33. This focus on ideology is unusual in diplomatic history, see, G. Bruce Strang,
    'The Spirit of Ulysses? Ideology and British Appeasement in the 1930s', Diplomacy
    and Statecraft, 19, 3 (2008), pp. 481-526.

100 Stone, *Responses*, p. 114.

101 G.T. Waddington, ' "An Idyllic and Unruffled Atmosphere of Complete Anglo-German Misunderstanding": Aspects of the Operations of the Dienststelle Ribbentrop in Great Britain, 1934–1938', *History*, 82, 265 (1997), pp. 44–72; David Lukowitz, 'George Lansbury's Peace Missions to Hitler and Mussolini in 1937', *Canadian Journal of History*, 15, 1 (1980), pp. 67–82; Stella Rudman, *Lloyd George and the Appeasement of Germany, 1919–1945* (Newcastle: Cambridge Scholars, 2011), pp. 186–263.

102 *Western Gazette*, 23 Oct. 1936, p. 16.

103 According to Griffiths, the following Conservative MPs were named in the document which purports to be the infamous 'red book' listing club members: Peter Agnew (originally an India diehard but declined to oppose the 1935 bill), Sir Samuel Chapman, Lord Colum Crichton-Stuart, Sir James Edmondson, Sir Thomas Hunter, John McKie, Harold Mitchell and J.J. Stourton, see, Richard Griffiths, *Patriotism Perverted: Captain Ramsay, the Right Club and British Anti-Semitism 1939–40* (London: Faber and Faber, 1998), pp. 143–164. Griffiths is cautious about placing too much reliance on the document's validity and veracity. See also, Robin Saikia, *The Red Book: The Membership List of The Right Club – 1939* (London: Foxley Books, 2010), pp. 97–132.

104 Pugh, 'Hurrah', pp. 192, 280–281; N.J. Crowson, *Facing Fascism: The Conservative Party and the European Dictators 1935–1940* (London: Routledge, 1997), p. 207; Griffiths, *Fellow*, pp. 307–317.

105 This draws on Pugh's list, see, Pugh, 'Hurrah', p. 270.

106 Webber, *Ideology*, pp. 73–88; Arthur Marwick, 'Middle Opinion in the Thirties: Planning, Progress and Political "Agreement" ', *English Historical Review*, 79, 311 (1964), pp. 285–298; Simon Ball, 'Mosley and the Tories in 1930: The Problem of Generations', *Contemporary British History*, 24, 4 (2009), pp. 445–459; Brian Girvin, *The Right in the Twentieth Century: Conservatism and Democracy* (London: Pinter, 1994), p. 80; Williamson, 'Conservative', pp. 73–97; Ball, *Portrait*, p. 80. See also, John Stevenson, 'Conservatism and the Failure of Fascism in Interwar Britain', in Martin Blinkhorn (ed.), *Fascists and Conservatives: The Radical Right and the Establishment in Twentieth-Century Europe* (London: Routledge, 1990), pp. 264–282.

107 Philip Murphy, *Alan Lennox-Boyd: A Biography* (London: I.B.Tauris, 1999), p. 43.

108 Paul Addison, 'Patriotism Under Pressure: Lord Rothermere and British Foreign Policy', in Chris Cook and Gillian Peele (eds), *The Politics of Reappraisal, 1918–1939* (London: Macmillan, 1975), pp. 189–208; Alan Foster, 'The Beaverbrook Press and Appeasement: The Second Phase', *European History Quarterly*, 21, 1 (1991), pp. 5–38.

109 Richard Thurlow, 'Anti-Nazi Anti-Semite: The Case of Douglas Reed', *Patterns of Prejudice*, 18, 1 (1984), pp. 23–34.

110 Franklin Reid Gannon, *The British Press and Germany 1936–1939* (Oxford: Clarendon Press, 1971), pp. 49–50; Elspeth Y. O'Riordan, *Britain and the Ruhr Crisis* (Basingstoke: Palgrave Macmillan, 2001), pp. 73, 89. Gwynne still wrote supportively to Neville Chamberlain, see, Gwynne to Chamberlain, 23 Feb. 1939, MS. Gwynne deposit 17. This might account for Janet Dack's contention that Gwynne 'encouraged and supported Chamberlain's policy of appeasement', see, Janet Dack, ' "It Certainly Isn't Cricket!" Media Responses to Mosley and the BUF', in Nigel Copsey and Andrzej Olechnowicz (eds), *Varieties of Anti-Fascism: Britain in the Inter-war Period* (Basingstoke: Palgrave Macmillan, 2010), pp. 141–161. However, it is clear that Gwynne's advice to Chamberlain, given following the closure in 1937 of the *Morning Post*, emphasized the need to deal with Germany from a position of strength, see, Gwynne to Chamberlain, 26 April 1938, MS. Gwynne deposit 17.

111 Gwynne to Sir John Reith, 22 Feb. 1937, MS. Gwynne deposit 21.

112 Richard Finlay, 'Scottish Conservatism and Unionism Since 1918', in Martin Francis and Ina Zweiniger-Bargielowska (eds), *The Conservatives and British Society, 1880–1990* (Cardiff: University of Wales Press, 1995), p. 114; Stephen M. Cullen, 'The Fasces and the Saltire: The Failure of the British Union of Fascists in Scotland, 1932–1940', *Scottish Historical Review*, 87, 2 (2008), pp. 306–331.

113 James Loughlin, 'Northern Ireland and British Fascism in the Inter-war Years', *Irish Historical Studies*, 29, 116 (1995), pp. 537–552. See also, Paul Corthorn, 'W.E.D. Allen, Unionist Politics and the New Party', *Contemporary British History*, 23, 4 (2009), pp. 509–525.

114 Ball, *Portrait*, p. 166.

115 *The Times*, 24 Feb. 1926, p. 14.

116 Croft, *Life*, p. 185.

117 Ball, *Portrait*, p. 344.

118 1922 Committee, minutes, 10 Dec. 1934, vol. 3, March 1934–July 1938, Bodleian Library, Oxford, Conservative Party Archive, 1922 Committee [hereafter 1922] 3. Raikes was still a controversial figure, see, *Daily Express*, 11 March 1935, p. 15. Wolmer received a complaint in 1935 about Raikes causing a destructive row in his constituency association, see, V. Cecil to Wolmer, 14 June 1935, third Earl of Selborne Papers [hereafter MS. Eng. hist. c. 1013].

119 'To the Electors of the Aldershot Division of Hampshire', 14 May 1929, MS. Eng. hist. c. 1013. Wolmer was afterwards rewarded in Baldwin's resignation honours list with appointment to the Privy Council, see, Baldwin to Wolmer, 21 June 1929, MS. Eng. hist. c. 1013.

120 *Morning Post*, 22 Oct. 1929, cutting, MS. Eng. hist. c. 1013.

121 'To the Electors of the Aldershot Division of Hampshire', 14 Oct. 1931, MS. Eng. hist. c. 1013.

122 *Manchester Guardian*, 3 Feb. 1934, p. 12.

123 Stuart Ball, 'The Legacy of Coalition: Fear and Loathing in Conservative Politics, 1922–1931', *Contemporary British History*, 25, 1 (2011), pp. 65–82; Stuart Ball, *The Conservative Party and British Politics 1902–1951* (London: Longman, 1995), p. 70.

124 Cowling, *Labour*, pp. 331–340.

125 'Analysis of Recent General Elections Together with By-Election Returns 1924' (n.d.), Bodleian Library, Oxford, Joseph Ball Papers, MS. Eng. c. 6652.

126 Ross McKibbin, *Classes and Cultures: England 1918–1951* (Oxford: Oxford University Press, 1998), p. 96.

127 Finlay, 'Scottish', pp. 112–114.

128 Lord Lloyd, memo., 4 March 1931, Williamson and Baldwin, *Baldwin Papers*, p. 254.

129 Marwick, 'Middle', pp. 285–298; W.H. Greenleaf, *The British Political Tradition, Volume II: The Ideological Heritage* (London: Methuen, 1983), pp. 245–254.

130 Cowling, *Labour*, p. 407. The Soviet Union now replaced Germany as the protagonist of invasion scares, see, Michael Hughes and Harry Wood, 'Crimson Nightmares: Tales of Invasion and Fears of Revolution in Early Twentieth-Century Britain', *Contemporary British History*, 28, 3 (2014), pp. 294–317; Tony Shaw, 'Early Warnings of the Red Peril: A Pre-history of Cold War British Cinema, 1917–1939', *Film History*, 14, 3/4 (2002), pp. 354–368.

131 Williamson, *Baldwin*, p. 177.

132 *House of Commons Debates*, 6 March 1925, vol. 181, cols 833–897; *The Times*, 7 March 1925, p. 12.

133 *The Times*, 3 Aug. 1925, p. 8.

134 *House of Commons Debates*, 6 Aug. 1925, vol. 187, cols 1581–1697.

135 Neville Chamberlain to Hilda Chamberlain, 9 Aug. 1925, Self, *Diary Letters, II*, p. 306.

136 Gwynne to Northumberland, 10 May 1926, MS. Gwynne deposit 32. See also, Churchill to Gwynne, 12 May 1926, MS. Gwynne deposit 17.

137 *The Times*, 8 Oct. 1926, p. 7.

138 Gwynne to Northumberland, 10 Dec. 1926, MS. Gwynne deposit 21.

139 David Dilks, *Neville Chamberlain, Volume I: Pioneering and Reform, 1869–1929* (Cambridge: Cambridge University Press, 1984), pp. 511–515.

140 Andrew Taylor, 'The Party and Trade Unions', in Anthony Seldon and Stuart Ball (eds), *Conservative Century: The Conservative Party Since 1900* (Oxford: Oxford University Press, 1994), pp. 506–507.

141 A.D. Steel-Maitland, 'Labour', in Earl of Malmesbury (ed.), *The New Order: Studies in Unionist Policy* (London: Francis Griffiths, 1908), pp. 335–376. See, Chapter 1.

142 Ball, *Portrait*, pp. 224–225.

143 *The Times*, 8 Oct. 1926, p. 7.

144 Geraint Thomas, 'Conservatives, the Constitution and the Quest for a "Representative" House of Lords, 1911–35', *Parliamentary History*, 31, 3 (2012), pp. 419–443.

145 David Jarvis, 'British Conservatism and Class Politics in the 1920s', *English Historical Review*, 111, 440 (1996), pp. 59–84.

146 See, Northumberland to Gwynne, 10 Oct. 1924, MS. Gwynne deposit 21; Bayford, diary, 18 May 1925, John Ramsden (ed.), *Real Old Tory Politics: The Political Diaries of Sir Robert Sanders, Lord Bayford, 1910–1935* (London: Historians' Press, 1984), p. 220.

147 *The Times*, 7 Oct. 1927, p. 7.

148 Bayford, diary, 3 June 1934, Ramsden, *Real*, p. 250.

149 David Jarvis, 'Mrs Maggs and Betty: The Conservative Appeal to Women Voters in the 1920s', *Twentieth Century British History*, 5, 2 (1994), pp. 129–152.

150 *The Times*, 21 Feb., 1925, p. 7.

151 Ball, *Portrait*, p. 423; Joni Lovenduski, Pippa Norris and Catriona Burness, 'The Party and Women', in Anthony Seldon and Stuart Ball (eds), *Conservative Century: The Conservative Party Since 1900* (Oxford: Oxford University Press, 1994), p. 612.

152 The other two were Sir George Cockerill and Samuel Samuel, see, *The Times*, 14 March 1928, p. 16.

153 *House of Commons Debates*, 29 March 1928, vol. 215, cols 1359–1481. Harmsworth's inclusion as a 'diehard' is complicated by his sharing a platform with Lloyd George at the 1922 general election, the result of a characteristic change of mind on the part of Rothermere, see, Cowling, *Labour*, p. 219. Boyd-Carpenter's son, John Boyd-Carpenter, a government minister under Harold Macmillan, makes no reference in his memoirs to Archibald being a diehard, preferring instead to attribute the end of his junior ministerial career to falling out with Baldwin, after which he was offered and declined the governorship of Kenya, see, John Boyd-Carpenter, *Way of Life* (London: Sidgwick and Jackson, 1980), p. 11. A letter from Amery to Lennox-Boyd, asking him to keep a hand on the coat tails of 'our impetuous young friend John Boyd Carpenter when the next meeting of the Oxford Committee takes place', suggests that John too was in close contact with the Right of the party in his younger years. See, Amery to Lennox-Boyd, 27 Oct. 1936, Bodleian Library, Oxford, Alan Lennox-Boyd Papers, MS. Eng. c. 3385.

154 *The Times*, 17 Nov. 1919, p. 9.

155 *The Times*, 31 March 1928, p. 14. Gretton subsequently supported another equally doomed amendment to the franchise bill which increased the age for both men and women voters to twenty-five, see, *The Times*, 19 April 1928, p. 16.

156 Lymington, *Ich*, p. 20.

157 *House of Commons Debates*, 29 March 1928, vol. 215, cols 1479–1481.

158 Stuart Ball, 'The 1922 Committee: The Formative Years 1922–45', *Parliamentary History*, 9, 1 (1990), pp. 129–157.

159 Ball, *Portrait*, p. 379.

160 *The Times*, 20 June 1924, p. 9.

161 Stuart Ball, 'The Conservative Party, the Role of the State and the Politics of Protection, c.1918–1932', *History*, 96, 323 (2011), pp. 280–303.

162 Sara L. Maurer, *The Dispossessed State: Narratives of Ownership in Nineteenth-Century Britain and Ireland* (Baltimore, MD: Johns Hopkins University Press, 2012), p. 7.

163 David Dutton, *A History of the Liberal Party Since 1900* (second edition, Basingstoke: Palgrave Macmillan, 2013), pp. 103–106.

164 Stephen Evans, 'The Conservatives and the Redefinition of Unionism, 1912–21', *Twentieth Century British History*, 9, 1 (1998), pp. 1–27.

165 Paul Canning, *British Policy Towards Ireland, 1921–1941* (Oxford: Clarendon Press, 1985), p. 81.

166 *The Times*, 5 Feb. 1929, p. 11; 10 Nov. 1930, p. 7; 20 May 1931, p. 11.

167 Ibid., 15 Feb. 1922, p. 10.

168 St John Ervine, *Craigavon: Ulsterman* (London: George Allen and Unwin, 1949), p. 473.

169 *House of Commons Debates*, 16 Feb. 1922, vol. 150, cols 1175–1376; 6 March 1922, vol. 151 cols 903–1034; 8 March 1922, vol. 151, cols 1362–1433.

170 Paul Bew, *Churchill and Ireland* (Oxford: Oxford University Press, 2016), pp. 113–130.

171 John Campbell, *F.E. Smith: First Earl of Birkenhead* (London: Jonathan Cape, 1983), pp. 584–585; Kevin Matthews, *Fatal Influence: The Impact of Ireland on British Politics, 1920–1925* (Dublin: University College Dublin Press, 2004), p. 75.

172 Cabinet Conclusions (Northern Ireland), 7 May 1924, Public Record Office of Northern Ireland, Cabinet Papers [hereafter NI CAB], 4/113/9.

173 See, first Baron Bayford [Robert Saunders], diary, 10 Aug. 1924, in Ramsden, *Real*, p. 216.

174 Thomas Jones, diary, 2 Aug. 1924, in Keith Middlemas (ed.), *Thomas Jones Whitehall Diary, Volume III: Ireland, 1918–1925* (London: Oxford University Press, 1971), p. 226.

175 *Senate Debates (Northern Ireland)*, 13 May 1924, vol. 4, col. 117; Jones, diary, 8 Aug. 1924, Middlemas, *Whitehall, III*, p. 235.

176 *The Times*, 5 Aug. 1924, p. 10; 8 Aug. 1924, p. 12.

177 Matthews, *Fatal*, p. 165.

178 Londonderry to Baldwin, 27 Aug. 1924, Cambridge University Library, Baldwin Papers [hereafter Bald.] 99, 128–129.

179 Cabinet Conclusions (Northern Ireland), 16 Sept. 1924, NI CAB/4/121.

180 *House of Lords Debates*, 8 Oct. 1924, vol. 59, cols 591–666.

181 Ibid., 9 Oct. 1924, vol. 59, cols 668–680.

182 Matthews, *Fatal*, pp. 205–209; Geoffrey J. Hand (ed.), *Report of the Irish Boundary Commission 1925* (Shannon: Irish Academic Press, 1969), pp. xii, xviii.

183 *House of Commons Debates,* 8 Dec. 1925, vol. 189, cols 309–363.

184 John Darwin, *The Empire Project: The Rise and Fall of the British World-System 1830–1970* (Cambridge: Cambridge University Press, 2009), pp. 444–445.

185 *House of Commons Debates,* 24 Nov. 1931, vol. 260, cols 303–355; 3 Dec. 1931, vol. 260, cols 1287–1413.

186 Philip Williamson, *National Crisis and National Government: British Politics, the Economy and the Empire, 1926–1932* (Cambridge: Cambridge University Press, 1992), p. 493; Deirdre McMahon, *Republicans and Imperialists: Anglo–Irish Relations in the 1930s* (London: Yale University Press, 1984), p. 289.

187 *House of Commons Debates,* 10 July 1935, vol. 304, cols 422–426. See, Richard Toye, ' "Phrases Make History Here": Churchill, Ireland and the Rhetoric of Empire', *Journal of Imperial and Commonwealth History,* 38, 4 (2010), p. 560.

188 'England's Peril Today' (May 1933), Churchill Archives Centre, Cambridge, Lord Lloyd Papers [hereafter GLLD] 11/2.

189 Croft to Churchill, 28 April 1938, CRFT 1/8.

190 *House of Commons Debates,* 5 May 1938, vol. 335, cols 1071–1185.

191 Canning, *British,* p. 316.

192 Earl of Lytton to Irwin, 20 Nov. 1929, in Williamson and Baldwin, *Baldwin Papers,* p. 224.

193 Sir Charles Fawcett [retired Bombay judge], 'The Provision of Safeguards under the Indian Federal Constitution', *Indian Empire Review* [hereafter *IER*], 1, 11 (1932), pp. 20–24.

194 Williamson, *Baldwin,* pp. 266–268.

195 Churchill to Croft, 31 March 1933, CRFT 1/8.

196 J.H.C. Harrison, 'Has Socialism Shaped our Indian Policy?', *IER,* 2, 12 (1933), pp. 33–35.

197 'The Simon Report: First Views in India', *The Times,* 11 June 1930, p. 14.

198 Viscount Simon, *Retrospect: The Memoirs of the Rt. Hon. Viscount Simon GCSI, GCVO* (London: Hutchinson, 1952), p. 153.

199 'Indian Empire Society: Statement of Policy', *IER,* 2, 3 (1933), pp. 43–49; H.M. Cowan, 'The Indian Executive and the Command Paper', *IER,* 2, 8 (1933), pp. 14–19; Michael O'Dwyer, 'A Sound Constitution for India', *IER,* 3, 4 (1934), pp. 147–150. There was a further irony in the diehards' fidelity to Simon's Commission given that he had resigned in January 1916, as Home Secretary, in opposition to conscription, an issue championed at the time by the Conservative Right.

200 Amery, diary, 9 March 1931, 16 March 1931, Barnes and Nicholson, *Empire,* pp. 153–156.

201 In June 1934 Baldwin remarked to a journalist that 'a good deal of the bitterness of the Die-hard agitation was due to Lord Sumner, who died a few weeks ago. He had been a Liberal, and, having been converted to Toryism, had become thoroughly narrow and bigoted', see, W.P. Crozier, interview notes, 12 June 1934,

Williamson and Baldwin, *Baldwin Papers*, p. 320. Sumner was president of the India Defence League (IDL), but his involvement in the precursor Indian Empire Society (IES) came in response to an invitation from Lords Sydenham and Salisbury, see, Antony Lentin, *The Last Political Law Lord: Lord Sumner (1859–1934)* (Newcastle: Cambridge Scholars Publishing, 2008), p. 219. Lord FitzAlan succeeded as president of the IDL.

202 *The Times*, 5 July 1930, p. 7.

203 Paul Stocker, ' "The Surrender of an Empire": British Imperialism in Radical Right and Fascist Ideology, 1921–1963', PhD, Teesside University (2016), pp. 99–100.

204 *House of Commons Debates*, 26 Jan. 1931, vol. 247, cols 698, 744–748.

205 Sarvepalli Gopal, 'Churchill and India', in Robert Blake and Wm. Roger Louis (eds), *Churchill* (Oxford: Clarendon Press, 1996), p. 458.

206 Winston S. Churchill, *India: Speeches and an Introduction* (London: Thornton Butterworth, 1931), pp. 15–28.

207 Austen Chamberlain to Hilda Chamberlain, 28 Oct. 1933, Self, *Correspondence*, pp. 251–252.

208 Richard Toye, *Churchill's Empire: The World that Made Him and the World He Made* (London: Macmillan, 2010), pp. 154–156.

209 Cowling, *Labour*, pp. 160–168.

210 Toye, *Empire*, pp. 181–182.

211 Cowling, *Labour*, p. 203.

212 Maurice Cowling, *The Impact of Hitler: British Politics and British Policy* (Chicago: University of Chicago Press, 1977), p. 272.

213 Ampthill to Lloyd, 1 May 1933, Mount Temple to Lloyd, 12 June 1933, Banbury to Lloyd, 1 May 1933, Malmesbury to Lloyd, 11 May 1933, GLLD 11/2.

214 Charmley, *Lloyd*, pp. 71, 93, 95, 105–106.

215 *House of Commons Debates*, 24 July 1929, vol. 230, cols 1301–1304; 29 July 1929, vol. 230, cols 1631–1646.

216 R.B.D. Blakeney, 'Egypt under Self-Determination', *IER*, 3, 11 (1934), pp. 458–462. Brigadier Blakeney was involved in fascist politics, see, Richard Thurlow, *Fascism in Britain: From Oswald Mosley's Blackshirts to the National Front* (London: I.B.Tauris, 1998), pp. 34–35.

217 See, GLLD 11/2.

218 Michael Bloch, *Closet Queens: Some 20th Century Politicians* (London: Little, Brown, 2015), pp. 115–116.

219 Compton Mackenzie, *Thin Ice* (London: Chatto and Windus, 1956), p. 78.

220 Hannon to Sir Malcolm Fraser, 13 June 1933, HNN/85/2.

221 Headlam, diary, 21 Oct. 1936, in Stuart Ball (ed.), *Parliament and Politics in the Age of Churchill and Attlee: The Headlam Diaries 1935–1951* (Cambridge: Cambridge University Press, 1999), p. 95.

222 Gretton to Churchill, 30 March 1930, CHAR 2/192/131–132; Lord Lloyd, memo., 4 March 1931, Williamson and Baldwin, *Baldwin Papers*, p. 254.

223 N.C. Fleming, 'Lancashire Conservatives, Tariff Reform, and Indian Responsible Government', *Contemporary British History*, 30, 2 (2016), p. 159.

224 Lloyd to Churchill, 20 April 1933, CHAR 2/197/28; 'Activities of the Indian Empire Society', *IER*, 1, 7 (1932); 'India Defence League', *The Times*, 2 June 1933, p. 7; 'The India Defence League', *IER*, 2, 7 (1933), pp. 2–3. Patrick Donner to Violet Milner, 2 May 1933, Bodleian Library, Oxford, Violet Milner Papers [hereafter VM] 39. Donner was made a director of the *National Review* in 1933.

225 Wolmer to Violet Milner, 29 June 1933, VM 26; Gretton to Churchill, 21 Sept. 1933, CHAR 2/197/114–116.

226 Donner, *Crusade*, pp. 41, 61.

227 Gwynne to Gretton, 5 April 1933; Gretton to Gwynne, 6 April 1933, MS. Gwynne deposit 17.

228 Wolmer to Lady Houston, 11 March 1935, MS. Eng. hist. c. 1013.

229 Gretton to Churchill, 7 March 1935, CHAR 2/240A/67.

230 Williamson, *National*, p. 182.

231 An article on Wolmer and the IDL had fun commenting on his 'long-winded' address, *Daily Express*, 22 July 1933, p. 6.

232 Ian St John, '*Writing to the Defence of Empire*: Winston Churchill's Press Campaign Against Constitutional Reform in India, 1929–1935', in Chandrika Kaul (ed.), *Media and the British Empire* (Basingstoke: Palgrave Macmillan, 2006), p. 110; Bracken to Beaverbrook, 14 Jan. 1931, in Richard Cockett (ed.), *My Dear Max: The Letters of Brendan Bracken to Lord Beaverbrook, 1925–1958* (London: Historians' Press, 1990), p. 35; Croft to Beaverbrook, 6 Oct. 1934, BBK C/101.

233 Bewdley Division Unionist Association, minutes, 14 April 1934, Worcestershire Archives, Bewdley Division Unionist Association Papers, 705.225/956/8.

234 Clarisse Berthezène, *Training Minds for the War of Ideas: Ashridge College, the Conservative Party and the Cultural Politics of Britain, 1929–54* (Manchester: Manchester University Press, 2015), p. 133; N.C. Fleming, 'Women and Lancashire Conservatism Between the Wars', *Women's History Review*, 26, 3 (2017), p. 335.

235 N.C. Fleming, 'Diehard Conservatism, Mass Democracy, and Indian Constitutional Reform, c.1918–1935', *Parliamentary History*, 32, 2 (2013), pp. 337–360.

236 Jeffrey Herf, *Reactionary Modernism: Technology, Culture, and Politics in Weimar and the Third Reich* (Cambridge: Cambridge University Press, 1984).

237 David Egerton, *England and the Aeroplane: Militarism, Modernity and Machines* (London: Penguin, 2013), pp. 74–79.

238 Patrick Zander, '(Right) Wings over Everest: High Adventure, High Technology and High Nationalism on the Roof of the World, 1932–1934', *Twentieth Century British History*, 21, 3 (2010), pp. 300–329.

239 Pugh, 'Hurrah', p. 190.

240 *House of Commons Debates*, 17 July 1933, vol. 280, cols 1632–1634.

241 Katherine C. Epstein, 'Imperial Airs: Leo Amery, Air Power and Empire, 1873–1945', *Journal of Imperial and Commonwealth History*, 38, 4 (2010), pp. 571–598.

242 Charmley, *Lloyd*, pp. 188–192; Wolmer to Lady Houston, 11 March 1935, MS. Eng. hist. c. 1013.

243 Lady Houston to Wolmer, 11 July 1934; Wolmer to Mr Allen, 13 July 1934, Lady Houston to Wolmer, 18 July 1934, MS. Eng. hist. c. 1013.

244 Gerald Studdert-Kennedy, 'The Christian Imperialism of the Die-Hard Defenders of the Raj, 1926–35', *Journal of Imperial and Commonwealth History*, 18, 3 (1990), pp. 342–362. See also, Croft, *Life*, p. 343.

245 Lymington, *Ich*, p. 29.

246 Gideon Murray, *A Man's Life: Reflections and Reminiscences of Experiences in Many Lands* (London: Hutchinson, 1934), pp. 251–252; Donner, *Crusade*, p. 63.

247 McKibbin, *Classes*, p. 293.

248 For Hannon's correspondence on Catholic matters see, HNN/80; Charles Lysaght, *Brendan Bracken* (London: Allen Lane, 1979), p. 186.

249 Charmley, *Lloyd*, p. 196.

250 Stone, *Responses*, pp. 132–138.

251 Webber, *Ideology*, p. 63.

252 For example, Custos [pseud.], 'India – Our Moral Obligation', *IER*, 1, 12 (1932); Dufadar [pseud.], 'Alas the Poor Indian: A Sidelight on the White Paper', *IER*, 2, 12 (1933), pp. 15–22; Hayter, 'The British and the "Scheduled Castes"', *IER*, 3, 3 (1934), pp. 117–119; George Milne, 'The Behar Earthquake', *IER*, 3, 6 (1934); Hubert Calvert, 'The Welfare of the Masses', *IER*, 4, 1 (1935), pp. 36–41.

253 Rahul Nair, 'The Construction of a "Population Problem" in Colonial India 1919–1947', *Journal of Imperial and Commonwealth History*, 39, 2 (2011), pp. 227–247; Katherine Mayo, *Mother India* (New York: Harcourt, Brace and Company, 1927).

254 Atholl to Lloyd, 12 Jan. 1934, GLLD 11/2; S.J. Hetherington, *Katherine Atholl, 1874–1960: Against the Tide* (Aberdeen: Aberdeen University Press, 1989), pp. 130–131, 142–43.

255 Stuart Ball, 'The Politics of Appeasement: The Fall of the Duchess of Atholl and the Kinross and West Perth By-Election, 1938', *Scottish Historical Review*, 69, 187 (1990), pp. 49–83.

256 *House of Commons Debates*, 22 Nov. 1933, vol. 283, cols 214–215; Croft also recommended, Patricia Kendall, *Come with Me to India!* (New York: Charles Scribner's Sons, 1931).

257 Mrinalini Sinha, *Specters of Mother India: The Global Restructuring of an Empire* (Durham, NC: Duke University Press, 2006), pp. 93, 288.

258 Katherine Mayo, 'The British in India as seen in America', IER, 1, 9 (1932), pp. 17–20.

259 Anne McClintock, *Imperial Leather: Race, Gender and Sexuality in the Colonial Contest* (New York: Routledge, 1995), pp. 71–72; Thomas R. Metcalf, *Ideologies of the Raj* (Cambridge: Cambridge University Press, 1995), pp. 66–112. See also, Dipesh Chakrabarty, *Provincializing Europe: Postcolonial Thought and Historical Difference* (Princeton, NJ: Princeton University Press, 2000).

260 Howard V. Brasted and Carl Bridge, 'The British Labour Party and Indian Nationalism, 1907–1947', *South Asia*, 2, 2 (1988), pp. 69–99; Nicholas Owen, *The British Left and India: Metropolitan Anti-Imperialism, 1885–1947* (Oxford: Oxford University Press, 2007), pp. 136–196.

261 Sir Verney Lovett [retired Indian Civil Service], 'The Proposed Transfer of Law and Order in Indian Provinces', *IER*, 1, 1 (1931); Lovett, 'Terrorism in Bengal', and 'A Retired Officer of the Force'; [anon.], 'Reading the Riot in India', *IER*, 1, 2 (1931); Hayter, 'Facts to be Faced in India', *IER*, 1, 5 (1932); Amiens [pseud.], 'Changes Since 1919 (2) The Indian Police', *IER*, 1, 7 (1932); Hayter, 'Law and Order in India and the Communal Question', *IER*, 1, 11 (1932); E.P.J. [pseud.], 'The White Paper Proposals with Regard to Law and Order', *IER*, 2, 10 (1933), pp. 24–28; Lovett, 'The Present Extent of Terrorism in India (a Critical Study)', *IER*, 2, 11 (1933), pp. 15–23; Lovett, 'The Present Extent of Terrorism II', *IER*, 3, 2 (1934), pp. 59–67; Hayter, 'Gradual Development', *IER*, 3, 4 (1934), pp. 165–167; Lovett, 'The Present Extent of Terrorism in India III', *IER*, 3, 5 (1934), pp. 187–195; Hayter, '*Vis consili expers mole ruit sua* [Brute Force Without Wisdom Falls by Its Own Weight]', *IER*, 3, 10 (1934), pp. 409–411; Hayter, 'The Police and the Law Courts', *IER*, 4, 1 (1935).

262 *House of Commons Debates*, 12 March 1931, vol. 249, col. 1425.

263 Lord Sydenham, 'The Effect of Indian Reform on Lancashire Trade', *IER*, 2, 4 (1933), pp. 22–25; Huck [pseud.], 'The Immorality of Examinations', *IER*, 2, 9 (1933), pp. 24–30.

264 Satoshi Mizutani, *The Meaning of White: Race, Class, and the 'Domiciled Community' in British India 1858–1930* (Oxford: Oxford University Press, 2011).

265 Ian Copland, *The Princes of India and the Endgame of Empire, 1917–1947* (Cambridge: Cambridge University Press, 2002), pp. 113–143; *Morning Post, Representative Indian States: A Series of Articles Reprinted from the* Morning Post (London: The Morning Post, 1935); C.L. Dunn, 'The Villagers of India', *IER*, 4, 6 (1935).

266 'Lord Sumner's notes', n.d. [*c.* Jan. 1934], GLLD 11/2.

267 Susan Pedersen, 'Modernity and Trusteeship: Tensions of Empire in Britain Between the Wars', in Martin Daunton and Bernard Rieger (eds), *Meanings of Modernity: Britain from the Late-Victorian Era to World War II* (Oxford: Berg, 2001), p. 204.

268 Hoare to Lord Willingdon, 19 May 1933, cited in Carl Bridge, *Holding India to the Empire: The British Conservative Party and the 1935 Constitution* (New Delhi: Sterling Publishers, 1986), p. 102.

269 Andrew Muldoon, ' "The Cow is Still the Most Important Figure in Indian Politics!" Religion, Imperial Culture and the Shaping of Indian Political Reform in the 1930s', *Parliamentary History*, 27, 1 (2008), p. 68.

270 O.C.G. Hayter, 'Trouble on the Borders', *IER*, 2, 4 (1933), pp. 30–34.

271 W.A. Rossignol, 'The Impartial Press', *IER*, 2, 10 (1933), pp. 38–40.

272 Neville Chamberlain to Hilda Chamberlain, 9 March 1933, in Robert C. Self (ed.), *The Neville Chamberlain Diary Letters, Volume IV: The Downing Street Years, 1934–1940* (Aldershot: Ashgate, 2005), pp. 118–119.

273 Neville Chamberlain to Ida Chamberlain, 5 Nov. 1932, *Diary Letters, III*, p. 356.

274 *The Times*, 12 Feb. 1935, p. 14. A similar observation is made of IMS objections to all-India government, see, Nair, 'Construction', pp. 227–228.

275 Elizabeth Buettner, 'From Somebodies to Nobodies: Britons Returning Home from India', in Martin Daunton and Bernard Rieger (eds), *Meanings of Modernity: Britain from the Late-Victorian Era to World War II* (Oxford: Berg, 2001), pp. 221–240; K.K. Lalkaka, 'The coming disintegration', *IER*, 2, 1 (1933), pp. 22–26.

276 Michael O'Dwyer, 'Non Co-operation by Sir T.B. Sapru and the Moderates', *IER*, 1, 9 (1932), pp. 12–16.

277 Louis Stuart, 'The Story of the Indian Empire Society', *IER*, 8, 12 (1939), pp. 465–474; A.H. Lane, *The Alien Menace* (London: Boswell, 1928).

278 N.C. Fleming, 'The Press, Empire and Historical Time: *The Times* and Indian Self-Government, *c.*1911–47, *Media History*, 16, 1 (2010), pp. 183–198; J.J. Astor to Churchill, 6 November 1933, CHAR 2/194/91–92.

279 D. George Boyce, *Decolonisation and the British Empire, 1775–1997* (Basingstoke: Macmillan, 1999), p. 19.

280 Gwynne to Patiala, 26 Dec. 1934, MS. Gwynne deposit 11.

281 See, correspondence and papers from 1932 to 1937, MS. Gwynne deposits 9, 10 and 11.

282 Douglas Dewar [ornithologist and formerly of the Indian Civil Service], 'The Anxieties of Pensioners', *IER*, 3, 5 (1934), pp. 196–203.

283 Evelyn Waugh, *Put Out More Flags* ([1942] London: Penguin, 2000), pp. 113–115.

284 Ian Copland, *India 1885–1947: The Unmaking of an Empire* (London: Longman, 2001), pp. 23, 33; Anthony Kirk-Greene, *Britain's Imperial Administrators, 1858–1966* (Basingstoke: Macmillan, 2000), pp. 98–99. See, Lalkaka, 'Europeans and the White Paper', *IER*, 2, 12 (1933), pp. 30–33.

285 *The Times*, 2 May 1933, p. 10.

286 Ibid., 7 Oct. 1932, p. 7; Hoare to MacDonald, 7 Oct. 1932, cited in Bridge, *Holding*, p. 92.

287 *House of Commons Debates*, 22 Feb. 1933, vol. 274, col. 1811.

288 *The Times*, 1 March 1933, pp. 9, 15; 'Editorial', *IER*, 2, 4 (1933), p. 13.

289 Baldwin to Atholl, 23 Feb. 1933, Williamson and Baldwin, *Baldwin Papers*, p. 306; Churchill to Salisbury, 1 April 1933 [copy], CRFT 1/8.

290 The five diehard places went instead to MPs Craddock and Sir Joseph Nall, and Lords Salisbury, Rankeillour and Burnham, all of whom dissented from the JSC's 1934 report.

291 *House of Commons Debates*, 16 April 1934, vol. 288, cols 714–728; Jones, diary, 28 Apr. 1934, in Thomas Jones, *A Diary with Letters 1931–1950* (London: Oxford University Press, 1954), pp. 126–127; W.P. Crozier's interview with Baldwin, 12 June 1934, Williamson and Baldwin, *Baldwin Papers*, pp. 317–322; *House of Commons Debates*, 13 June 1934, vol. 290, cols 1711–1808.

292 Copland, *Princes*, p. 142.

293 Salisbury to Gwynne, 13 Oct. 1933; Gwynne to Salisbury, 17 Oct. 1933; Salisbury to Gwynne, 7 Nov. 1933; Gwynne to Salisbury, 13 Nov. 1933, MS. Gwynne deposit 11.

294 Gwynne to Patiala, telegram, 5 Feb. 1934, MS. Gwynne deposit 11.

295 *The Times*, 16 Feb. 1934, p. 8. He was succeeded at Basingstoke by Patrick Donner, see, Donner, *Crusade*, pp. 157–180.

296 Lymington, *Ich*, p. 12.

297 Ibid., pp. 13, 118.

298 Ibid., p. 119.

299 Ibid., pp. 120, 124–125.

300 Stone, *Responses*, pp. 148–188.

301 Martin Pugh, *Tories and the People, 1880–1935* (Oxford: Blackwell, 1985), pp. 189–190; *The Times*, 6 May 1933, p. 9.

302 Wolmer to Gwynne, 7 Feb. 1936, MS. Gwynne deposit 10.

303 *House of Commons Debates*, 10 April 1933, vol. 276, col. 2251.

304 *The Times*, 29 June 1933, p. 8.

305 Croft to Churchill, 22 Sept. 1933, CHAR 2/194/6; Croft to Churchill, n.d. [Sept. 1933], CHAR 2/194/7–8.

306 Neville Chamberlain to Hilda Chamberlain, 7 Oct. 1933, *Diary Letters, III*, pp. 405–406.

307 *The Times*, 7 Oct. 1933, pp. 7, 12.

308 Neville Chamberlain to Hilda Chamberlain, 7 Oct. 1933, *Diary Letters, III*, pp. 405–406.

309 *The Times*, 5 Oct. 1934, p. 14; Croft to Churchill, 8 Oct. 1934, CHAR 2/225/24.

310 Amery, diary, 1 Nov. 1934, in Barnes and Nicholson, *Empire*, pp. 387–388.

311 Neville Chamberlain to Ida and Hilda Chamberlain, 9 Dec. 1934, *Diary Letters, IV*, pp. 104–105; *The Times*, 5 Dec. 1934, p. 14. Rallies and meetings continued nevertheless, see, 'Activities of the India Defence League', *IER*, 4, 5 (May 1935), p. 178; *IER*, 4, 6 (June 1935), p. 245.

312 Agnew to Wolmer, 3 Dec. 1934, published in *The Times*, 5 Dec. 1934, p. 10.

313 Neville Chamberlain to Ida and Hilda Chamberlain, 9 Dec. 1934, *Diary Letters, IV,* pp. 104–105.

314 *House of Commons Debates,* 12 Dec. 1934, vol. 296, col. 531; *House of Lords Debates,* 12 Dec. 1934, vol. 95, cols 248–308. The House of Lords contained over a hundred IDL members; 'Conservatives and India: Sir A. Chamberlain's advice', *The Times,* 5 Dec. 1934, p. 9.

315 *Manchester Guardian,* 2 Jan. 1935, p. 8.

316 Lord Templewood [Samuel Hoare], *Nine Troubled Years* (London: Collins, 1954), p. 86; O'Dwyer, 'All-India Federation', *IER,* 4, 1 (Jan. 1935), pp. 7–11.

317 Croft to Churchill, 23 July 1934, CHAR 2/215/29–30.

318 Lancashire, Cheshire and Westmorland Divisional Association, minutes of quarterly meetings, 14 Jan. 1933, 29 April 1933, 14 Oct. 1933, 5 May 1934, Bodleian Library, Oxford, Conservative Party Archive, ARE 3/1/2. Lancashire MPs opposed to the India bill included, Frederick Wolfe Astbury (Salford West); Eric Alfred George Bailey (Gorton); John Broadbent (Ashton-under-Lyne); Alan Ernest Leofric Chorlton (Platting); C.C. Erskine-Bolst (Blackpool); Edward Lascelles Fleming (Withington); Albert G. Fuller (Ardwick); John Lees-Jones (Manchester Blackley); Sir Joseph Nall (Manchester Hulme); Reginald Purbrick (Liverpool Walton); Sir A.N. Stewart Sandeman (Middletown and Prestwich); and Linton Theodore Thorp (Nelson and Colne).

319 *The Times,* 28 June 1934, p. 15. Gretton gave his backing to Churchill, see, Gretton to Churchill, 1 Nov. 1934, CHAR 2/215/97.

320 Sir Thomas White to Purbrick, 15 Dec. 1934; Purbrick to Mr Cox, 4 Feb. 1935, Churchill Archives Centre, Cambridge, Randolph Churchill Papers 5/2; White to Derby, 16 June 1933, Liverpool Record Office, Lord Derby Papers [hereafter 920 DER (17)] 2/14; Derby to White, 19 June 1933, 920 DER (17) 6/34; Liverpool Record Office, Liverpool Constitutional Association, Board of Management Meeting, 26 June 1933, 329 CON/1/1/3.

321 Winston Churchill to Randolph Churchill, 2 Feb. 1935, CHAR 2/246/48; Wolmer to Viscount FitzAlan, 1 Feb. 1935, MS. Eng. hist. c. 1013; Wolmer to Violet Milner, 11 March 1935, VM 26; Neville Chamberlain to Hilda Chamberlain, 26 Jan. 1935, in *Diary Letters, IV,* p. 113; *Citizen* [Gloucester], 26 Jan. 1935, p. 1; *Aberdeen Press and Journal,* 1 Feb. 1935, p. 7. Goodman still opposed the India bill.

322 Prestwich Constituency Association Annual General Meeting, 3 March 1933, 4 March 1933; General Purposes Committee, 25 May 1930, 20 June 1933; Committee, 28 Sept. 1933, 29 Nov. 1934, 28 Feb. 1935, 15 March 1935, 16 Sept. 1935, Lancashire Archives, Middleton and Prestwich Conservative Association Papers, PLC 1/2. See also, Waterloo, Crosby, Seaforth, and Litherland Women's Central Committee Meeting, 15 March 1935, 12 April 1935, Lancashire Archives, Waterloo, Crosby, Seaforth, and Litherland Women's Central Committee Papers, DDX 806/2/2.

323 *Daily Mirror*, 24 Jan. 1935, p. 2; 30 Jan. 1935, p. 4; 2 Feb. 1935, p. 4; 4 Feb. 1935, p. 4; 5 Feb. 1935, p. 4; 6 Feb. 1935, p. 2.

324 Derby to Thomas White, 26 Aug. 1935, 29 Aug. 1935, 22 Sept. 1935, 10 Oct. 1935, Liverpool Record Office, 920 DER (17) 6/34; White to Derby, 28 Aug. 1935, 30 Sept. 1935, 7 Nov. 1935, 920 DER (17) 6/33.

325 Wolmer to Lady Houston, 11 March 1935, MS. Eng. hist. c. 1013; Wolmer to Violet Milner, 11 March 1935, VM 26; Charmley, *Lloyd*, p. 190.

326 Seventy-nine Conservative MPs voted against, in addition three paired, and two served as tellers, *The Times*, 12 Feb. 1935, p. 9; 13 Feb. 1935, p. 12.

327 Patiala to Gwynne, 27 Feb. 1935, MS. Gwynne deposit 11; Gwynne to Courtauld, 15 Jan. 1935, MS. Gwynne deposit 17; the E.G. Spencer-Churchill – Edward Russell Report, 1 July 1934, republished in Donner, *Crusade*, pp. 363–372.

328 Gwynne to Patiala, 3 April 1935, 9 May 1935, MS. Gwynne deposit 11.

329 Atholl, Todd, Astbury, Nall and Thorp to Baldwin, 1 May 1935, Bald. 107, 82–87; *The Times*, 24 May 1935, pp. 16, 18.

330 Hoare to Wolmer, 15 May 1935, MS. Eng. hist. c. 1013.

331 *House of Commons Debates*, 5 June 1935, vol. 302, col. 2015. The seventy-nine include: Gilbert Acland-Troyte (Tiverton), Sir William Alexander (Glasgow Central), Frederick Wolfe Astbury (Salford West), Duchess of Atholl (Kinross and West Perthshire), Eric A.G. Bailey (Manchester Gorton), George Balfour (Hampstead), M.W. Beaumont (Aylesbury, Buckinghamshire), Sir Reginald Blaker (Spelthorne, Surrey), Brendan Bracken (North Paddington), Albert Newby Braithwaite (Buckrose, East Riding of Yorkshire), John Broadbent (Ashton-under-Lyne, Lancashire), Brig. Gen. Howard Clifton Brown (Newbury), Alexander Crawford Browne (Belfast West), John George Burnett (Aberdeen North), Henry Walter Burton (Sudbury), G.R. Hall-Caine (East Dorset), Major William H. Carver (Howdenshire), Alan Ernest Leofric Chorlton (Bury), Winston Churchill (Epping), Sir Cyril Cobb (Fulham West), John Sewell Courtauld (Chichester), Sir Reginald Craddock (Combined English Universities), A.C. Critchley (Twickenham), Henry Page Croft (Bournemouth), Sir William Henry Davison (Kensington South), Herbert Dixon (Belfast East), Patrick Donner (Islington West), Charles E.G.C. Emmott (Glasgow Springburn), C.C. Erskine-Bolst (Blackpool), W. Lindsay Everard (Melton), Edward Lascelles Fleming (Manchester Withington), Sir Patrick J. Ford (Edinburgh North), Albert G. Fuller (Manchester Ardwick), Albert W. Goodman (Islington North), William P.C. Greene (Worcester), John Gretton (Burton), W.G. Howard Gritten (Hartlepool), Marquess of Hartington (Derbyshire West), Joseph Hepworth (Bradford East), Michael John Hunter (Brigg), Sir George W.H. Jones (Stoke Newington), Admiral Sir Roger Keyes (North Portsmouth), Lawrence Kimball (Loughborough), Sir Alfred Knox (Wycombe), John Lees-Jones (Manchester Blackley), Alan Lennox-Boyd (Mid-Bedfordshire), Thomas Levy

(Elland), J.H. Lockwood (Shipley), Sir Joseph McConnell (County Antrim), Adam Maitland (Faversham), Arthur Marsden (Battersea North), Sir J.S.P. Mellor (Tamworth), Sir Joseph Nall (Manchester Hulme), William Graham Nicholson (Petersfield), William Nunn (Whitehaven, Cumberland), Sir Charles Oman (Oxford University), Sir Basil Peto (Barnstaple), Reginald Purbrick (Liverpool Walton), Victor Raikes (South East Essex), Sir Cooper Rawson (Brighton), David D. Reid (County Down), John R. Remer (Macclesfield), Sir A.N. Stewart Sandeman (Middletown and Prestwich), Sir Frank Barnard Sanderson (Ealing), Thomas Somerset (North Belfast), Annesley A. Somerville (Windsor), Charles S. Taylor (Eastbourne), Vice-Admiral Ernest A. Taylor (Paddington South), William P. Templeton (Coatbridge), Linton Theodore Thorp (Nelson and Colne), Alfred J.K. Todd (Berwick-on-Tweed), Gordon Cosmo Touche (Reigate), Sir William A. Wayland (Canterbury), Sydney Richard Wells (Bedford), Charles Williams (Torquay), Herbert G. Williams (South Croydon), Alfred Wise (Smethwick), Viscount Wolmer (Aldershot), and Hebert Wragg (Belper).

332 Wolmer to Violet Milner, 25 April 1935, VM 26.
333 Editorial, *IER*, 4, 10 (1935), p. 382.
334 S.C. Ghosh, 'Decision-Making and Power in the British Conservative Party: A Case Study of the Indian Problem 1929-34', *Political Studies*, 13, 2 (1965), pp. 204-205. In his memoirs, Donner argued that by delaying implementation of the 1935 constitution the diehard campaign had helped to avoid Indian neutrality in the Second World War and allowed 'the 60 million Untouchables ... time to organize and thereby secure for themselves a better fate than would otherwise have been the case', Donner, *Crusade*, p. 130.
335 J.A. Spender, *Great Britain, Empire and Commonwealth: 1886-1935* (London: Cassell, 1936), pp. 757-758.
336 Copland, *Princes*, pp. 142-143.
337 Cowling, *Labour*, p. 2.
338 K. Veerathappa, *British Conservative Party and Indian Independence 1930-1947* (New Delhi: Ashish Publishing House, 1976), pp. 109-112.
339 Gwynne, diary, 1932, MS. Gwynne deposit 29.

Chapter 5   Consensus and disunity, 1935–40

1 Nick Smart, *The National Government, 1931-40* (Basingstoke: Macmillan, 1999), p. 122.
2 'The Labour Party's Call to Power', in F.W.S. Craig (ed.), *British General Election Manifestos 1918-1966* (Chichester: Political Reference Publications, 1970), pp. 81-83.

3   Paul Addison, 'Patriotism Under Pressure: Lord Rothermere and British Foreign Policy', in Chris Cooke and Gillian Peele (eds), *The Politics of Reappraisal, 1918–1939* (London: Macmillan, 1975), p. 94.

4   Maurice Cowling, *The Impact of Labour 1920–1924: The Beginning of Modern British Politics* (Cambridge: Cambridge University Press, 1971), p. 301; Keith M. Wilson, *A Study in the History and Politics of the* Morning Post *1905–1926* (Lampeter: Edwin Mellon, 1991), pp. 193–228.

5   David Dilks, ' "The Unnecessary War"? Military Advice and Foreign Policy in Great Britain, 1931–1939', in Adrian Preston (ed.), *General Staffs and Diplomacy Before the Second World War* (London: Croom Helm, 1978), pp. 98–132; Paul Kennedy, *The Rise and Fall of the Great Powers: Economic Change and Military Conflict from 1500 to 2000* (London: Unwin Hyman, 1988), pp. xix–xx.

6   Richard Toye, 'The Rhetorical Culture of the House of Commons After 1918', *History*, 99, 335 (2014), pp. 270–298.

7   *National Review*, Nov. 1919, p. 285.

8   Lord Croft, *My Life of Strife* (London: Hutchinson, 1948), p. 254. See also, Henry Page Croft, 'Empire Unity – Defence', *Indian Empire Review*, 5, 11 (1936), pp. 398–400.

9   Keith Middlemas and John Barnes, *Baldwin: A Biography* (London: Weidenfeld and Nicolson, 1969), pp. 358–362.

10 *The Times*, 20 Oct. 1933, p. 8.

11 Brett Holman, *The Next War in the Air: Britain's Fear of the Bomber, 1908–1941* (Abingdon: Routledge, 2016).

12 *Chelmsford Chronicle*, 14 Oct. 1938, p. 9.

13 Croft, *Life*, p. 98.

14 Maurice Hankey to Selborne, 13 Nov. 1933; 26 March 1936, Bodleian Library, Oxford, second Earl of Selborne Papers [hereafter MS. Selborne] 87.

15 Salisbury to Irwin, 13 Sept. 1927, in Stuart Ball (ed.), *Conservative Politics in National and Imperial Crisis: Letters from Britain to the Viceroy of India 1926–31* (Aldershot: Ashgate, 2014), pp. 176–177; Gaynor Johnson, *Lord Robert Cecil: Politician and Internationalist* (Farnham: Ashgate, 2013), p. 246.

16 Viscount Lymington, *Ich Dien: The Tory Path* (London: Constable, 1931), p. 108.

17 *House of Lords Debates*, 8 May 1930, vol. 77, cols 444–451.

18 John Charmley, *Lord Lloyd and the Decline of the British Empire* (London: Weidenfeld and Nicolson, 1987), pp. 174, 205. The political outlook of the NL on this question convinced the India Defence League to consider the former's senior members a likely source of sympathizers for its 'social list', see, P. Tatham to Lloyd, 18 Jan. 1935, Churchill Archives Centre, Cambridge, Lord Lloyd Papers [hereafter GLLD] 11/2.

19 Uri Bialer, 'Elite Opinion and Defence Policy: Air Power Advocacy and British Rearmament During the 1930s', *Review of International Studies*, 6, 1 (1980), pp. 32–51;

Nicholas Crowson, 'Citizen Defence: The Conservative Party and Its Attitude to National Service, 1937–57', in Abigail Beach and Richard Weight (eds), *The Right to Belong: Citizenship and National Identity in Britain, 1930–1960* (London: I.B.Tauris, 1998), pp. 205–222; D.J. Mitchell, 'The Army League, Conscription and the 1956 Defence Review', PhD, University of East Anglia (2012), pp. 75–106.

20 Neville Chamberlain to Hilda Chamberlain, 7 Oct. 1933, in Robert C. Self (ed.), *The Neville Chamberlain Diary Letters, Volume III: The Heir Apparent, 1918–1933* (Aldershot: Ashgate, 2002), pp. 405–406.

21 N.C. Fleming, 'Cabinet Government, British Imperial Security, and the World Disarmament Conference, 1932–1934, *War in History*, 18, 1 (2011), pp. 62–84.

22 Martin Ceadel, 'Interpreting East Fulham', in Chris Cook and John Ramsden (eds), *By-Elections in British Politics* (London: Macmillan, 1973), pp. 118–139.

23 *The Times*, 5 Oct. 1934, p. 15.

24 *House of Commons Debates*, 10 Nov. 1932, vol. 270, cols 525–641; Raikes to editor, 'To Bomb or Not', *Saturday Review*, 26 Aug. 1933, p. 232.

25 *Daily Mirror*, 25 Oct. 1935, p. 6. The interruptions are not mentioned in the official record, see, *House of Commons Debates*, 24 Oct. 1935, vol. 305, cols 369–468.

26 Memo., 3 May 1935, Churchill Archives Centre, Cambridge, Winston Churchill Papers [hereafter CHAR] 2/243/57–58.

27 Lord Winterton MP to Violet Milner, 27 May 1935, Bodleian Library, Oxford, Violet Milner Papers [hereafter VM] 52.

28 Richard Carr, *Veteran MPs and Conservative Politics in the Aftermath of the Great War: The Memory of All That* (Aldershot: Ashgate, 2013), p. 168.

29 Ronald Hyam, *Understanding the British Empire* (Cambridge: Cambridge University Press, 2010), pp. 86–87.

30 Wolfe W. Schmokel, *Dream of Empire: German Colonialism, 1919–1945* (New Haven: Yale University Press, 1964), pp. 76–136.

31 *Empire and India Defence League Bulletin*, 2 (Feb. 1936); 3 (March 1936); 4 (April 1936).

32 Gretton, memo., 3 July 1935, CHAR 2/241B/183–187.

33 *House of Commons Debates*, 7 Dec. 1936, vol. 318, cols 1641–1644.

34 Adrian Phillips, 'Chronicle of a Conspiracy Foretold: MI5, Churchill and the "King's Party" in the Abdication Crisis', *Conservative History Journal*, 2, 5 (2017), p. 19.

35 Philip Zeigler, 'Churchill and the Monarchy', in Robert Blake and Wm. Roger Louis (eds), *Churchill* (Oxford: Clarendon Press, 1996), pp. 191–194.

36 James J. Sack, *From Jacobite to Conservative: Reaction and Orthodoxy in Britain, c.1760–1832* (Cambridge: Cambridge University Press, 2002), p. 137.

37 Sir Clive Wigram to Lord Irwin, 27 March 1931, cited in Harold Nicolson, *King George the Fifth: His Life and Reign* (London: Constable, 1952), p. 507.

38 Gretton to Croft, 12 May 1936; 15 May 1936, Churchill Archives Centre, Cambridge, Croft Papers [hereafter CRFT] 1/12.

39 Gretton to Croft, 12 May 1936; 15 May 1936; Croft to Gretton, 16 May 1936, CRFT 1/12.

40 Hugh Orr-Ewing to EIDL members, 23 July 1936 (circulated minutes of EIDL meeting on 16 July 1936), GLLD 11/2.

41 Maurice Cowling, *The Impact of Hitler: British Politics and British Policy* (Chicago: University of Chicago Press, 1977), p. 128.

42 Collin Brooks records a 1938 debate at the English Speaking Union on the mandates, during which his advocacy of transfer 'brought Duncan Sandys to my metaphorical throat', see, Collin Brooks, diary, 30 Nov. 1938, in N.J. Crowson (ed.), *Fleet Street, Press Barons and Politics: The Journals of Collin Brooks, 1932–1940* (Cambridge: Cambridge University Press, 1998), pp. 232–233.

43 See, Churchill Archives Centre, Cambridge, Duncan Sandys Papers, DSND 1/10.

44 J.H. Swales to Derby, 10 July 1935, Liverpool Record Office, Lord Derby Papers, 920 DER (17) 16/3.

45 N.J. Crowson, *Facing Fascism: The Conservative Party and the European Dictators 1935–1940* (London: Routledge, 1997), pp. 74, 109.

46 Memo., 18 Feb. 1936, CHAR 2/251/69–72.

47 Stuart Ball, *Portrait of a Party: The Conservative Party in Britain, 1918–1945* (Oxford: Oxford University Press, 2013), p. 238.

48 Lancashire and Cheshire Division Minutes, 1932–65, Bodleian Library, Oxford, Conservative Party Archive, ARE/3/1/2.

49 See, Lennox-Boyd papers for minutes and ephemera on Chamberlain Centenary Committee, Bodleian Library, Oxford, Lennox-Boyd Papers [hereafter MS. Eng. c. 3385].

50 Gary Love, 'The British Movement, Duncan Sandys, and the Politics of Constitutionalism in the 1930s', *Contemporary British History*, 23, 4 (2009), pp. 543–558.

51 Clarisse Berthezène, *Training Minds for the War of Ideas: Ashridge College, the Conservative Party and the Cultural Politics of Britain, 1929–54* (Manchester: Manchester University Press, 2015), pp. 123–140.

52 Peter Brooke, *Duncan Sandys and the Informal Politics of Britain's Late Decolonisation* (Basingstoke: Palgrave Macmillan, 2017), p. 27; *The Times*, 6 March 1935, p. 16.

53 *The Times*, 6 Feb. 1936, pp. 7, 14.

54 Ibid., 12 Feb. 1936, p. 14.

55 Ibid., 13 Feb. 1936, p. 6.

56 Ibid., 15 Feb. 1936, p. 11.

57 R.A.C. Parker, *Chamberlain and Appeasement: British Policy and the Coming of the Second World War* (Basingstoke: Palgrave Macmillan, 1993), p. 70–71.

58 *House of Commons Debates*, 6 April 1936, vol. 310, col. 2415.

59 Ibid., 27 April 1936, vol. 311, cols. 552–553.

60 Dick Brooman-White to Lennox-Boyd, 28 April 1936, MS.. Eng. c. 3385.

61 Cited in Patrick Donner, *Crusade: A Life Against the Calamitous Twentieth Century* (London: Sherwood, 1984), pp. 192–195.

62 Amery, diary, 7 May 1936, in John Barnes and David Nicholson (eds), *The Empire at Bay: The Leo Amery Diaries 1929–1945* (London: Hutchinson, 1988), p. 416.

63 Neville Chamberlain to Ida Chamberlain, 13 April 1936, in Robert C. Self (ed.), *The Neville Chamberlain Diary Letters, Volume IV: The Downing Street Years, 1934–1940* (Aldershot: Ashgate, 2005), pp. 186.

64 *The Times*, 25 June 1936, p. 13. See also, *Daily Mirror*, 25 June 1936, p. 13; Amery, diary, 24 June 1936, Barnes and Nicholson, *Empire*, p. 422.

65 *Western Daily Press*, 25 June 1936, p. 7.

66 *The Times*, 25 June 1936, p. 13. See also, *Daily Mirror*, 25 June 1936, p. 13; Amery, diary, 24 June 1936, Barnes and Nicholson, *Empire*, p. 422.

67 *Scotsman*, 6 July 1936, p. 13.

68 *The Times*, 17 July 1936, p. 14.

69 Crowson, *Facing*, pp. 75–76.

70 Amery, diary, 16 July 1936, Barnes and Nicholson, *Empire*, p. 425.

71 House of Commons Library, Notice of Early Day Motion, 22 July 1936, no. 128, pp. 2881–2884.

72 *House of Commons Debates*, 27 July 1936, vol. 315, col. 1132.

73 Zara Steiner, *The Triumph of the Dark: European International History 1933–1939* (Oxford: Oxford University Press, 2011), pp. 305–306.

74 A.L. Kennedy, diary, 30 June 1936, Gordon Martel (ed.), The Times *and Appeasement: The Journals of A.L. Kennedy, 1932–1939* (Cambridge: Cambridge University Press, 2000), pp. 235–236.

75 Scott Newton, *Profits of Peace: The Political Economy of Anglo–German Appeasement* (Oxford: Clarendon Press, 1996), p. 77.

76 1922 Committee, minutes, 27 July 1936, vol. 3, March 1934–July 1938, Conservative Party Archive, Bodleian Library, Oxford, 1922 Committee [hereafter 1922] 3.

77 *The Times*, 1 Oct. 1936, p. 12; Amery diary, 1 Oct. 1936, Barnes and Nicholson, *Empire*, p. 427.

78 *The Times*, 2 Oct. 1936, p. 8. See also, *Daily Mirror*, 2 Oct. 1936, p. 6.

79 Schmokel, *Dream*, p. 100.

80 Jones to Lady Grigg, 12 Feb. 1937, in Thomas Jones, *A Diary with Letters 1931–1950* (London: Oxford University Press, 1954), p. 313.

81 House of Commons Library, Notice of Early Day Motion, 15 Feb. 1937, no. 55, 1259.

82 *The Times*, 24 Feb. 1937, p. 8.

83 Ibid., 22 July 1937, p. 14.

84 Schmokel, *Dream*, pp. 102–104.

85 John Charmley, *Chamberlain and the Lost Peace* (London: Ivan R. Dee, 1989), p. 20.

86 Ritchie Ovendale, *'Appeasement' and the English Speaking World: Britain, the United States, the Dominions and the Policy of 'Appeasement', 1937–1939* (Cardiff: University of Wales Press, 1975), p. 38.

87 Charmley, *Chamberlain*, p. 32.

88 N.C. Fleming, *The Marquess of Londonderry: Aristocracy, Power and Politics in Britain and Ireland* (London: I.B.Tauris, 2005), p. 187; Martin Pugh, *'Hurrah for the Blackshirts!' Fascists and Fascism in Britain Between the Wars* (London: Jonathan Cape, 2005), p. 272; Andrew Chandler, 'Munich and Morality: The Bishops of the Church of England and Appeasement', *Twentieth Century British History*, 5, 1 (1994), pp. 77–99.

89 Andrew J. Crozier, *Appeasement and Germany's Last Bid for Colonies* (London: Macmillan, 1988), pp. 226–227.

90 Leonard Barnes, *Empire or Democracy? A Study of the Colonial Question* (London: Victor Gollancz, 1939), pp. 236, 264.

91 *The Times*, 18 Oct. 1937, p. 10.

92 Schmokel, *Dream*, p. 83.

93 *The Times*, 18 Oct. 1937, p. 10; see, David Olusoga and Casper W. Erichsen, *The Kaiser's Holocaust: Germany's Forgotten Genocide and the Colonial Roots of Nazism* (London: Faber, 2011).

94 *The Times*, 1 Oct. 1936, p. 8.

95 Gerwin Strobl, *The Germanic Isle: Nazi Perceptions of Britain* (Cambridge: Cambridge University Press, 2000), pp. 172–173. Citing Strobl, Professor Sarkisyanz goes so far as to argue that Hitler was 'inspired' by the example of the British empire, see, Manuel Sarkisyanz, *Hitler's English Inspirers: Based on Lectures Given in Heidelberg University, South Asia Institute* (Belfast: Athol Books, 2003).

96 *The Times*, 24 Feb. 1937, p. 8.

97 Ibid., 18 Oct. 1937, p. 10.

98 Ibid., 8 Oct. 1937, pp. 8–9.

99 *Scotsman*, 8 Oct. 1937, p. 12.

100 *The Times*, 9 Oct. 1937, p. 12.

101 Ibid., 2 Dec. 1937, p. 7.

102 Neville Chamberlain to Hilda Chamberlain, 5 Dec. 1937, *Diary Letters, IV*, p. 289.

103 Schmokel, *Dream*, p. 108.

104 Neville Chamberlain to Ida Chamberlain, 26 Nov. 1937, *Diary Letters, IV*, pp. 286–287.

105 Schmokel, *Dream*, pp. 112, 118.

106 Andrew Roberts, *'The Holy Fox': The Life of Lord Halifax* (London: Weidenfeld and Nicolson, 1991), p. 77.

107 Neville Chamberlain to Ida Chamberlain, 20 March 1938, *Diary Letters, IV*, p. 307.

108 *Daily Mirror*, 14 Oct. 1938, p. 2. Churchill's speech on Munich, a week earlier, raised the analogy of Danegeld, see, *House of Commons Debates*, 5 Oct. 1938, vol. 339, col. 367. For colonies discussion in the lead up to the Munich agreement, see, Neville Chamberlain to Hilda Chamberlain, 2 Oct. 1938, *Diary Letters, IV*, p. 350.

109 Selborne to editor of *The Times* (draft), 18 Oct. 1938, MS. Selborne 87; *The Times*, 19 Oct. 1938, p. 13.

110 *The Times*, 17 Nov. 1938, pp. 14, 19; 25 Nov. 1938, pp. 11, 14.

111 *House of Commons* Debates, 14 Nov. 1938, vol. 341, cols 491–493.

112 *The Times*, 15 Nov. 1938, p. 14.

113 1922 Committee, minutes, 14 Nov. 1938, vol. 4, Nov. 1938–May 1943, 1922/4.

114 House of Commons Library, Notice of Early Day Motion, 14 Nov. 1938, no. 5, p. 118.

115 Schmokel, *Dream*, pp. 121–124.

116 Neville Chamberlain to Hilda Chamberlain, n.d. [1–2 April 1939], *Diary Letters, IV*, p. 402; Neville Chamberlain to Ida Chamberlain, 23 July 1939, ibid., p. 431; 8 October 1939, ibid., p. 455.

117 Donner, *Crusade*, pp. 207.

118 *The Times*, 6 Feb. 1939, p. 14; 28 Feb. 1939, p. 14.

119 *The Times*, 14 June 1939, p. 14; 17 June 1939, p. 12; 17 Oct. 1939, p. 9; 11 Nov. 1939, p. 6.

120 Donner, *Crusade*, pp. 207–211.

121 *Empire and India Defence League Bulletin*, 3 (March 1936).

122 Neville Thompson, *The Anti-Appeasers: Conservative Opposition to Appeasement in the 1930s* (Oxford: Clarendon Press, 1971), pp. 69, 84; Andrew David Stedman, ' "A Most Dishonest Argument"? Chamberlain's Government, Anti-Appeasers and the Persistence of League of Nations' Language Before the Second World War', *Contemporary British History*, 25, 1 (2011), pp. 83–99.

123 Parker, *Chamberlain*, pp. 319–321; R.A.C. Parker, *Churchill and Appeasement* (London: Macmillan, 2000), p. 117.

124 Churchill to Croft, 29 Oct. 1938, CRFT 1/8.

125 Croft to Churchill, 31 Oct. 1938, CRFT 1/8.

126 Crossley diary, 20 Sept. 1938, in Martin Gilbert (ed.), *Winston S. Churchill, Volume V: Companion Documents, Part 3* (London: Heinemann, 1981), p. 1170.

127 *Evening Standard*, 10 Dec. 1937, p. 10.

128 'Cato', *Guilty Men* ([1940] London: Penguin, 1998), pp. 18–19.

129 Evelyn Waugh, *Brideshead Revisited* ([1945] London: Penguin, 2000), pp. 261–262; 278–280. Patrick Donner took exception to the novel's depiction of Oxford: 'his characters represented a tiny minority', Donner, *Crusade*, p. 54.

130 *House of Commons Debates*, 22 July 1935, vol. 304, cols 1523–1524.

131 *Daily Mirror*, 23 July 1935, p. 3.

132 John Ruggiero, *Neville Chamberlain and British Rearmament: Pride, Prejudice, and Politics* (Westport, CT: Greenwood Press, 1999), p. 77.

133 *Daily Mirror*, 11 July 1935, p. 3.

134 *House of Commons Debates*, 10 July 1935, vol. 304, cols 422–426.

135 Ibid., 5 May 1938, vol. 335 col. 1112–1116.

136 Parker, *Churchill*, p. 147.

137 *House of Commons Debates*, 25 June 1937, vol. 325, cols 1574–1577.

138 Ibid., 2 Nov. 1938, vol. 340, cols 332–336.

139 Stuart Ball, 'The Politics of Appeasement: The Fall of the Duchess of Atholl and the Kinross and West Perth By-Election, 1938', *Scottish Historical Review*, 69, 187 (1990), pp. 49–83.

140 *House of Commons Debates*, 22 July 1935, vol. 304, col. 1523.

141 Ibid., 19 Dec. 1935, vol. 307, cols 2087–2090.

142 Ibid., 2 Nov. 1938, vol. 340, cols 238–239.

143 David Waley, *British Public Opinion and the Abyssinian War 1935-6* (London: Temple Smith, 1975), p. 53.

144 Wolmer to Edward Mackie [of the *Statesman*, Calcutta], 9 Sept. 1935, Bodleian Library, Oxford, third Earl of Selborne Papers, MS. Eng. hist. c. 1013.

145 Donner to Violet Milner, 2 Oct. 1935, VM 39.

146 Dan Stone, *Responses to Nazism in Britain, 1933-1939: Before War and Holocaust* (Basingstoke: Palgrave Macmillan, 2003, p. 114.

147 *House of Commons Debates*, 14 March 1938, vol. 333, cols 72–73.

148 Ibid., 3 Oct. 1938, vol. 339, cols 29–40; John Charmley, *Duff Cooper: The Authorised Biography* (London: Phoenix, 1997), p. 127.

149 *House of Commons Debates*, 5 Oct. 1938, vol. 339, cols 374–383.

150 Ibid., 3 Oct. 1938, vol. 339, cols 94–97.

151 Amery, diary, 3 Oct. 1938, Barnes and Nicholson, *Empire*, p. 525.

152 Amery, diary, 17 March 1936, ibid., p. 411; Henry Channon, diary, 2 Aug. 1939, in Robert Rhodes James (ed.), *Chips: The Diaries of Sir Henry Channon* (London: Weidenfeld and Nicolson, 1967), p. 207.

153 *House of Commons Debates*, 6 Oct. 1938, vol. 339, cols 558–561. The other nine were the Duchess of Atholl, Brendan Bracken, Winston Churchill, John Courtauld, William Davison, Roger Keyes, John Lees-Jones, Thomas Somerset, and Viscount Wolmer.

154 Halifax to Selborne, 18 Oct. 1938, MS. Selborne 87; *The Times*, 19 Oct. 1938, p. 13.

155 *House of Commons Debates*, 19 May 1939, vol. 347, cols 1850–1855; Raikes criticized Churchill's association with Labour on foreign policy, see, Thompson, *Anti-Appeasers*, p. 171, citing *House of Commons Debates*, 25 May 1938, vol. 336, col. 1294.

156 *House of Commons Debates*, 15 March 1939, vol. 345, 465–467.

157 *The Times*, 18 March 1939, p. 8.

158 Ibid., 31 March 1939, p. 10.

159 *Aberdeen Journal*, 13 April 1939, p. 7.

160 *House of Commons Debates*, 3 Sept. 1939, vol. 351, cols 300–301.

161 Croft to Margesson, 7 Sept. 1939, CRFT 1/16.

162 *The Times*, 5 April 1940, p. 5.

163 Larry L. Witherell, 'Lord Salisbury's 'Watching Committee' and the Fall of Neville Chamberlain, May 1940', *English Historical Review*, 116, 469 (2001), pp. 1134–1166.

164 Londonderry to Lord Swinton, 23 March 1940, Public Record Office of Northern Ireland, Londonderry Papers, D/3099/4/56.

165 *House of Commons Debates*, 7 May 1940, vol. 360, cols 1125–1130. He made his concerns plain to Churchill in advance, Keyes to Churchill, 30 April 1940, in Paul G. Halpern (ed.), *The Keyes Papers: Selections from the Private and Official Correspondence of Admiral of the Fleet Baron Keyes of Zeebrugge* (London: George Allen and Unwin, 1981), pp. 40–43. Churchill had supported Keyes's candidature at Portsmouth in 1934, Churchill to Croft, 19 Jan. 1934, CRFT 1/8.

166 N.A.P. Johnson, 'The Roles of the Conservative Party and the National Government During the 'Phoney War', September 1939–May 1940', M Phil, University of Birmingham (2002), pp. 88–89; John D. Fair, 'The Norwegian Campaign and Winston Churchill's Rise to Power in 1940: A Study of Perceptions and Attribution', *International History Review*, 9, 3 (1987), pp. 410–437.

167 Stuart Ball, *The Conservative Party and British Politics 1902–1951* (London: Longman, 1995), pp. 98–99. See also, Harshan Kumarasingham, ' "For the Good of the Party": An Analysis of the Fall of British Conservative Party Leaders from Chamberlain to Thatcher', *Political Science*, 58, 2 (2006), pp. 43–63.

168 *House of Commons Debates*, 8 May 1940, vol. 360, cols 1364–1365. In addition to Gretton and Davison, four others, who had not before abstained, were prepared to do so on this occasion: Charles Emmott, Lindsay Everard, Howard Gritten and Reginald Purbrick, none of whom addressed the two-day debate.

169 *House of Commons Debates*, 8 May 1940, vol. 360, cols 1364–1365.

170 Ibid., 7 May 1940, vol. 360, col. 1088; 8 May 1940, vol. 360, cols 1291–1292.

171 Amery, diary, 7 May 1940, Barnes and Nicholson, *Empire*, p. 592.

172 *House of Commons Debates*, 7 May 1940, vol. 360, cols 1106–1107. See also, *Daily Mirror*, 17 April 1940, p. 2.

173 Harold Nicolson, diary, 7 May 1940, in *Nicolson Diaries*, p. 76.

174 Winston S. Churchill, *The Second World War, Volume I: The Gathering Storm* (revised edition, London: Cassell, 1949), pp. 74, 76, 205. For Churchill's presentation of his relationship with the front and back benches in 1930s see David Reynolds, *In*

Command of History: Churchill Fighting and Writing the Second World War (London: Allen Lane, 2004), pp. 91–110.

175 Wolmer's opposition to Chamberlain was criticized by local constituency members, see, Parker, *Churchill*, p. 192.

176 Cowling, *Hitler*, pp. 91–93, 139; Robert Self, *Neville Chamberlain: A Biography* (Aldershot: Ashgate, 2006), pp. 239–241; Fleming, 'Cabinet', p. 71.

Retrospect and prospect

1 Colin Loader, *The Intellectual Development of Karl Mannheim: Culture, Politics, and Planning* (Cambridge: Cambridge University Press, 1985), p. 78.

2 See, Camilla Schofield, ' "A Nation or No Nation?" Enoch Powell and Thatcherism', in Ben Jackson and Robert Saunders (eds), *Making Thatcher's Britain* (Cambridge: Cambridge University Press, 2012), pp. 95–110; Stephen Howe, 'Decolonisation and Imperial Aftershocks', in Ben Jackson and Robert Saunders (eds), *Making Thatcher's Britain* (Cambridge: Cambridge University Press, 2012), pp. 234–251.

Bibliography

Primary sources

1 Personal papers

Bodleian Library, Oxford
Joseph Ball
1st Viscount Boyd of Merton [Alan Lennox-Boyd]
H.A. Gwynne
1st Viscount Milner
Violet, Viscountess Milner
Charles Oman
John Sandars
2nd Earl of Selborne
3rd Earl of Selborne [Viscount Wolmer]

British Library, St Pancras
1st Earl of Balfour [Arthur Balfour]
1st Earl of Halsbury
1st Baron Sydenham of Combe

Churchill Archive Centre, Cambridge
Randolph Churchill
Winston Churchill
1st Baron Croft of Bournemouth [Henry Page Croft]
Baron Duncan-Sandys
1st Baron Lloyd of Dolobran [George Lloyd]

Cambridge University Library
1st Earl Baldwin of Bewdley [Stanley Baldwin]

Durham County Record Office, Durham
Theresa, Marchioness of Londonderry

Liverpool Record Office
17th Earl of Derby

National Maritime Museum, Greenwich
Lionel Graham Horton Horton-Smith
Arnold White

Parliamentary Archive, Westminster
1st Baron Beaverbrook
Andrew Bonar Law
Patrick Hannon
1st Lord Wargrave [Edward Goulding]
19th Baron Willoughby de Broke

Public Record Office of Northern Ireland, Belfast
Baron Carson of Duncairn [Edward Carson]
7th Marquess of Londonderry

2 State, institutional and organizational records

British Library, St Pancras
Imperial Maritime League
Indian Empire Society

Conservative Party Archive, Bodleian Library, Oxford
East Midlands Area (National Union of Conservative and Unionist Associations)
1922 Committee
North-Western Area (National Union of Conservative and Unionist Associations)

House of Commons Library, Westminster
Early Day Motions

Lancashire Archives, Preston
Middleton and Prestwich Conservative Association
Waterloo, Crosby, Seaforth, and Litherland Women's Central Committee

Liverpool Record Office
Liverpool Constitutional Association

Private Papers
Gretton Group (copies provided to Professor Stuart Ball, University of Leicester, by Mrs
    Elizabeth Meynell, grand-daughter of the 1st Baron Gretton)

Public Record Office of Northern Ireland, Belfast
Cabinet Conclusions (Northern Ireland)
Ulster Unionist Council

Worcestershire Archives, Worcester
Bewdley Division Unionist Association

3 Newspapers, journals and periodicals

Aberdeen Press and Journal
Bournemouth Echo
Boy's Own Paper
Chelmsford Chronicle
Citizen
Daily Express
Daily Mirror
Empire and India Defence League Bulletin
Evening Standard
Fleet
Idler
Indian Daily Mail
Indian Empire Review
Jewish Chronicle
Manchester Guardian
Morning Post
National Review
Navy League Journal/Navy
Nineteenth Century
Outlook
Referee
Saturday Review
Scotsman
Star
The Times
Western Daily Press (Yeovil)
Western Gazette

4 Published letters, diaries and autobiographies

Amery, L.S., *My Political Life, Volume I: England Before the Storm 1896–1914* (London: Hutchinson, 1953).

Ball, Stuart (ed.), *Parliament and Politics in the Age of Churchill and Attlee: The Headlam Diaries 1935–1951* (Cambridge: Cambridge University Press, 1999).

Ball, Stuart (ed.), *Conservative Politics in National and Imperial Crisis: Letters from Britain to the Viceroy of India 1926–31* (Aldershot: Ashgate, 2014).

Barnes, John, and David Nicholson (eds), *The Leo Amery Diaries, Volume I: 1896–1929* (London: Hutchinson, 1980).

Barnes, John, and David Nicholson (eds), *The Empire at Bay: The Leo Amery Diaries 1929–1945* (London: Hutchinson, 1988).

Blumenfeld, R.D., *R.D.B.'s Diary, 1887–1914* (London: Heinemann, 1930).

Bond, Brian, and Simon Robbins (eds), *Staff Officer: The Diaries of Walter Guinness (First Lord Moyne) 1914–1918* (London: Leo Cooper, 1987).

Boyce, D. George (ed.), *The Crisis of British Unionism: Lord Selborne's Domestic Political Papers, 1885–1922* (London: Historians' Press, 1987).

Boyd-Carpenter, John, *Way of Life* (London: Sidgwick and Jackson, 1980).

Brett, Maurice V. (ed.), *Journals and Letters of Reginald, Viscount Esher, Volume III: 1910–1915* (London: Nicholson and Watson, 1938).

Brooks, David (ed.), *The Destruction of Lord Rosebery: From the Diary of Sir Edward Hamilton, 1894–1895* (Gloucester: Historians' Press, 1986).

Buckland, Patrick (ed.), *Irish Unionism 1885–1923: A Documentary History* (Belfast: HMSO, 1973).

Cecil of Chelwood, Viscount [Lord Robert Cecil], *All the Way* (London: Hodder and Stoughton, 1949).

Churchill, Winston S., *The Second World War, Volume I: The Gathering Storm* (revised edition, London: Cassell, 1949).

Clark, Alan (ed.), *A Good Innings: The Private Papers of Viscount Lee of Fareham* (London: John Murray, 1974).

Cockett, Richard (ed.), *My Dear Max: The Letters of Brendan Bracken to Lord Beaverbrook, 1925–1958* (London: Historians' Press, 1990).

Croft, Lord [Henry Page Croft], *My Life of Strife* (London: Hutchinson, 1948).

Crowson, N.J. (ed.), *Fleet Street, Press Barons and Politics: The Journals of Collin Brooks, 1932–1940* (Cambridge: Cambridge University Press, 1998).

Donner, Patrick, *Crusade: A Life Against the Calamitous Twentieth Century* (London: Sherwood, 1984).

Gilbert, Martin (ed.), *Winston S. Churchill, Volume V: Companion Documents, Part 3* (London: Heinemann, 1981).

Gordon, Peter (ed.), *The Red Earl: The Papers of the Fifth Earl Spencer 1835–1910, Volume I: 1885–1910* (Northampton: Northamptonshire Record Society, 1986).

Haldane, Richard Burdon, *An Autobiography* (London: Hodder and Stoughton, 1929).

Halpern, Paul G. (ed.), *The Keyes Papers: Selections from the Private and Official Correspondence of Admiral of the Fleet Baron Keyes of Zeebrugge* (London: George Allen and Unwin, 1981).

Hamilton, [Lord] George, *Parliamentary Reminiscences and Reflections 1886–1906* (London: John Murray, 1922).

Hazlehurst, Cameron, and Christine Woodland (ed.), *A Liberal Chronicle: Journals and Papers of J.A. Pease, 1908 to 1910* (London: Historians' Press, 1994).

Hewins, W.A.S., *The Apologia of an Imperialist: Forty Years of Empire Policy* (2 volumes, London: Constable, 1929).

Jeffery, Keith (ed.), *The Military Correspondence of Field Marshal Sir Henry Wilson, 1918–1922* (London: Bodley Head for the Army Records Society, 1985).

Johnson, Nancy E. (ed.), *The Diary of Gathorne Hardy, later Lord Cranbrook, 1866–1892: Political Selections* (Oxford: Clarendon Press, 1981).

Jones, Kennedy, *Fleet Street and Downing Street* (London: Hutchinson, 1920).

Jones, Thomas, *A Diary with Letters 1931–1950* (London: Oxford University Press, 1954).

Lansbury, George, *My Life* ([1928] London: Constable, 1931).

Long of Wraxall, Viscount [Walter Long], *Memories* (London: Hutchinson, 1923).

Low, David, *Low's Autobiography* (London: Michael Joseph, 1956).

Lucy, Henry W., *A Diary of the Unionist Parliament 1895–1900* (Bristol: J.W. Arrowsmith, 1901).

Lucy, Henry W., *The Balfourian Parliament 1900–1905* (London: Hodder and Stoughton, 1906).

Mackail, J.W., and Guy Wyndham, *Life and Letters of George Wyndham, Volume II* (London: Hutchinson, 1925).

Macmillan, Harold, *Winds of Change 1914–1939* (London: Macmillan, 1966).

Martel, Gordon (ed.), The Times *and Appeasement: The Journals of A.L. Kennedy, 1932–1939* (Cambridge: Cambridge University Press, 2000).

Middlemas, Keith (ed.), *Thomas Jones Whitehall Diary, Volume III: Ireland, 1918–1925* (London: Oxford University Press, 1971).

Midleton, Earl of, *Records and Reactions 1856–1939* (London: John Murray, 1939).

Morgan, Kenneth O., *Lloyd George Family Letters 1885–1936* (Cardiff: University of Wales Press, 1973).

Mosley, Oswald, *My Life* (London: Thomas Nelson and Sons, 1968).

Murray, Gideon [Viscount Elibank], *A Man's Life: Reflections and Reminiscences of Experiences in Many Lands* (London: Hutchinson, 1934).

Nicolson, Nigel (ed.), *Harold Nicolson: Diaries and Letters, 1939–1945* (London: Collins, 1967).

Oxford and Asquith, Earl of [H.H. Asquith], *Memories and Reflections 1852–1927, Volume II* (London: Cassell, 1928).

Ramsden, John (ed.), *Real Old Tory Politics: The Political Diaries of Sir Robert Sanders, Lord Bayford 1910–1935* (London: Historians' Press, 1984).

Rhodes James, Robert (ed.), *Chips: The Diaries of Sir Henry Channon* (London: Weidenfeld and Nicolson, 1967).

Rhodes James, Robert (ed.), *Memoirs of a Conservative: J.C.C. Davidson's Memoirs and Papers 1910–37* (London: Weidenfeld and Nicolson, 1969).

Self, Robert C. (ed.), *The Austen Chamberlain Diary Letters: The Correspondence of Sir Austen Chamberlain with His Sisters, Hilda and Ida, 1916–1937* (Cambridge: Cambridge University Press, 1995).

Self, Robert C. (ed.), *The Neville Chamberlain Diary Letters, Volume I: The Making of a Politician, 1915–1920* (Aldershot: Ashgate, 2000).

Self, Robert C. (ed.), *The Neville Chamberlain Diary Letters, Volume II: The Reform Years, 1921–1927* (Aldershot: Ashgate, 2000).

Self, Robert C. (ed.), *The Neville Chamberlain Diary Letters, Volume III: The Heir Apparent, 1928–1933* (Aldershot: Ashgate, 2002).

Self, Robert C. (ed.), *The Neville Chamberlain Diary Letters, Volume IV: The Downing Street Years, 1934–1940* (Aldershot: Ashgate, 2005).

Shackleton Bailey, D.R., *Cicero, Letters to Friends, Volume I: Letters 1–113* (Cambridge, MA: Harvard University Press, 2001).

Simon, Viscount [Sir John], *Retrospect: The Memoirs of the Rt. Hon. Viscount Simon GCSI, GCVO* (London: Hutchinson, 1952).

Sydenham of Combe, Lord, *My Working Life* (London: John Murray, 1927).

Templewood, Viscount [Samuel Hoare], *Nine Troubled Years* (London: Collins, 1954).

Vincent, John (ed.), *The Crawford Papers: The Journals of David Lindsay Twenty-Seventh Earl of Crawford and Tenth Earl of Balcarres, 1871–1940, During the Years 1892 to 1940* (Manchester: Manchester University Press, 1984).

Williams, Robin Harcourt (ed.), *Salisbury–Balfour Correspondence: Letters Exchanged Between the Third Marquess of Salisbury and His Nephew, Arthur James Balfour 1869–1892* (Ware: Hertfordshire Record Society, 1988).

Williamson, Philip, and Edward Baldwin (eds), *Baldwin Papers: A Conservative Statesman 1908–1947* (Cambridge: Cambridge University Press, 2004).

Willoughby de Broke, Lord, *The Passing Years* (London: Constable, 1924).

Wilson, Keith (ed.), *The Rasp of War: The Letters of H.A. Gwynne to the Countess Bathurst, 1914–1918* (London: Sidgwick and Jackson, 1988).

Wilson, Trevor (ed.), *The Political Diaries of C.P. Scott 1911–1928* (London: Collins, 1970).

Winterton, Earl, *Pre-War* (London: Macmillan, 1932).

Winterton, Earl, *Orders of the Day* (London: Cassell 1953).

5 Contemporary works and works by contemporaries

Anon., *Who's Who, 1933* (London: A. & C. Black, 1933).

Barnes, Leonard, *Empire or Democracy? A Study of the Colonial Question* (London: Victor Gollancz, 1939).

Belloc, Hilaire, and Cecil Chesterton, *The Party System* (London: Stephen Swift, 1911).

'Cato', *Guilty Men* ([1940] London: Penguin, 1998).

Churchill, Randolph S., *Lord Derby 'King of Lancashire': The Official Life of Edward, Seventeenth Earl of Derby 1865–1948* (London: Heinemann, 1959).

Churchill, Winston S., *India: Speeches and an Introduction* (London: Thornton Butterworth, 1931).

Colvin, Ian, *The Life of Lord Carson, Volume II* (London: Victor Gollancz, 1934).

Comyn-Platt, Thomas, 'Foreign Policy', in the Earl of Malmesbury (ed.), *The New Order: Studies in Unionist Policy* (London: Francis Griffiths, 1908), pp. 145–172.

Craig, F.W.S. (ed.), *British General Election Manifestos 1918–1966* (Chichester: Political Reference Publications, 1970).

Dicey, A.V., *Lectures on the Relation Between Law and Public Opinion in England During the Nineteenth Century* (London: Macmillan, 1905).

Dugdale, Blanche E.C., *Arthur James Balfour, First Earl of Balfour, KG, OM, FRS, Volume II: 1906–1930* (London: Hutchinson, 1936).

Froude, J.A., *Oceana, or England and Her Colonies* (London: Longmans, 1886).

Hand, Geoffrey J. (ed.), *Report of the Irish Boundary Commission 1925* (Shannon: Irish Academic Press, 1969).

Hobson, J.A., *Imperialism: A Study* (New York: James Pott, 1902).

Holland, Bernard, *The Life of Spencer Compton, Eighth Duke of Devonshire, Volume II* (London: Longmans, Green and Co., 1911).

Horton-Smith, L.G.H., *Perils of the Sea: How We Kept the Flag Flying: A Short History of a Long Fight* (London: Imperial Maritime League, 1920).

Kendall, Patricia, *Come with Me to India!* (New York: Charles Scribner's Sons, 1931).

Lane, A.H., *The Alien Menace* (London: Boswell, 1928).

Lloyd, George, and Edward Wood, *The Great Opportunity* (London: John Murray, 1919).

Londonderry, Marchioness of [Edith Vane-Tempest-Stewart], *Henry Chaplin: A Memoir* (London: Macmillan, 1926).

Lymington, Viscount, *Ich Dien: The Tory Path* (London: Constable, 1931).

Malmesbury, Earl of (ed.), *The New Order: Studies in Unionist Policy* (London: Francis Griffiths, 1908).

Marjoribanks, Edward, *The Life of Lord Carson, Volume I* (London: Victor Gollancz, 1932).

Mayo, Katherine, *Mother India* (New York: Harcourt, Brace and Company, 1927).

Morning Post, *Representative Indian States: A Series of Articles Reprinted from the Morning Post* (London: Morning Post, 1935).

Newton, Lord, *Lord Lansdowne: A Biography* (London: Macmillan, 1929).

Nicolson, Harold, *King George the Fifth: His Life and Reign* (London: Constable, 1952).

Plunkett, H.C., *The Irish Convention: Confidential Report to His Majesty The King by the Chairman* (Dublin: HMSO, 1918).

Rudlin, W.A., *The Growth of Fascism in Great Britain* (London: George Allen and Unwin, 1935).

Spender, J.A., *Great Britain, Empire and Commonwealth: 1886–1935* (London: Cassell, 1936).

White, Arnold, *Society, Smart Society, and Bad Smart Society: Their Influence on Empire, Being Seven Letters Written to the Editor of the 'Daily Chronicle'* (London: Daily Chronicle, 1900).

White, Arnold, *The Views of 'Vanoc': An Englishman's Outlook* (London: Keegan Paul, Trench, Trübner, 1910).

Willoughby de Broke, Lord, 'A Plea for an Unreformed House of Lords', *National Review*, 49 (1907), pp. 770–771.

Willoughby de Broke, Lord, 'The Coming Campaign', *National Review*, 56 (1910), pp. 59–70.

Willoughby de Broke, Lord, 'The House of Lords and After', *National Review*, 57 (1911), pp. 394–404.

Willoughby de Broke, Lord, 'The Tory Tradition', *National Review*, 57 (1911), pp. 201–213.

Willoughby de Broke, Lord, 'National Toryism', *National Review*, 58 (1912), pp. 413–427.

Willoughby de Broke, Lord, 'The Restoration of the Constitution', *National Review*, 58 (1912), pp. 857–868.

Willoughby de Broke, Lord, 'The Unionist Position', *National Review*, 62 (1913), pp. 212–224.

Willoughby de Broke, Lord, 'The Comfortable Classes and National Defence', *National Review*, 63 (1914), pp. 419–442.

Willoughby de Broke, Lord, 'The Unionist Party and the General Election', *National Review*, 63 (1914), pp. 775–786.

Woolf, Leonard, *After the Deluge: A Study of Communal Psychology* ([1931] Harmondsworth: Pelican, 1937).

Wyatt, Harold Frazer, 'The Ethics of Empire', *Nineteenth Century* (April 1897), pp. 516–530.

Wyatt, Harold Frazer, 'War as the Supreme Test of National Value', *Nineteenth Century* (Feb. 1899), pp. 216–225.

Wyatt, Harold Frazer, 'The Army and the Empire', *Idler* (June 1900), pp. 55–62.

Wyatt, Harold Frazer, 'Peace and War', *Boy's Own Paper*, 26 Dec. 1885, p. 207.

Wyatt, Harold Frazer, and L.G.H. Horton-Smith, *The Passing of the Great Fleet* (London: Sampson Low, Marston, 1909).

Wyatt, Harold Frazer, and L.G.H. Horton-Smith, *The True Truth About the Navy* (London: Imperial Maritime League, 1909).

Wyatt, Harold Frazer, and L.G.H. Horton-Smith, *The Imperial Maritime League: The Secret of Its Success* (London: Imperial Maritime League, 1910).

6 Literature, fiction and film

Disraeli, Benjamin, *Sybil, or the Two Nations* ([1845] Oxford: Oxford University Press, 1998).

Mackenzie, Compton, *Thin Ice* (London: Chatto and Windus, 1956).

Powell, Michael, and Emeric Pressburger (dir.), *The Life and Death of Colonel Blimp* (The Archers, 1943).

Trollope, Anthony, *The Eustace Diamonds* ([1871–73] London: Folio Society, 1990).

Trollope, Anthony, *Phineas Redux* ([1873–74] London: Folio Society, 1990).

Waugh, Evelyn, *Black Mischief* ([1932] London: Penguin, 2000).

Waugh, Evelyn, *Put Out More Flags* ([1942] London: Penguin, 2000).

Waugh, Evelyn, *Brideshead Revisited: The Sacred and Profane Memories of Captain Charles Ryder* ([1945] London: Penguin, 2000).

7 Official papers

Hansard, *House of Commons Debates*
Hansard, *House of Lords Debates*
Hansard, *Senate Debates (Northern Ireland)*

Secondary sources

8 Articles, biographies and monographs

Adams, R.J.Q., 'The National Service League and Mandatory Service in Edwardian Britain', *Armed Forces and Society*, 12, 1 (1985), pp. 53–74.

Adams, R.J.Q., *Bonar Law* (London: John Murray, 1999).

Addison, Paul, 'Patriotism Under Pressure: Lord Rothermere and British Foreign Policy', in Chris Cook and Gillian Peele (eds), *The Politics of Reappraisal, 1918–1939* (London: Macmillan, 1975), pp. 189–208.

Adonis, Andrew, *Making Aristocracy Work: The Peerage and the Political System in Britain 1884–1914* (reprinted edition, Oxford: Clarendon Press, 2002).

Arnstein, Walter L., *Protestant Versus Catholic in Mid-Victorian England* (Columbia, MO: University of Missouri Press, 1982).

Ash, Bernard, *The Lost Dictator: A Biography of Field-Marshal Sir Henry Wilson Bart GCB DSO MP* (London: Cassell, 1968).

Aston, Nigel, 'The Tories and France, 1714–60: Faith and Foreign Policy', in Jeremy Black (ed.), *The Tory World: Deep History and the Tory Theme in British Foreign Policy, 1679–2014* (Farnham: Ashgate, 2015).

Aubel, Felix, 'The Conservatives in Wales, 1880–1935', in Martin Francis and Ina Zweiniger-Bargielowska (eds), *The Conservatives and British Society, 1880–1990* (Cardiff: University of Wales Press, 1995), pp. 96–110.

Auerbach, Sascha, 'Negotiating Nationalism: Jewish Conscription and Russian Repatriation in London's East End, 1916–1918', *Journal of British Studies*, 46, 3 (2007), pp. 594–620.

Baker, David, 'The Extreme Right in the 1920s: Fascism in a Cold Climate, or "Conservatism with Knobs On"?', in Mike Cronin (ed.), *The Failure of British Fascism: The Far Right and the Fight for Political Recognition* (Basingstoke: Palgrave Macmillan, 1996), pp. 12–28.

Ball, Simon, 'Mosley and the Tories in 1930: The Problem of Generations', *Contemporary British History*, 24, 4 (2009), pp. 445–459.

Ball, Stuart, *Baldwin and the Conservative Party: The Crisis of 1929–1931* (London: Yale University Press, 1988).

Ball, Stuart, 'The 1922 Committee: The Formative Years 1922–45', *Parliamentary History*, 9, 1 (1990), pp. 129–157.

Ball, Stuart, 'The Politics of Appeasement: The Fall of the Duchess of Atholl and the Kinross and West Perth By-Election, 1938', *Scottish Historical Review*, 69, 187 (1990), pp. 49–83.

Ball, Stuart, *The Conservative Party and British Politics 1902–1951* (London: Longman, 1995).

Ball, Stuart, 'The Conservative Party, the Role of the State and the Politics of Protection, c.1918–1932', *History*, 96, 323 (2011), pp. 280–303.

Ball, Stuart, 'The Legacy of Coalition: Fear and Loathing in Conservative Politics, 1922–1931', *Contemporary British History*, 25, 1 (2011), pp. 65–82.

Ball, Stuart, *Portrait of a Party: The Conservative Party in Britain, 1918–1945* (Oxford: Oxford University Press, 2013).

Ballinger, Chris, 'Hedging and Ditching: The Parliament Act 1911', *Parliamentary History*, 30, 1 (2011), pp. 19–32.

Barker, Rodney, *Politics, Peoples and Government: Themes in British Political Thought Since the Nineteenth Century* (Basingstoke: Palgrave Macmillan, 1994).

Barker, Rodney, *Political Ideas in Modern Britain: In and After the Twentieth Century* (2nd edition, London: Routledge, 1997).

Barnes, John, 'Ideology and Factions', in Anthony Seldon and Stuart Ball (eds), *Conservative Century: The Conservative Party Since 1900* (Oxford: Oxford University Press, 1990), pp. 315–345.

Beckett, J.C., *The Anglo–Irish Tradition* (London: Faber and Faber, 1976).

Belich, James, *Replenishing the Earth: The Settler Revolution and the Rise of the Anglo-World, 1783–1939* (Oxford: Oxford University Press, 2009).

Bell, Duncan, 'Empire and International Relations in Victorian Political Thought', *Historical Journal*, 49, 1 (2006), pp. 281–298.

Bell, Duncan, *The Idea of Greater Britain: Empire and the Future of World Order, 1860–1900* (Princeton, NJ: Princeton University Press, 2007).

Bentley, Michael, *Lord Salisbury's World: Conservative Environments in Late Victorian Britain* (Cambridge: Cambridge University Press, 2001).

Benyon, John, ' "Intermediate" Imperialism and the Test of Empire: Milner's "Excentric" High Commission in South Africa', in Donal Lowry (ed.), *The South African War Reappraised* (Manchester: Manchester University Press, 2000), pp. 84–103.

Berthezène, Clarisse, *Training Minds for the War of Ideas: Ashridge College, the Conservative Party and the Cultural Politics of Britain, 1929–54* (Manchester: Manchester University Press, 2015).

Bew, Paul, *Churchill and Ireland* (Oxford: Oxford University Press, 2016).

Bialer, Uri, 'Elite Opinion and Defence Policy: Air Power Advocacy and British Rearmament During the 1930s', *Review of International Studies*, 6, 1 (1980), pp. 32–51.

Biggs-Davison, John, *George Wyndham: A Study in Toryism* (London: Hodder and Stoughton, 1951).

Black, Jeremy, 'Introduction', in Jeremy Black (ed.), *The Tory World: Deep History and the Tory Theme in British Foreign Policy, 1679–2014* (Farnham: Ashgate, 2015), pp. 1–20.

Blake, Robert, *The Unknown Prime Minister: The Life and Times of Andrew Bonar Law 1858–1923* (London: Eyre and Spottiswoode, 1955).

Blake, Robert, *Disraeli* (New York: St Martin's Press, 1967).

Blake, Robert, *The Conservative Party from Peel to Churchill* (London: Fontana, 1972).

Blewett, Neal, *The Peers, the Parties and the People: The General Elections of 1910* (London: Macmillan, 1972).

Blinkhorn, Martin (ed.), *Fascists and Conservatives: The Radical Right and the Establishment in Twentieth Century Europe* (London: Routledge, 1990).

Blinkhorn, Martin, *Fascism and the Right in Europe, 1919–1945* (London: Routledge, 2000).

Bloch, Michael, *Closet Queens: Some 20th Century Politicians* (London: Little, Brown, 2015).

Bowman, Timothy, *Carson's Army: The Ulster Volunteer Force, 1910–22* (Manchester: Manchester University Press, 2007).

Boyce, D. George, *Englishmen and Irish Troubles: British Public Opinion and the Making of Irish Policy 1918–22* (Cambridge, MA: Massachusetts Institute of Technology Press, 1972).

Boyce, D. George, 'Edward Carson (1845–1935) and Irish Unionism', in Ciaran Brady (ed.), *Worsted in the Game: Losers in Irish History* (Dublin: Lilliput Press, 1989), pp. 145–157.

Boyce, D. George, *Decolonisation and the British Empire, 1775–1997* (Basingstoke: Macmillan, 1999).

Brasted, Howard V., and Carl Bridge, 'The British Labour Party and Indian Nationalism, 1907–1947', *South Asia*, 2, 2 (1988), pp. 69–99.

Brettle, Adrian, '1864: The Genesis of a New Conservative World?', in Jeremy Black (ed.), *The Tory World: Deep History and the Tory Theme in British Foreign Policy, 1679–2014* (Farnham: Ashgate, 2015), pp. 187–202.

Bridge, Carl, *Holding India to the Empire: The British Conservative Party and the 1935 Constitution* (New Delhi: Sterling Publishers, 1986).

Brooke, Peter, *Duncan Sandys and the Informal Politics of Britain's Late Decolonisation* (Basingstoke: Palgrave Macmillan, 2017).

Buckland, Patrick, *Irish Unionism: One: The Anglo-Irish and the New Ireland 1885–1922* (Dublin: Gill and Macmillan, 1972).

Buettner, Elizabeth, 'From Somebodies to Nobodies: Britons Returning Home from India', in Martin Daunton and Bernard Rieger (eds), *Meanings of Modernity: Britain from the Late-Victorian Era to World War II* (Oxford: Berg, 2001), pp. 221–240.

Burness, Catriona, 'The Making of Scottish Unionism, 1886–1914', in Stuart Ball and Ian Holliday (eds), *Mass Conservatism: The Conservatives and the Public Since the 1880s* (London: Routledge, 2002), pp. 16–35.

Butler, Lord (ed.), *The Conservatives: A History from Their Origins to 1965* (London: George Allen and Unwin, 1977).

Cain, Peter, 'The Conservative Party and "Radical Conservatism", 1880–1914: Incubus or Necessity?', *Twentieth Century British History*, 7, 3 (1996), pp. 371–381.

Cain, Peter, 'Empire and the Language of Character and Virtue in Later Victorian and Edwardian Britain', *Modern Intellectual History*, 4, 2 (2007), pp. 249–273.

Cain, Peter, and A.G. Hopkins, *British Imperialism: Crisis and Decolonisation, 1914–1990* (2nd edition, London: Longman, 2002).

Campbell, John, *F.E. Smith: First Earl of Birkenhead* (London: Jonathan Cape, 1983).

Cannadine, David, *The Decline and Fall of the British Aristocracy* (reprinted edition, London: Papermac, 1996).

Cannadine, David, *Ornamentalism: How the British Saw Their Empire* (London: Allen Lane, 2001).

Canning, Paul, *British Policy Towards Ireland, 1921–1941* (Oxford: Clarendon Press, 1985).

Carey, John, *The Intellectuals and the Masses: Pride and Prejudice Among the Literary Intelligentsia, 1880–1939* (London: Faber and Faber, 1992).

Carr, Richard, *Veteran MPs and Conservative Politics in the Aftermath of the Great War: The Memory of All That* (Aldershot: Ashgate, 2013).

Catherwood, Christopher, *Winston's Folly: Imperialism and the Creation of Modern Iraq* (London: Constable, 2004).

Catterall, Peter, 'The Party and Religion', in Anthony Seldon and Stuart Ball (eds), *Conservative Century: The Conservative Party Since 1900* (Oxford: Oxford University Press, 1990), pp. 637–670.

Cawood, Ian, *The Liberal Unionist Party: A History* (London: I.B.Tauris, 2012).

Ceadel, Martin, 'Interpreting East Fulham', in Chris Cook and John Ramsden (eds), *By-Elections in British Politics* (London: Macmillan, 1973), pp. 118–139.

Cesarani, David, 'The Anti-Jewish Career of Sir William Joynson-Hicks, Cabinet Minister', *Journal of Contemporary History*, 24, 3 (1989), pp. 461–482.

Chakrabarty, Dipesh, *Provincializing Europe: Postcolonial Thought and Historical Difference* (Princeton, NJ: Princeton University Press, 2000).

Chandler, Andrew, 'Munich and Morality: The Bishops of the Church of England and Appeasement', *Twentieth Century British History*, 5, 1 (1994), pp. 77–99.

Charmley, John, *Lord Lloyd and the Decline of the British Empire* (London: Weidenfeld and Nicolson, 1987).

Charmley, John, *Chamberlain and the Lost Peace* (London: Ivan R. Dee, 1989).

Charmley, John, *Duff Cooper: The Authorised Biography* (London: Phoenix, 1997).

Charmley, John, *A History of Conservative Politics Since 1830* (2nd edition, Basingstoke: Palgrave Macmillan, 2008).

Cheyette, Bryan, 'Racism and Revision: Hilaire Belloc and the "Marconi Scandal" 1900–1914: A Reassessment of the Interactionist Model of Racial Hatred', in Tony Kushner and Kenneth Lunn (eds), *The Politics of Marginality: Race, the Radical*

Right and Minorities in Twentieth Century Britain (London: Routledge, 1990), pp. 131–142.

Clark, Alan, *The Tories: Conservatives and the Nation State 1922–1997* (London: Weidenfeld and Nicolson, 1998).

Clarke, P.F., *Lancashire and the New Liberalism* (Cambridge: Cambridge University Press, 1971).

Claydon, Tony, 'Toryism and the World in the Later Stuart Era, 1679–1714', in Jeremy Black (ed.), *The Tory World: Deep History and the Tory Theme in British Foreign Policy, 1679–2014* (Farnham: Ashgate, 2015), pp. 21–32.

Coetzee, Frans, *For Party or Country: Nationalism and the Dilemmas of Popular Conservatism in Edwardian England* (Oxford: Oxford University Press, 1990).

Coetzee, Frans, 'Faction and Failure: 1905–1910', in Stuart Ball and Anthony Seldon (eds), *Recovering Power: The Conservatives in Opposition Since 1867* (Basingstoke: Palgrave Macmillan, 2005), pp. 92–112.

Coetzee, Frans, and Marilyn S. Coetzee, 'Rethinking the Radical Right in Germany and Britain Before 1914', *Journal of Contemporary History*, 21, 4 (1986), pp. 515–537.

Coleman, Bruce, *Conservatism and the Conservative Party in Nineteenth-Century Britain* (London: Edward Arnold, 1988).

Colley, Linda, *Britons: Forging the Nation 1707–1837* (reprinted edition, London: Yale University Press, 2005).

Constantine, Stephen, 'Amateur Gardening and Popular Recreation in the 19th and 20th Centuries', *Journal of Social History*, 14, 3 (1981), pp. 387–406.

Copland, Ian, *India 1885–1947: The Unmaking of an Empire* (London: Longman, 2001).

Copland, Ian, *The Princes of India and the Endgame of Empire, 1917–1947* (Cambridge: Cambridge University Press, 2002).

Corthorn, Paul, 'W.E.D. Allen, Unionist Politics and the New Party', *Contemporary British History*, 23, 4 (2009), pp. 509–525.

Cowling, Maurice, *The Impact of Labour 1920–1924: The Beginning of Modern British Politics* (Cambridge: Cambridge University Press, 1971).

Cowling, Maurice, *The Impact of Hitler: British Politics and British Policy 1933–1940* (Chicago: University of Chicago Press, 1977).

Crowson, N.J., *Facing Fascism: The Conservative Party and the European Dictators 1935–1940* (London: Routledge, 1997).

Crowson, N.J., 'Citizen Defence: The Conservative Party and Its Attitude to National Service, 1937–57', in Abigail Beach and Richard Weight (eds), *The Right to Belong: Citizenship and National Identity in Britain, 1930–1960* (London: I.B.Tauris, 1998), pp. 205–222.

Crozier, Andrew J., *Appeasement and Germany's Last Bid for Colonies* (London: Macmillan, 1988).

Cruickshanks, Eveline, *Political Untouchables: The Tories and the '45* (London: Duckworth, 1979).

Cullen, Stephen M., 'The Fasces and the Saltire: The Failure of the British Union of Fascists in Scotland, 1932–1940', *Scottish Historical Review*, 87, 2 (2008), pp. 306–331.

Cunningham, Hugh, 'The Conservative Party and Patriotism', in Robert Colls and Philip Dodd (eds), *Englishness: Politics and Culture 1880–1920* (London: Croom Helm, 1986), pp. 283–307.

Dack, Janet, ' "It Certainly Isn't Cricket!" Media Responses to Mosley and the BUF', in Nigel Copsey and Andrzej Olechnowicz (eds), *Varieties of Anti-Fascism: Britain in the Inter-war Period* (Basingstoke: Palgrave Macmillan, 2010), pp. 141–161.

Darwin, John, 'Fear of Falling: British Politics and Imperial Decline Since 1800', *Transactions of the Royal Historical Society*, fifth series (1986), pp. 27–43.

Darwin, John, *After Tamerlane: The Rise and Fall of Global Empires, 1400–2000* (London: Allen Lane, 2007).

Darwin, John, *The Empire Project: The Rise and Fall of the British World-System 1830–1970* (Cambridge: Cambridge University Press, 2009).

Daunton, Martin, and Bernard Rieger, 'Introduction', in Martin Daunton and Bernard Rieger (eds), *Meanings of Modernity: Britain from the Late-Victorian Era to World War II* (Oxford: Berg, 2001), pp. 1–7.

Defries, Harry, *Conservative Party Attitudes to Jews, 1900–1950* (London: Routledge, 2001).

Dilks, David, ' "The Unnecessary War"? Military Advice and Foreign Policy in Great Britain, 1931–1939', in Adrian Preston (ed.), *General Staffs and Diplomacy Before the Second World War* (London: Croom Helm, 1978), pp. 98–132.

Dilks, David, *Neville Chamberlain, Volume I: Pioneering and Reform, 1869–1929* (Cambridge: Cambridge University Press, 1984).

Douglas, Roy, 'The National Democratic Party and the British Workers' League', *Historical Journal*, 15, 3 (1972), pp. 533–552.

Dutton, David, *Austen Chamberlain: Gentleman in Politics* (Bolton: Ross Anderson, 1985).

Dutton, David, 'His Majesty's Loyal Opposition': The Unionist Party in Opposition 1905–1915 (Liverpool: Liverpool University Press, 1992).

Dutton, David, *A History of the Liberal Party Since 1900* (second edition, Basingstoke: Palgrave Macmillan, 2013).

Egerton, David, *England and the Aeroplane: Militarism, Modernity and Machines* (London: Penguin, 2013).

Eldridge, C.C., *Disraeli and the Rise of a New Imperialism* (Cardiff: University of Wales Press, 1996).

English, Jim, 'Empire Day in Britain, 1904–1958', *Historical Journal*, 49, 1 (2006), pp. 247–276.

Epstein, Katherine C., 'Imperial Airs: Leo Amery, Air Power and Empire, 1873–1945', *Journal of Imperial and Commonwealth History*, 38, 4 (2010), pp. 571–598.

Ervine, St John, *Craigavon: Ulsterman* (London: George Allen and Unwin, 1949).

Evans, Brendan, and Andrew Taylor, *From Salisbury to Major: Continuity and Change in Conservative Politics* (Manchester: Manchester University Press, 1996).

Evans, Stephen, 'The Conservatives and the Redefinition of Unionism, 1912–21', *Twentieth Century British History*, 9, 1 (1998), pp. 1–27.

Fair, John D., *British Interparty Conferences: A Study of the Procedure of Conciliation in British Politics, 1867–1921* (Oxford: Clarendon Press, 1980).

Fair, John D., 'The Norwegian Campaign and Winston Churchill's Rise to Power in 1940: A Study of Perceptions and Attribution', *International History Review*, 9, 3 (1987), pp. 410–437.

Fair, John D., and John A. Hutcheson, 'British Conservatism in the Twentieth Century: An Emerging Ideological Tradition', *Albion*, 19, 4 (1987), pp. 549–578.

Fanning, Ronan, ' "Rats" versus "Ditchers": The Die-hard Revolt and the Parliament Bill of 1911', in Art Cosgrove and J.I. Maguire (eds), *Parliament and Community: Historical Studies XIV* (Belfast: Appletree Press, 1983), pp. 191–210.

Farr, Barbara Storm, *The Development and Impact of Right-Wing Politics in Britain, 1903–1932* (London: Garland, 1987).

Fest, Wilfried, 'Jingoism and Xenophobia in the Electioneering Strategies of British Ruling Elites Before 1914', in Paul Kennedy and Anthony Nichols (eds), *Nationalist and Racialist Movements in Britain and Germany Before 1914* (London: Macmillan, 1981), pp. 171–189.

Feuchtwanger, E.J., *Disraeli, Democracy and the Tory Party: Conservative Leadership and Organization After the Second Reform Bill* (Oxford: Clarendon Press, 1968).

Finlay, Richard, 'Scottish Conservatism and Unionism Since 1918', in Martin Francis and Ina Zweiniger-Bargielowska (eds), *The Conservatives and British Society, 1880–1990* (Cardiff: University of Wales Press, 1995), pp. 111–126.

Fleming, N.C., *The Marquess of Londonderry: Aristocracy, Power and Politics in Britain and Ireland* (London: I.B.Tauris, 2005).

Fleming, N.C., 'The Press, Empire and Historical Time: *The Times* and Indian Self-Government, c.1911–47', *Media History*, 16, 1 (2010), pp. 183–198.

Fleming, N.C., 'Cabinet Government, British Imperial Security, and the World Disarmament Conference,' 1932–1934, *War in History*, 18, 1 (2011), pp. 62–84.

Fleming, N.C., 'Diehard Conservatism, Mass Democracy, and Indian Constitutional Reform, c.1918–1935', *Parliamentary History*, 32, 2 (2013), pp. 337–360.

Fleming, N.C., 'Diehard Conservatives and the Appeasement of Nazi Germany, 1935–1940', *History*, 100, 441 (2015), pp. 412–435.

Fleming, N.C., 'The Imperial Maritime League: British Navalism, Conflict and the Radical Right, c.1907–1920', *War in History*, 23, 3 (2016), pp. 296–322.

Fleming, N.C., 'Lancashire Conservatives, Tariff Reform, and Indian Responsible Government', *Contemporary British History*, 30, 2 (2016), pp. 151–176.

Fleming, N.C., 'Women and Lancashire Conservatism Between the Wars', *Women's History Review*, 26, 3 (2017), pp. 329–349.

Ford, Robert, 'Who Might Vote for the BNP? Survey Evidence on the Electoral Potential of the Extreme Right in Britain', Roger Eatwell and Matthew J. Goodwin (eds), *The New Extremism in 21st Century Britain* (Abingdon: Routledge, 2010), pp. 145–168.

Foster, Alan, 'The Beaverbrook Press and Appeasement: The Second Phase', *European History Quarterly*, 21, 1 (1991), pp. 5–38.

France, John, 'Salisbury and the Unionist Alliance', in Lord Blake and Hugh Cecil (eds), *Salisbury: The Man and His Policies* (London: Palgrave Macmillan, 1987), pp. 219–251.

Fraser, Peter, 'The Liberal Unionist Alliance: Chamberlain, Hartington, and the Conservatives 1886–1904', *English Historical Review*, 77, 302 (1962), pp. 53–78.

Gamble, Andrew, 'Europe and America', in Ben Jackson and Robert Saunders (eds), *Making Thatcher's Britain* (Cambridge: Cambridge University Press, 2012), pp. 218–233.

Gambles, Anna, *Protection and Politics: Conservative Economic Discourse 1815–1852* (Woodbridge: Boydell and Brewer, 1999).

Gannon, Franklin Reid, *The British Press and Germany 1936–1939* (Oxford: Clarendon Press, 1971).

Gash, Norman, *Aristocracy and People: Britain, 1815–1865* (Cambridge MA: Harvard University Press, 1979).

Gaunt, Richard A., 'From Country Party to Conservative Party: The Ultra-Tories and Foreign Policy', in Jeremy Black (ed.), *The Tory World: Deep History and the Tory Theme in British Foreign Policy, 1679–2014* (Farnham: Ashgate, 2015), pp. 149–165.

Ghosh, S.C., 'Decision-Making and Power in the British Conservative Party: A Case Study of the Indian Problem 1929–34', *Political Studies*, 13, 2 (1965), pp. 198–212.

Gilmour, David, *Curzon: Imperial Statesman, 1855–1925* (reprinted edition, London: John Murray, 2003).

Girvin, Brian, 'The Party in Comparative and International Context', in Anthony Seldon and Stuart Ball (eds), *Conservative Century: The Conservative Party Since 1900* (Oxford: Oxford University Press, 1990), pp. 695–725.

Girvin, Brian, *The Right in the Twentieth Century: Conservatism and Democracy* (London: Pinter, 1994).

Glickman, Harvey, 'The Toryness of English Conservatism', *Journal of British Studies*, 1 (1961), pp. 111–143.

Glover, David, *Literature, Immigration, and Diaspora in Fin-de-Siècle England: A Cultural History of the 1905 Aliens Act* (Cambridge: Cambridge University Press, 2012).

Gollin, Alfred M., *The Observer and J.L. Garvin 1908–1914: A Study in a Great Editorship* (London: Oxford University Press, 1960).

Gollin, Alfred M., *Proconsul in Politics: A Study of Lord Milner in Opposition and Power* (London: Anthony Blond, 1964).

Gollin, Alfred M., *Balfour's Burden: Arthur Balfour and Imperial Preference* (London: Anthony Blond, 1965).

Gopal, Sarvepalli, 'Churchill and India', in Robert Blake and Wm. Roger Louis (eds), *Churchill* (Oxford: Clarendon Press, 1996), pp. 457–471.

Gorman, Daniel, *Imperial Citizenship: Empire and the Question of Belonging* (Manchester: Manchester University Press, 2006).

Green, E.H.H., *The Crisis of Conservatism: The Politics, Economics and Ideology of the British Conservative Party, 1880–1914* (reprinted edition, London: Routledge, 1996).

Green, E.H.H., *Ideologies of Conservatism: Conservative Political Ideas in the Twentieth Century* (Oxford: Oxford University Press, 2002).

Greenleaf, W.H., *The British Political Tradition, Volume II: The Ideological Heritage* (London: Methuen, 1983).

Gregory, Adrian, *The Last Great War: British Society and the First World War* (Cambridge: Cambridge University Press, 2008).

Griffin, Roger, *The Nature of Fascism* (London: Routledge, 1993).

Griffiths, Richard, *Fellow Travellers of the Right: British Enthusiasts for Nazi Germany 1933–9* (London: Constable, 1980).

Griffiths, Richard, *Patriotism Perverted: Captain Ramsay, the Right Club and British Anti-Semitism 1939–40* (London: Faber and Faber, 1998).

Guttsman, W.L., *The British Political Elite* (London: MacGibbon and Kee, 1965).

Haidt, Jonathan, *The Righteous Mind: Why Good People Are Divided by Politics and Religion* (London: Allen Lane, 2012).

Hall, Catherine, and Sonya Rose (eds), *At Home with the Empire: Metropolitan Culture and the Imperial World* (Cambridge: Cambridge University Press, 2006).

Hamer, D.A., *The Politics of Electoral Pressure: A Study in the History of Victorian Reform Agitations* (Hassocks: Harvester Press, 1977).

Hamilton, W. Mark, 'The "New Navalism" and the British Navy League, 1895–1914', *Mariner's Mirror*, 64, 1 (1978), pp. 37–44.

Hanham, H.J., *Elections and Party Management: Politics in the Time of Disraeli and Gladstone* (Hassocks: Harvester Press, 1978).

Hart, Bradley W., and Richard Carr, 'Sterilization and the British Conservative Party: Rethinking the Failure of the Eugenics Society's Political Strategy in the Nineteen-Thirties', *Historical Research*, 88, 242 (2015), pp. 716–739.

Hawkins, Angus, *Parliament, Party and the Art of Politics in Britain, 1855–1859* (Stanford, CA: Stanford University Press, 1987).

Hayek, F.A., *The Road to Serfdom: Text and Documents [The Collected Works of F.A. Hayek, Volume II, ed. Bruce Caldwell]* (London: University of Chicago Press, 2007).

Hazlehurst, Cameron, Sally Whitehead and Christine Woodland (eds), *A Guide to the Papers of British Cabinet Ministers 1900–1964* (Cambridge: Cambridge University Press, 1996).

Heffernan, Michael, 'The French Right and the Overseas Empire', in Nicholas Atkin and Frank Talbot (eds), *The Right in France, 1789–1997* (London: I.B.Tauris, 1998), pp. 89–113.

Hendley, Matthew, ' "Help Us to Secure a Strong, Healthy, Prosperous and Peaceful Britain": The Social Arguments of the Campaign for Compulsory Military Service in Britain, 1899–1914', *Canadian Journal of History*, 30, 2 (1995), pp. 261–288.

Hendley, Matthew, *Organized Patriotism and the Crucible of War: Popular Imperialism in Britain, 1914–1932* (Montreal and Kingston: McGill-Queen's University Press, 2012).

Herf, Jeffrey, *Reactionary Modernism: Technology, Culture, and Politics in Weimar and the Third Reich* (Cambridge: Cambridge University Press, 1984).

Hetherington, S.J., *Katherine Atholl, 1874–1960: Against the Tide* (Aberdeen: Aberdeen University Press, 1989).

Holman, Brett, *The Next War in the Air: Britain's Fear of the Bomber, 1908–1941* (Abingdon: Routledge, 2016).

Holmes, Colin, *John Bull's Island: Immigration and British Society, 1871–1971* (Basingstoke: Macmillan, 1988).

Holmes, Colin, *Anti-Semitism in British Society, 1876–1939* (reprinted edition, Abingdon: Routledge, 2016).

Howe, Stephen, 'Decolonisation and Imperial Aftershocks', in Ben Jackson and Robert Saunders (eds), *Making Thatcher's Britain* (Cambridge: Cambridge University Press, 2012), pp. 234–251.

Hughes, Michael, and Harry Wood, 'Crimson Nightmares: Tales of Invasion and Fears of Revolution in Early Twentieth-Century Britain', *Contemporary British History*, 28, 3 (2014), pp. 294–317.

Humphries, Michael, ' "The Eyes of an Empire": The Legion of Frontiersmen, 1904–14', *Historical Research*, 85, 227 (2012), pp. 133–158.

Hutcheson, John A., *Leopold Maxse and the* National Review, *1893–1914* (New York: Garland, 1989).

Hutchison, I.G.C., *A Political History of Scotland 1832–1924: Parties, Elections, Issues* (Edinburgh: Jon Donald, 1986).

Hyam, Ronald, 'The British Empire in the Edwardian Era', in Judith M. Brown and Wm. Roger Louis (eds), *The Oxford History of the British Empire, Volume IV: The Twentieth Century* (Oxford: Oxford University Press, 1999), pp. 47–63.

Hyam, Ronald, *Understanding the British Empire* (Cambridge: Cambridge University Press, 2010).

Jackson, Alvin, *The Ulster Party: Irish Unionists in the House of Commons, 1884–1911* (Oxford: Oxford University Press, 1989).

Jackson, Alvin, *Sir Edward Carson* (Dundalk: Dundalgan Press, 1993).

Jackson, Daniel, *Popular Opposition to Irish Home Rule in Britain* (Liverpool: Liverpool University Press, 2009).

Jaggard, Edwin, 'Lord Falmouth and the Parallel Political Worlds of Ultra-Toryism, 1826–32', *Parliamentary History*, 33, 2 (2014), pp. 300–320.

James, Lawrence, *Warrior Race: A History of the British at War from Roman Times to the Present* (London: Abacus, 2001).

Jarvis, David, 'Mrs Maggs and Betty: The Conservative Appeal to Women Voters in the 1920s', *Twentieth Century British History*, 5, 2 (1994), pp. 129–152.

Jarvis, David, 'British Conservatism and Class Politics in the 1920s', *English Historical Review*, 111, 440 (1996), pp. 59–84.

Jeffery, Keith, *Field Marshal Sir Henry Wilson: A Political Soldier* (Oxford: Oxford University Press, 2006).

Jenkinson, Jacqueline, 'The 1919 Riots', in Panikos Panayi (ed.), *Racial Violence in Britain, 1840–1950* (Leicester: Leicester University Press, 1993), pp. 92–111.

Johnson, Gaynor, *Lord Robert Cecil: Politician and Internationalist* (Farnham: Ashgate, 2013).

Johnson, Matthew, *Militarism and the British Left, 1902–1914* (Basingstoke: Palgrave Macmillan, 2013).

Jones, Emily, 'Conservatism, Edmund Burke and the Invention of a Political Tradition, c.1885–1914', *Historical Journal*, 58, 4 (2015), pp. 1115–1139.

Kaul, Chandrika, *Reporting the Raj: The British Press and India, c.1880–1922* (Manchester: Manchester University Press, 2003).

Kendle, John, *Ireland and the Federal Solution: The Debate over the United Kingdom Constitution, 1870–1921* (Kingston and Montreal: McGill-Queen's University Press, 1989).

Kennedy, Paul, *The Rise and Fall of the Great Powers: Economic Change and Military Conflict from 1500 to 2000* (London: Unwin Hyman, 1988).

Kennedy, Thomas C., 'Troubled Tories: Dissent and Confusion Concerning the Party's Ulster Policy, 1910–1914', *Journal of British Studies*, 46, 3 (2007), pp. 570–593.

Keohane, Nigel, *The Party of Patriotism: The Conservative Party and the First World War* (Aldershot: Ashgate, 2010).

Kinnear, Michael, *The Fall of Lloyd George: The Political Crisis of 1922* (London: Macmillan, 1973).

Kirk-Greene, Anthony, *Britain's Imperial Administrators, 1858–1966* (Basingstoke: Macmillan, 2000).

Koss, Stephen, *The Rise and Fall of the Political Press in Britain* (London: Fontana, 1990).

Kumarasingham, Harshan, ' "For the Good of the Party": An Analysis of the Fall of British Conservative Party Leaders from Chamberlain to Thatcher', *Political Science*, 58, 2 (2006), pp. 43–63.

Lawrence, Jon, *Electing Our Masters: The Hustings in British Politics from Hogarth to Blair* (Oxford: Oxford University Press, 2009).

Lebzelter, Gisela C., 'Anti-Semitism: A Focal Point for the British Radical Right', in Paul Kennedy and Anthony Nicholls (eds), *Nationalist and Racialist Movements in Britain and Germany Before 1914* (London: Macmillan, 1981), pp. 88–105.

Lentin, Antony, *The Last Political Law Lord: Lord Sumner (1859–1934)* (Newcastle: Cambridge Scholars, 2008).

Lindsay, T.F., and Michael Harrington, *The Conservative Party, 1918–1970* (London: Macmillan, 1974).

Loader, Colin, *The Intellectual Development of Karl Mannheim: Culture, Politics, and Planning* (Cambridge: Cambridge University Press, 1985).

Loughlin, James, 'Northern Ireland and British Fascism in the Inter-war Years', *Irish Historical Studies*, 29, 116 (1995), pp. 537–552.

Loughlin, James, *Ulster Unionism and British National Identity Since 1885* (London: Pinter, 1995).

Love, Gary, 'The British Movement, Duncan Sandys, and the Politics of Constitutionalism in the 1930s', *Contemporary British History*, 23, 4 (2009), pp. 543–558.

Lovenduski, Joni, Pippa Norris and Catriona Burness, 'The Party and Women', in Anthony Seldon and Stuart Ball (eds), *Conservative Century: The Conservative Party Since 1900* (Oxford: Oxford University Press, 1994), pp. 611–635.

Lukowitz, David, 'George Lansbury's Peace Missions to Hitler and Mussolini in 1937', *Canadian Journal of History*, 15, 1 (1980), pp. 67–82.

Lysaght, Charles, *Brendan Bracken* (London: Allen Lane, 1979).

McClintock, Anne, *Imperial Leather: Race, Gender and Sexuality in the Colonial Contest* (New York: Routledge, 1995).

McDonough, Frank, *The Conservative Party and Anglo–German Relations, 1905–1914* (Basingstoke: Palgrave Macmillan, 2007).

McDowell, R.B., *The Irish Convention, 1917–18* (London: Routledge and Keegan Paul, 1970).

McEwen, J.M., ' "Brass-Hats" and the British Press During the First World War', *Canadian Journal of History*, 18, 1 (1983), pp. 43–67.

McKenzie, R.T., *British Political Parties: The Distribution of Power Within the Conservative and Labour Parties* (2nd edition, London: Heinemann, 1967).

McKibbin, Ross, *Classes and Cultures: England 1918–1951* (Oxford: Oxford University Press, 1998).

McKibbin, Ross, *Parties and People: England 1914–1951* (Oxford: Oxford University Press, 2010).

McMahon, Deirdre, *Republicans and Imperialists: Anglo–Irish Relations in the 1930s* (London: Yale University Press, 1984).

McNally, Patrick, *Parties, Patriots and Undertakers: Parliamentary Politics in Early Hanoverian Ireland* (Dublin: Four Courts Press, 1997).

Mackenzie, John M., *Propaganda and Empire: The Manipulation of British Public Opinion, 1880–1960* (Manchester: Manchester University Press, 1984).

MacRaild, Donald M., *Faith, Fraternity and Fighting: The Orange Order and Irish Migrants in Northern England, c.1850–1920* (Liverpool: Liverpool University Press, 2005).

Mansergh, Nicholas, *The Unresolved Question: The Anglo–Irish Settlement and Its Undoing 1912–72* (London: Yale University Press, 1991).

Manton, Kevin, 'Edwardian Conservatism and the Constitution: The Thought of Lord Hugh Cecil', *Parliamentary History*, 34, 3 (2015), pp. 365–382.

Marder, A.J., *From the Dreadnought to Scapa Flow: The Royal Navy in the Fisher Era, 1904–1919, Volume I: The Road to War, 1904–1914* (London: Oxford University Press, 1961).

Marsh, Peter, *The Discipline of Popular Government: Lord Salisbury's Domestic Statecraft, 1881–1902* (Hassocks: Harvester Press, 1978).

Marsh, Peter, *Joseph Chamberlain: Entrepreneur in Politics* (London: Yale University Press, 1994).

Marwick, Arthur, 'Middle Opinion in the Thirties: Planning, Progress and Political "Agreement"', *English Historical Review*, 79, 311 (1964), pp. 285–298.

Matthews, Kevin, *Fatal Influence: The Impact of Ireland on British Politics, 1920–1925* (Dublin: University College Dublin Press, 2004).

Maurer, Sara L., *The Dispossessed State: Narratives of Ownership in Nineteenth-Century Britain and Ireland* (Baltimore MD: Johns Hopkins University Press, 2012).

Mayer, A.J., 'Internal Crisis and War Since 1870', in C.L. Bertrand (ed.), *Revolutionary Situations in Europe 1917–22: Germany, Italy, Austria-Hungary* (Montreal: Centre interuniversitaire d'études européennes, 1977), pp. 206–211.

Mazower, Mark, *Dark Continent: Europe's Twentieth Century* (London: Allen Lane, 1998).

Metcalf, Thomas R., *Ideologies of the Raj* (Cambridge: Cambridge University Press, 1995).

Middlemas, Keith, and John Barnes, *Baldwin: A Biography* (London: Weidenfeld and Nicolson, 1969).

Mizutani, Satoshi, *The Meaning of White: Race, Class, and the 'Domiciled Community' in British India 1858–1930* (Oxford: Oxford University Press, 2011).

Mock, Wolfgang, 'The Function of "Race" in Imperialist Ideologies: The Example of Joseph Chamberlain', in Paul Kennedy and Anthony Nichols (eds), *Nationalist and Racialist Movements in Britain and Germany Before 1914* (London: Macmillan, 1981), pp. 190–203.

Monger, David, *Patriotism and Propaganda in First World War Britain: The National War Aims Committee and Civilian Morale* (Liverpool: Liverpool University Press, 2012).

Moore, Simon, 'The Agrarian Conservative Party in Parliament, 1920–1929', *Parliamentary History*, 10, 2 (1991), pp. 342–362.

Morgan, Kenneth O., *Consensus and Disunity: The Lloyd George Coalition Government 1918–1922* (Oxford: Clarendon Press, 1979).

Morgan, Kenneth O., *Wales in British Politics, 1868–1922* (Cardiff: University of Wales Press, 1980).

Morris, A.J.A., *The Scaremongers: The Advocacy of War and Rearmament, 1896–1914* (London: Routledge and Keegan Paul, 1984).

Muldoon, Andrew, ' "The Cow Is Still the Most Important Figure in Indian Politics!" Religion, Imperial Culture and the Shaping of Indian Political Reform in the 1930s', *Parliamentary History*, 27, 1 (2008), pp. 67–81.

Murphy, Philip, *Alan Lennox-Boyd: A Biography* (London: I.B.Tauris, 1999).

Murphy, Richard, 'Faction in the Conservative Party and the Home Rule Crisis, 1912–14', *History*, 71, 232 (1986), pp. 222–234.

Nair, Rahul, 'The Construction of a "Population Problem" in Colonial India 1919–1947', *Journal of Imperial and Commonwealth History*, 39, 2 (2011), pp. 227–247.

Newton, Scott, *Profits of Peace: The Political Economy of Anglo–German Appeasement* (Oxford: Clarendon Press, 1996).

Norton, Philip, 'The Parliamentary Party and Party Committees', in Anthony Seldon and Stuart Ball (eds), *Conservative Century: The Conservative Party Since 1900* (Oxford: Oxford University Press, 1990), pp. 97–144.

Norton, Philip, 'Resisting the Inevitable? The Parliament Act 1911', *Parliamentary History*, 31, 3 (2012), pp. 444–459.

Norton, Philip, and Arthur Aughey, *Conservatives and Conservatism* (London: Temple Smith, 1981).

O'Day, Alan, *Irish Home Rule 1867–1921* (Manchester: Manchester University Press, 1998).

O'Gorman, Frank, *British Conservatism: Conservative Thought from Burke to Thatcher* (London: Longman, 1986).

O'Leary, Cornelius, and Patrick Maume, *Controversial Issues in Anglo–Irish Relations, 1910–1921* (Dublin: Four Courts Press, 2004).

O'Riordan, Elspeth Y., *Britain and the Ruhr Crisis* (Basingstoke: Palgrave Macmillan, 2001).

Offer, Avner, *Property and Politics 1870–1914: Landownership, Law, Ideology and Urban Development in England* (Cambridge: Cambridge University Press, 1981).

Olusoga, David, and Casper W. Erichsen, *The Kaiser's Holocaust: Germany's Forgotten Genocide and the Colonial Roots of Nazism* (London: Faber, 2011).

Otte, T.G., ' "We Are Part of the Community of Europe": The Tories, Empire and Foreign Policy, 1874–1914', in Jeremy Black (ed.), *The Tory World: Deep History and the Tory Theme in British Foreign Policy, 1679–2014* (Farnham: Ashgate, 2015), pp. 203–227.

Ovendale, Richie, *'Appeasement' and the English Speaking World: Britain, the United States, the Dominions and the Policy of 'Appeasement', 1937–1939* (Cardiff: University of Wales Press, 1975).

Owen, Nicholas, *The British Left and India: Metropolitan Anti-Imperialism, 1885–1947* (Oxford: Oxford University Press, 2007).

Packer, Ian, 'The Conservatives and the Ideology of Landownership, 1910–1914', in Martin Francis and Ina Zweiniger-Bargielowska (eds), *The Conservatives and British Society, 1880–1990* (Cardiff: University of Wales Press, 1995), pp. 39–57.

Panayi, Panikos, 'Anti-German Riots in Britain During the First World War', in Panikos Panayi (ed.), *Racial Violence in Britain in the Nineteenth and Twentieth Centuries* (Leicester: Leicester University Press, 1993), pp. 65–91.

Panayi, Panikos, 'Anti-Immigrant Violence in Nineteenth- and Twentieth-Century Britain', in Panikos Panayi (ed.), *Racial Violence in Britain in the Nineteenth and Twentieth Centuries* (Leicester: Leicester University Press, 1993), pp. 1–25.

Parker, R.A.C., *Chamberlain and Appeasement: British Policy and the Coming of the Second World War* (Basingstoke: Palgrave Macmillan, 1993).

Parker, R.A.C., *Churchill and Appeasement* (London: Macmillan, 2000).

Peatling, G.K., *British Opinion and Irish Self-Government, 1865–1925: From Unionism to Liberal Commonwealth* (Dublin: Irish Academic Press, 2001).

Pedersen, Susan, 'Modernity and Trusteeship: Tensions of Empire in Britain Between the Wars', in Martin Daunton and Bernhard Rieger (eds), *Meanings of Modernity: Britain from the Late-Victorian Era to World War II* (Oxford: Berg, 2001), pp. 203–217.

Peele, Gillian, 'St George's and the Empire Crusade', in Chris Cook and John Ramsden (eds), *By-Elections in British Politics* (London: Macmillan, 1973), pp. 79–108.

Peele, Gillian, 'Revolt over India', in Chris Cook and Gillian Peele (eds), *The Politics of Reappraisal, 1918–1939* (London: Macmillan, 1975), pp. 114–145.

Phillips, Adrian, 'Chronicle of a Conspiracy Foretold: MI5, Churchill and the "King's Party" in the Abdication Crisis', *Conservative History Journal*, 2, 5 (2017), pp. 17–23.

Phillips, Gregory D., *The Diehards: Aristocratic Society and Politics in Edwardian England* (Cambridge, MA: Harvard University Press, 1979).

Phillips, Gregory D., 'Lord Willoughby de Broke and the Politics of Radical Toryism, 1909–1914', *Journal of British Studies*, 20, 1 (1980), pp. 205–224.

Porter, Bernard, *The Absent-Minded Imperialists: Empire, Society and Culture in Britain* (Oxford: Oxford University Press, 2004).

Porter, Bernard, *Critics of Empire: British Radicals and the Imperial Challenge* (London: I.B.Tauris, 2008).

Porter, Bernard, *Empire Ways: Aspects of British Imperialism* (London: I.B.Tauris, 2016).

Porter, Dilwyn, ' "A Trusted Guide of the Investing Public": Harry Marks and the *Financial News* 1884–1916', *Business History*, 28, 1 (1986), pp. 1–17.

Pugh, Martin, *Electoral Reform in War and Peace 1906–1918* (London: Routledge and Keegan Paul, 1978).

Pugh, Martin, *The Tories and the People, 1880–1935* (Oxford: Blackwell, 1985).

Pugh, Martin, *'Hurrah for the Blackshirts!' Fascists and Fascism in Britain Between the Wars* (London: Jonathan Cape, 2005).

Quinault, Roland, 'Portrait of a "Diehard": Greville Verney, Nineteenth Lord Willoughby de Broke', in Robert Bearman (ed.), *Compton Verney: A History of the House and Its Owners* (Stratford-upon-Avon: Shakespeare Birthplace Trust, 2000), pp. 157–174.

Quinault, Roland, *British Prime Ministers and Democracy: From Disraeli to Blair* (London: Bloomsbury Academic, 2011).

Ramsden, John, *The Age of Balfour and Baldwin, 1902–1940* (London: Longman, 1978).

Ramsden, John, *An Appetite for Power: A History of the Conservative Party Since 1830* (London: Harper Collins, 1999).

Readman, Paul, 'Conservatives and the Politics of Land: Lord Winchelsea's National Agricultural Union, 1893–1901', *English Historical Review*, 121, 490 (2006), pp. 25–69.

Redford, Duncan, 'Collective Security and Internal Dissent: The Navy League's Attempts to Develop a New Policy Towards British Naval Power Between 1919 and the 1922 Washington Naval Treaty', *History*, 96, 321 (2011), pp. 48–67.

Rempel, Richard A., *Unionists Divided: Arthur Balfour, Joseph Chamberlain and the Unionist Free Traders* (Newton Abbot: David and Charles, 1972).

Reynolds, David, *In Command of History: Churchill Fighting and Writing the Second World War* (London: Allen Lane, 2004).

Rhodes James, Robert, *Lord Randolph Churchill* (reprinted edition, London: Phoenix, 1994).

Rich, Paul B., *Race and Empire in British Politics* (2nd edition, Cambridge: Cambridge University Press, 1990).

Roberts, Andrew, *'The Holy Fox': The Life of Lord Halifax* (London: Weidenfeld and Nicolson, 1991).

Roberts, Andrew, *Salisbury: Victorian Titan* (London: Weidenfeld and Nicolson, 1999).

Roberts, Matthew, 'Popular Conservatism in Britain, 1832–1914', *Parliamentary History*, 26, 3 (2007), pp. 387–410.

Robinson, Francis, 'The British Empire and the Muslim World', in Judith M. Brown and Wm. Roger Louis (eds), *The Oxford History of the British Empire, Volume IV: The Twentieth Century* (Oxford: Oxford University Press, 1999), pp. 398–420.

Rodner, William S., 'Leaguers, Covenanters, Moderates: British Support for Ulster, 1913–1914', *Éire-Ireland*, 17, 3 (1982), pp. 68–85.

Rubenstein, William D., 'Henry Page Croft and the National Party 1917–22', *Journal of Contemporary History*, 9, 1 (1974), pp. 129–148.

Rudman, Stella, *Lloyd George and the Appeasement of Germany, 1919–1945* (Newcastle: Cambridge Scholars, 2011).

Ruggiero, John, *Neville Chamberlain and British Rearmament: Pride, Prejudice, and Politics* (Westport CT: Greenwood Press, 1999).

Sack, James J., *From Jacobite to Conservative: Reaction and Orthodoxy in Britain, c.1760–1832* (Cambridge: Cambridge University Press, 2002).

Saikia, Robin, *The Red Book: The Membership List of The Right Club – 1939* (London: Foxley Books, 2010).

Sarkisyanz, Manuel, *Hitler's English Inspirers: Based on Lectures Given in Heidelberg University, South Asia Institute* (Belfast: Athol Books, 2003).

Sayer, Derek, 'British Reaction to the Amritsar Massacre 1919–1920', *Past and Present*, 131 (1991), pp. 130–164.

Schmokel, Wolfe W., *Dream of Empire: German Colonialism, 1919–1945* (London: Yale University Press, 1964).

Schofield, Camilla, ' "A Nation or No Nation?" Enoch Powell and Thatcherism', in Ben Jackson and Robert Saunders (eds), *Making Thatcher's Britain* (Cambridge: Cambridge University Press, 2012), pp. 95–110.

Schwarz, Bill, 'The Language of Constitutionalism: Baldwinite Conservatism', in Martin Langan and Bill Schwarz (eds), *Formations of Nation and People* (London: Hutchinson, 1984), pp. 1–18.

Schwarz, Bill, 'Politics and Rhetoric in the Age of Mass Culture', *History Workshop Journal*, 46 (1998), pp. 129–159.

Schwarz, Bill, *Memories of Empire, Volume I: The White Man's World* (Oxford: Oxford University Press, 2011).

Searle, G.R., *The Quest for National Efficiency: A Study in British Politics and Political Thought, 1899–1914* (Oxford: Wiley Blackwell, 1971).

Searle, G.R., 'Critics of Edwardian Society: The Case of the Radical Right', in Alan O'Day (ed.), *The Edwardian Age: Conflict and Stability 1900–1914* (London: Macmillan, 1979), pp. 79–96.

Searle, G.R., 'The "Revolt from the Right" in Edwardian Britain', in Paul Kennedy and Anthony Nicholls (eds), *Nationalist and Racialist Movements in Britain and Germany Before 1914* (London: Macmillan, 1981), pp. 21–39.

Searle, G.R., *Corruption in British Politics, 1895–1930* (Oxford: Clarendon Press, 1987).

Self, Robert, *Neville Chamberlain: A Biography* (Aldershot: Ashgate, 2006).

Shannon, Richard, *The Age of Salisbury 1881–1902: Unionism and Empire* (London: Longman, 1996).

Shaw, Tony, 'Early Warnings of the Red Peril: A Pre-history of Cold War British Cinema, 1917–1939', *Film History*, 14, 3/4 (2002), pp. 354–368.

Shields, Andrew, *The Irish Conservative Party, 1852–1868: Land, Politics and Religion* (Dublin: Irish Academic Press, 2007).

Silverfarb, Daniel, *Britain's Informal Empire in the Middle East: A Case Study of Iraq, 1929–1941* (Oxford: Oxford University Press, 1986).

Simes, D.G.S., 'A Long and Difficult Association: The Ultra Tories and "the Great Apostate"', *Wellington Studies*, 3 (1999), pp. 56–87.

Sinha, Mrinalini, *Specters of Mother India: The Global Restructuring of an Empire* (Durham, NC: Duke University Press, 2006).

Smart, Nick, *The National Government, 1931–40* (Basingstoke: Macmillan, 1999).

Smith, Jeremy, *The Tories and Ireland 1910–1914: Conservative Party Politics and the Home Rule Crisis* (Dublin: Irish Academic Press, 2000).

Smith, Paul, *Disraelian Conservatism and Social Reform* (London: Routledge and Keegan Paul, 1967).

Smith, Paul, *Disraeli: A Brief Life* (Cambridge: Cambridge University Press, 1996).

Soloway, Richard, 'Counting the Degenerates: The Statistics of Race Deterioration in Edwardian England', *Journal of Contemporary History*, 17, 1 (1982), pp. 137–164.

Soloway, Richard, *Demography and Degeneration: Eugenics and the Declining Birth Rate in Twentieth Century Britain* (Chapel Hill, NC: University of North Carolina Press, 1995).

Southern, David, 'Lord Newton, the Conservative Peers and the Parliament Act of 1911', in Clyve Jones and David Lewis Jones (eds), *Peers, Politics and Power: The House of Lords, 1603–1911* (London: Hambledon Press, 1986), pp. 519–525.

Southgate, Donald (ed.), *The Conservative Leadership 1832–1932* (London: Macmillan, 1974).

St John, Ian, 'Writing to the Defence of Empire: Winston Churchill's Press Campaign Against Constitutional Reform in India, 1929–1935', in Chandrika Kaul (ed.), *Media and the British Empire* (Basingstoke: Palgrave Macmillan, 2006), pp. 108–119.

Stedman, Andrew David, ' "A Most Dishonest Argument"? Chamberlain's Government, Anti-Appeasers and the Persistence of League of Nations' Language Before the Second World War', *Contemporary British History*, 25, 1 (2011), pp. 83–99.

Steiner, Zara, *The Triumph of the Dark: European International History 1933–1939* (Oxford: Oxford University Press, 2011).

Stenton, Michael (ed.), *Who's Who of British Members of Parliament, Volume I, 1832–1885* (Hassocks: Harvester Press, 1976).

Stenton, Michael, and Stephen Lees (eds), *Who's Who of British Members of Parliament, Volume III, 1919–1945* (Hassocks: Harvester Press, 1979).

Stevenson, John, 'Conservatism and the Failure of Fascism in Interwar Britain', in Martin Blinkhorn (ed.), *Fascists and Conservatives: The Radical Right and the Establishment in Twentieth-Century Europe* (London: Routledge, 1990), pp. 264–282.

Stewart, Graham, *Burying Caesar: Churchill, Chamberlain and the Battle for the Tory Party* (London: Weidenfeld and Nicolson, 1999).

Stewart, Robert, *The Foundation of the Conservative Party, 1830–1867* (London: Longman, 1978).

Stone, Dan, *Responses to Nazism in Britain, 1933–1939: Before War and Holocaust* (Basingstoke: Palgrave Macmillan, 2003).

Strang, G. Bruce, 'The Spirit of Ulysses? Ideology and British Appeasement in the 1930s', *Diplomacy and Statecraft*, 19, 3 (2008), pp. 481–526.

Strobl, Gerwin, *The Germanic Isle: Nazi Perceptions of Britain* (Cambridge: Cambridge University Press, 2000).

Stubbs, John, 'Lord Milner and Patriotic Labour, 1914–1918', *English Historical Review*, 87, 345 (1972), pp. 717–754.

Stubbs, John, 'The Impact of the Great War on the Conservative Party', in Chris Cook and Gillian Peele (eds), *The Politics of Reappraisal, 1918–1939* (London: Macmillan, 1975), pp. 14–38.

Studdert-Kennedy, Gerald, 'The Christian Imperialism of the Die-Hard Defenders of the Raj, 1926–35', *Journal of Imperial and Commonwealth History*, 18, 3 (1990), pp. 342–362.

Summers, Anne, 'Militarism in Britain Before the Great War', *History Workshop Journal*, 21 (1976), pp. 104–123.

Summers, Anne, 'The Character of Edwardian Nationalism: Three Popular Leagues', in Paul Kennedy and Anthony Nicholls (eds), *Nationalist and Racialist Movements in Britain and Germany Before 1914* (London: Macmillan, 1981), pp. 68–87.

Sykes, Alan, 'The Confederacy and the Purge of the Unionist Free Traders, 1906–1910', *Historical Journal*, 18, 2 (1975), pp. 349–366.

Sykes, Alan, *Tariff Reform in British Politics 1903–1913* (Oxford: Clarendon Press, 1979).

Sykes, Alan, 'The Radical Right and the Crisis of Conservatism Before the First World War', *Historical Journal*, 26, 3 (1983), pp. 661–676.

Sykes, Alan, 'Goulding, Edward Alfred, Baron Wargrave (1862–1936)', *Oxford Dictionary of National Biography* (Oxford: Oxford University Press, 2004).

Sykes, Alan, *The Radical Right in Britain: Social Imperialism to the BNP* (Basingstoke: Palgrave Macmillan, 2005).

Taylor, Andrew, 'The Party and Trade Unions', in Anthony Seldon and Stuart Ball (eds), *Conservative Century: The Conservative Party Since 1900* (Oxford: Oxford University Press, 1994), pp. 499–543.

Thackeray, David, 'The Crisis of the Tariff Reform League and the Division of "Radical Conservatism", c.1913–1922', *History*, 91, 301 (2006), pp. 45–61.

Thackeray, David, 'Rethinking the Edwardian Crisis of Conservatism', *Historical Journal*, 54, 1 (2011), pp. 191–213.

Thackeray, David, 'Building a Peaceable Party: Masculine Identities in British Conservative Politics, c.1903–24', *Historical Research*, 85, 230 (2012), pp. 651–673.

Thackeray, David, *Conservatism for the Democratic Age: Conservative Cultures and the Challenge of Mass Politics in Early Twentieth-Century England* (Manchester: Manchester University Press, 2013).

Thomas, Geraint, 'Conservatives, the Constitution and the Quest for a "Representative" House of Lords, 1911–35', *Parliamentary History*, 31, 3 (2012), pp. 419–443.

Thomas, Geraint, 'The Conservative Party and Welsh Politics in the Inter-war Years', *English Historical Review*, 128, 533 (2013), pp. 877–913.

Thompson, Andrew S., 'The Language of Imperialism and the Meanings of Empire: Imperial Discourse in British Politics, 1895–1914, *Journal of British Studies*, 36, 2 (1997), pp. 147–177.

Thompson, Andrew S., *Imperial Britain: The Empire in British Politics, c.1880–1932* (London: Longman, 2000).

Thompson, J. Lee, *Northcliffe: Press Baron in Politics, 1865–1922* (London: John Murray, 2000).

Thompson, Neville, *The Anti-Appeasers: Conservative Opposition to Appeasement in the 1930s* (Oxford: Clarendon Press, 1971).

Thurlow, Richard, 'Anti-Nazi Anti-Semite: The Case of Douglas Reed', *Patterns of Prejudice*, 18, 1 (1984), pp. 23–34.

Thurlow, Richard, *Fascism in Britain: From Oswald Mosley's Blackshirts to the National Front* (London: I.B.Tauris, 1998).

Toczek, Nick, *Haters, Baiters and Would-Be Dictators: Anti-Semitism and the UK Far Right* (Abingdon: Routledge, 2016).

Toye, Richard, *Churchill's Empire: The World that Made Him and the World He Made* (London: Macmillan, 2010).

Toye, Richard, ' "Phrases Make History Here": Churchill, Ireland and the Rhetoric of Empire', *Journal of Imperial and Commonwealth History*, 38, 4 (2010), pp. 549–570.

Toye, Richard, 'The Rhetorical Culture of the House of Commons After 1918', *History*, 99, 335 (2014), pp. 270–298.

Turner, John, 'The Politics of Business', in John Turner (ed.), *Businessmen and Politics: Studies of Business Activity in British Politics, 1900–1945* (London: Heinemann, 1984), pp. 1–19.

Turner, John, *British Politics and the Great War: Coalition and Conflict 1915–1918* (London: Yale University Press, 1992).

Urbach, Karina, 'Age of No Extremes? The British Aristocracy Torn Between the House of Lords and the Mosley Movement', in Karina Urbach (ed.), *European Aristocracies and the Radical Right, 1918–1939* (Oxford: Oxford University Press, 2007), pp. 53–71.

Veerathappa, K., *British Conservative Party and Indian Independence 1930–1947* (New Delhi: Ashish Publishing House, 1976).

Waddington, G.T., ' "An Idyllic and Unruffled Atmosphere of Complete Anglo–German Misunderstanding": Aspects of the Operations of the Dienststelle Ribbentrop in Great Britain, 1934–1938', *History*, 82, 265 (1997), pp. 44–72.

Waley, David, *British Public Opinion and the Abyssinian War 1935–6* (London: Temple Smith, 1975).

Warren, Alan, 'Disraeli, the Conservatives and the National Church, 1837–1881', *Parliamentary History*, 19, 1 (2000), pp. 96–117.

Webber, G.C., *The Ideology of the British Right, 1918–1939* (London: Croom Helm, 1986).

Weston, Corinne C., 'Salisbury and the Lords 1868–1895', *Historical Journal*, 25, 1 (1982), pp. 103–129.

Weston, Corinne C., *The House of Lords and Ideological Politics: Lord Salisbury's Referendal Theory and the Conservative Party, 1846–1922* (Philadelphia, PA: American Philosophical Society, 1995).

Weston, Corinne C., and Patricia Kelvin, 'The "Judas Group" and the Parliament Bill of 1911', in Clyve Jones and David Lewis Jones (eds), *Peers, Politics and Power: The House of Lords, 1603–1911* (London: Hambledon Press, 1986), pp. 527–539.

Whiting, Richard, 'The Empire and British Politics', in Andrew Thompson (ed.), *Britain's Experience of Empire in the Twentieth Century* (Oxford: Oxford University Press, 2012), pp. 161–210.

Williams, A. Susan, *Ladies of Influence: Women of the Elite in Interwar Britain* (London: Allen Lane, 2000).

Williams, Rhodri, *Defending the Empire: The Conservative Party and British Defence Policy 1899–1915* (London: Yale University Press, 1991).

Williamson, Philip, *National Crisis and National Government: British Politics, the Economy and the Empire, 1926–1932* (Cambridge: Cambridge University Press, 1992).

Williamson, Philip, *Stanley Baldwin: Conservative Leadership and National Values* (Cambridge: Cambridge University Press, 1999).

Williamson, Philip, 'The Conservative Party, Fascism and Anti-Fascism 1918–1939', in Nigel Copsey and Andrzej Olechnowicz (eds), *Varieties of Anti-Fascism: Britain in the Inter-war Period* (Basingstoke: Palgrave Macmillan, 2010), pp. 73–97.

Wilson, Keith M., *A Study in the History and Politics of the Morning Post 1905–1926* (Lampeter: Edwin Mellon, 1991).

Wilson, Keith M., 'National Party Spirits: Backing into the Future', in Matthew Hughes and Matthew Seligmann (eds), *Leadership in Conflict 1914–1918* (Barnsley: Leo Cooper, 2000), pp. 209–226.

Windscheffel, Alex, *Popular Conservatism in Imperial London 1868–1906* (Woodbridge: Boydell and Brewer, 2007).

Witherell, Larry L., *Rebel on the Right: Henry Page Croft and the Crisis of British Conservatism, 1903–1914* (London: Associated University Presses, 1997).

Witherell, Larry L., 'Lord Salisbury's "Watching Committee" and the Fall of Neville Chamberlain, May 1940', *English Historical Review*, 116, 469 (2001), pp. 1134–1166.

Witherell, Larry L., 'Sir Henry Page Croft and Conservative Backbench Campaigns for Empire, 1903–1932', *Parliamentary History*, 25, 3 (2006), pp. 357–381.

Woods, Philip, 'Lionel Curtis, the Round Table Movement and the Montagu– Chelmsford Reforms (1919)', in Andrea Bosco and Alex May (eds), *The Round Table, the Empire/Commonwealth and British Foreign Policy* (London: Lothian Foundation Press, 1997), pp. 369–379.

Young, John W., 'Conservative Leaders, Coalition, and Britain's Decision for War in 1914', *Diplomacy and Statecraft*, 25, 2 (2014), pp. 214–239.

Zander, Patrick, '(Right) Wings over Everest: High Adventure, High Technology and High Nationalism on the Roof of the World, 1932–1934', *Twentieth Century British History*, 21, 3 (2010), pp. 300–329.

Ziegler, Philip, 'Churchill and the Monarchy', in Robert Blake and Wm. Roger Louis (eds), *Churchill* (Oxford: Clarendon Press, 1996), pp. 187–198.

9 Unpublished theses

Crutchley, J.L., 'E Is for Empire? Imperialism and British Public Elementary School Curricula, 1902–1931', PhD, University of Worcester (2016).

Jarvis, David, 'Stanley Baldwin and the Ideology of the Conservative Response to Socialism, 1918–1931', PhD, Lancaster University (1991).

Johnson, N.A.P., 'The Roles of the Conservative Party and the National Government During the 'Phoney War', September 1939–May 1940', MPhil, University of Birmingham (2002).

Kowol, C.P., 'The Lost World of British Conservatism: The Radical Tory Tradition, 1939–1951', DPhil, University of Oxford (2013).

Mitchell, D.J., 'The Army League, Conscription and the 1956 Defence Review', PhD, University of East Anglia (2012).

Porter, Dilwyn, 'The Unionist Tariff Reformers, 1903–1914', PhD, University of Manchester (1976).

Stocker, Paul, '"The Surrender of an Empire": British Imperialism in Radical Right and Fascist Ideology, 1921–1963', PhD, Teesside University (2016).

Index